Building N-Tier Applications with COM and Visual Basic® 6.0

Ash Rofail
Tony Martin

Wiley Computer Publishing

John Wiley & Sons, Inc.

NEW YORK · CHICHESTER · WEINHEIM · BRISBANE · SINGAPORE · TORONTO

Publisher: Robert Ipsen

Editor: Theresa Hudson

Assistant Editor: Kathryn A. Malm

Managing Editor: Micheline Frederick

Electronic Products, Associate Editor: Mike Sosa

Text Design & Composition: North Market Street Graphics

Designations used by companies to distinguish their products are often claimed as trademarks. In all instances where John Wiley & Sons, Inc., is aware of a claim, the product names appear in initial capital or ALL CAPITAL LETTERS. Readers, however, should contact the appropriate companies for more complete information regarding trademarks and registration.

This book is printed on acid-free paper. ∞

Published by John Wiley & Sons, Inc.

Published simultaneously in Canada.

This publication is designed to provide accurate and authoritative information in regard to the subject matter covered. It is sold with the understanding that the publisher is not engaged in professional services. If professional advice or other expert assistance is required, the services of a competent professional person should be sought.

Library of Congress Cataloging-in-Publication Data:

Rofail, Ash, 1966–
 Building N-Tier applications with CD-ROM and Visual Basic 6.0 /
Ash Rofail, Tony Martin.
   p. cm.
  ISBN 0-471-29549-3 (pbk. : alk. paper/CD-ROM)
   1. Application software—Development. 2. CD-ROMs. 3. Microsoft
Visual BASIC. I. Martin, Tony, 1963– . II. Title.
QA76.76.A65R665 1999
005.1—dc21   98-55320
                  CIP

Printed in the United States of America.

10 9 8 7 6 5 4 3 2 1

To my wife Amy, and my children Alexander and Kristina.

—ASH ROFAIL

*To Mom and Dad, for everything they've done for me,
especially the stuff I don't know about.*

—TONY MARTIN

CONTENTS

v

ACKNOWLEDGMENTS

We would like to thank Yasser Shohoud for writing Chapter 10, "Inside Microsoft Transaction Server." His work was critical in getting this book out in a timely fashion. When you reap the many benefits of that chapter, remember it was Yasser who shared his knowledge and skill with you.

Thank you very much to Dave Gunnell for providing the technical review of this book. You are the sharpest engineer we know, and are held in high esteem indeed.

Very important thanks go to Terri Hudson, Kathryn Malm, Gerrie Cho, and the rest of the crew at Wiley. Without their support and input, this book would not be nearly as useful, easy to read, or entertaining as it is. You're the best in the business.

Thanks also to the Best Software FPG software development team for putting up with us while we wrote this book. We know we owe you a great debt for your forbearance, and some day we'll think of a way to pay you back for it.

A special thanks to Kim "Sweetness" Houser for suggesting the idea for the example program in Chapter 14. You thought we were kidding about using your idea, didn't you?

Thanks to my family for your support, encouragement, patience, and love. Even after long days of hard work, you still accepted my crankiness. You are my world.

Thanks to Tony Martin, my coauthor, for agreeing to help me with this project. I've learned a lot from your discipline, commitment, and knowledge.

Thanks to Jose Mojica, who promoted the book idea with me, for all the hard work he put into getting the book started. I'm only sorry you had to move to other projects and couldn't be involved in writing the book with me.

Many thanks to Claire Horne at Moore Literary Agency. Your hard work in refining the book idea and concept shaped this book.

                                                                    Ash

Thanks to my coauthor, Ash Rofail, for bringing me into this project. I had a great time. Given the option, I would do it all over again.

A special thanks from me to Kathryn Malm, whose editing of this book has made me into a much better writer. Thanks, and accept my apologies for never quite learning to use *because* instead of *since*.

Thanks to my entire family, including Mom, Dad, Lise, Wayne, Nico, Alex, and Hanna, for living with this project almost as much as I did. They got updates from me on a regular basis, whether they asked or not. And thanks for asking.

Thanks to my pals, Warren and David, for moral and other valuable types of support. Thanks also go to Ann Ferraro for her kind attention and friendship, without which I might not have been able to complete my share of this tome. Thanks to Mary Balmer for pretending to be interested while I ranted about the book on a daily basis. And thanks to Tirith for keeping me awake during long, late nights of writing, begging to go out just one more time.

Thanks to Bob Crane, Werner Klemperer, John Banner, Robert Clary, Larry Hovis, Richard Dawson, Ivan Dixon, Kenneth Washington, Leon Askin, and Howard Caine for getting me through this. I would not have made it without your talent.

Finally, thanks to my grandfather, Chester A. Downs, who passed away during the writing of this book, for 86 years of gracing myself and this planet with his presence. He was a quiet hero, and I will miss him.

                                                                    Tony

Ash Rofail has been developing mission-critical client/server solutions since 1986. During the past 10 years he has been involved in developing financial applications for mid- to high-end markets using C++, Visual Basic, and Java. Over the course of his career he has developed several language translators, code generators, and compilers to help migrate legacy systems into the Windows world. Ash is a frequent contributing author for Visual Basic Programmers Journal (VBPJ) and Enterprise Development magazines. He is also a speaker in several industry conferences such as VBits.

Tony Martin has been programming since 1981, when CP/M was king and PC-DOS was a young upstart. Since then he has been involved in many aspects of software development and innumerable development projects. His major areas of interest and specialty include user interface programming, design, and theory; the software engineering process, its study, and improvement; C++ development; Basic and Visual Basic programming, for about 15 years; and software usability. More recent interests and work include COM and other new Microsoft technologies, web development, and programming for the Internet. Tony lives in Northern Virginia, works at Best Software, Inc. as a senior software engineer, and shares his home with a Border terrier. At any given moment, you'll probably find him wandering the woods with his camera, photographing the splendor of the world around us. His most valuable possession is his sense of wonder, which he exercises regularly.

N-tier technology is good stuff. It allows you to create your program as independent components, spread it across any number of computers around the world, and accommodate the needs and whims of thousands or millions of users. N-tier architectures are currently in use by huge corporations that process thousands of transactions per second, each of which may be critical to the user and the company. Every person on the Internet who makes a purchase through the Web is using an N-tier system located somewhere on the planet, while the software ensures that each transaction is handled securely, completely, and simultaneously with many others. And the demand for faster transaction processing and higher volumes of throughput is increasing rapidly.

With the advent of the Internet and the Web, the need for N-tier technology will be even higher. The online population is growing quickly, and as more people discover the convenience of electronic transactions and remote computing, N-tier applications will be required to fill the demand. It will be up to people like you to build these systems of today and tomorrow.

It's exciting to be involved in the construction of a major N-tier application. You get to use the latest technologies, work on typically large applications that will be used by many people and have far-reaching effects, and often get involved with Internet development. Sound like something you want to be part of? If so, then this book will help you get there.

Overview of the Book and Technology

Designing and constructing N-tier systems is demanding, and several technologies are required to create these complex programs. However, recent developments in the software technology world have made building N-tier systems a more approachable task. Among the most important are Microsoft Visual Basic 6.0 and the Component Object Model, or COM.

COM provides us with a standard specification for creating reusable software components that can work together to get a job done. It makes the process of creating distributed applications much easier, because components can be located on different computers and can be updated in a central location instead of on thousands of client computers. Until recently, COM development has resided in the realm of the C++ programmer. However, newer versions of Visual Basic have begun to support COM development, and Visual Basic 6.0 adds more of this capability and makes things even easier.

This book will teach you all about N-tier development using COM and Visual Basic 6.0 as your primary tools. You'll quickly come to realize that N-tier development is within the reach of anyone who can use these tools and who spends a little time to understand how they work. You will find that as you read this book and learn more about the technology, ideas for new software systems and new ways to implement them will start forming in your mind. And we don't mean screen savers, either. We're talking about big, complex systems that can handle very large jobs and numbers of users.

There is a lot of information in this book, covering many topics and areas of N-tier technology. Don't let it intimidate you! As with any endeavor, knowledge is power, and we'll give you N-tier development knowledge. We like to share; we can't help it. Just dive in and have a ball.

How This Book Is Organized

This book is organized into three primary sections: Overview, Digging Deeper, and Putting It All Together.

Overview includes chapters that introduce the N-tier architecture and the technologies involved. Each introduction chapter includes a beginner's description and overview of the technology being detailed, a discussion of the pros and cons of the technology, and a complete code example that illustrates the primary concepts of the technology. Topics include COM, DCOM, and MTS.

The **Digging Deeper** section goes into much deeper detail about N-tier technologies. These include COM, DCOM, MTS, client technologies, all aspects of databases, and Visual Basic tools. This is the meat of the book, especially if you are an advanced reader.

Putting It All Together is composed of one chapter that brings together many of the technologies covered in the book into a single example N-tier application. While the other chapters in the book cover the various topics that are critical to N-tier development, this chapter combines them to illustrate how they work together.

What Should You Read First?

The book is organized in a more or less sequential fashion, first by the reader's level of knowledge and then by technology. The first four chapters introduce the reader to the technologies involved, with an overview of N-tier architectures followed by introductions to COM, DCOM, and MTS. In order to understand DCOM, you must first learn about COM. A working knowledge of COM and DCOM are useful before you dive into MTS.

The next nine chapters present more in-depth information about the technologies involved. The COM, DCOM, MTS order of precedence applies here as well. However, feel free to skip around in the client and database chapters as you like.

The Chapters

It's always nice to have an overview of the chapters before you invest time in reading them. Programmers especially prefer to get a quick summary before spending valuable coding time reading a whole chapter. Therefore, we provide here a capsule version of each chapter in the book. Using this guide, you can skip around in the book as you see fit.

Chapter 1, "Overview of N-Tier Applications." In case you are new to the world of N-tier applications, we have provided an overview of the architecture, as well as some useful and interesting insights into programming N-tier software. Even if you are already familiar with N-tier architecture, we recommend this chapter. It explains not only the architecture, but our approach to it and programming for it.

Chapter 2, "Introduction to COM." This chapter provides a thorough introduction to COM and COM programming with Visual Basic. Topics include what COM is; how it came about; the pros and cons of COM; how to program COM objects with Visual Basic; some nice Visual Basic tools and shortcuts; and a complete, working COM example.

Chapter 3, "Introduction to DCOM." This chapter picks up where the previous one leaves off, and covers the distributed version of COM. It discusses what DCOM is; how it differs from COM; how it works; the basics of marshaling; in- and out-of-process components; passing data in a DCOM world; error handling; security; deployment of remote components; and a complete, working example in Visual Basic.

Chapter 4, "Introduction to MTS." This chapter introduces Microsoft Transaction Server, a major player in the world of N-tier applications. Details include transactions—what they are and why they are important; an overview of the MTS environment; the pros and cons of MTS; the MTS mechanism; programming MTS components; MTS security; the installation of MTS components; how to build MTS components using Visual Basic; and a complete, working MTS example program.

Chapter 5, "Creating Business Rules." Business rules are an important part of N-tier applications because they drive a large portion of the functionality of the business tier. This chapter covers exactly what business rules are; some techniques for discovering your business rules; where business rules reside in your program; a working example of one way to implement business rules; and some tips for planning and implementing your business rules.

Chapter 6, "Thin and Fast Clients." You've probably heard about thin and fast clients. They are all the rage in N-tier computing. More often than not, people speak about thin clients without really understanding what they are and why they are interesting. This chapter explains all this, as well as how to determine whether or not thin clients are appropriate for your application; what types of clients are available to you and their pros and cons; performance issues; and a few helpful (and possibly interesting) examples.

Chapter 7, "Web and Internet Clients." This chapter covers the client component of your application from the Internet perspective. It discusses in great detail the technologies available for Web and Internet clients; how they work; how to program them; and a bunch of entertaining examples. It presents information on Dynamic HTML, the Document Object Model, ActiveX documents, and how to program it all using Visual Basic.

Chapter 8, "Understanding COM Internals." This chapter gets into the dark recesses of COM and its internals. It discusses COM interfaces;

component design and interaction; object-oriented techniques; object models and their creation; and the ADO COM model.

Chapter 9, "DCOM Details." DCOM will set you free from the shackles of a single computer, and this chapter will tell you all about it. Topics include DCOM marshaling; how DCOM communications work; security; and the new VB6 IIS Classes.

Chapter 10, "Inside Microsoft Transaction Server." MTS is an important part of many N-tier applications, and provides transactional support for your program. This chapter covers it in detail, including how MTS components work; the MTS environment and using MTS components within it; distributed transactions and the Microsoft Distributed Transaction Controller; building stateless components; debugging MTS components; and MTS security.

Chapter 11, "The Database Server." The database is a central component of almost any N-tier application, and is covered in detail here and in the next chapter. The information in this chapter includes database design; stored procedures; wrapping stored procedures in COM components; COM and SQL Server; SQL-DMO; SQL NameSpace; SQL Server performance optimizations; and SQL Server security.

Chapter 12, "Data Access with Visual Basic 6." Visual Basic 6 has added a host of amazingly useful database tools and technologies to its suite of capabilities. This chapter makes sure you know about them all, including the Data Project; the Data Environment and its designer and data view; the Data Object Wizard; the ADO data control; the Data Repeater; and the Data Form Wizard. It also shows you how to create a data-bound ActiveX control.

Chapter 13, "MSMQ as Another Tier." N-tier architecture allows you to have any number of tiers in your application, creating them as appropriate. This chapter teaches the use of Microsoft Message Queue as another tier, and covers what MSMQ is; how it fits in as another tier; what it can do for you; using and programming MSMQ; how to set up MSMQ; and using MSMQ events and transactions.

Chapter 14, "Putting It Together." This chapter puts many of the technologies and techniques covered in previous chapters together in the form of a complete sample N-tier application. It walks through the entire process of creating an N-tier application, from requirements to construction.

Appendix A, "What's New In Visual Basic 6.0." While you can find out this information from the Visual Basic CD-ROM, it takes a while to weed through. Therefore we have done it for you, and have detailed some of the new features that are specifically applicable to N-tier development.

Appendix B, "Project Considerations." N-tier projects tend to be large, and large projects require special management and development techniques. This chapter illustrates the basics of how to run and manage a large development effort and covers how to set up teams; keep communications going; put solid development practices in place; create and manage schedules; and develop and implement standards.

Appendix C, "About the CD-ROM." This appendix contains information about the contents of the companion CD-ROM for this book. It lists the examples that are included with the book, as well as what software is included.

Who Should Read this Book

Almost anyone can read this book and learn something from it. The only thing we assume you already have is a working knowledge of Visual Basic. We won't be teaching you how to design forms or write code behind events. As long as you know Visual Basic well enough to turn out some programs of your own, you should be all set.

There are a few different types of readers who will probably be drawn to this book. If you are one of them, you can follow these guidelines to help you jump to the correct portions of the book, maximizing your learning experience.

The Visual Basic hobbyist turned professional. You will probably want to read this book from cover to cover. The first four chapters were written with you in mind. The first part of the book will introduce you to the newer Microsoft technologies, including COM, DCOM, and MTS. There we will lay the groundwork for more advanced topics that will come in later chapters.

The Visual Basic professional moving to distributed applications. Most of this book will appeal to this type of professional. In the first section, where all the introductions are made, feel free to read through the chapters that cover the technologies you have not had exposure to. Others might make a good refresher. Later chapters, starting with Chapter 7, are full of advanced topics that will help propel you to the heights of N-tier development.

The advanced Visual Basic professional. You may want to skip the introductory chapters if you are familiar with COM, DCOM, and MTS. Beginning with Chapter 7, you will learn the inner details and techniques for the client, business, database, and other tiers. Most of the chapters stand well on their own, and you can jump around to the topics in which you are most interested. If you are a hot-shot Visual Basic programmer, but are still unfamiliar with the Microsoft component technologies, feel free to read or skim Chapters 2, 3, and 4, which will give you a working knowledge of these technologies.

Tools You Will Need

The primary tool you will need for the content and examples in this book is Microsoft Visual Basic Enterprise Edition version 6.0. The Enterprise Edition is the version that contains all of the remote programming capabilities, which are key to N-tier development. Make sure this program is installed and running smoothly before you try out any of the code in this book.

If you are using Windows NT 4.0 or later, then you will need the Windows NT Option Pack. This will provide you with MTS and MSMQ. You can obtain this software from Microsoft, usually for free or at a low cost. When you get it, install MTS as well as MSMQ on your local machine or a server. When installing MSMQ on a local computer, make sure you set it up with an independent queue, so you can create local queues. See Chapter 13 for more information on setting up MSMQ.

If you are using Windows95, then you will need DCOM for Windows95. This is a free add-on for Windows95 that adds DCOM capabilities to the operating system. You can get this from Microsoft's Web site (www.microsoft.com).

What's on the CD-ROM

There are two types of content on the companion CD-ROM for this book: example source code and software.

All the source code for every example in the book is included on the CD-ROM, located under the \Examples directory. Under this directory are other directories, one for each chapter that has examples. If a chapter has more than one example, there will be another directory for each example in that chapter. Each example includes all the source code and project files needed to rebuild the program, as well as compiled, ready-to-run versions of each program. Of course, a few of the programs will require some configuration, such as installing a component in MTS, before they will run correctly. Such are the minor woes of building N-tier applications.

There are also a few software packages on the CD-ROM, either full working versions or trial versions. Among the programs included are:

- *Rational Software's Visual Quantify.* An advanced performance profiling tool that automatically pinpoints application performance bottlenecks. Visual Quantify also delivers repeatable timing data for all parts of an application, including components, not just the parts for which you have the source code. It provides graphical views of performance data, and integrates directly with Visual Basic.

- *Rational Software's Visual PureCoverage.* Visual PureCoverage for Windows NT is an easy-to-use coverage analysis tool that automatically pinpoints untested code in your C, C++, Java or Visual Basic components and applications.

- *Riverton Software's HOW.* HOW is a component modeling tool and deployment framework for building business applications. HOW makes it straightforward for mainstream developers to build distributed and Internet applications using Visual Basic, Microsoft Transaction Server, DCOM, and other enterprise technologies from Microsoft.

- *Platinum Technologies' Platinum ERwin.* PLATINUM ER*win*, the industry leader, is a powerful, award-winning, easy-to-use database design tool. Its rich set of design techniques and unique iterative approach provide exceptional productivity for implementing transactional systems and data warehouses across the enterprise. This fully functional evaluation version of ER*win* 3.5.2 will help jump-start you into data modeling and database design. To activate this product evaluation you will need to use an evaluation key code. You can obtain an evaluation key code by contacting PLATINUM technology at 800-442-6861 or 630-620-5000.

- *Methods Bay's Infraset.* A repository-driven and model-based COM business object framework and RDBMS persistence layer for component-based architectures. The InfraSet business object framework enables any middle-tier business class to Create, Retrieve, Update, and Delete its objects within standard relational databases through the developer's configuration of an Active Repository of design information.

- *A link to Microsoft Internet Explorer, latest version.* Many of the technologies and example programs used in this book require Microsoft Internet Explorer. We have included a link to it on the CD-ROM, just in case you don't have it.

- *A link to DCOM for Windows95.* This add-on allows you to build and run DCOM components on a Windows95 computer. This will be required if you are running Windows95.

- *Allaire Homesite.* This program is one of the best HTML editors we have ever seen. The version included on the CD-ROM is a 30-day evaluation copy that will convince you to buy it.

- *The CSS Style Sheet Editor.* This program is an HTML style sheet editor that helps you to easily create and edit CSS1 style sheets for use with Web clients. We wrote it just for you. See Chapter 7 for more details about it.

Feel free to cruise around the CD-ROM and run the examples or play with the software. It will give you a feel for what's to come in the book, and hopefully get you fired up about N-tier development.

Heading Out

The next few chapters will lay the groundwork for your N-tier experience and prepare you for the more detailed core topics to come. Unless you are extremely careful, you will learn plenty about building N-tier applications and the technology behind them.

Now that you have a roadmap for the book, you can start on your journey to N-tier guru-hood. It is our hope that you will learn enough here to participate in or lead an N-tier development project, make informed decisions about what technologies to use and how to use them, and impress everyone around with your new knowledge. Have a great trip!

PART ONE

Overview

CHAPTER 1

Overview of N-Tier Applications

D esigning and building client/server applications is a bit like raising children. As all parents will tell you, their methodology is a proven approach used by their parents and is the only successful way to bring up children. Application developers have a similar theory. We tend to follow what we think is a proven method of development and hope the cookie-cutter approach used to build our previous application pays off again.

There is no doubt experience plays a big role in the design and development of applications. As a matter of fact, several architectural models have been devised for this purpose, from a single-tier, monolithic application to the traditional three-tier approach. However, the demands and complexities of today's systems exceed the solutions presented by these models. Today's applications need to be scalable, component based, and able to accommodate distributed or multiple tiers in order to address changing business needs. If you don't have a clear road map of these characteristics, or the requirements of these types of business applications, the task can be overwhelming.

In this book we explain the benefits of a multitier system and architecture, as well as the trade-offs involved in adopting such an approach. We discuss the desired goals for an N-tier application and how to achieve them.

Before we dive in, we need to review a few basic concepts—application architecture, components, and how Visual Basic fits in with both. These concepts are important, and they help to lay the foundation for future chapters, so please pay attention!

What Is an Application Architecture?

An application architecture is a mechanism to explain and communicate to your development team as well as to the outside world how your application was constructed. It explains the structure of your application and lists its pieces. It's like describing your home by saying, "I live in a two-story house with four bedrooms and a finished basement." The developers who are going to work on your application need such a description of the components that make up your application architecture before you actually build the application. It basically sets the vision for building the application.

A common conception is that an application architecture describes the application's state after development is complete. In fact, an application architecture is not the result of something but rather the cause of it. Your application architecture causes your application to be built. When designing your home, at some point you told the construction architect that you wanted a two-story house with four bedrooms and a finished basement. One of the main objectives in developing an application is to adopt an architectural vision for that application.

It is crucial to think of your application architecture when designing applications in COM. Building an entire system on interfaces—which we will discuss throughout this book—is very dangerous and difficult to change down the road if you don't think of all the aspects of your application. We have heard of a major COM application that was constructed without anyone thinking about what transactions were going to work and where they were going to live. That particular system was designed in a way that would allow users to enter and track transactions: The surprise came when the customers wanted to reverse the transaction. The system was not able to do it, because all the interfaces were in place and there was no way to add support to the architecture to make this feature possible. Don't let things like this happen to you! Think of your application architecture in detail so that you can cover all the requested features. Going back one more time to the house analogy, if you decide to build a two-story house and lay the foundation to do so, do not come back when the house is almost complete and request to have it made into a skyscraper.

There are several types of architectural models to choose from to provide just the framework for you to build upon. They are similar to prefabricated construction in that most of the plans are usually developed and then modified to fit a specific need. In the next few sections we will be looking at some of these plans, such as three-tier architecture, as well as providing you with the N-tier architectural framework that we will follow in this book.

Let's start off by looking at application architecture in terms of traditional building architecture again. Before a building can be constructed, an architect must design a set of plans or blueprints that depict every detail and piece of that particular building. Without detailed blueprints to guide the construction, there is no guarantee that the end result will match the architect's vision for the building.

The importance of blueprints also applies to software architecture. In the case of application development, the architecture acts as the blueprint or master plan for your application. It provides the outline or framework for the infrastructure components, methodologies, and procedures the application developer uses to create the application.

A sound architecture will facilitate change. Because change is inevitable due to lack of robust requirements or shifts in user needs, the architecture of your application should be able to support and implement these changes. Architectures are used for all types of applications, but in this book we focus on client/server applications.

Client/Server Application Architecture

Client/server applications and architectures have been around for years, but only in the last decade have they gained popularity on PC platforms. Statistics show that over 65 percent of all enterprise applications run on top of a client/server architecture.

Two-Tier Architecture

A client/server architecture is divided into client and server computers. In the simplest terms, the client requests services and the server processes the requests. The client is the computer and software the user sees and interacts with. For example, a person who works in phone sales uses a client computer to look up your phone number to call you with his or her sales pitch. A separate server computer talks to the client in order to request data. The user doesn't see the server. In our phone sales example, the salesperson's client computer sends a SQL request to the server and requests your phone number. The server looks the information up in its database, and then sends the requested phone number back to the client. It's then displayed on the client machine via a user interface, and the salesperson calls you up. In this scenario, the client machine handles both the user interface and any processing that is performed; the server hosts and operates the database. This configuration is a basic, two-tier client/ server system. A typical two-tier architecture consists of a GUI (the client on tier 1) and a database (the server on tier 2). Two-tier architecture is also referred to as a fat client because the majority of the application runs on the client side.

As we indicated, two-tier architectures have been around for years. Their purpose is to provide a centralized database that many clients can talk to. The database handles multiple connections to the clients and services their requests as they come in. Two-tier architecture is great for building applications quickly with visual builder tools like Visual Basic. This configuration promised to make remote transactional computing a grand reality: However, there were problems. The number of connections a database had to manage grew far beyond the architecture's capabilities. Inefficient clients held on to too many connections, which resulted in overloaded databases and servers. To offload some of the processing to the server, more functionality was moved from the clients to the database in the form of stored procedures. Although this enabled the clients to operate more efficiently, it resulted in even more server overload. Simple two-tier architectures could not handle growing, enterprise-wide, mission-critical applications.

Three-Tier Architecture

Enter a new solution called three-tier client/server architecture. The basic idea for three-tier architecture is that the client computer or GUI continues to talk to the server, but the client no longer talks directly to the database. Instead it speaks with an application server that acts like a broker on a new tier called the middle tier. You may have also heard the middle tier referred to as the business tier or component tier. The middle tier typically contains the bulk of the business logic—the functionality related to the core purpose of the program, and it also talks to the database. Figure 1.1 illustrates a three-tier architecture.

Here's how it works: The client talks to the middle tier. The middle tier uses a database connection pool to manage the communication with the database. If the client makes a request for data, the middle tier grabs a connection to the database. It completes the request, passes the data back, and then (here's the clever bit) releases the connection the client uses. The next time the client needs to request a data service, it allocates another connection. Why this new complexity? In the three-tier architecture, a client does not hold on to one or more connections continuously because it would hog bandwidth and memory resources. The middle tier can thus accommodate 100 clients using about 10 concurrent connections, because the client does not need the database 100 percent of the time. With three-tier as opposed to two-tier architecture the bulk of the processing is moved to the server. This is referred to as a thin client. Table 1.1 further highlights the differences between two- and three-tier architectures.

NOTE

Microsoft manages the communication between components across tiers and the management of resources on the server using Microsoft Transaction Server (MTS) and SQL Server. MTS, in conjunction with the COM components you write as part of your application, manages connections between the database and your components. It allocates resources on an as-needed basis and releases them on an as-soon-as-possible basis, maximizing resource availability. SQL Server, Microsoft's database, integrates very tightly with MTS to ensure that resources are used effectively and data

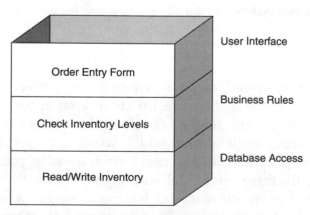

Figure 1.1   The three-tier architecture.

Table 1.1 Two-Tier versus Three-Tier Architecture

	TWO-TIER	THREE-TIER
System administration	Complex (more logic on the client to manage)	Less complex (the application can be centrally managed on the server—application programs are made visible to standard system management tools)
Security	Low (data-level security)	High (fine-tuned at the service or method level)
Encapsulation of data	Low (data tables are exposed)	High (the client invokes services or methods)
Performance	Poor (many SQL statements are sent over the network; selected data must be downloaded for analysis on the client)	Good (only service requests and responses are sent between the client and server)
Scale	Poor (limited management of client communications links)	Excellent (concentrates incoming sessions; can distribute loads across multiple servers)
Application reuse	Poor (monolithic application or client)	Excellent (can reuse services and objects)
Ease of development	High	Getting better (standard tools can be used to create the clients, and tools are emerging that can be used to develop both the client and server sides of the application)

transactions are secure and safe. When Windows 2000 is released, MTS and COM will become part of the operating system, and the two will be jointly known as COM+.

N-Tier Architecture

Traditionally, when you embark on a new client/server project, a lot of time is spent researching the best architecture to fit your application. If you've done this before, you'll remember sifting through a variety of cookie-cutter approaches to determine which would best service the needs of both your application and end users. Undoubtedly, your most common choice was the three-tier model. Although the three-tier model is a robust application architecture model, it is positioned as a general-purpose approach to solving what can be very sophisticated problems involving application upgrades and enhancements, and the scalability

	TWO-TIER	THREE-TIER
Server-to-server infrastructure	No	Yes (via server-side middleware)
Legacy application integration	No	Yes (via gateways encapsulated by services or objects)
Internet support	Poor (Internet bandwidth limitations make it harder to download fat clients and exacerbate the already noted limitations)	Excellent (thin clients are easier to download as applets or beans; remote service invocations distribute the application load to the server)
Heterogeneous database support	No	Yes (three-tier applications can use multiple databases within the same business transaction)
Rich communication choices	No (only synchronous, connection-oriented RPC-like calls)	Yes (supports RPC-like calls, but can also support connectionless messaging, queued delivery, publish-and-subscribe, and broadcast)
Hardware architecture flexibility	Limited (you have a client and a server)	Excellent (all three tiers may reside on different computers, or the second and third tiers may both reside on the same computer, with component-based environments that can be distributed on the second tier across multiple servers as well)
Availability	Poor (can't fail over to a backup server)	Excellent (can restart the middle-tier components on other servers)

Used with permission by John Wiley & Sons, Inc., New York, NY from 3-Tier Client/Server at Work by Jeri Edwards, ©1999.

of your application when suddenly it is being accessed by twice the expected number of users.

N-tier architecture is an extension of the three-tier model. It further splits the three core tiers into additional layers. These layers are based on either a logical or physical service that the application performs. For example, when designing a user interface that communicates with a business component in a traditional three-tier model, the architect can further break down the client and middle tiers into three tiers: a client that displays the user interface, a new layer that handles the formatting of the data sent by the middle tier and that communicates with the client in a very generic way, and the business tier. The purpose of this split is to change the type of user interface without going back to modify the business components. This is an example of a logical tier. The reason it is logical is because the new tier between the client and the middle tier can physically reside on the client machine or wherever the middle tier is located. In this case, we are not locked into a specific physical location for that new tier, as long as it can efficiently do its job. On the other hand, the creation of a new tier can be physical. Let's say you are on the road and you need to enter orders in an order entry module. You don't want to worry about what the system does under the hood. It could be checking the inventory level in a certain warehouse; then, if there are not enough items on hand, it will check other warehouses and then issue a transfer from one warehouse to the other, and so on. As you can see, this can take a while, so the need to create a physical tier that can handle this type of operation behind the scenes and inform you of the results later on presents a valuable solution. An example of a new physical tier is Microsoft Message Queue (MSMQ), which we discuss in greater detail in Chapter 13, "MSMQ as Another Tier." It is important to note that because we are talking about N-tier architecture, where N can be an odd or even number, there is no such thing as a middle tier. Middle tier is a term that commonly refers to the business tier, so from now on we will not be using the term middle tier, but will refer to the tier by its service name.

The key to understanding N-tier architecture is to use the three-tier model as a framework to architect your application. However, you're not limited to living inside just three tiers. Imagine that you just finished building a very large house on the water. You thought long and hard about your needs and decided that three rooms of 50 by 50 feet would fit them perfectly. Once you moved in, though, you found that the rooms were too big and inefficient—there is no TV big enough to fill any room that size. If you rented this home, you'd be stuck with it until the lease was up. But remember, this is *your* house; you can do whatever you want with it. So, you decide to renovate. You don't knock down the house and start from scratch, but work within the building's frame and partition the larger rooms into smaller, more efficient-sized areas that make your big-screen TV look, well, big.

The same architectural approach we used on this waterfront property applies to constructing client/server applications. We want to stay within the guidelines of the three-tier architecture model, but we want to have control over reconstructing these tiers into additional tiers to form our new, more efficient N-tier application.

Most developers live only within the three tiers because they approach the situation as if renting the architecture, not buying it. The basis of a successful implementation is a solid understanding of what type of application you build. Most people design a house by choosing the number of rooms they want, rather than considering what they need. You can build a much more efficient house if you know what type of activities you will be performing there. For example, no doubt you will sleep in the house, so you need a bedroom. You may work from the house, so you will need an office. Perhaps you will play and record music in your spare time, so you will need a room opposite the bedroom and office, and so on. Building rooms that meet your needs results in a more efficient house.

How does this apply to building client/server applications? Consider it a new way of thinking about your application architecture. This new way of thinking is what we call service-based architecture.

Service-Based Architecture

Today's business applications carry heavy requirements. This is mainly due to the competitive nature of the software industry. Each independent software vendor wants to be the first to market with its product. All also want to keep a competitive edge by adapting to business requirement changes and user requirements in a fast and efficient manner. The standard way of version update is not sufficient; users can no longer wait 12 to 18 months for a new version of a product. Therefore, the need to develop and ship incremental releases across services is increasing and will be the deciding factor in the life of the application.

Let's go back to our waterfront property for a moment. When we planned what rooms we needed in the house, we thought about what we were going to do there. What we were really doing was taking a service-based approach to building our home; we thought about what services our house would be used for, and that determined what rooms, or parts, our house had to contain. So the services were derived from our needs and what operations we were going to perform. This is similar to identifying the application's functionality and services to create a service-based architecture.

If you think of the traditional three-tier architecture you can easily identify the services each layer provides. When you spend time architecting your application, you will realize that you need to further break down your traditional three tiers and create additional physical or logical tiers. By doing this, you will also be breaking the tiers into components and repartitioning them to fit the new service-oriented approach you are building. This process is very similar to remodeling a house. As your needs change—for example, your kids leave the house or you construct new additions—you find that you now need to either combine rooms by tearing down walls or partition rooms by putting new walls up. This remodeling action is simply done to enable a new type of service that your house will need to support. Although this analogy helps explain the concepts of redesign, it still leaves the question: How do you then identify your application services?

Application services are derived from business modeling. Business modeling is the process that you go through to fully understand how your application will work and what types of services will be provided. Services are equivalent to functionality, so you need to understand and model the application's functions. When you come up with a high-level design of the services or functions of your application, you start to dissect these services into smaller pieces called components. You then move into the detailed design of these components, as we do in Chapter 8, "Understanding COM Internals." Once the components are designed, you can then start to fit them into the N-tier architecture based on efficiency and deployment needs.

Using this service-based approach, we can look at an application as a set of services that are required to support a specified business problem. Rather than concentrating on creating levels of tiers first, we identify the services the application should perform and partition or layer them. However, the services-based architectural model is not a strictly layered model. As services are packaged into more and finer-grained components, the layers simply become useful ways to partition the services. The services themselves are implemented as a collection of cooperating components that can be distributed and reconfigured dynamically across one or n computing tiers. Cooperation among components is based not on an interface at the layer boundaries but rather on following the rules of well-behaved component interfaces. We'll discuss these rules in detail in Chapter 8, "Understanding COM Internals," when we develop our business components.

This leads us to a discussion of reuse. What if two applications require the same service? They simply share the component that implements the service.

Application layering models stress packaging services and distributing them for a specific application. However, they do little to directly address opportunities for reuse. If an application's logical structure is used to express the application as invocations of services, rather than concentrating on creating the tiers first, a robust-tiered application is the resulting architecture. In such a model, the services an application requires become the basis for assessing the availability of components that deliver those services. Where reuse is not possible, services are packaged into component implementations based on heuristics that consider technology options, anticipated usage patterns, process and data distribution, performance, and other projected application characteristics, as well as reuse goals. In either case, the mapping of services to components can be one-to-one but is generally one-to-many.

Figure 1.2 illustrates the service-based architecture.

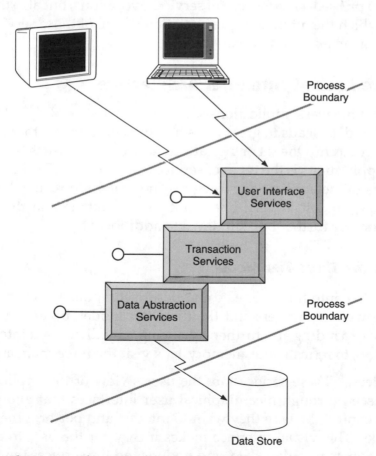

Figure 1.2   The service-based architecture.

One aspect of a component-based approach to building software is that multiple components may participate in a service request. Transaction analysis is a part of the process of making decisions about how components are packaged together. For example, if delivering a service to the user involves several business services, you should consider packaging these services in the same component because component coordination can be complex. In Chapter 10, "Inside Microsoft Transaction Server," we discuss how Microsoft Transaction Server can help us with packaging such services, known as business transactions. Business transactions require an infrastructure that provides component coordination services within transaction boundaries. This technology must monitor the successful creation of components, including notifications in the event of failure. Business transactions may last for milliseconds—or minutes, days, or weeks—and perform work in a variety of business locations. Component coordination must support not only transactions explicitly expressed as sequences of service invocations, but also the situation in which the internal implementation of one of those services in turn relies on an autonomous service.

A Retrospective Look at Three-Tier Architecture

The fact that business applications share characteristics of their logical structure (models) leads to great ways to reuse components that implement that structure. One set of logical structure characteristics typical of business applications is the types of services they provide. These are the main layers of the application structure. They might look like they are just three-tier, but it is very important to understand the three-tier model before we further break it down to additional tiers.

Revisiting the Three-Tier Model

Before we dive into how to create and design components, we need to make sure we fully understand the three-tier model, because we are going to be expanding and further enhancing it by dividing it into multiple tiers. So, to refresh your memory, let's visit the three main areas.

User services.   These services are the user's view of the application, usually seen through nice graphical user interfaces that allow end users to control the way they want to interact and perform the business tasks. This visual interface makes it easy for the user to access information, manipulate data, and understand the services the application can offer.

Business services.   These services are the heart of the application. They implement the business rules that define how the application is going to work and control how data is accessed, manipulated, and interpreted for making business decisions. While user services are very specific to the end user, business services affect all aspects of the application.

NOTE   You can build business services using different types of tools and technologies, and you can even mix and match between them. For example, user services typically reside on a client workstation, have a graphical user interface, and are usually prototyped first so that end users can give input before the actual coding is done. Data services require almost no user input and are designed by developers who have experience in data modeling and database design. Business processes and rules are modeled through interaction with business knowledge workers you can call "domain experts," and may require complex analysis, design, and coding.

Data services.   These services control access to the corporate data. Their job is to protect the client from having to know a lot about the format and structure of the database and where it's located. Many of these services can be provided directly by reusable components such as Database Management Systems (DBMSs), but sometimes applications have specific performance needs or data replication or migration requirements that might force you to use custom services that will manage all access to data. We will explore this topic in more depth in Chapter 11, "The Database Server."

NOTE   Large application development teams tend to include designers and developers who specialize in each of these areas. On small development projects, all of these services may be designed and constructed by the same person, although even small development teams tend to acknowledge differences in techniques and tools appropriate for graphical user interaction design versus database modeling and service design and implementation.

After breaking your application down into sets of services, the next step is to break these down further into components.

Component-Based Development

Services represent the high-level design of the application. The next step is to take every service or function and develop the detail design in the form of components.

A component is a chunk of software that offers related services accessible through a standard interface. Components can live on different machines and across networks, yet they still know about each other and interact very well. This is somewhat like a telephone conversation: Just because your friends are not visible to you in the same room doesn't mean they don't exist. Components are the same way: They don't have to be on the same machine to communicate. They can be implemented and tested independently, increase the reusability and maintainability of your program, and are easily replaceable. They work easily with Microsoft Transaction Server (MTS) and other Microsoft architectures.

Components make your development life a lot easier. They are very cohesive, meaning they are dedicated to a single, well-defined purpose. Because of this, multiple components can be developed at the same time. While the components are being developed, you can publish their interfaces and everyone can code to them without requiring the complete functionality. Then, when the components are ready to be put into the project, they can be added to the system, and suddenly your client has new functionality available to it.

Component-based development refers to the techniques and tools that allow the construction of applications from new and preexisting components. It is, in a sense, the next generation of client/server computing. The key characteristic of component-based applications is that the layering model is no longer two-tier or three-tier and tied closely to a physical platform configuration, but is instead multitier (or N-tier) and able to be distributed and dynamically reconfigured across a heterogeneous environment. As you will learn thoughout this book, efficient component interaction is very important. To make components effective, they need to be grouped according to the services they provide in order to minimize interaction across a distributed environment. So far we have discussed high-level services and lower-level components and why it is important to understand how your applications work, but the question now is: How do you come up with the services and components? Traditionally, the most senior people would sit in a room and brainstorm about what the applications should do. This approach is not recommended, however, because when people leave they take their knowledge with them. Therefore, we recommend performing what is called the process of modeling business objects, sometimes referred to as domain modeling. This is where you extract the services and detailed requirements for your application.

Business objects are meaningful real-world items—customers, forms, orders—that users and developers alike can understand. Business objects describe the behavior of real-world items. A business object is a design abstraction, not a piece of code. The ability to describe behavior formally allows us to write software that acts like real-world objects. For example, a software company might need to represent system objects such as users, access tokens, or print queues consistently across platforms. Class libraries (collections of components) for these objects are increasingly available to programmers and power users. Business objects provide a useful foundation for building standard software components because they capture semantics that are understandable by real business personnel in the real world. They also add value over other representations by providing a way to manage software complexity by grouping behavior with the objects that exhibit it. They provide a model of the business, independent of the business processes that operate on the business objects. Business objects also serve as building blocks for new software projects.

When you've built a solid business model, the resulting software components offer a set of related services that are more likely to be added to your software project. This makes it easier to manage change, because each component is a well-encapsulated implementation of operations on business objects. It provides the basis for sharing business rules and data across application boundaries. If the business user is to be involved in the development process from construction to assembly, then software components must be equally understandable and recognizable in business terms. Business objects thus provide a consistent semantic to the business models and, by implication, have the potential to bring this benefit to the software components that implement them.

NOTE The reverse is not true. That is, software components aren't business objects just because they implement some business process semantics and rules.

Business object modeling is a discovery technique for identifying core business concepts and their associated business semantics. By building components that encapsulate the behavior of a business object, we expect to increase the possibility of component reuse and make it easier to manage change.

Because of the realities of how business applications are used and deployed, it is unlikely that there will be a one-to-one mapping between business objects and components. Rather, components will reflect a better design on how they are actually used, code performance characteristics, or deployment partitioning opportunities. Visual Basic 6 makes it easier to manage the structure of applications, construction, and deployment, as well as ways to locate and reuse components.

Significant benefits can be gained from design time and source code reuse, but the ultimate vision is based on runtime reuse—location- and implementation-independent service that is mapped at runtime to the component (or a selected component) that implements it.

Structuring Components

Now that we know what services are and how we can create components from high-level services, it is important to note that the structure of the business application is a complex one. When done right, creating this structure can be as easy as we have made it sound. There are still some influencing factors when designing a business application, mainly because it is hard to view a business application from just one angle.

The structure of a business application is viewed differently by different people. From the administrator's perspective, an application's structure is a bunch of pieces, such as dynamic link libraries (DLLs), that fit together to make up the functionality of the application. From the developer's perspective, an application's structure is expressed in terms of the source code files that are used to generate components. From the business analyst's perspective, an application's structure is expressed in terms of the business process, objects, and data models that represent the logic of the developing application, regardless of where the pieces are going to fit.

The business process and data models may be the most stable view of the application, but they nevertheless will change to reflect changing business requirements. The bottom line is that the structure of an application encompasses all these views and their interrelationships.

One of the complexities of component-based development is that a change in a given component may have implications for any related component. If the relationship is purely descriptive, meaning the developer using or calling a certain component does not know much about your internal implementation (what the code inside your component looks like), then the implication may be simply that the related component—for example, a document—needs to be updated. For example, imagine you are at a restaurant and you like the service you are getting from your waiter. Every time you go you ask for that person by name to get you water. There is a dependency here on the name of the waiter. For example, what happens when the waiter quits? Does this mean you will die of thirst? You could, if you keep insisting that person gets your water. But, if you are flexible enough to just ask for water from "a waiter," then you are safe. You don't need to worry about what happens to any particular waiter as long as you are guaranteed to get your drink. In the same manner, if a relationship includes a dependency on a third-party software component for which the business organization does not have the source code, then you're in trouble and your application might no longer work or its functionality will change.

Understanding an application's structure will become very important in a component-based development environment. These structures can be complex, involving configuration of components in determining where they reside and how they interact. These are some of the issues we will address when designing and developing our components in Chapter 8, "Understanding COM Internals," and when looking at how we create our application object model.

Reusing Components

Most opportunities for reusing software components today occur when the semantics are reasonably well agreed upon—that is, when the object models, were they to be constructed formally, would meet with little objection. This involves largely technology services rather than business services, where technology services include services to handle print, list box, and other infrastructure objects with business-neutral semantics and rules. Third-party component building blocks today, from ActiveX controls to database management systems (DBMSs), are largely technology services. Interest in what have been called commercial lines of business objects will continue to increase, but will require agreement on business interfaces and semantics across companies. A large percentage of business software reuse opportunities today involve reuse of source code. Often, this reuse is informal rather than formal. Individual programmers reuse algorithms and data validation routines, sharing code with other members of their development teams or companies through source code control systems. Code is copied, tailored, and modified for new uses or new deployment constraints.

Reuse of source code will continue to be important for component builders because there will be areas of code that are hard to reimplement or difficult to understand.

Layering Your Components

There are several architectural layering models you can follow to develop a client/server solution. Some of the popular ones are the two-tier remote data access model (business processing on the client) and the database server model (business processing in database stored procedures), as well as the three-tier application server model (business processing independent of both the client and the database). In particular, the three-tier model suggests that shared business processes and business logic should reside neither on the client nor the database server, but rather on a business tier of servers, to maximize distributed processing and guard all access to and manipulation of corporate data.

The right partitioning model will depend on the application's requirements. For example, an N-tier layering model will service applications that require high levels of customization, need remote or disconnected access, and are highly scalable in enterprise-wide settings.

The SCUBA Approach

The layering model also services business applications directed toward taking advantage of the emerging popularity of the Internet. Throughout the book we will be exploring the different layers of and approaches to developing a highly scalable, component-based, UI-independent, business-oriented architecture. (We call this the SCUBA approach for short.) The SCUBA approach fits every type of business application. It is particularly helpful for applications that have the following requirements:

Scalability requirements. Scalability is a key aspect of the N-tier environment. Ideally, to address performance requirements, each client request should be serviced on demand. In order to address requirements, developers should be able to plan on having the ability to service an ever increasing number of client requests. The business tier should support unlimited on-demand concurrency.

Component requirements. We feel that components offer developers the best way to build distributed applications. Their object-oriented

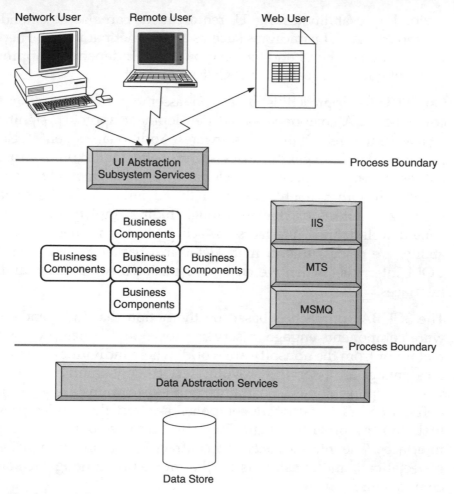

Figure 1.3   The SCUBA architecture.

properties of modularity and information hiding make them easy to extend and to maintain. Because they're large, they very naturally implement entire business entities such as customers, products, or employees. So, at development time they're easily reused, and at deployment time they simplify application partitioning and distribution. In addition, Transaction Server assumes component-based applications and a component-based approach to development.

UI requirements.   In business applications, the UI can be a very vulnerable area. End users demand control over the UI; they want to be able to customize it to fit their business needs. Developers also need the flexibility to change the UI seamlessly based on feedback provided by usability testing. UI requirements can also be extended to support new UI paradigms such as an Internet paradigm. Therefore, separation of the UI and focusing on the UI-independent approach is one of our main goals in the SCUBA approach.

Our SCUBA approach is based on assembly of applications from components. A component-based development approach significantly increases the reusability of software. Additional benefits relate to improved development processes, such as better logical problem analysis and decomposition, parallel development, and incremental replacement of software. Other benefits stem from the advantages of encapsulation— minimizing effects of change through hiding implementation details behind well-defined interfaces—which positively influences maintainability. We discuss this in more detail in Chapter 8, "Understanding COM Internals," when we create our business components and their interfaces.

The SCUBA approach is based on the notion that independent software components engage in service provision. Service provision is a metaphor from the nonsoftware world, where individuals and companies engage in a service provider–service consumer relationship in which responsibilities, constraints, and expectations are governed by defined contracts. Software components reflect the service provision metaphor by providing logically related services defined in exposed interfaces. The interface acts as a contract, specifying responsibilities, expectations, and constraints on the interaction among the software components.

Constructing applications by assembling software components has benefits in many areas, including maintainability, reusability, parallel development, outsourcing component supply, and taking advantage of distributed computing. Grouping services into categories helps establish useful guidelines for developers as to how these benefits may be achieved. For example, division into task support and visual interface, business rules, and data appears to provide a useful basis for software component design and construction that meets the needs of a broad set of business applications.

Business object modeling provides the rationale for the sound design of reusable, easily maintained software components. Business objects are object-oriented business modeling concepts that encapsulate business rules, policies, and decision making. As they exist in business models and software design models, they provide a consistently meaningful link for business users from their business models through to executable software components.

The activities of many possibly diverse and distributed software components may require coordination to complete a given service. A special kind of service—a business transaction—is often a key operation of a business object, and may require the services of special infrastructure components to manage, track, and coordinate its successful completion. Transaction coordination is an example of an infrastructure service that needs to be provided by software components independent of any particular business application.

SCUBA Complements the DNA Model

Windows DNA architecture is not just one product or one technology. It is the first application architecture that integrates the Internet, client/server, and PC models of computing into a framework of distributed computing solutions. Windows DNA represents a unified approach for building distributed, scalable N-tier applications. Windows DNA applications use a standard set of Windows-based services that address the requirements of all tiers of the distributed applications: user interface and navigation, business processes, and storage.

The heart of Windows DNA is the integration of Web and client/server application development models through a common object model. Windows DNA uses a common set of services such as components, Dynamic HTML, Web browser and server, scripting, transactions, message queuing, security, directory, database and data access, systems management, and user interface. These services are exposed in a unified way at all tiers for applications to use.

To implement our SCUBA approach, we rely on the tools, technologies, and services that Windows DNA makes available to us. We will highlight the services of Windows DNA that we are reusing as we discuss them in chapters.

Does DNA Fit Your Business Application Needs?

Because Windows DNA is an application architecture that unifies the development of Web applications and traditional client/server applications, you might find that some of its services might not apply to your specific application needs, especially if your application has light Web requirements or none at all.

The following questionnaire will help you assess whether or not your application can benefit from the Windows DNA set of services and architecture. When developing applications today it is easy to get too involved in technology and forget about your users' needs and business needs. The questionnaire will help you identify what is important to your users and your business.

Does your business application need to be Web ready? Windows DNA applications can take advantage of key Internet innovations such as the World Wide Web. Through Microsoft Internet Information Server, Windows DNA applications can present user interfaces created in Dynamic HTML, the standard language for creating interactive Web interfaces. This offers a simplified browser interface, centralized maintenance, and the efficiency of a just-in-time software delivery model that gives users the most up-to-date software. And, by targeting Microsoft Internet Explorer 4.0, Windows DNA applications support a wide variety of client operating systems, including Windows NT, Windows95, Windows 3.1, Windows CE, Macintosh, and Unix.

Does your business application require a high degree of maintenance? Through Microsoft's Zero Administration initiative, Windows DNA architecture and its component elements can be managed centrally. This allows network administrators to install and update applications without having to adjust each user's PC manually.

Does your business application need to be dynamically configured? Windows DNA architecture can change its configuration and capabilities dynamically by using the new interception enhancements in COM+. So, as business conditions or other environmental factors change, the application logic itself can change, too.

Does your business application need to work in a disconnected or mobile mode? Windows DNA includes capabilities to allow mobile computers to intelligently partition and store data and functionality while connected to the corporate network, so users can take advantage of business applications even while disconnected from that network.

If you answered yes to any of these questions, then Windows DNA will be a good application methodology to adopt. Throughout the coming chapters we will be validating the promise of Windows DNA with our SCUBA approach.

Visual Basic and the Architecture Process

There is a fundamental commitment you must make when architecting N-tier client/server solutions in Visual Basic: You must adhere to the COM guidelines. When you decide to use VB to build implementations of an N-tier product, you in fact sign a COM agreement that states that you agree to follow the guidelines and concepts involved in whatever COM feature VB supports. This is the basis for this book, and we go into these guidelines in detail in future chapters.

The standard paradigm recommended for Visual Basic client/server applications is that of a series of tiers or layers. In this section we explain the strengths and weaknesses of that approach when it comes to VB. First, we need to understand the layers of a typical Visual Basic application.

Visual Basic Layers

Just to get your feet wet, we'll explore what a VB-tiered program looks like. Let's take the three-tier model that is common among client/server development and extend it with one additional layer that provides abstraction interfaces. In future chapters we discuss not only how to create logical component layers, but also how we can move these components into physical layers using technologies such as Microsoft Transaction Server (MTS) and Microsoft Message Queue (MSMQ). Let's first start by understanding the responsibilities for the layers and what should and shouldn't be part of each. I suggest copying the layer guidelines and keeping them next to your computer so that as we develop the different layers you are always reminded of the dos and don'ts. After each layer description, we supply a short coding example that outlines how an update to a customer record is processed from the front end all the way through the database. This example is intended to show how the control of a process can be subdivided into the four layers of a VB application.

User interface layer. This layer is the topmost layer and is where all user interaction occurs. It supports no dependents and is directly dependent on the data interface. This layer is almost entirely non-reusable and is completely contained within the application boundary.

```
Sub cmdSaveRecord_Click ()
    'Begin by changing some of the UI Visual Elements
    cmdSaveRecord.Enabled = False
    pnlStatus.Caption = "Processing Request..."
    'Call the SaveRecord function
    SaveRecord
    pnlStatus.Caption = "Processing Complete"
    cmdSaveRecord.Enabled = True
End Sub
```

Data interface layer. This layer is where all data is contained or manipulated in memory. It directly supports the user interface and is directly dependent on the business interface. This layer is mostly nonreusable and is usually contained completely within the application boundary. However, in the case of distributed, reusable component areas, the component can manage its own data.

```
'This function verifies the data in the UI meets certain preliminary
'criteria for a save. Then it calls the save transaction.
Sub SaveRecord ()
Dim sCustcode As String
Dim sCustName As String
...
        If txtCustcode.Text <> icCustLen Then
        'Call the error the error handler
        ErrDisplay "Custcodes must be " & Str$(icCustLen) Exit Sub
    End If
    sCustCode = Trim$(txtCustcode.Text)
    ...
    if UpdateCustomer (sCustCode, sCustName, ....) then
    ...
End Sub
```

Business interface layer. This layer is where all transaction-based processing of data occurs. It coordinates all permanent storage of data either through file or database access. This layer supports the data interface and is dependent on the external access interface. It may be reusable and can extend past the application boundary in the same way as the data interface.

```
'This function does the update of a customer.
Function UpdateCustomer (ByVal sCustcode As String, ....)
Dim sParam As String
UpdateCustomer = False
'Validate Customers
'If The Customer Code is Valid then
```

```
            UpdateCustomer = True
      Else
            'The update failed, so call the error handler
ErrDisplay "An Error occurred while updating Customer" & sCustName
End
If
Else
      'The validation Failed
      'Call the error display module
      ErrDisplay "An Error occurred while updating Customer" & sCustName
End
If
...
```

External access and component interface layer. This layer provides abstraction interfaces to the user interface, the data interface, or external data sources in the form of files, databases, or hardware. It supports the business interface and in most cases is completely reusable. This layer can also be managed strictly by a component area that falls outside the component boundary.

```
Function ExecSQL (ByVal sSQLQry As String) As Integer
ExecSQL = False
      'Check Valid connection
      If SQLConnectionDead(iSQLConn) = NUM_ERR_DEADCONN Then
         ...
      End If
      ...
      iRes = SQLCmd(iSQLConn, sSQLQry)
      iRes = SQLExec(iSQLConn)
      Do Until (Results(iSQLConn) = NOMORERESULTS)
      Do Until (NextRow(iSQLConn) = NOMOREROWS)
            If Val(SQLData(giSQLConn, 1)) = NUM_EXEC_SUCCESS Then
            ExecSQL = True
            Else
            ExecSQL = False
                'Error data could be in column 2
            End If
         Loop
      Loop
End Function
```

User Interface Layer

The user interface layer is the only portion of the application that is responsive to user interaction. The user interface layer is where all data is presented to the user by means of window objects. The user interface is also where all inputs or modifications to data are made by means of window objects. The user interface is one of two layers that reference window objects such as controls, forms, and so forth. In the best-case scenario, the user interface layer is the only layer that references window objects. However, in reality, allowing the data interface layer to reference the window objects directly can significantly reduce the amount of code and help to simplify code paths. Since there are many aspects of a design that must balance out (maintainability, reusability, performance, and simplicity), tradeoffs such as this are often considered.

What Should the User Interface Layer Include?

- All event handlers or events. These subroutines are called in response to some user action—a click, a mouse move—to change the status of a window object such as Form_Resize or Lost_Focus or to call back procedures. It also includes procedures that either fill controls with data or retrieve data from controls. As stated previously, the line between the user interface and data interface layers is often very fine when it comes to the issues of filling controls or retrieving data from controls. The responsibilities of the user interface layer include operations such as the presentation of data to end users in a way that makes it easy to understand and manipulate. This includes decisions about which controls and objects are included on the form and how these controls are organized.

- Acting on any changes that occur on the user interface layer, such as repainting the controls and forms when the view changes and enabling, disabling, and activating the Windows controls on the form.

- Processing user requests by packaging these requests and sending them to another component that handles the actual processing.

What Should the User Interface Layer Not Include?

VB makes it extremely easy to get carried away with placing all kinds of nonrelated user interface logic into forms and controls such as business logic or database logic. To design a truly scalable system, we need to get rid of some of the bad habits that VB lets us get away with. Some of these habits are also the types of things that shouldn't be in the user interface layer, such as:

- Code that directly interfaces with database files.

- Processing of business rules, such as finance charges, and validation of the results.

- Enforcing business processing and the flow of transactional logic. An example would be placing code in the user interface layer that forces the end user to perform a business action before processing the initial request.

Data Interface Layer

The data interface layer is where an application completes all of its in-memory data manipulation. This layer is responsible for validating and manipulating all of an application's data, and also supplies all data to the user interface layer for display in window objects. This layer supplies all data to the business interface layer for use in the supervision of the external access interface. This includes SQL strings and parameters. The data interface layer can use locally stored data sources such as registry entries or caches to store operational parameters and data. However, all external access is achieved through the business interface.

What Should the Data Interface Layer Include?

The data interface layer includes any routines that perform operations on the data of an application. The responsibilities of the data interface layer include such operations as:

- Loading and setting stored operational parameters. These functions retrieve user or application settings from a table or registry.
- Sorting, validating, and formatting data in arrays or structures. When the user interface layer makes requests for data, it's the responsibility of the data interface layer to sort the data before it is presented to the client. This can be done based on parameters supplied by the client.
- Formatting data for use in the business interface. The data interface layer should not only be responsible for formatting data back to the client, but also for taking data from the client and performing the same operation but this time presenting the data to a business layer.
- Enforcing data interface business rules, such as the verification of data existence. The data layer also needs to enforce validation rules. These rules can also come from another lower-level data layer such as a metadata layer, which we discuss in Chapter 12, "Data Access with Visual Basic 6."

What Should the Data Interface Layer Not Include?

Because the data interface layer interacts with data, it is easy to get carried away and claim a larger territory for it than you are actually allowed. The data interface layer should not take control over every component that deals with data. The success of an N-tier component-based architecture depends on how disciplined and responsible each layer is and how well each layer respects its area of responsibility. To achieve this goal, it's very important to understand what you should not include in the data interface layer. This includes operations such as:

- Displaying application data or information via window objects. The data interface layer's job is not to display data, but to present it to the user interface layer and let the user interface layer handle the display of the data. The data interface layer performs the delivery; the user interface layer accepts or rejects the delivery and then presents it to the UI controls.

- Enforcing business processes and transactional flow of logic. The data interface layer should not attempt to enforce any operations that control or influence the business logic. The data interface layer will aid the business interface layer in making decisions by presenting data and posting data when the business logic asks for it.

Business Interface Layer

The business interface layer is part of the working internals of a client/ server application. The business interface layer controls all data accessed by the application from the database. In addition, it controls *all* updates to the data in the database that are initiated by the application. The business interface layer uses the external access interface layer to process its communication with the external data source and uses the data interface layer as its application data repository.

What Should the Business Interface Layer Include?

The business interface layer oversees the external access interface in the transfer or manipulation of all data to and from an external data source. The responsibilities of the business interface layer include such operations as:

- Initiating or building queries. The business interface layer is responsible for most of the implementation work of the business rules. A portion of the business rules tasks involve the building of queries.

- Enforcing business processes. The business interface layer takes full responsibility for enforcing the business rules and transactional logic. It is the one centralized place where all core operations happen.

- Handling violations of external access business rules, such as triggers that fire or write permissions. Seeing that the business interface layer enforces the processing of business rules, it also makes sense to let that tier handle exceptions and violation to the rules.

What Should the Business Interface Layer Not Include?

Since the business rules are the application's brain, it is natural to attempt to use them to control all other components and functionality. This is where you need an understanding of what each layer is responsible for. It is critical that the business interface layer not control any of the following areas:

- Handling of presentation logic. The business interface layer should not dictate how data is displayed to the user interface layer.

- Performing data manipulation operations such as sorting arrays or formatting data. The business interface layer should suggest data formatting based on business rules, but should not perform these specific tasks.

- Setting or resetting parameters. In some cases the business interface layer will find it necessary to set certain parameters to ensure the integrity of the operation. Although this is valid, it should be limited to initiating requests and not include performing the operation itself.

External Access Interface and Component Interface Layer

The external access interface layer embodies the communication of an application with an external data source. The external access interface layer is the specific transport or transports the application uses to communicate with an external data source. Some common transports are ADO and ODBC. These transports require different code to complete specific functions. By encapsulating a series of external function calls or methods within modular functions, you can build reusable code that reliably completes certain component operations. For example, the component operation of logging into a database can be encapsulated in some general fashion. This same code can be used without modification in every application that uses an identical transport. The architecture used to call this function can be used even in applications that use a different transport. This preserves the consistency of a code base and allows for enhanced reusability and extensible architectures.

There are several benefits to coding a specific external access interface layer. The first is the demonstrated benefit of reusability. A second benefit derives from an application that has a central pipe where all its external communication is completed: The ability to tap into a central location for logging and error handling can be a tremendous time-saver. A third major benefit is that encapsulating transport-specific code makes it extremely easy to replace an existing transport's code with code from a different transport. This method also allows an application to make modifications to the implementation of a transport without modifications to the application-specific code.

What Should the External Access Interface Layer Include?

The external access interface layer directly handles *all* communication with an external data source. The responsibilities of the external access interface layer should include such operations as:

- Executing all queries. There is a key difference between this function and that of the business interface layer. The business interface layer built the query based on business criteria. The external access interface layer is responsible for executing the query.

- Retrieving all information from the external access interface layer such as GetNextCustomerRecord. The external access interface layer is responsible for executing all the navigational and operational types of database interaction.

- Passing along all external data source messages, errors, and so forth. When an error occurs in processing any of the database activities, the components have the responsibility of raising any type of errors or messages back to the calling function.

- Opening and closing files or databases such as OpenFile and DBConnect. One of the major responsibilities of this interface layer is the handling of file operations and database connects. This layer is also used to create abstractions for accessing a variety of database types, so that business components and clients don't need to know anything about data location or data types. One day the client is talking to Microsoft Access, the next day to Microsoft SQL Server.

What Should the External Access Interface Layer Not Include?

One of the objectives to aim for with the external access interface layer is to preserve the abstraction it provides. We want to be very cautious not to disturb this functionality and to keep it as pure as possible. We can achieve this by keeping the following distractions out:

- Displaying application data or information via window objects. Again, we want to ensure that the interface limits its interaction only to the database and not to the user interface layer.

- Performing data manipulation operations such as sorting arrays or formatting data. This interface's job is executing tasks. It has absolutely no data manipulation or formatting responsibilities.

- Controlling the flow of transactional logic. The external access interface layer services the requests of the business interface layer, but it does not control the logic and functional operation of that layer.

External Component Interfaces

External component interfaces are components that exist outside an application boundary and provide some service to those applications that instantiate them. External component interfaces are becoming much more common with the onset of OCX controls and OLE server functionality in Visual Basic.

Where do external component interfaces fit into the layered paradigm? With so much functionality being encapsulated and reused in these external component interfaces, the need to position them within the layered paradigm is very real. Fortunately, the layered paradigm facilitates the use of such components with ease.

External component interfaces are positioned entirely on the basis of how much ownership they exert over their own display mechanisms such as data storage and manipulation, transactional logic, and external data access. If an external component interface is responsible for its own data, as for example an object encapsulating customers, it may require an application's data interface to interface with its data. If it only manipulates data—for instance, the calculation of accumulated interest for a credit card over a certain period—it may not require the data access interface layer to interact with it at all. It may, however, require the business interface layer to interface with it to generate a match code for an example, or it may require the external access interface layer to interface with it via a SQL connection.

External component interfaces fit in smoothly with the layered paradigm. The only point that deserves special consideration is that of consistency. When you use an external component interface, we recommend that your application implement a standard, reusable set of core functions if at all possible. This consistency throughout the application adds significant value when code bases are compared, code is reused, and complex applications are debugged.

Caution about the Layered Paradigm

As with any paradigm, there are also limitations. Some potential dangers relate to component operations. This happens when component operations become so small that they become core functions in disguise.

Module overload is another pitfall that you should avoid. This happens when the number of module component operations becomes too great to keep track of easily. You can combat this by grouping modular component operations that support the same component area into the same module. For example, rather than using 14 types of inserts, updates, and deletes, it would be preferable to move the component operations for a product into the same modular grouping. The operations for an insert, update, and delete on a product will all go into a single product maintenance module. This becomes a component module.

Our final caution has to do with mixing layers. Problems occur when layers are mixed in some areas and not in others. For example, in the data interface layer for implementing product maintenance, the code may reference a window object. Conversely, in the data access interface layer for implementing customer maintenance, the code does not reference a window object. This situation can be confusing and is not very maintainable. Consistency is the key to overcoming this and a great many other programming trouble spots.

Winding Up

Let's order pizza. We suggest a pizza for two reasons. First, you can see that there is a lot of work ahead for us in architecting the application, designing our COM components, and understanding all the implementation details for a successful N-tier component-based application. The most important reason for ordering a pizza, however, is that it helps us present a real-life example of the concepts of layers and responsibilities.

When you order a pizza, you make a phone call and say, "I need one large pizza with extra anchovies." Chances are the person taking your order is not the one who is going to eventually make the pizza. Think of the person taking your order as the UI-centric business component. You don't tell this person how to make the pizza or where the cheese and tomato sauce go, you just give him or her your request.

After you hang up the telephone, the person who took your order turns around and gives your order to the cook. The cook is the one who performs the work. He or she may delegate some tasks to an assistant, but for the most part the cook is ultimately responsible for the work. Once the cook completes the task and the pizza is ready, another person enters the scenario and promises to deliver your pizza on time. That person drives the car and comes to your door and hands you the pizza. He or she does not come in, set the table, or help you chew the pizza. His or her task is to simply deliver the pizza to you. As the UI person, it is now your responsibility to present the pizza to your family.

Now, imagine that there are no predefined roles and guidelines for ordering and making a pizza. Each person with a role in our earlier scenario can choose what he or she wants to do. You will end up with a scenario where you call to place your order and the cook answers the phone and says, "I'll be right over to cook the pizza and serve it to you and your family; I'll do it all." Although this may sound nice, it's not efficient when the cook has 10 people calling at the same time.

The most important aspect of a successful N-tier system is design. You need to understand your application requirements and user needs in depth. You also need to examine your application services and components closely to determine the most efficient way to develop your application.

In the following chapters we discuss in detail the discipline involved in building a robust N-tier application. By the way, it's not a bad idea to order a pizza for real.

CHAPTER 2

Introduction to COM

C OM? Who cares about COM? As Visual Basic programmers, our job is to write great applications at top speed. COM was never necessary before, so why should we use it now? It's only going to slow us down.

Well, there are actually some very good reasons to learn about and use COM. It addresses some of the needs of modern business applications very well. Today, more than ever, business requirements change frequently. Components make it easier to replace functionality without having to completely reinstall your software. In this age of reduced development budgets, COM also helps out by making reusable software more of a reality.

One of the common misconceptions about COM is that it is difficult to learn and use. COM can be very straightforward, and when used with Visual Basic, downright easy. You just have to get beyond that learning curve and get enough of it under your belt to become comfortable with it. This chapter will cover much of this, including the following:

- An overview of COM and components, how they came about, and the major aspects of component-based software development.
- The pros and cons of COM and components.
- The basic process of creating COM components in Visual Basic.

What Is COM?

When Visual Basic first came out, the world of Windows programming opened to the masses. It presented a simpler model of event-driven programming that anyone could use. Even your little brother or sister could write a simple program. No longer were you required to learn more complex programming languages and write large quantities of code in order to get the simplest of Windows programs working. You could create a useful program in a fraction of the time it used to take.

To some degree, this is still true. Visual Basic still makes Windows programming much easier and more productive for all programmers, from beginner to expert. The same basic concept of drawing your user interface and writing code behind it is still the core of Visual Basic. However, the tasks we are asked to perform as developers are now much more complex than they used to be. Our software has to support multiple simultaneous users, access more complex databases, operate in multicomputer environments across networks, and take advantage of new technologies. Visual Basic has evolved with the world of advanced software requirements and new technology, but it can't handle everything by itself.

In order to address some of the modern business requirements, such as easily modifiable functionality and reusable functionality, the concept of software components was devised. A component is a discrete piece of software that does some specific, predefined work that your program (or anyone else's program) can make use of. It is self-contained and thus easily replaceable. The idea was great, because it allowed you to write a component once and then use it everywhere, while giving you the ability to correct or enhance the component's functionality simply by updating and replacing the component. Making this work, however, would require a formal standard that everyone could use to create components, ensuring that they would be compatible and interchangeable.

The COM/CORBA Wars

The concept of developing a component standard came into fashion with several groups all at once. The two largest and most prominent were the Object Management Group (OMG) and Microsoft. The OMG, a consortium of companies that banded together, created a component standard called Common Object Request Broker Architecture (CORBA), which originally led the way, gaining major industry support. Microsoft, or course, had its own ideas about creating a component standard. Its answer, called Component Object Model (COM), immediately started gaining ground on CORBA, especially in the Windows world.

Both standards cover the basics of creating reusable software components. In the software industry, the two standards each have their own distinct supporters, who feel very strongly about the merits of their chosen standard. Discussions about the pros and cons of these two standards on Internet forums can become quite heated. The COM versus CORBA debate is second only to the PC versus Mac debate in emotion and intensity. Both support the separation of business functionality from the client software, as well as software reuse. There are distinct differences between the two standards, but they are not really relevant here. The important point is that while CORBA is popular in the Unix environment, COM is the predominant standard in use on Windows platforms. If you are using Microsoft tools, including Visual Basic, COM is your answer.

The Component Object Model

Of course, COM stands for Component Object Model, the Microsoft standard for creating software components. This tells you who made it and how to spell it, but not what it really is. COM is a specification for the construction and binary compilation of software components. This means that COM is not a programming language; it is not a library of code; and it is not compiler. The COM specification tells you how to build components so that they can communicate with each other and with your application, and it tells a compiler manufacturer how to create the binary-compiled components so that they can be used by any COM-compliant application. COM is kind of like a rule book. If you follow the COM rules, your components will be able to work with other COM components, whether you or someone else wrote them.

COM has several important characteristics, including the following:

- Component code
- Interfaces
- GUIDs
- Binary compatibility

Component code is the actual work your component does. Once you get the component infrastructure set up, your component has to do something. If your component is intended to perform work related to invoices, then you'll have to create component code to calculate totals, do inventory lookups, and so on.

Interfaces allow any program to access the functionality of your component. An interface is a collection of public function definitions that your component makes available to your program and other components. The interface tells the rest of the world what your component can do and how to make use of its functionality.

A Globally Unique Identifier, or GUID (rhymes with "squid"), is assigned to every COM component and interface ever created, uniquely identifying it to the operating system and other software. When you change your component or interface in any way, you get a new GUID for it. GUIDs are ugly, superlong codes that look like this: 6262D3A0-11CF-91F6-C2863C385E30. This is the GUID for the Microsoft MSFlexGrid control. Usually, you will not have to worry about the GUID; Visual Basic will create one for you.

It is important to note that COM components conform to a binary standard. This means that regardless of the language you use to create your COM component, it will be compatible and usable by other COM components. If your astronomical calculations component is written in C++ and your telescope control component is written in Visual Basic, they can still use each other's services.

COM = Components + Interfaces

A COM component is nothing without its interface. The interface defines the public functionality that other software and components can use. Typically, when you are planning your components, you design the interfaces first. This is important, because the interaction between components is the most complex part of building a component-based application. It takes time and planning to define all the interfaces so that the components provide all the functionality needed by the rest of the software.

Personal computer (PC) hardware provides a good analogy to help you understand COM. Your computer is expandable, allowing you to add or remove functionality in the form of additional hardware. This additional hardware is similar to software components. If, for example, you need more display capabilities, you can replace the video board with a more advanced one. Simply buy a new one and put it into an open bus slot in the computer.

The bus slot is the interface. IBM designed the original PC as an open architecture, thus making it easy to add or remove hardware. In order to ensure that new hardware would work correctly with the computer, IBM created a standard interface to the computer in the form of a bus on the computer's motherboard. Each slot conforms to the standard that IBM created and defines how other hardware can communicate with the computer. As long as any new hardware obeys the rules of the interface standard, the hardware will be able to communicate with the computer.

The same thing applies to software components. You first create a component that has an interface defined for it. For example, you might create a component that calculates the total energy output of a laser your company manufactures. Part of your interface would include access to the function CalculateLaserOutput, which takes a power input value and a laser model number as input parameters. It might look like this:

```
Public Function CalculateLaserOutput(Power As Single, Model _
as Integer) As Single
```

Other parts of your program, including other components, can access this functionality by calling it through the interface. Now suppose that you add some new models to your line of lasers, and you have to update the functionality of the CalculateLaserOutput function. As long as you don't change the interface (in this case, you won't have to), you can update the component code, recompile the component, and replace only the component. Everything else in the program, components or otherwise, now has access to the new functionality without requiring changes.

It is important to note that once an interface is defined and published (made available to the world at large), it cannot be changed. One of the rules of COM guarantees that software can rely on an interface remaining the same once it has been published. This helps to prevent compatibility problems. However, even though you cannot change an existing interface, you can extend it by adding functionality.

You can see why it's important to plan your interfaces carefully. If you do a good job of thinking ahead, you will reduce the likelihood of having to change the code that uses a particular component. As long as the interface does not change, the code that uses the interface does not have to change. If you do not plan your interfaces well, then it is more likely that they will change, requiring changes to the surrounding code as well. If part of your plan is to accommodate frequently changing business functionality, then you'll want to be able to simply drop in a new component that updates the software. If your interfaces do not change, this will be a piece of cake.

The Two Faces of COM

COM has both pros and cons. It's important to know when to use COM and when to ignore it. The information and guidelines presented in this section will help you to distinguish between a situation that calls for COM and one that does not.

The Benefits of COM

Understanding the benefits of COM will make it easier to decide when it is important to use COM for your software project. When you see all that COM has to offer, you will be convinced of its usefulness.

COM components are easily replaceable.   There's an old cliché to the effect that the only two certainties in life are death and taxes. We'll add one more thing that you can be sure of: Software changes. No matter what the reason, software will require changes, and when it does, you will be called upon to make them.

COM makes this much easier than updating your entire program. Without components, you would most likely make changes to code and build them into a large application that lives on all your users' machines. Once you make the changes and rebuild the program, you will have to assemble it into a new release that can be installed on all the client computers. If your program was built using COM components, you can rebuild and ship a single component.

COM components are ideal for changing business requirements. The business requirements of software are usually fairly fluid. During development, as well as after software has been deployed, new requirements and changes to existing ones are constantly flooding in. User's requests, bug fixes, and new requirements from marketing and management need to be accommodated. Your particular application, because of its nature, may also require updates and frequent changes to business rules. For example, a program that calculates taxes would have to be updated at least once a year to implement new tax law changes.

Because COM components are easy to replace, you could localize your business rules into a few components. If the business rules change, you can make the changes in the components, rebuild them, and distribute the new components. This would prevent you from having to make changes throughout the program, as long as your interfaces don't change. Your work will be localized—and so will the likelihood of errors propagating through the program.

Suppose you built those tax law calculations into a single component called TaxCalcs. Your update for the end of the year would be a single component that you could send to your users instead of a complete program, which would have to be tested from head to toe. The component would isolate the changes so that only the component and the code that directly uses it would have to be retested.

COM components help make reusability a reality.   One of the best things about COM is that it makes it fairly easy to write some code once and then use it all over the place. For example, you could create a component that handles all your string functions. Over time, you can make any corrections or additions to the functionality of the component. Any application can make use of the component.

COM components make parallel development easier.   Typical COM development means that you develop the component interfaces first, to make sure that everything will work together. Then you implement everything that the interfaces say you should. The nice thing about this is that once the interfaces are designed, distributing them to several programmers allows the implementation of the components to proceed in parallel. You might have a strings component, a calculations component, and a data retrieval component. All can be built at the same time, and if the interfaces are designed properly, they'll all work together when they're done.

The Trouble with COM

Although COM is good, COM is not perfect. You'll need to address some annoying things about the mechanics of COM, or COM will bite you.

COM component versions are a pain. Every COM component gets a GUID, a unique ID that the operating system uses to identify your component. These GUIDs are stored in the Windows system registry. Normally, this would not be a problem. However, every time that you change your component's interface, a new GUID is assigned to it. This mechanism is used as a version number to indicate to the software using the component that the interface has changed. It ensures that once you start using a component, you'll always be using the same version of the component. If you want to use an upgraded version, you get its new GUID.

The problem is that these component versions cause as many problems as they cure. During development, you have to pay careful attention to the versions of the components you are using. Every new build of the component results in a new version. It is very easy to get out of synch, which can cause real debugging problems. Make it a common practice to check your component versions during development each time a new build is created.

Old interfaces must hang around. One of the requirements of COM is that once an interface is created, it never goes away, thus ensuring that once a program makes use of a specific version of a component, that version's functionality is always supported. For example, making use of a specific function in a component, such as a quadratic equation function, guarantees that this function will always be there with the same number and type of parameters, regardless of the component version.

As COM developers, we are required to keep old versions of component interfaces intact. You can add functionality to a component or update existing functionality, but you cannot remove existing functionality. The only real problem this causes is the evolution of a bloated component. At some point you may have to move your functionality to a new component altogether if it gets too large or has too much old functionality dragging it down.

COM interfaces require careful planning. As mentioned before, interfaces are an integral part of COM components. The interfaces are the communication mechanisms that components use to talk to each other and to access each others' functionality. We have also seen that every time a component or its interface changes, a new version is associated with the component.

Careful planning of interfaces will help prevent too many versions of your interfaces from proliferating during development. If the components and the software that makes use of them are to have any hope of working together, the interfaces have to be designed correctly the first time. While a couple of changes in an interface are usually not a problem, the more often you make changes, the more versions you get, and the more confusing it may become to keep track of which one you should be using.

COM and Visual Basic

With COM, Visual Basic makes a repeat performance. It made Windows programming a heck of a lot easier for many people, and more productive as well. Now it does the same thing with COM components. Many of the tedious and problematic details, such as reference counting, are done for you automatically, letting you concentrate primarily on the functionality provided by the component.

Some programmers get a kick out of those details. They enjoy writing code to handle threads, managing COM interfaces at the lowest level, and writing their own message-handling systems. However, most programmers have business-related work to do, and using COM components with Visual Basic makes this easier than ever. Visual Basic provides you with many tools to make component building easier. We'll give you an overview of these tools in this chapter and in Chapter 8.

Visual Basic Classes

If you haven't had the chance to toy with Visual Basic classes yet, make sure you find the time soon. First, Visual Basic classes are fun. They allow you to create your own object extensions to Visual Basic. You'd be surprised how organized your program can become by using classes. The class modules can also be used by other Visual Basic projects. Second, Visual Basic classes are the mechanism by which COM components are created. If you expect to be writing COM components with Visual Basic (and we hope you do!), classes are the key.

What's a Class?

Classes are a combination of regular old Visual Basic code (called *methods* and *events*), properties, and data, all packaged into one unit. In Visual Basic, once you have created and compiled a class, you have created a COM component, which can be reused by other programs as well as the one you're currently building. Classes are also extremely convenient and are excellent organizational tools.

Sometimes, a class contains information and functionality that are related to each other and treated as an object. For example, you might create a class called TaxReturn, which has the following attributes:

Class: TaxReturn

Properties: TaxPayer, Salary, Year, SSN, Address, TaxesWithheld

Methods: CalcTaxes, FileTaxes

Once you build your data and methods into a Visual Basic class, you create an instance of it in the code that needs to use it. It can be used just like any other intrinsic Visual Basic object, such as the Printer or Screen objects. As soon as you type the name of the object followed by the period, a list of your classes' properties and methods appears. They work just like an extension of the Visual Basic language.

The Anatomy of a Class

As mentioned, classes are composed of methods, properties, and data. As with any programming language, Visual Basic has specific language constructs and rules you can use to implement these features of components. We'll be taking you on a crash course of class implementation that should get you up to speed in no time.

Class Data

A class can contain any sort of data that it requires. A DiskDrive class might store such obvious data as a drive letter, disk size, and amount of free space. It might also store less obvious data, such as unique disk label and volume information that only the class, not everyone else, needs to know. The difference between data that the class makes available to others and data it uses strictly for internal purposes is delineated by the public and private keywords. They are declared in the public area of the class module, outside of any functions or procedures. The implementation looks like this:

```
Public sDriveLetter As String * 1
Public dDiskSize As Double
Public dFreeSpace As Double
Dim sDiskLabel As String
Dim sVolume As String
```

The private data items, declared with the Dim statement, cannot be seen outside the code for the class module. The public data items are not only visible to the outside world, but can also be changed by anyone. Public data items in a class become properties. They are simple to implement, but also dangerous, because anyone can change them without your knowledge. A better way to implement items that the other components and code can change is as formal properties.

Class Properties

Class properties are data items you can set and retrieve within a class. More abstractly, they represent attributes of a class that other code can set. The Caption property of a Label control is an example of a property. While you can implement properties as a public data item, as mentioned previously, you do not have any control over the data that someone assigns to the property. The best classes protect themselves from bad data, and you can only do this with code.

In order to do this, Visual Basic provides three types of class properties: Get, Let, and Set. They are each used in the following manner.

Get. Used to retrieve the current value of a property. The safety feature you typically build into a Get property is that it returns a safe default value if no value has yet been set for the property. A Get property would be implemented as follows:

```
Public Property Get DiskSize () As Double
    If dDiskSize < 1 Then
        DiskSize = 0
    Else
        DiskSize = dDiskSize
    End If
End Property
```

Let. This type of property is used to set the value of a data item in the class. You should always build a data-validation safety check into this property to help the class protect itself from bogus data. A Let property implementation is illustrated here:

```
Public Property Let DiskSize (dNewSize As Double)
    If dNewDize < 0 Then
        dDiskSize = 0
    Else
        dDiskSize = dNewSize
    End If
End Property
```

Set.   Much like the Let property, a Set property sets the value of a data item in a class, but Set is used only to set an object reference. This type of property should always check the incoming object reference to make sure it is not equal to Nothing.

```
Public Property Set WhichForm (f As Form)
    If Not f Is Nothing Then
        Set ClassForm = f
    End If
End If
```

One of the most important points here is that a class should protect itself from bad data being sent in. Before a class can help others, it needs to be able to help itself. Because we have the power to protect ourselves, it makes sense to use it.

Class Methods

Class method is another name for procedures and functions located in a class. Class methods have direct access to the data members, public and private, of the class. They can themselves be declared public and private. Public methods can be accessed by the users of the class, while private methods can only be called by other methods of the class itself. All the real work of the class is done by its methods.

There's no real trick to methods. They look just like regular functions and procedures. As with properties, they should do as much error handling as possible to help protect the class from the dangers of invalid data.

Visual Basic is so class- and component-oriented that it provides a host of tools to help you out. The Class Builder helps you create classes quickly, in line with the whole Visual Basic concept of rapid development. The Object Browser helps you to navigate through your classes. And the entire Visual Basic language makes building COM components simpler than it's ever been.

The Object Browser

The Object Browser, a valuable tool built into Visual Basic, may be unfamiliar to you, especially if you haven't dealt with classes yet. It allows you to explore any object known to the Visual Basic system, whether it's part of Visual Basic or your project. Figure 2.1 illustrates what the Object Browser window looks like. To view it, press the F2 key in Visual Basic.

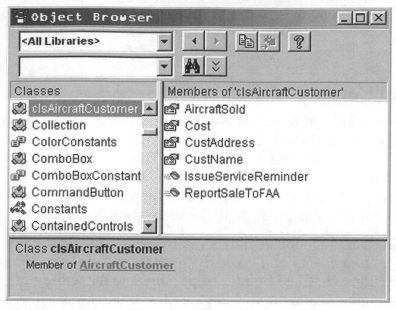

Figure 2.1   The Visual Basic Object Browser.

Take a quick tour of the dialog. Starting in the upper left, we begin with the Library list. From here you can select the major library you want to view, including All Libraries. Under that is the Search field. Enter any search phrase you like in this field, and click the Search button. Any references to your search phrase will be listed in the window. Next is the toolbar, which contains Next and Previous buttons, a Copy button, a View Definition button, and Help. Under that are the Search and Show Search Results buttons.

The major components of the window are the two large panes. The left one contains all the classes available in the selected library. The right pane lists all the members (methods, properties, events, types, etc.) available in the selected class. At the bottom of the screen is a short listing that displays some details about the selected items.

The Object Browser becomes more useful as your project gets larger. This is a good thing, because N-tier applications tend to be large ones. As the number of components and classes in your system grows, you will begin to appreciate how easy it is to navigate your project using the Object Browser. It acts as a directory of everything in your project.

It can also be a marvelous tool for exploring what's available in the Visual Basic system components. Spend some time one afternoon just browsing through all the objects and classes in the list. You might be surprised what sort of goodies you run across.

The Class Builder

Classes are integral to Visual Basic 6.0. If you delve into Visual Basic beyond even the shallowest depth, you will encounter classes and find that you need to be able to create them. The designers of Visual Basic knew that you'd be creating classes all the time and that many aspects of classes, such as implementing Get, Let, and Set methods, are tedious. To help out with this problem, they created the Class Builder.

Class Builder is a tool that allows you to create and edit the properties, methods, and events of a class. By generating code from the settings you provide to it, Class Builder helps eliminate the tedium of creating classes. Figure 2.2 illustrates what the Class Builder looks like.

A quick walkthrough of a few of Class Builder's features will help make its benefits clearer. We'll be creating a simple little class to represent the customers of an aircraft manufacturing company. If you'd like, feel free to load the project (AircraftCustomer.vbp) we already typed in for you on the companion CD-ROM in the \examples\ch02ex01 directory.

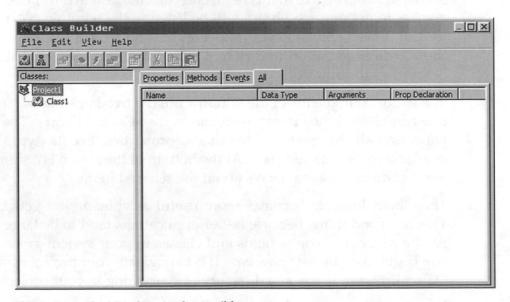

Figure 2.2 The Visual Basic Class Builder.

We'll need to track some information about the customers, as well as to perform some actions on that data. The following list details the attributes of our class:

Class: AircraftCustomer

Properties: CustName, CustAddress, AircraftSold, Cost

Methods: IssueServiceReminder, ReportSaleToFAA

For now, we'll just be building the COM object itself. Later in the chapter, under Using Your COM Component, we'll show you how to make use of it. We'll be performing the following steps with Class Builder in order to construct the AircraftCustomer class:

1. Plan your component and its interface.
2. Create an ActiveX DLL project in Visual Basic and set its properties.
3. Fire up Class Builder.
4. Use Class Builder to add our data items and properties to the class.
5. Use Class Builder to add our methods to the class.
6. Create the code.
7. Compile the project to a DLL.

As we have mentioned, it is very important to give your component and its interface careful thought before implementing it, because you don't want to change it once it has been published. If you're building your component in a team environment, make sure it provides all the services and interfaces required by the rest of the system. Holding design reviews with your team members can be very helpful in this regard.

Our class represents a customer of a company that sells aircraft. After careful consideration, we have concluded that our component needs the properties and methods listed in Table 2.1.

Table 2.1 Our Class and Interface Definitions

CLASS: AIRCRAFT CUSTOMER PROPERTIES	METHODS
Customer Address (Get, Let)	IssueServiceReminder
Aircraft Sold (Get, Let)	ReportSaleToFAA
Cost (Get, Let)	

The next step is to create the project in Visual Basic. To do this, start Visual Basic. When it's ready for you, it will ask what type of project you want to create. Select ActiveX DLL. Figure 2.3 shows the Visual Basic project dialog and the correct selection to make. The ActiveX DLL is the typical project type you will use to create a COM component DLL that other projects can use.

Once the project has been created, the important class property to set is the Instancing property. Make sure it is set to something other than Private or PublicNotCreatable. These setting values will prevent other classes or programs from creating an instance of the COM component. The default value is MultiUse, which should be fine for most purposes.

Set the name of the Project to AircraftCustomer and the name of the class to clsAircraftCustomer.

Because we already have a class to work with, we start Class Builder by highlighting our class in the project explorer window and selecting it from the Add-Ins menu. It may give you some warning dialog about the fact that the class was not created with Class Builder—whatever. Just clear it and Class Builder will start.

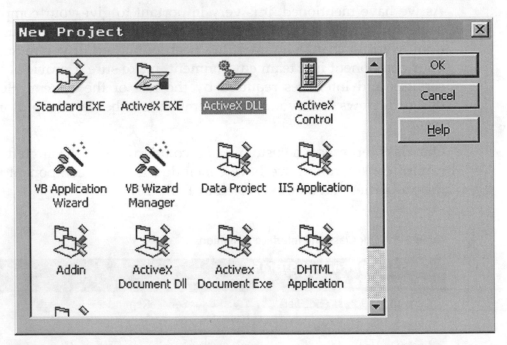

Figure 2.3 The ActiveX DLL project selection.

It is a distinct possibility that Class Builder will not be available on the Add-Ins menu. To correct this problem, select Add-In Manager from the Add-Ins menu. A dialog will appear, which is illustrated in Figure 2.4. Select the VB 6 Class Builder Utility and check the Loaded/Unloaded and Load on startup options on the dialog. This will load the Class Builder now, as well as every subsequent time Visual Basic is started.

You could also start Class Builder by adding a new class to the project, even though this is not how our example is doing it. In the Project Explorer window of Visual Basic, right-click on the project and select Add Class Module from the context menu (you could also select Add Class Module from the Project menu). Double-click the VB Class Builder icon in the dialog box, as shown in Figure 2.5. Class Builder will start and we can start to add our properties and methods.

Once Class Builder has started, we can create and edit properties and methods easily. We need to add four properties to the class: CustName, CustAddress, AircraftSold, and Cost. To add the CustName to the class, click the Properties tab to make sure we're on the right page, then click the class name in the left-hand pane to give us the right focus. Click the

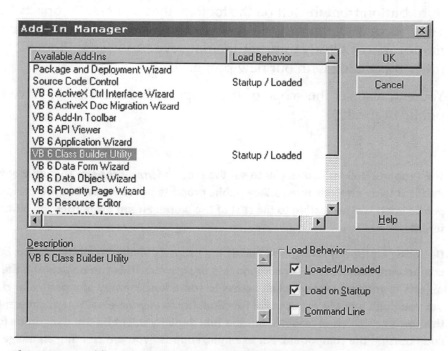

Figure 2.4   Adding Class Builder via the Add-In Manager.

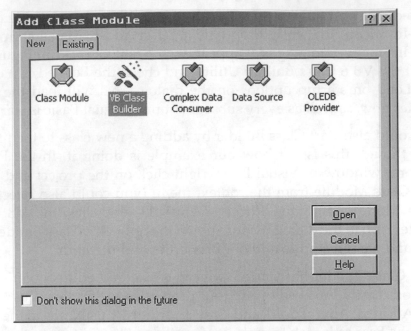

Figure 2.5 The Class Builder selection in the Add Class Module dialog.

third button from the left on the toolbar, the Add New Property button. The Property Builder dialog will be displayed. Fill in the name of the first property, CustName. Set the data type to string. Figure 2.6 illustrates this dialog with our new property.

You can also set the scope of the property here. For now, leave it as a public property.

TIP

The Property Builder allows you to set the scope of your property to public or friend. Public is fairly straightforward. Any public property becomes part of the component's public interface, accessible to the rest of the world. Friend properties are a little different.

Declaring a property as a friend makes the property visible to all the objects in your component, but not to other components or software. This can be useful if the other objects in your component need access to some functionality of a particular class but you don't want to expose that functionality to anyone else. You might want to do this for organizational reasons, but the functionality might be too dangerous for the code outside the component. For example, suppose you are creating an Image class that stores and operates on a graphical image. One class might store all the graphics

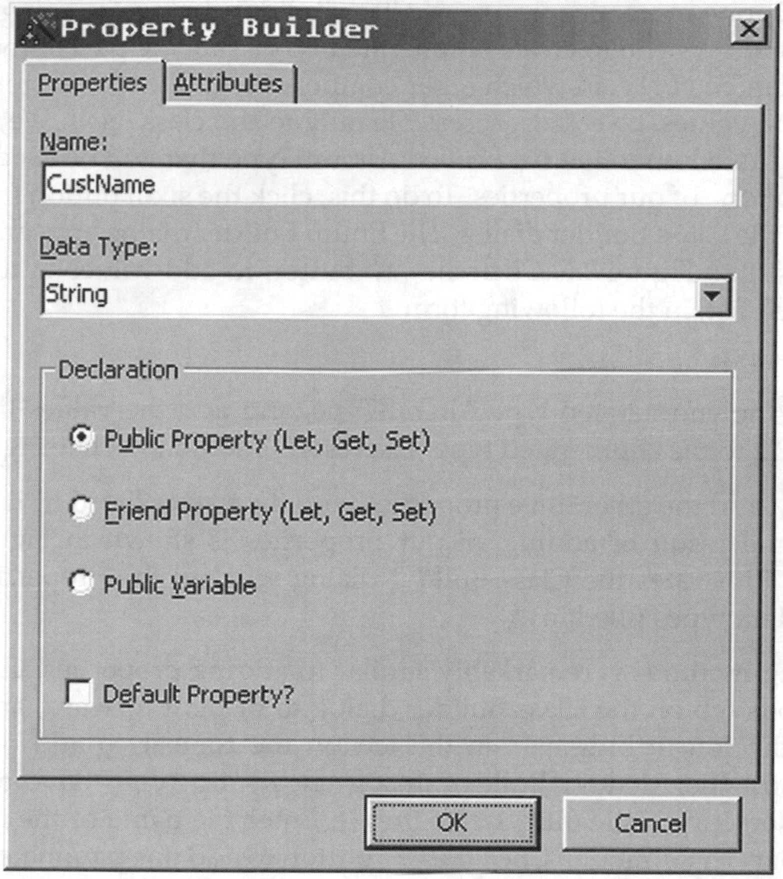

Figure 2.6 The Property Builder dialog.

data and make it available to other classes in the component through friend functions. However, we would not want other components or software to have direct access to the data, because they could do anything to it—even corrupt it.

Because the friend property is not part of the class's public interface, it cannot be accessed using late binding, where an instance of the component is assigned to a generic object variable. If you declare an object variable as

```
Dim x As MyClass
```

the friend functions are available for use in the rest of the component. However, if you declare it generically and assign it using late binding, as in

```
Dim x As Object
```

the friend functions are not available to the rest of the component.

There is one more nice feature of Class Builder that we're going to use here. It allows you to create enumerated types that are part of the class. They can be *public*, in which other components and code can reference the type values, or *private*, accessible only to the class itself. We will be adding an enumerated type called AircraftType that will be used as the type for one of our properties. To do this, click the sixth button from the left on the Class Builder dialog. The Enum Builder dialog appears, looking just like Figure 2.6. Click the "+" button to add values to the enumerated list, in the following form:

```
Name=Value
```

Name the enumerated type AircraftType, and add the values listed in Table 2.2 to the enumerated type. The results should look like Figure 2.7.

Finally, add the other three properties with the values listed in Table 2.3. The final result of adding all our properties is shown in Figure 2.8, which illustrates the Class Builder dialog with all the properties and their data types filled in.

Adding methods is remarkably similar to adding properties. Click the Methods tab on the Class Builder dialog to bring it forward, and then click the fourth button from the left on the toolbar to add our first method. The Method Builder dialog shows up (they have a lot of "Builders" in this feature, don't they?). Enter the name of the method IssueServiceReminder. Click the "+" button to add one parameter to the method. The Add Argument dialog pops up, illustrated in Figure 2.9. Enter "frequency" in the Name field, check the ByVal box to turn it on, and set the Data Type to integer. This parameter represents the number of months that signify the type of service we are reminding the owner about (a 6-month service, a 12-month service, etc.).

When you click the OK button, the parameter will be added to the Method Builder dialog, which should now look like Figure 2.10.

Table 2.2 The AircraftType Enumerated Values

NAME	VALUE
PiperCub	1
CessnaCitationJet	2
Mig21	3
LockheedVega	4
DouglasDC3	5

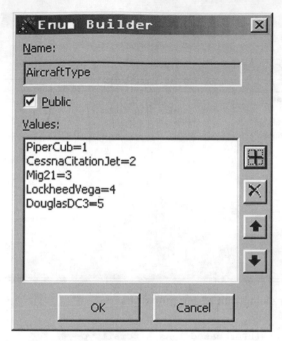

Figure 2.7   The Enum Builder dialog.

Add our remaining method, called ReportSaleToFAA. It has no parameters. Click the OK button to close the dialog. You can cruise around the Class Builder dialog to see all our settings. If you click the All tab, you'll see our properties, methods, and the enumerated type all on one page. This is illustrated in Figure 2.11.

NOTE

When using Class Builder to add an enumerated type to your class, you need to be aware of a problem in Visual Basic. When you create a Get property using Class Builder that returns a value of your enumerated type, the generated code will have an error in it. This code fragment illustrates what it will generate:

Table 2.3   The Remaining Class Properties

PROPERTY	DATA TYPE
CustAddress	String
AircraftSold	AircraftType
Cost	Currency

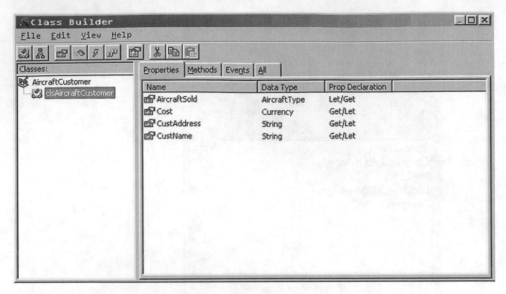

Figure 2.8 The Class Builder dialog with all our properties.

```
Public Property Get AircraftPurchased() As AircraftType
'used when retrieving value of a property, on the right
'side of an assignment.
'Syntax: Debug.Print X.AircraftPurchased
    Set AircraftPurchased = mvarAircraftPurchased
End Property
```

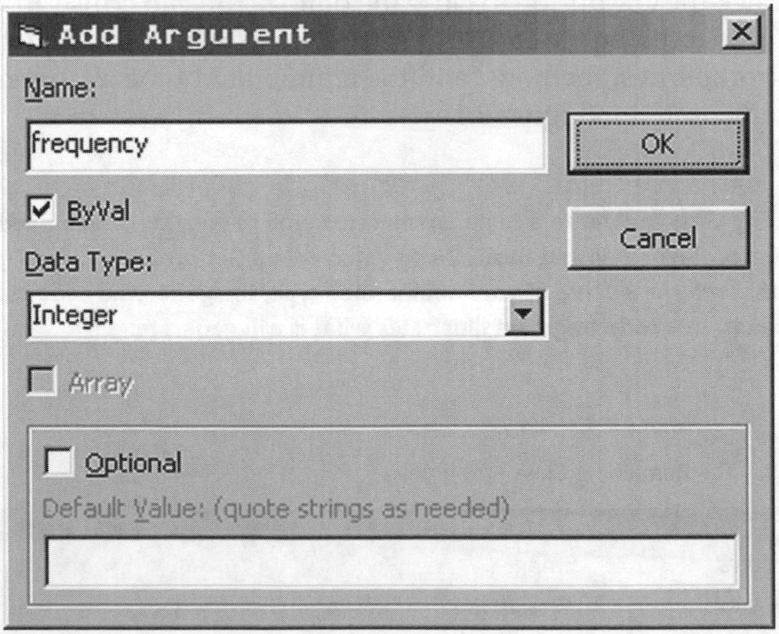

Figure 2.9 The Add Argument dialog.

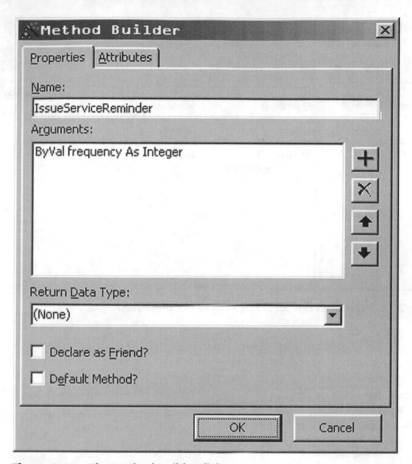

Figure 2.10   The Method Builder dialog.

Note the use of Set in the assignment statement. This is not correct. Set is only used when an Object assignment is being made. You'll have to remove the Set part of the expression before the code will compile or run correctly.

Now that we have all our settings for the new class, we have to let it do the real work and create the code from our settings. Select the Update Project item from the Class Builder File menu. It will generate code and dump it into the class code window. The listing it generates follows:

```
'local variable(s) to hold property value(s)
Private mvarCustName As String 'local copy
Private mvarCustAddress As String 'local copy
Private mvarAircraftSold As AircraftType 'local copy
Private mvarCost As Currency 'local copy
```

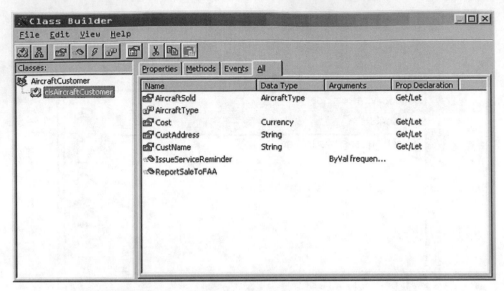

Figure 2.11 The Class Builder dialog with all our attributes.

```
Public Enum AircraftType
    PiperCub = 1
    CessnaCitationJet = 2
    Mig21 = 3
    LockheedVega = 4
    DouglasDC3 = 5
End Enum

Public Sub ReportSaleToFAA()
End Sub

Public Sub IssueServiceReminder(ByVal frequency As Integer)
End Sub

Public Property Let Cost(ByVal vData As Currency)
'used when assigning a value to the property, on the left side
'of an assignment.
'Syntax: X.Cost = 5
    mvarCost = vData
End Property

Public Property Get Cost() As Currency
'used when retrieving value of a property, on the right side
'of an assignment.
'Syntax: Debug.Print X.Cost
    Cost = mvarCost
End Property
```

```
Public Property Let AircraftSold(ByVal vData As AircraftType)
'used when assigning a value to the property, on the left side
'of an assignment.
'Syntax: X.AircraftSold = 5
    mvarAircraftSold = vData
End Property

Public Property Get AircraftSold() As AircraftType
'used when retrieving value of a property, on the right side
'of an assignment.
'Syntax: Debug.Print X.AircraftSold
    Set AircraftSold = mvarAircraftSold
End Property

Public Property Let CustAddress(ByVal vData As String)
'used when assigning a value to the property, on the left side
'of an assignment.
'Syntax: X.CustAddress = 5
    mvarCustAddress = vData
End Property

Public Property Get CustAddress() As String
'used when retrieving value of a property, on the right side
'of an assignment.
'Syntax: Debug.Print X.CustAddress
    CustAddress = mvarCustAddress
End Property

Public Property Let CustName(ByVal vData As String)
'used when assigning a value to the property, on the left side
'of an assignment.
'Syntax: X.CustName = 5
    mvarCustName = vData
End Property

Public Property Get CustName() As String
'used when retrieving value of a property, on the right side
'of an assignment.
'Syntax: Debug.Print X.CustName
    CustName = mvarCustName
End Property
```

Interestingly enough, the Get AircraftSold property created a Set statement in the code instead of a normal assignment, as in

```
Set AircraftSold = mvarAircraftSold
```

This code will not compile correctly, because AircraftSold is not an object. Simply remove the Set from the expression and everything will compile just fine.

Notice that there is no code in the ReportSaleToFAA and IssueServiceReminder methods. The Class Builder just put in placeholders for us. For the purposes of this example, we're just going to put message boxes in there that state the function has been carried out. Modify these two methods to add the following code.

```
Public Sub ReportSaleToFAA()

    MsgBox "Sale of aircraft to:" & vbCrLf & vbCrLf & _
        mvarCustName & vbCrLf & mvarCustAddress & _
        vbCrLf & "has been reported to the FAA.", _
        vbOKOnly, "AircraftCustomer COM Component"

End Sub

Public Sub IssueServiceReminder(ByVal frequency As Integer)

    MsgBox "A " & Trim(frequency) & "-month service " & _
    "reminder has been issued to " & vbCrLf & vbCrLf & _
    mvarCustName & vbCrLf & mvarCustAddress, _
    vbOKOnly, "AircraftCustomer COM Component"

End Sub
```

Our final step is to compile the project to a DLL. Select the Make AircraftCustomer.DLL option from the file menu. Click OK to build the DLL. Visual Basic creates a GUID for it, known as a CLSID, or class ID. It builds the CLSID into the DLL and writes it into the system registry so the rest of the world knows about it. It writes to several locations in the registry, but you can find them fairly easily. Run REGEDIT (in your Windows\System directory) to perform a search for AircraftCustomer. The first location it finds should be off the root directory called HKEY_CLASSES_ROOT, the key being called AircraftCustomer. It will list the CLSID for the COM DLL we just built. Ours came out to

```
95B9D6BE-403E-11D2-9ADC-444553540001
```

Once you know the CLSID, you can navigate to the following location in the registry:

```
\HKEY_CLASSES_ROOT\CLSID\xxx
```

where xxx is the CLSID we just found. This entry will list the location of the physical DLL file on the disk, in our case,

c:\src\ch02ex01\AircraftCustomer.dll

as well as the threading mode chosen for the component (it should read Apartment, the default for Visual Basic COM DLLs). This is a good way to hunt down exactly where your DLL went if you should lose it. A word of caution however: Don't make any changes to your registry while you're poking around. You could inadvertently change something you didn't intend to, possibly rendering your system unusable. Stick to read-only mode while in the registry.

And that completes the creation of your COM component. If this is your first one, congratulations! You've made your first foray into a larger world. And it was fairly painless, wasn't it? Of course, we still haven't made use of the component, but that's coming up next.

Using Your COM Component

This new component is now sitting on our computer. It's been fun so far, but we need a good ending to the story. It's time to realize the benefits of our COM component. We're going to write a little test program to utilize the services and properties we built into our component. If you don't like typing, you can load the ch02ex01.vbp project from the companion CD-ROM, located in the \examples\ch02ex01 directory.

The process of building our example will go something like this:

1. Create a new Standard EXE project in Visual Basic.
2. Add a reference to our new COM component.
3. Build the form.
4. Add code to the form.
5. Run the program.

First, we'll create a new Standard EXE project in Visual Basic. Select Create new Project from the Visual Basic File menu. When the New Project dialog appears, select the Standard EXE project type. Click OK to create the project.

The Windows system, and Visual Basic to some degree, knows about our component we created earlier. However, our new project does not. In order to imbue it with this knowledge, we need to add a reference to it in our project. Select References from the Project menu. The References dialog appears, illustrated in Figure 2.12.

Find the reference to our AircraftCustomer component and check it on. Our project now understands that the component exists and what it has to offer.

Next, we have to build the form. Visual Basic created a default form for us when we created the project. Add controls to the form until it looks

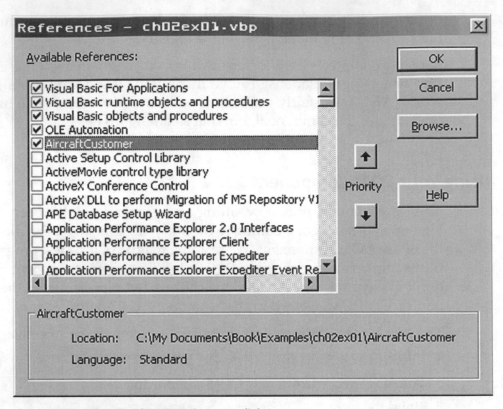

Figure 2.12 The Visual Basic References dialog.

like the illustration in Figure 2.13. The controls and their names are listed in Table 2.4.

We need to add code to handle events on the form and to create and talk to our component. Enter the code from the following listing into the code window for the main form. Read through the commentary in the code, as it explains some of the finer details of what's going on.

```
Option Explicit
' Create an object variable that will point to an
' instance of our COM component.
Dim ac As clsAircraftCustomer

Private Sub cmdExit_Click()

    Unload Me

End Sub

Private Sub cmdReport_Click()
```

```
        ' Collect data from form and stuff it into the
        ' component.
        CollectData
        ' Tell the component to report the purchase to
        ' the FAA. We here in the client don't need to
        ' know how it's done—the component knows.
        ac.ReportSaleToFAA

End Sub

Private Sub cmdService_Click()

        ' Collect data from form and stuff it into the
        ' component.
        CollectData

        ' Tell the component to send out the service
        ' reminder.
        ac.IssueServiceReminder 12

End Sub

Private Sub Form_Load()

        ' Allocate a new instance of clsAircraftCustomer.
        Set ac = New clsAircraftCustomer

        ' Fill in the aircraft combo box.
        cmbAircraft.AddItem "Piper Cub"
        cmbAircraft.AddItem "Cessna CitationJet"
        cmbAircraft.AddItem "MiG-21"
        cmbAircraft.AddItem "Lockheed Vega"
        cmbAircraft.AddItem "Douglas DC-3"

End Sub

Private Sub Form_Terminate()

        ' Free up the memory used when we allocated a
        ' new instance of clsAircraftCustomer.
        If Not ac Is Nothing Then
            Set ac = Nothing
        End If

End Sub
' Take the data from the form and stuff it into
' the clsAircraftCustomer component.
Private Sub CollectData()

        ac.CustName = txtName.Text
        ac.CustAddress = txtAddress.Text
        ac.Cost = txtCost.Text
        ac.AircraftSold = cmbAircraft.ListIndex

End Sub
```

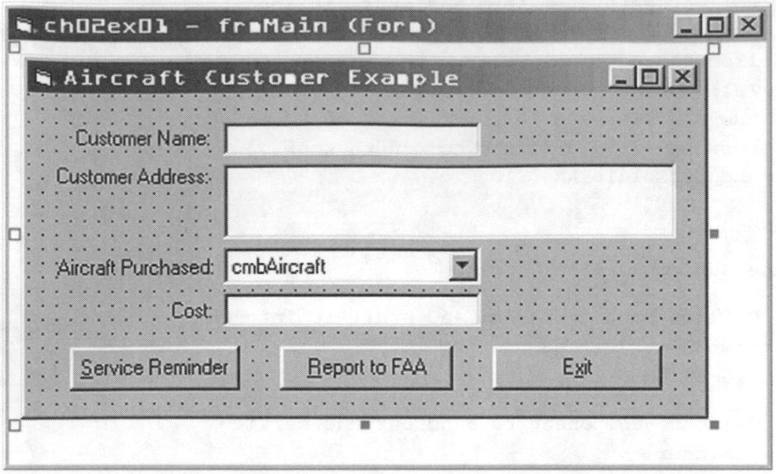

Figure 2.13 The AircraftCustomer test form.

The code brings up a couple of points worth mentioning. First, notice that we create an object variable called ac at the beginning of the program code. It is not of type AircraftCustomer, but instead of type clsAirCraft-Customer. AircraftCustomer is the name of the COM component we created, whereas clsAircraftCustomer is a class within that component.

Second, the FormLoad event actually creates an instance of our class by using the New keyword. With object variables, such as our clsAircraft-Customer variable ac, we need to create a variable to point to it and then actually create an instance of the class with the New keyword. This could have been done in one step using the following statement:

```
Dim ac As New clsAircraftCustomer
```

Table 2.4 Controls for the AircraftCustomer Test Program Form

CONTROL	NAME	RELEVANT SETTINGS
Text Box	txtName	none
Text Box	txtAddress	Multiline=True
ComboBox	cmbAircraft	Style=2
Text Box	txtCost	none
Command Button	cmdService	none
Command Button	cmdReport	none
Command Button	cmdExit	

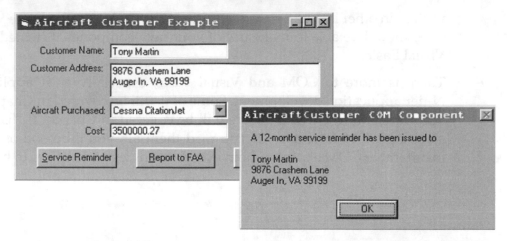

Figure 2.14   Our test program during execution.

Note that this allocates memory that needs to be freed before the program ends and, ideally, as soon as is practical. In the Terminate event for the form, we free the memory occupied by the object by setting the object variable to a value of Nothing.

Hit the F5 key and run this thing. You can enter information into all the fields and click the Service Reminder and Report To FAA buttons. You'll see that the functions in the component display the message boxes we built into it using the data in its properties. Note that we really didn't build much into our component in the way of error handling, so don't stress it out too much. Figure 2.14 shows the program during execution, along with one of the message boxes displayed by the component.

Our little test program had no trouble using this nifty COM component. Any other program, including a complex one, could make use of it just as easily.

Winding Up

You've had a taste of COM now—we hope a pleasant, flavorful one. Visual Basic makes it fairly easy to do the COM thing, allowing you to reap the benefits of COM combined with the rapid development that Visual Basic affords you. You have the beginnings of what you need to start making COM-based reusable components. Heck, even programs written in other languages that conform to the COM standard, like Visual C++, should be able to make use of your new components created with Visual Basic.

There is more to COM and Visual Basic, especially as it applies to N-tier application development. Some of it will be covered in Chapter 3, "Introduction to DCOM." More will be covered in Chapter 8, "Understanding COM Internals." If you read them all, you'll be one of those insufferable COM experts whom everyone envies and aspires to be.

CHAPTER 3

Introduction to DCOM

I f you read the last chapter, you've been exposed to a whole new world of reusable and extensible COM components. It's a new way to think about software construction. Your brain is probably racing back and forth, considering all the new possibilities and cool programming techniques you can play with. You're just settling in to a comfortable understanding of all that COM stuff.

Now we're going to throw a wrench into that comfort zone you've established. While COM allows you to create reusable components, what happens if you want those components to be located on a machine other than the client computer? After all, that's the goal of an N-tier application. Microsoft already thought of this long ago and created a slightly different flavor of COM, called Distributed COM, or DCOM. We'll be providing you with the tourist version of DCOM in this chapter and the detailed version in Chapter 9, "DCOM Details." If you're new to COM or DCOM, we'd recommend starting in this chapter. Resist the urge to jump to Chapter 9 to get the details, because it assumes that you know everything presented in this chapter.

This DCOM overview will cover the following:

- What DCOM is, why you should care, and how it works

- Some more information on DCOM-specific subjects (for example, passing data and error handling) and how DCOM differs from plain old COM

- How you create installations to deploy that distributed application

- How Visual Basic allows you to build DCOM components and applications that use them

NOTE

For most of the functionality referred to in this chapter, you will need the Enterprise Edition of Visual Basic. Only this version includes the remote, distributed capabilities used with DCOM. Visual Basic is sold as three separate versions: the Learning Edition, the Professional Edition, and the Enterprise Edition. Each of these has progressively more capabilities and a higher price tag. All of the remote capabilities are hosted in the Enterprise Edition.

DCOM is worthy of some careful scrutiny, so let's dive in.

What Is DCOM?

DCOM is not a complicated mystery. DCOM is just COM with a long-distance carrier. DCOM allows your components to run on a computer other than the one using your DCOM component. A standard COM component runs on the same machine and in the same process space (more on this later in this chapter) as the software that uses it. A DCOM component usually runs on a different machine (but it doesn't have to) and runs in its own process space. Whether it runs locally or remotely, the functionality of your component is available to your program or other components.

While the concept of DCOM is not much different from that of COM, quite a few surrounding details are different. To master DCOM is to understand these details and how they affect the software you are building. For example, error handling becomes a different issue when using DCOM, because the error has to be sent to the client, located on a different computer. Passing data over the network from the component to the client requires rethinking, because sending small quantities of data many times generates a great deal of network traffic. And because we're talking to another computer over a network, we have to consider security issues.

So, while the basic concept is the same as for COM, the remote nature of DCOM forces us to deal with some ancillary issues such as network traffic and security. We'll provide an overview of most of these issues in this chapter, and we'll clarify the intimate details in Chapter 9, "DCOM Details."

What's the Point?

As Visual Basic programmers embarking on an N-tier project, DCOM can be your ticket to the distributed part of your application. It provides you with the ability to talk to services on a machine other than the client computer. This is a big step forward for Visual Basic programmers, who have previously been shackled to the client machine with no access to other computers.

In the past, all your functionality was hosted on the client machine. If you were creating advanced enterprise applications, perhaps the database was on a server somewhere. With DCOM, you can now place actual functionality on the server and access it almost as if it were local. This provides some major benefits to the application programmer and the user:

- You can write a component once and have many programmers use it.

- You can design and implement only the component's interface, and other programmers can code to that interface while you run off and implement the code behind it that does actual work.

- When components change, you can replace them once in a single place—on a server instead of on every client machine. All clients get the update when the server-side component is in place.

Of course, along with benefits come trade-offs. DCOM is pretty darn good, but it's not perfect. You'll have to decide if the negative aspects of DCOM are worth the benefits it provides. Some of the cons of DCOM include the following:

- As a programmer, you have to change focus from being property-oriented to being service-oriented (see the next section in this chapter for more information on this). This requires you to think sideways a little until you get used to it.

- Installation of DCOM components is more involved than are traditional application installations. You have to make sure that the client knows about the server-side components and where they are located.

- Components located on a server are slower than components located on a client because of the network traffic turnaround time.

- Debugging DCOM components when they are located on a server is more difficult than debugging a local component.

Despite the drawbacks of DCOM, it's a great technology that you can put to work for your remote computing needs. Because N-tier applications are by nature loaded with remote component access, DCOM is probably in your future. If you ever begin to doubt whether DCOM is worth it, consider the alternative: implementing the remote communications, data passing, and coordination yourself. You might spend all the time allotted to your project on this aspect alone.

The Focus Changes

When first created, Visual Basic was a major advance for Basic programmers, because they could transfer most of their knowledge of the Basic language to a Windows environment. They had to learn about event-driven programming, a different paradigm than they were used to, but they made the transition. As Visual Basic advanced, it became more and more object-oriented. Programmers adjusted to this also. The Visual Basic system contained a large number of objects, such as the Screen, the Form, and every control known to humankind. They all had their own sets of properties that could be set or accessed. For a long time, Visual Basic was object-oriented and property-focused. It still is for the most part, except where DCOM is now involved. Properties make it very convenient and easy to save and access information about a particular object.

Now Visual Basic supports the development of DCOM components, which typically live on a server computer. This introduces a dilemma for the Visual Basic programmer, now so used to setting and accessing properties as a way of life. Accessing a few typical property settings looks like this:

```
rType = RobotComponent.Type
rSpeed = RobotComponent.Speed
rState = RobotComponent.State
```

Normally, the RobotComponent would sit on the same computer as the software that was accessing its properties. Instead, we make the Robot-

Component a DCOM component and host it on a different computer. Now, each time a property is accessed or set, a complete round-trip across the network is executed. For example, accessing the Robot-Component.Type property causes the software to run across the network to the server and ask the RobotComponent what its Type value is, which sends the value back across the network to the software that called it. Simply accessing these three properties creates three network round-trips. This is not an acceptable situation in a typical distributed application.

In order to address this problem, Visual Basic programmers have to make yet another paradigm shift, although this one seems like a step backward. When building DCOM components, your focus has moved away from property-oriented components to *service-oriented* components. This means that instead of writing components that rely on many properties, you should create components that send back large amounts of data with a single service call. Using our previous example, we would create a component that returned all the information formerly accessed by using multiple properties in a single call, like this:

```
' This Enum is a public Enum in our RobotComponent
Public Enum RobotInfoType
    RobotType As Integer
    Speed As Integer
    State As Boolean
End Enum
...
' This code is located in the client that uses the
' RobotComponent.
Dim ri As RobotInfoType
RobotComponent.RobotInfo ri
```

When you execute the RobotInfo call located in the server-side Robot-Component, it collects all the information necessary and packs it into the passed-in RobotInfoType enumerated type. Once it returns, the calling program can access all the information it needs, and only one network trip was generated. This is a good general practice to use when creating DCOM components.

While you are moving from *public* properties to services, there is nothing wrong with creating *private* services in the server-side DCOM component for use by the component itself. When the component accesses properties within itself, no network traffic is generated, and performance is not affected. For example, our RobotComponent might contain the following code, which it uses to implement the RobotInfo method:

```
Public Enum RobotInfoType
    RobotType As Integer
    Speed As Integer
    State As Boolean
End Enum

Dim rbtType As Integer
Dim rbtSpeed As Integer
Dim rbtState As Boolean

Public Sub GetRobotInfo (ri As RobotInfoType)
    ri.RobotType = Me.RobotType
    ri.Speed = Me.Speed
    ri.State = Me.State
End Sub

Private Property Get RobotType() As Integer
    RobotType = rbtType
End Property

Private Property Get Speed() As Integer
    Speed = rbtSpeed
End Property

Private Property Get State() As Boolean
    State = rbtState
End Property
```

While it may not be possible or appropriate to avoid properties all the time, attempt to reduce the amount of network traffic you generate by keeping a service focus instead of a property focus.

The Basic DCOM Mechanism

Just so you'll have a frame of reference as we continue our introduction to DCOM, we're giving you the quick-and-dirty DCOM picture. As you saw in Chapter 2, "Introduction to COM," a COM component is created in Visual Basic as an ActiveX DLL project, which contains classes your program can access through the COM component. This component is then registered on the client system in the Windows registry. In this way, you can add a simple reference to the client program project. It knows all about the component through the registry entries, including exactly where the DLL file is located on the machine, so it can be loaded and executed.

DCOM is similar, but there are differences. DCOM components are built as ActiveX EXEs. They still need to be registered, but they reside on a different machine. When the component gets registered on the client machine, information about its location contains not only the directory but also the computer in which the component is located. Using this information, the client software knows which computer to contact to access the component.

On the client side, an instance of the DCOM component is created, just as with any other component. The runtime system pops over to the registry and looks for the registry entry of the component you're trying to create. Assuming it finds what it's looking for, the system now knows on which machine the component is located. When you make a request of the component, it connects to that machine across the network and passes on the request. Any required data is transferred back across the network and sent to your client software.

You don't have to worry about the communication mechanism or locating the component. The operating system handles this for you. However, you do need to deal with the remote nature of the component during installation and deployment. We'll cover this in detail later in this chapter.

DCOM Discussion Topics

Earlier we alluded to the fact that, while DCOM is similar to COM, there are a handful of practical differences to deal with. Issues such as scalability, passing of data, and setting up and distributing the components are all handled differently from standard COM components. These differences are the subject of this section.

In- and Out-of-Process

You've probably heard of the terms *in-process* and *out-of-process* before. Perhaps you looked further into it, or maybe you just scanned right over them, not interested in what they really were. If you venture into the world of DCOM, you'll have to bite the bullet and learn exactly what these terms mean. Fortunately, we are going to tell you what they mean, why they are significant, and why you should care.

In-process. This means that a component is running in the same process space as the application that is using it. They share the same address space. In-process components are built as DLLs. All Visual Basic ActiveX DLL projects are in-process. This term is usually shortened to *in-proc*.

Out-of-process. This means that the component is running in a different process space from the application that is using it. They do not share the same process space. Visual Basic ActiveX EXE projects function as out-of-process components. This term is usually shortened to *out-of-proc*.

Why is this significant? The important point is that in order for a DCOM component to be able to run on a different machine, it cannot be part of the same address space as the client software. Therefore, all the DCOM components you create with Visual Basic will be ActiveX EXE projects, allowing them to run out-of-process. This will allow the components to execute on another machine in its own address space, yet still make its services available to your software.

The Surrogate

There is one exception to the fact that EXEs are out-of-process components and DLLs are in-process components. When writing components for Microsoft Transaction Server, you are required to create DLLs. This makes it difficult to create multipurpose components that can run in MTS or as standalone server-side DCOM components, because the DLLs cannot be accessed across the network as out-of-process components.

In order to address this problem, Microsoft created a utility called Surrogate that runs on a Windows NT server. Its purpose is to wrap a DLL component in an EXE so that it can be run as an out-of-process DCOM component. This exception allows you to use components that were built as ActiveX DLLs on a server as DCOM components. This utility is covered in more detail in Chapter 9, when DCOM is dissected.

Passing Data

Passing data to and from DCOM components is slightly different than for normal COM components because of the intervening network between the client and the component. This affects us in two ways. When you are passing data into DCOM components you need to pay careful attention to the passing mechanism you use. When you pass back data from a DCOM component, you need to do it in a more service-oriented fashion, as well as to select an appropriate mechanism for passing back large amounts of data.

Passing Data into DCOM Components

We don't want to hang onto connections across the network for any significant length of time. Doing so reduces available resources for other programs. Whenever we send data to a component, we want to make sure the data is sent and the connection dropped as quickly as possible, especially if the component will be busy for a while before it finished what we asked it to do.

To drop connections when speaking to DCOM components, make sure you pass your arguments into the component using the ByVal method. If you use ByRef, a reference to the data is passed to the component, and the connection to that reference is maintained until the method in the component completes its task. It does this in case it has to modify the value stored in the reference passed in. Instead, pass the value using the ByVal method. This will pass a simple copy of the value required by the method, which requires no continuous connection. The component method will still receive the value it needs, and we accomplish our goal of passing data in without maintaining any network connections.

Passing Data out of DCOM Components

We don't want to access properties too often, because every time a property is accessed or set, it creates network traffic. Instead, pass your data back in packages through methods. This will prevent numerous trips across the network by packaging all your data into one big chunk that can be sent using a single call across the network. You can use several mechanisms to do this, including arrays, strings, and Recordsets.

Arrays.   You can use arrays as a method for passing back large amounts of data from a server-side component. This has the advantages of being simple to understand and implement and can contain as much information as you like. However, arrays can be tricky to use. If you use arrays to pass back data that is not all of the same nature, both the component and the client have to know the organization scheme. For example, say you use an array to pass back a stock price, quantity available, and a broker code, arranged like this:

```
Dim stockData(3) As Single
stockData(0) = stockPrice
stockData(1) = stockQuantity
stockData(2) = stockBrokerCode
```

This will work, but the client software needs to know the layout of the array. This is not a good situation to be in, because the component cannot be reused by other components or clients that do not know the organization of the array. If the layout of the data has to change, so do all the clients and components that use it. It is a good idea to hide all the implementation details from a client so that the component is as reusable as possible.

If you are returning many instances of the same type of data, such as a list of 50 stocks, an array works fine, because it does not require any special client-side knowledge of the data layout.

Strings. You could easily package your data as a single string, concatenating all your data together with a separator to segregate the fields. Code to do this might look like this:

```
Dim returnData As String
Dim sep As String
sep = ";"
returnData = stockPrice & sep & stockQuantity & sep & _
stockBrokerCode
```

This is also easy to implement. However, as with arrays, it requires the client to know the layout of the string data. It has the added disadvantage that string concatenation is a slow process. There are occasions when you may not be able to avoid this, such as when the data is intended to be posted to a text box on the client. The key is to use it as necessary and appropriate.

Recordsets. You can use ADO Recordsets to pass data back to a client. The record does not have to be created by a database, but can be created manually in code. The great advantage of this technique is that the client does not have to know the specific layout of the data. This information, including the field name, the data type, and the data itself, can be extracted from the Recordset. Code to implement a Recordset in a component and pass it back to the client looks like this:

```
' This code is in a DCOM out-of-process component. Notice that the
' function has an ADO Recordset as its return type.
Public Function LoadSettings() As ADODB.Recordset

    ' 1. Create our Recordset object.
    Dim rs As New ADODB.Recordset
```

```
' 2. Set up the fields you want the Recordset to contain.
'    We have only two in this case.
rs.Fields.Append "SettingName", adChar, 32
rs.Fields.Append "SettingValue", adChar, 255

' 3. Open the Recordset. Note that this must
'    be done AFTER the fields have been
'    defined for the Recordset.
rs.Open

' 4. Add records to the Recordset. Here we are adding 3
'    rows to the Recordset.
rs.AddNew
rs!SettingName = "BodyFont"
rs!SettingValue = "Verdana"

rs.AddNew
rs!SettingName = "TitleFont"
rs!SettingValue = "Rictus"

rs.AddNew
rs!SettingName = "BodyFontColor"
rs!SettingValue = Str(RGB(100, 120, 140))

' 5. Send the Recordset back to the client.
Set LoadHomePageSettings = rs

End Function

' The following code is located somewhere in the client.
...
' Create an ADO Recordset object variable, but don't
' actually allocate it with New yet. The component function
' will do this for us.
Dim rs As ADODB.Recordset

' Create an instance of the DCOM component that will send us
' back a Recordset.
Dim x As New MyComponent

' Get the Recordset from the component.
Set rs = x.LoadSettings()
```

For small amounts of data or single values, use a user-defined structure type or a function return value. If you need to return larger quantities of data, consider using a Recordset or an array.

Passing data around from clients to DCOM components will work with the familiar BrRef parameters and properties. However, these are inefficient when used with DCOM, and other mechanisms (such as those previously discussed) are required if you're going to create scalable, performance-oriented N-tier applications.

Error Handling

Errors happen everywhere. In a common, standard EXE application on one computer, you can write a quick Visual Basic error handler to deal with system errors like file not found errors and to check return values of your own functions for local errors. This is fairly straightforward and easy to implement.

When you introduce server-side components into the mix, things get a little more complicated, but not so much so that we can't deal with it. You just have to understand the details. There are two particular issues to consider. First, we need to be able to deal with errors in general across a network when the error occurs in the component. Second, and a slightly more complex case, we must address errors that occur in another component referenced by the component the client is using.

In general, it is desirable for components to handle all errors. Whether the error occurs in the component itself or is an unhandled error from another component referenced by the base component, it should be handled at the component level. If this is not possible or is not appropriate, you can raise the error to the level of the client. The general method is to use the Visual Basic Err object to raise the error and to write code in the client to deal with it. If a component raises errors to the client, it is important for the programmer of the component to publish a list of the possible errors, their codes, and the reasons they are occurring.

The following example illustrates some code from a DCOM component and a client that is calling it. One important point to learn from this discussion is that if your component raises an error, you need to add the value of the vbObjectError constant to the error code you are passing back. This will allow the client to easily distinguish between local errors and those that occur in a server-side component.

```
Public Sub ChangeServerDirectory()
    ' This code is in the DCOM component, and generates an error.
    On Error Goto ErrTrap
    Chdir "\NonexistentDirectory"
    On Error Goto 0
    ...
ErrTrap:
    ' Components should handle all their own errors, but for this
```

```
        ' example, we're passing on to the client. We're using our own
        ' error code to indicate that the error occurred in the
        ' component, not in the client itself. We leave the error
        ' description intact.
        Err.Raise vbObjectError + Err.Number
End Sub

' This code is in the client.
Dim x As New MyComponent
Dim RealError As Long
On Error Goto ClientErrTrap
' Change to bad local directory
Chdir
' Change to bad server-side directory
x.ChangeServerDirectory()
On Error Goto 0
...
ClientErrTrap:
    RealError = Err.Number - vbObjectError
    Select Case RealError
    Case 76    ' Path not found error
        MsgBox "Error occurred changing local directories."
    Case vbObject + 76
        MsgBox "Error occurred changing server directories."
    End Select
```

The last important point about component-based error handling: Plan it carefully. In order for error handling to function correctly from numerous server-side components across networks and back to the client, you'll need to plan your error codes and their meanings to make sure they are consistent across the system. Establish your error list and their codes before you code a single component.

Marshaling

Marshaling is another of those terms that, if you haven't used DCOM before, is clouded in mystery, and something that's important only to other people. However, marshaling is easily explained, as well as important to grasp.

When you pass data from your application to a regular, in-process COM component, the components stack is used to store the parameters. This works just like calling a function in the application itself. However, when passing arguments to an out-of-process DCOM component, this is not possible. We need a different mechanism to effect parameter passing—a technique that allows us to move the data across the process boundary. This mechanism is called *marshaling*.

Marshaling works by a mechanism called *proxy/stub*. There is a proxy function built into the client and a stub function built into the component. The proxy marshals the data and prepares it for shipment across the process boundary to the component. The stub function in the component *un*marshals the data for use by the component. All this is transparent to you as a Visual Basic programmer and is built into the client and component for you. Don't worry about trying to implement it yourself. However, the fact that this mechanism exists and that marshaling is occurring is important to understand, as we'll see right now.

ByRef versus ByVal

Data coming into a component can be passed either by value or by reference. When dealing with regular local functions or an in-process COM object, you usually pass data based on which mechanism results in smaller amounts of data being sent. For instance, a large string or array of data is usually passed by reference in order to prevent sending the whole chunk of data on the call stack. This will result in a small pointer being passed instead of the entire string or array, which is faster. As Visual Basic programmers, we sort of got used to this and made it a normal practice.

Now with DCOM, things have flip-flopped again. The act of marshaling a reference takes longer than passing a string or an array of data (depending on the size of the array or string, of course). If you pass a reference to a large chunk of data, the address cannot be sent directly across the process boundary to the server-side component, because the address spaces are different. The marshaling mechanism has to create a duplicate reference that fits the target address space of the DCOM component and then send it over. This is a slow process and is usually not efficient.

To prevent the slow marshaling mechanism from bogging down your application, pass as much data by value as is possible. Sending larger amounts of data, such as an array or a large user-defined type, will actually be faster than the marshaling mechanism. This may vary depending on the quantity of data being sent across the process boundary. Try out some timing trials to see which is faster if you plan on sending large amounts of data from the server to the client.

Security

Security is an important issue when it comes to distributed applications. You and your customers have to be assured that only authorized users and applications will be creating and running the components that are installed on a server. The last thing you want to worry about is to have some unauthorized user calling the public interfaces of objects that could ruin critical data or even creating so many instances of a component that it brings a server to its electronic knees. Implementing security properly is the key to making your components run safely.

Providing security in your distributed application is not so much an issue of programming as it is of configuring security options correctly. It's more of a setup issue than a programming one, although you can program specific security details if you need to. There are two primary areas of security you need to worry about:

The client side.   The client software needs to know where the components are located—on which server machine and where on that machine. The administrator can set this up on each client computer.

The server side.   This is the really important part. The system administrator must configure each component, telling the system which user accounts have permission to create and execute the server-side components.

All this configuration is accomplished by using the DCOM Configuration Utility.

DCOM Configuration Utility

The DCOM Configuration Utility allows you to configure the location of applications and components and to set permissions for applications and components as well as the user accounts that have access to the applications and components installed on either a client or server computer. You will use this utility to configure access permissions for specific user accounts.

If you have Windows NT, the DCOM Configuration Utility is located in the Windows\System32 directory. You should be able to start it simply by hitting Start, Run from Windows NT, and typing in the following command:

```
DCOMCNFG.EXE
```

However, if you are running the DCOM Configuration Utility from Windows95 or Windows98, things work a little differently. If you are using Windows98, DCOMCNFG is included on your computer in the Windows\System directory. However, in order to make it work, you need to enable user-level security. You can do this through Control Panel, Network. Select the Access Control tab, then select the User-level Access Control option. Enter the name of your computer in the edit box. Getting DCOM onto a Windows95 machine is a little more involved. It does not come with DCOM capabilities or the DCOM Configuration Utility. However, you can download it from Microsoft's Web site at www.microsoft.com/com/dcom/dcom1_2/default.htm.

Once you download it, you can install it and follow the on-screen instructions to get DCOM for Windows95 running. You'll then be able to use DCOMCNFG.

Now we get to the utility itself. You'll probably spend some time here during the development of your distributed application, especially as you learn and experiment with the utility and security in general. You'll be an old hand once you've played around with it a little. Feel free to experiment; just make sure you stick to setting the rights of your own components and stay away from others you don't recognize, especially components and programs that look like system services.

Now that you have the DCOM Configuration Utility running, you'll see the main dialog, as shown in Figure 3.1. Looking at the screen, you see a list of ugly class IDs and some program names. There are also three tabs across the top: Applications, Default Properties, and Default Security. Each one will be covered in turn.

Applications

The Applications tab lists all the applications and objects on the system that can be launched or created on a remote machine. If the object or application has a *program ID*, it will be listed by its easy-to-understand name (for example, Microsoft Word). If not, it will be listed by its less friendly CLSID. From here you can find out where the actual DLL or EXE is located, set where the component will execute, and set up access permissions for the component.

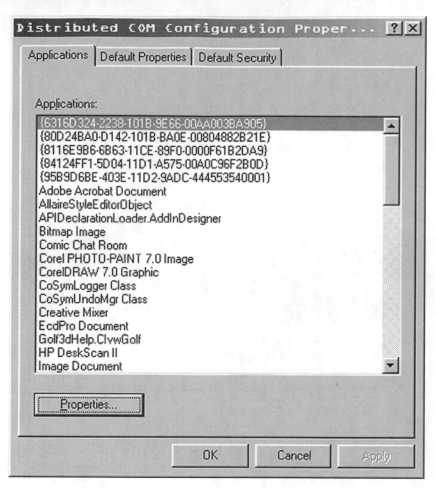

Figure 3.1   The DCOM Configuration Utility.

Highlight any component you like and click on the Properties button. A dialog will appear, as illustrated in Figure 3.2. Now we have three more tabs to deal with. Will this ever let up? Sure. We'll just touch on these three and move on.

The General tab tells you the name and the type of application or component, as well as where the component file, be it a DLL or an EXE, is located. It is strictly an informational tab. The Location tab is where you set the machine on which the component will run. You can choose the current computer or another one, and then specify it by machine name. Figure 3.3 shows the available settings.

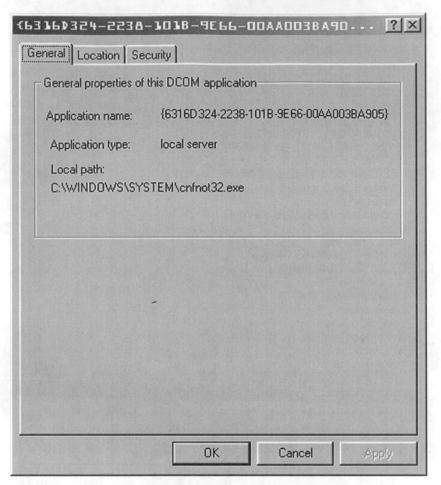

Figure 3.2   The Application/Component Properties dialog.

The last tab, Security, allows you to specify the security settings for the component. You can choose to use the default access permissions, which you can also set up using this utility, or edit the security settings, listing specific users who can access the component. This is where you can really restrict access to any component once it is installed on a computer. This tab is illustrated by Figure 3.4.

Default Properties

The Default Properties tab allows you to set DCOM communications properties as well as some of the security settings. The dialog appears in Figure 3.5. The first item on the agenda is the checkbox labeled "Enable

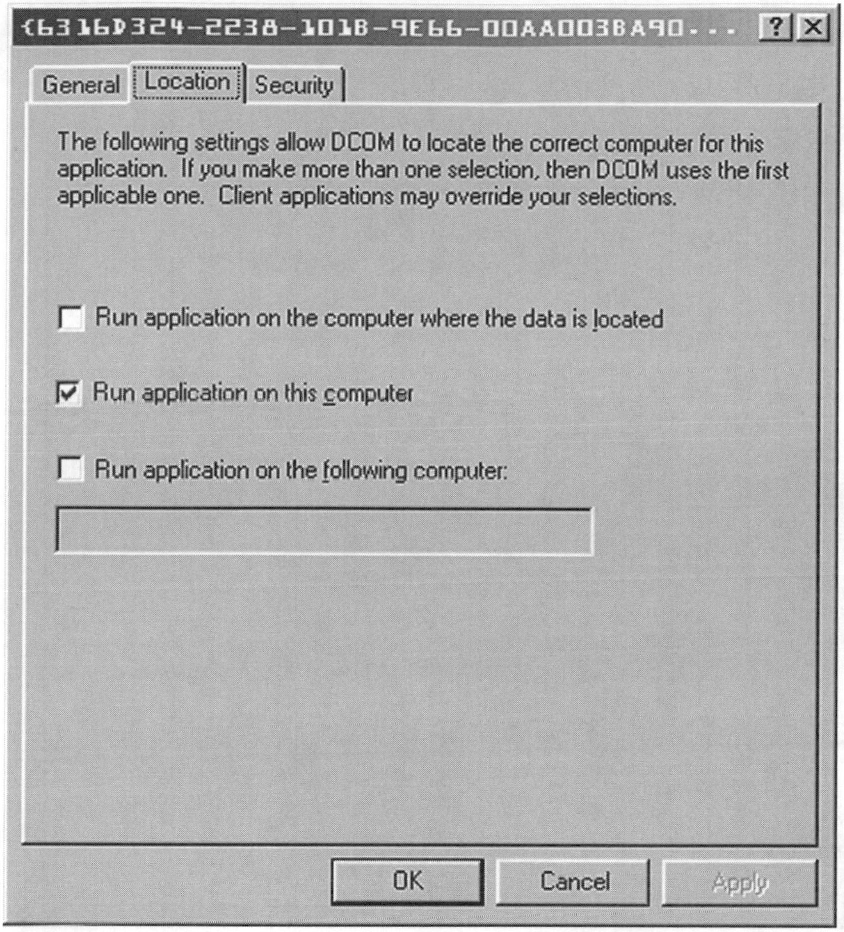

Figure 3.3   The Location Settings dialog.

Distributed COM on this computer." Turning this on allows DCOM objects to be created on this computer. It is a global setting that affects the entire machine. It will allow applications on other computers to create and access components on this one.

The other two settings on this dialog are Default Authentication Level and Default Impersonation Level. The Default Impersonation Level determines the packet-level security you want when applications and components communicate. There are a number of possible settings, but only when running DCOMCNFG on Windows NT. The choices in Windows95 or Windows98 are limited to None and Connect. The options are listed in Table 3.1.

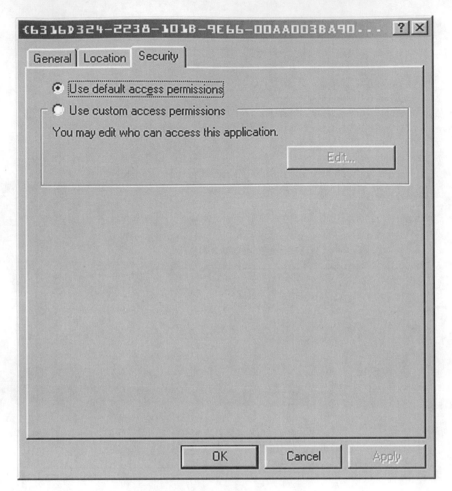

Figure 3.4   The Security Settings tab.

The Default Impersonation Level determines whether applications or components can determine who is calling them and whether they can perform operations on behalf of the client. The possible settings for this option are listed in Table 3.2.

Default Security

The Default Security tab allows you to set the default security settings for the computer or server on which DCOMCNFG is running. In the event that components do not have their own specific security settings, the settings specified on this tab are used. On this tab you can set the following:

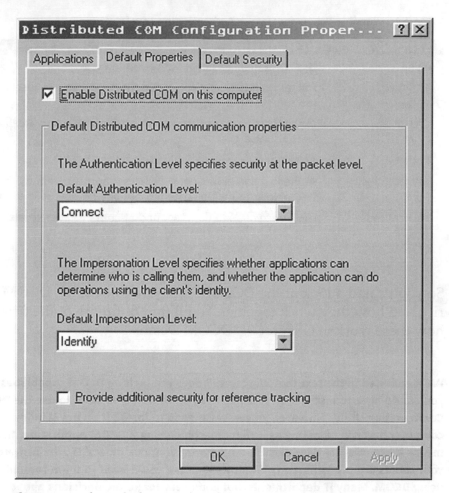

Figure 3.5   The Default Properties tab.

- Default Access Permissions, or who can access applications with no settings of their own
- Default Launch Permissions, or who can start or run an application of component with no settings of their own
- Default Configuration Permissions, or who is allowed to change the configuration of existing components or install new components

The Default Security tab is illustrated in Figure 3.6. Note that as a user of the DCOM Configuration utility, you will need sufficient right, usually Administrator rights, to make changes to the settings for which the utility provides access.

Table 3.1 Possible Values for Default Authentication Level

SETTING	DESCRIPTION
None	Use no authentication at the packet level.
Connect	Authentication occurs only when the application connects with the server.
Call	Authentication occurs only when a call is made and accepted by the server.
Packet	Authenticates every packet that comes across the wire.
Packet Integrity	Authentication occurs on all packets that come from the client. It also ensures that the data has not been modified in any way.
Packet Privacy	Adds encryption to the other packet authentication levels.

So you've had a look at the DCOM Configuration Utility, DCOM security, and how they work together. You'll find out more of the details on how these work in Chapter 9, "DCOM Details."

TIP

We mentioned in the text that Windows95 does not include DCOM capabilities, and you would have to install it on a Windows95 machine if you want to use the DCOM Configuration Utility. However, you will also need to install it on any Windows95 computer that will be acting as a client machine using a DCOM application. This means a trip to every Windows95 computer for your customers' IT administrators. If your clients are predominantly Windows95 users, you'll want to think carefully about using DCOM. Many IT departments, not end users, make the decisions about whether to purchase distributed software, often based on the workload it will create for them (among other things, of course). This is not an issue with Windows98 clients. Windows98 includes DCOM.

Table 3.2 Possible Values for Default Impersonation Level

SETTING	DESCRIPTION
Identify	The server can check for permissions but can't access any system objects.
Impersonate	The server can access system objects as if they were the client.
Delegate	Just like Impersonate, but can also represent the client when calling other servers.

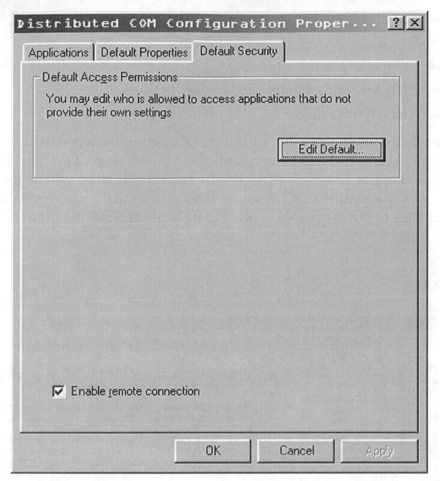

Figure 3.6   The Default Security tab (Windows NT).

OLE View

We thought we'd mention just in passing that there is another utility you can use to browse through your components and get information about them. It has quite a bit more information than DCOMCNFG. It's called OLE View, and it comes with Visual Basic. When you run it, you'll see an Explorer-like application, illustrated in Figure 3.7.

Some of the things you can find out about your components, or any components on your computer, include the following:

- CLSIDs
- ProgIDs
- Component version number
- All the interfaces supported by the component
- Activation settings

Feel free to explore this utility more thoroughly when you have the time. You'll find it to be very useful as you develop COM- and DCOM-based applications. The DCOM Configuration utility will be used in a realistic example in Chapter 9, "DCOM Details," where you'll get a chance to put it to use and observe its benefits firsthand.

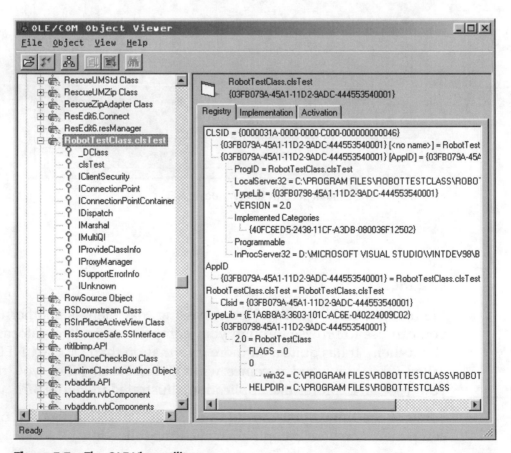

Figure 3.7   The OLE View utility.

Deployment

If you've ever fooled around creating your own utilities and programs with Visual Basic and ended up with one you wanted to share with others, then you probably used the Setup Toolkit. This is the installation utility included with Visual Basic. It is very useful because Visual Basic has several runtime files that have to be distributed with the applications you create using Visual Basic. The Setup Toolkit makes it easier to create installations of your program by walking you through a simple wizard, automatically including the Visual Basic runtime files, and compressing it all into a self-running setup program. It does the job, but is very simple, not too pretty, and cannot handle special situations.

This same utility is part of Visual Basic 6.0, but has a new look, more capability, and a new name. Now you use the Packaging and Deployment Wizard. It not only creates installations, which are still simple (though not as simple as they used to be), but also dependency files. It will also deploy an application for you to some location, such as a network server or a Web server, and it handles the deployment and installation of distributed components.

When creating installations for distributed applications, you create one installation for the client software and a second one for the remote components that will be installed on the server. For example, you have a project called MyClass.vbp that contains a Visual Basic DCOM component (ActiveX EXE), and another project that is a standard EXE that makes use of the MyClass component. You would run the Packaging and Deployment Wizard once on the MyClass project, which would create an installation for it. It will ask if you want to include the remote automation support files as you're walking through the steps in the Wizard, to which you should answer yes. There will also be a question about whether this component file should be installed as a shared file. If you say yes by checking this option, the component can be used by other applications and will not be removed from the system while any applications are still using it. The rest of the installation creation proceeds normally. This installation would then be run on the target server by the server administrator.

Next, create another installation by running the Packaging and Installation Wizard again on the client software. This is a standard installation that you can create by walking through the steps in the Wizard without any special considerations. Once it is complete, it can be installed on the client machines.

Note that for this sort of distributed installation to work, you need to make sure that the VBR file associated with the component is located in the same directory as the component EXE itself. We'll go into more detail about VBR files and how to generate them in the Visual Basic example later in this chapter. We'll also show you a complete installation for the example program we create.

TIP

The Packaging and Installation Wizard will also create dependency files. These are text files that you can browse through to see all the component dependencies pertaining to your project. Try running through the Wizard and creating a dependency file on your DCOM component project. When you are finished, load it into Notepad and take a peek. You'll see all kinds of hideous GUIDs. If you are brave enough, you'll be able to find references to some interesting items, including your component EXE, any classes it contains, their CLSIDs and versions, and even more interestingly, the CLSIDs for the proxy stubs. Remember those? They perform all the marshaling for your component. Visual Basic created them for you. They aren't just ethereal figments of our imagination. They really exist, and they really handle the ugliness of marshaling without your intervention.

DCOM and Visual Basic

Visual Basic allows you to create DCOM components as well as applications that use them. As with other aspects of Windows application development, DCOM programming is much easier with Visual Basic than with other languages like C++. It handles many of the seamier issues for you, such as creating proxy stubs and marshaling. In fact, you can't write your own marshaling code in Visual Basic. If for some reason (such as talking to legacy systems) you need to write your own, you'll need Visual C++ for the job.

Now we'll turn to the basics of creating DCOM components with Visual Basic. Our complete example will walk you through the creation of a DCOM component, a test application that puts it to use, and a pair of installations that will work for the client and the component. If you'd like to see the sneak preview before we get to it, you can find all the code for the example on the companion CD-ROM in the \examples\ ch03ex01 directory.

As we've mentioned, COM components run in the same process space as the application that makes use of them; they are in-process. They can be implemented as DLLs. DCOM components run in their own process space; they are out-of-process. So that they may run by themselves, they are implemented as EXEs. Visual Basic uses a project type called ActiveX EXE that you use to build DCOM components.

Project Settings

You need to know about three important settings regarding the project and the class you create. We'd be remiss if we neglected to explain their details. So put on your studious face for just a minute and pay attention.

The first is the Unattended Execution Project Property. This is a project-level setting that is available to ActiveX projects. It indicates whether the component is meant to run by itself, without any user intervention. You will probably turn this option on for most of your DCOM components. Projects that have this option set cannot have any user interface elements in them. Figure 3.8 shows the Visual Basic Project Properties dialog with the General tab. The Unattended Execution setting is down the left side. For now, just make sure this setting is turned on for new ActiveX EXE projects.

The Remote Server Files Project Setting tells Visual Basic to create the special files required if you plan to install or run your component from a remote machine. It is located on the Project Properties dialog on the Components tab. We use this setting in the example deployment later in this chapter.

The Instancing class property is set using the properties window of Visual Basic, while your class is selected in the project explorer window. It determines if and how other applications can create instances of your component. The possible values and their meanings are listed in Table 3.3. The default value for a class in an ActiveX EXE project is MultiUse, which works fine for most cases. You can leave it on this setting until you develop a need for the other settings.

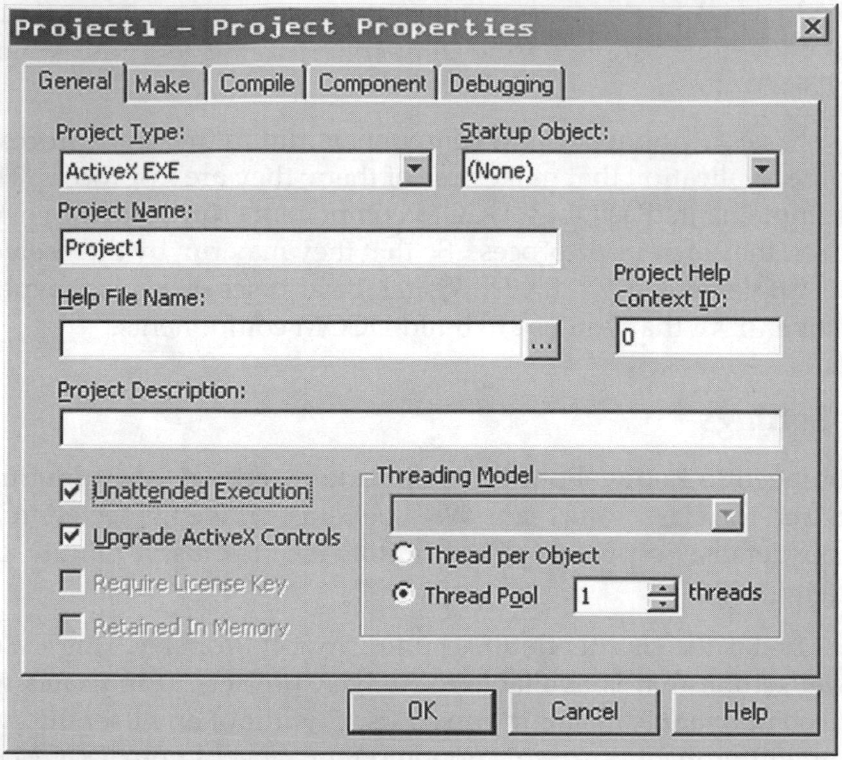

Figure 3.8 The Project Properties tab.

TIP

Make sure your DCOM components are user interface–free! Suppose you create a DCOM component, an error occurs, and you display a message box alerting the user about the error. Will the user ever see the warning? Nope. The component is located—and is executing—on the server, and that's where the message box will be displayed. There are occasions to do this, such as when the component needs the attention of the server administrator (perhaps the server has run out of disk space or the component contains a status panel that can be accessed from the server). However, if the message, or any user interface feature, is intended for the end user, it should not be located in the component. Put it in the client application so that the user will actually be able to see it.

The Example Program

Our example program for this chapter calculates HTML color codes when a color is selected from a dialog box. It could be used by any appli-

Table 3.3   Possible Values for the Instancing Property

SETTING	DESCRIPTION
1—Private	Nobody can create instances of your class or even find out about it. Use this setting for classes that are completely private to your project.
2—PublicNotCreatable	Other applications can have access to the class in your component, but only if a class in your component creates them first. You must use New or CreateObject to instantiate them before anyone has access to those instances.
3—SingleUse	Other applications can create instances of the class. However, every time an instance is created, a new instance of the entire component is started. You cannot use this setting in an ActiveX DLL project.
4—GlobalSingleUse	Other applications can create instances of the class. However, every time an instance is created, a new instance of the entire component is started. However, properties and methods are accessed like global functions. You cannot use this setting in an ActiveX DLL project.
5—MultiUse	Other applications can create instances of the class. A single instance of the component can create multiple instances of the class.
6—GlobalMultiUse	Other applications can create instances of the class. A single instance of the component can create multiple instances of the class. All properties and methods are accessed as global functions. You don't even need to create an instance of a class with this setting. One will be created automatically.

cation that generated HTML for Web pages, reports, or other Web features. This example illustrates the basic DCOM principles of creating a DCOM component as a Visual Basic ActiveX EXE, creating an instance of a DCOM component for use in your own code, and passing data to and from DCOM components, including an array to contain return values.

If you'd like to take the shorter route instead of typing all this in manually, you can load the example code from the companion CD-ROM. Located in the \examples\ch03ex01 directory, it contains everything we're going to do here.

In case you are not familiar with HTML color codes, they are hexadecimal representations of red, green, and blue values that combine to make a single color value. Each red, green, and blue value has a range of 0 to 255 and can be represented in the range of hexadecimal values from 00 to FF. They are combined as a six-digit hexadecimal string preceded by a # character. For example, if we use red, green, and blue values of 100, 120, and 140, respectively, they yield hexadecimal values of 64, 78, and 8C. When combined into an HTML color code, it looks like this:

```
#64788C
```

Our component's job will be to accept a value from the common color selector dialog and convert it to an HTML color string. We'll add a couple other methods to the component as we go along to make it more generically useful.

These are the basic steps we'll be following to build both our DCOM component and the standard EXE test program to try out our component:

1. Create an ActiveX EXE project that will be our DCOM component, and set its properties.
2. Configure the class in the component that will contain our functionality.
3. Write code in the class to do all the color calculations.
4. Build the DCOM component.
5. Add a Standard EXE project to the workspace that will act as our test bed for the component.
6. Design the simple form for our test bed user interface.
7. Add code to the test bed to use our component.
8. Compile the test bed and run the whole shooting match.

Let's dive in! This is going to be cool, especially when you see just how easy it is to create DCOM components for your N-tier application using Visual Basic.

Get Visual Basic going and select the ActiveX EXE project type. Figure 3.9 shows the Visual Basic New Project dialog with the correct selection highlighted. It will create the project for us, as well as a single, empty, placeholder class. Adjust the properties of the project so that its name is HTMLColorComponent.

The class that Visual Basic created for us needs a name. In the properties window, fill in the name HTMLColor and set its Instancing property to

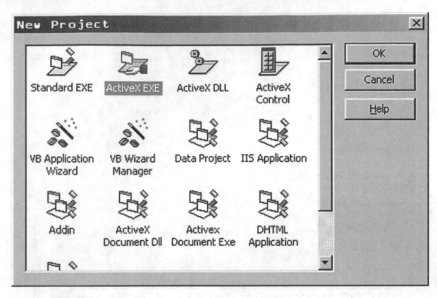

Figure 3.9 The Visual Basic New Project dialog.

MultiUse if it is not there already. At this point, you might want to save your project and the class file. Name the project file HTMLColorComponent.vbp and the class file HTMLColor.cls.

From the Visual Basic Properties menu, select HTMLColorComponent Properties. On the Component tab, turn on the Remote Server Files checkbox. This tells Visual Basic to create the additional files necessary to install and host the component on another machine. Figure 3.10 shows this dialog with the setting turned on.

The code we add to the class needs to perform our HTML color calculations. We're going to add several variations of the calculation that returns color data in a couple different formats, including the following:

- Accepting a long color value (from the Common Color Selector dialog) and returning an HTML color string (BuildHtmlColor).

- Accepting a red, a green, and a blue value and returning an HTML color string (RGBtoHTML).

- Accepting an HTML color string and splitting it into its component red, green, and blue values, which will be returned in a three-element array (HTMLtoRGB).

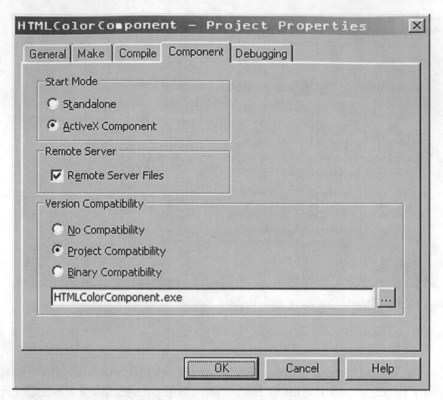

Figure 3.10   The Component Project Properties dialog.

Type the following code into the class module:

```
Public Sub HTMLtoRGB(ByVal HTMLColor As String, ByRef rgb() As _
Integer)

    Dim sClr As String
    sClr = HTMLColor

    ' The HTML Color string should be in the format
    ' #RRGGBB. Strip the leading # from the string.
    If Left(sClr, 1) = "#" Then
        sClr = Right(sClr, Len(sClr) - 1)
    End If

    ' Convert the color from HTML to three color values.
    rgb(0) = CInt("&H" & Left(sClr, 2))
    rgb(1) = CInt("&H" & Mid(sClr, 3, 2))
    rgb(2) = CInt("&H" & Right(sClr, 2))

End Sub
```

```
Public Function RGBtoHTML(ByVal r As Integer, ByVal g As Integer _
,ByVal b As Integer) As String

    ' Convert the color values to an HTML color string.
    Dim sClr As String

    ' The red component
    sClr = "#" & Hex(r) & Hex(g) & Hex(b)

End Function
Public Function BuildHtmlColor(ByVal lColor As Long) As String

    Dim sHexColor As String
    Dim sClr As String

    ' Make a hexadecimal string out of our color value. Make
    ' sure it has leading zeroes on it, or the color value
    ' will be bogus!
    sHexColor = Right("000000" & Hex$(lColor), 6)

    ' The bytes come in reversed, so we have a BGR string
    ' instead of an RGB string. Peel the values off as
    ' string values.

    ' The Red component
    sClr = "#" & Right(sHexColor, 2)
    ' The Blue component
    sClr = sClr & Mid(sHexColor, 3, 2)
    ' The Green component
    sClr = sClr & Left(sHexColor, 2)

    ' Return the string value
    BuildHtmlColor = sClr

End Function
```

We now have three public functions in our DCOM class interface, as well as implementations for them. The last step for the component is to compile it.

From the Visual Basic File menu, select Make HTMLColorCompo-nent.exe. Your component will be compiled into an ActiveX EXE and will be registered on your local system so that it can be used. That's it— you've created your first DCOM component. If you'd like to prowl around a bit, open the DCOM Configuration Utility or OLE View and look for the HTMLColorComponent.HTMLColor entry to find all kinds of information about your component.

Now that our component has been built, we need to create a test program to try it out. We'll use the ability of Visual Basic to create a *project group*, which is a set of related projects that are loaded simultaneously. From the Visual Basic File menu, select Add Project. When the Add Project dialog comes up, select Standard EXE and click on OK. In the Project Properties window, change the name of the project to ch03ex01.

When we use a project group, we have to tell Visual Basic which project in the list is the startup project, the one that executes when you click on the Run button. To do this, right-click on the ch03ex01 project in the Project Explorer window. From the context menu that appears, select Set As Startup.

Next we need to design the form for our user interface. Visual Basic created a default form for us when it created the project. We'll go ahead and use it, but change its name to frmMain. Add the controls listed in Table 3.4 to the form with the specified properties, and arrange them so that the form looks like Figure 3.11. You may have to add the Microsoft Common Dialog control to the project using the Components feature of Visual Basic. From the Visual Basic Project menu, Select the Components option. When the dialog appears, click the Microsoft Common Dialog Control item to add it to your project.

The next step is to add code to the test form to use our component. First, we're going to need a way to access the functionality of our DCOM component. To get at it, we create a generic object variable (hc in our code listing) and then create an instance of our component in the Form_Load event. You could create the instance anywhere you like. In fact, you should normally create the instance as late as possible and free it up as soon as possible. However, because creating an instance takes time, you might want to do this when the user can tolerate delays (for

Table 3.4 Test Form Controls

CONTROL	NAME	RELEVANT PROPERTIES
Label	lblColorValue	Text: "<none yet>"
Label	lblHTMLColor	Text: "<none yet>"
Label	lblRGB	Text: "<none yet>"
Button	btnSelectColor	Caption: Select Color
Button	btnExit	Caption: Exit
CommonDialog	cd1	

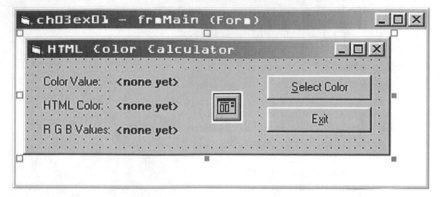

Figure 3.11   The test form for our example.

example, when a form loads). Use the CreateObject function to create an instance of our component and assign it to our object variable hc. Whenever we need access to the functionality, we can now get it through hc.

Also notice that in the Form_Terminate event we set the hc object variable to a value of Nothing. This action frees the memory we allocated when we called CreateObject. It is important to do this to make sure that we don't hold onto resources any longer than necessary.

Add the following code in the code window for the form we just created. The commentary in the code explains a little about the code itself.

```
Option Explicit

' This object variable will point to an instance of
' our HTMLColorComponent when we create one later.
Dim hc As Object

Private Sub btnExit_Click()

    ' End the program when the user clicks the
    ' Exit button.
    Unload Me

End Sub

' This code is executed when the user clicks the
' Select Color button. It does all the real work
' of our example.
Private Sub btnSelectColor_Click()
```

```
        Dim rgbValues(3) As Integer

        ' Setup and load the color selector
        cd1.CancelError = False
        cd1.ShowColor

        ' Now we have a color, so do the calculations using
        ' our DCOM component.
        lblColorValue.Caption = cd1.Color
        lblHTMLColor.Caption = hc.BuildHtmlColor(cd1.Color)
        hc.HTMLtoRGB lblHTMLColor.Caption, rgbValues()
        lblRGB.Caption = _
            Trim(rgbValues(0)) & ", " & _
            Trim(rgbValues(1)) & ", " & _
            Trim(rgbValues(2))

End Sub

Private Sub Form_Load()

    ' Create an instance of our out-of-process DCOM
    ' HTMLColorComponent. We'll use it when the user
    ' clicks the Select Color button.
    Set hc = CreateObject("HTMLColorComponent.HTMLColor")

End Sub

Private Sub Form_Terminate()

    ' If the HTMLColorComponent is still hanging around
    ' (and it should be), then free the memory it is
    ' holding on to.
    If Not hc Is Nothing Then
        Set hc = Nothing
    End If

End Sub
```

Finally, let's compile the test program and run everything. From the Visual Basic File menu, select Make ch03ex01.exe. This will compile our project into a standalone EXE. This is our client program. Press the F5 key or click the Run button on the toolbar to fire up the program. If all goes normally, you'll see our program executing, looking very much like Figure 3.12. Try it out! Click the Select Color button to pop up the Common Color Selector dialog. Pick something interesting, and click on OK. Our component will calculate all the color values and display them on the test dialog.

The nifty thing about this test program is that you could easily install the component on a server and the thing would still work. Read on to find out how to create installations to deploy our component and test client.

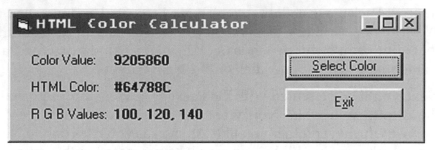

Figure 3.12   Our functioning program and component.

TIP

If you'd like to see one of the benefits of DCOM firsthand, try modifying some functionality in the component. For example, you could change the way that the Build-HTMLColor method is implemented so that instead of a plain color code it calculates a color code and surrounds it with an HTML background color tag, as in <BODY BGCOLOR="#FF00FF">. Then replace the component and run the client program. You'll see that the functionality has now been updated and is reflected in the client. If your component is hosted in the server, you can replace it once, and all clients get the updated functionality without requiring any changes to the client machines.

Deploying the Example Program

To install our program and component, we need to run the Packaging and Deployment Wizard twice: once for the component and again for the client test program. Start the Packaging and Deployment Wizard and follow the steps and settings.

First we'll build the installation for the component. Run the Microsoft Packaging and Deployment Wizard. When it comes up, select the component project file. In this case, the project is called HTMLColorComponent.vbp. Click on the Package button to continue. We'll be working through a total of 11 steps in this wizard.

Next is the selection of the Packaging Script. The only real option available is Standard Setup Package 1, which is already selected for us. Click on the Next button to continue.

Next, we fill in the Package Type. You can choose a Standard Setup Package, which is a standard installation from disks or a CD-ROM, an

Internet Package Installation, which can be posted and installed from a Web site or server, or a Dependency File. This lists all the runtime files that your component depends on. We want a Standard Setup Package, so highlight that one and click on the Next button.

Next, you'll be presented with the Package Folder step. Here you select the directory in which you want the installation files to be created. Choose whichever folder you like. As soon as you click on the Next button, which you should do now, you'll be presented with a message box that asks if you want to include the Remote Automation Support files. If you want your component to be hosted on a remote machine, which we do in this case, then answer yes to this question.

Next is the Included Files step. In this dialog you can add any additional support files your application might need, such as external graphics or data files. We don't need any for this component, so just accept the default settings and click on the Next button.

Now you select what sort of CAB files you want the wizard to build for you. CAB files are compressed files containing the files that make up your application. The choices are a Single CAB file or Multiple CAB files. If you will be distributing your component installation on floppy disks, select the Multiple option. If it will be deployed over the network or on a CD-ROM, then a Single CAB file will be fine. Select the option that makes sense for your needs and click on the Next button.

The next wizard step asks you for an installation title. This is the title that appears at the top of the installation window while the component is being installed. Enter whatever you like, or accept the default, and click on the Next button.

The Start Menu Items option is next. Because we are building an installation for a component, we don't need any Start Menu items. Just click on the Next button.

Next are the options for file Installation Locations. Using these settings, you can tell the installation utility where you want the component or application to be installed. The settings are filled in with defaults that should be fine. If you need to change one of the settings, highlight it and enter a new directory. Note that you can use predefined variable names for standard directories, such as $(WinSysPath), to represent the target machine's Windows\System directory, whatever it is for that machine.

Everything should be fine as it is for our component installation, so click on the Next button to move on.

Next is the shared Files option. If you would like any of the components listed here to be used by other applications, then turn on the checkbox for that component. We should have only our one component listed there, so click the checkbox to turn it on. Then click on the Next button.

Finally, the last step! If you would like to save all these settings in a script file so you won't have to enter them again the next time you build an installation for this component, then enter a name for the script file. It will be saved when you click on the Finish button, which you can do right now. When you click on the Finish button, the wizard will compress all the files that are part of your installation, including your application or component files, the Visual Basic runtime files, the Remote Automation Support files, and the supporting files for the setup program itself. Everything you need to put on a disk will be either built or copied into the Installation path you specified previously in the wizard. Once the build is complete, you can copy the files to a disk, CD-ROM, or a network server and run them to install the component.

Once the component installation is complete, we can proceed with the installation for the client program. Follow the same steps we did previously, but use the following settings for each wizard step.

1. *Project Selection.*   Enter the ch03ex01.vbp project file.
2. *Packaging Script.*   Choose the default, Standard Package Setup 1.
3. *Package Type.*   Select Standard Setup Package.
4. *Package Folder.*   Enter any default directory you like.
5. *Included Files.*   There are not extra files, so accept the default values.
6. *CAB Options.*   Select Single or Multiple, whichever suits your needs.
7. *Installation Title.*   Enter any title you like. The default, ch03ex01 is kind of lame, so something better might be in order, such as Chapter 3 DCOM Client Example.
8. *Start Menu Items.*   Again, you get a pretty boring default of ch03ex01. Feel free to change it to something better.
9. *Installation Locations.*   The default will work fine. Change it if you feel the need.

10. *Shared Files.* There aren't any for the client, so leave the checkbox turned off.

11. *Finish.* Enter a script name if you like. Click on the Finish button to build the client installation.

Once the installation packages are complete, you can install them wherever you like. While the Visual Basic Packaging and Setup Wizard is fairly limited, it will handle most of your needs for test programs and small component-based projects. Look into a more complete setup software package for a large or commercial product.

Winding Up

You're cruising through our introduction chapters with ease, quickly gaining the ability to throw out terminology and concepts in conversation with a casual flair. DCOM is now clear, and some of those peculiar terms now have real meaning. Plus, you've had the grand tour of creating DCOM components with Visual Basic and building installations for them. You even have access to the tools that will allow you to poke around in any components on your computer.

There is one last major component of N-tier architectures in a Microsoft world that you need to understand: Microsoft Transaction Server. The next chapter will give you the overview of this technology, what it means to you and your projects, and an example of how to put an MTS component together. Once the MTS introduction is complete, you'll be ready to dive into the guts of the various applications tiers, starting with the client.

Introduction to MTS

Microsoft Transaction Server, or MTS, is yet another part of the Microsoft DNA architecture that Visual Basic N-tier application developers need to be familiar with. MTS provides us with some marvelous programming benefits, which we'll be covering in this chapter. Many details fit together to form the whole MTS picture, and we need to understand them before we can dive in and start coding. As we discuss these details, the complete story of MTS and how it works will become clear.

In this chapter, we'll cover the following:

- Transactions, what they are, and why they are important
- Microsoft's solution to the transaction issue
- MTS pros and cons
- The MTS programming model
- MTS security
- MTS Explorer
- MTS and Visual Basic, including a quick example program

Even though transactions and MTS seem complicated at first, they will readily become clear as you read this chapter. A little background on transactions will start us off on the right foot.

Transactions

Now that you understand COM and DCOM, you can write applications that are component-based as well as distributed on other computers. Your components containing your business rules and other functionality can reside on servers and are easily replaceable. You're a distributed, component-oriented programming powerhouse, ready to tackle just about any problem your customers and users can throw at you. However, yet another aspect of distributed, N-tier, enterprise application programming has thus far gone unmentioned: transactions.

Contrary to popular belief, transactions apply to more than the world of financial applications. Transactions entail more than simply moving money from one place to another. A transaction can be part of just about any N-tier application. The definition of a transaction follows.

Transaction.   A task or unit of work that is either completed in total or canceled entirely. A successful transaction is guaranteed to be completed, no matter how many steps it takes or how many computers are involved. If the transaction is not successful, it is guaranteed to be completely undone, as if it were never even started.

Transactions are very important to a large percentage of N-tier enterprise applications. Any software that needs to guarantee the completion or failure of a transaction as a whole can benefit from transaction handling. Transactions have traditionally been handled by the database. An application could start a transaction in the database and then perform whatever database actions were required. Sometimes transactions would involve many steps, but all the steps were database actions, such as a data retrieval, modifying the data, and putting it back in its new form. Once the database activity was complete, the application could commit the transaction, which would tell the database to make all your changes permanent. If any database action occurring after the start of the transaction failed, then the entire transaction could be rolled back to the point at which the transaction began. This worked fine for transactions that took place in a single database. But what about transactions that involved multiple databases on multiple servers, or even transactions that did not involve databases at all?

Suppose, for example, that your client software makes a single request to one of your server-side components. It asks your component to save information the user has just entered about a new employee, including basic information, insurance-provider selection, 401(k) enrollment, and salary. Your company (or customer) keeps general information, salary, and 401(k) enrollment on one server in a specific database, and the insurance selection on a different server in another database. To save all of the employee-related information, updates have to occur on two computers in two separate databases. The server-side component has to make two updates. In one scenario, the component first updates one server, which is successful. It then updates the second computer, which is also successful. Because both parts of the transaction are successful, the transaction as a whole is successful.

In a second scenario, the first update succeeds, but the component is unable to perform the second update because the server is down temporarily and cannot write the data as requested. In this case, the transaction as a whole fails because a single part of it has failed. It is the responsibility of the application to undo the first update, canceling the entire transaction and removing the data it wrote to the first database.

The various applications for transactions can become complex and difficult to manage. For example, imagine implementing a transaction that is composed of eight separate updates to a database as well as two major data transmission activities that send data to other sites. If any one step fails, the transaction as a whole fails. Writing code to manage all these steps would not be our idea of fun. You'd have to be able to back out any number of successfully completed steps at the point where a single step fails. Even worse, try writing a generic system to handle any sort of multistep transaction in your application. This huge task would eat your entire development schedule for lunch.

The good news is that you don't have to write your own transaction-handling system. Someone we all know very well has already done this for us.

Microsoft's Solution: MTS

Microsoft Transaction Server was designed to handle the work and the details of managing and executing complex transactions. It is a system for processing transactions in a robust and reliable fashion. It runs on a server and makes use of components that you write. The really great thing about MTS is that it handles the details of executing transactions for you so that you can concentrate on writing software to solve your business problems rather than on creating a transaction-handling infrastructure.

To gain the transaction-processing capabilities of MTS, you have to accept two facts of life with MTS. First, you have to learn about MTS, what it's all about, its terminology, and how it works. This isn't too taxing, but you need to understand several aspects of MTS for the complete picture to gel in your mind. We'll take care of this for you in this chapter. Second, you need to subscribe to and adopt the MTS programming model. This isn't so bad either, and if you are planning to use COM components as a major part of your application architecture, then you're already halfway there.

ACID

An acronym used in the industry to describe the four primary properties of a transaction is *ACID*, which stands for Atomicity, Consistency, Isolation, and Durability.

Atomicity refers to the fact that a transaction either succeeds or fails as a single, or atomic, unit. If any part fails, the whole thing fails. The atom part means that a transaction, though potentially composed of many tasks, is treated as one task by the system.

Consistency means that the state of the durable data modified by a component (usually the data stored in the database) matches the state expected by the component. That is, the state of the database is consistent.

Isolation ensures that concurrent transactions are not aware of each other's state. It is important to isolate transactions from each other, because knowledge of each other's intermediate state could result in application inconsistencies. If one transaction acts based on the state of another, and the other's state later changes, then the action taken by the first may no longer be valid. The goal is to create transactions that function by themselves, without regard for any other transactions.

Durability means that no matter what failures might occur during a transaction, the committed changes, such as data saved to a database, will endure despite the problem that occurred. This ensures that even if a network crashes or a lightning strike takes out a server, the changes that a transaction has committed will not be lost.

Microsoft Transaction Server accounts for all of these transaction attributes through one or more of its parts. Any transaction that conforms to the MTS way of life will inherit these desirable traits as well.

MTS Overview

There's a lot going on behind the scenes when MTS is used as part of your application. Although you don't need to track every detail while you are creating code and components for use with MTS, it is extremely helpful to have an understanding of the MTS activities and tasks. MTS does a lot of work to make our lives as programmers easier, but you and MTS will work better as a team if you know what it's doing behind your back. You'll be able to make better decisions about your MTS components if you know how they fit into the whole MTS puzzle.

MTS is described as a transaction-processing *system*, which implies that there are several parts to it. MTS is composed of the following major pieces:

- MTS execution environment
- MTS Explorer
- APIs
- Resource dispensers
- Application components

All these components of MTS play an important role in making distributed, robust transactions work for your application, and each needs some explanation. After defining the parts, we'll put them together to see how the whole MTS system works together.

MTS execution environment.   This is the MTS runtime environment that executes on a server and hosts all the MTS components that you create to contain and run your business logic. It manages the creation and destruction of objects, threads, and security. The runtime environment interacts with applications components, resource dispensers, and the database to execute transactions. The MTS environment also establishes an address or process space in which your components execute.

MTS Explorer.   This is a graphical administration tool that allows you to manage your MTS components and the packages in which they reside. It allows you to install and distribute your components as well as to define the security configurations for each. Using MTS Explorer, you can create packages of MTS components and set them up for execution on the server. You can also create installation programs for client computers. When the client installations are run on the client machines, they will then know on which server the components reside, allowing the client software to use the MTS components. You can even use MTS Explorer to monitor the execution of the installed components, tracking statistics about their usage and load on the server.

APIs.   MTS provides several application programming interfaces that allow you to build components that fit into the MTS model and allow MTS to manage transactions involving your components. You have access to several important calls through the MTS API, which allows your components to work in the MTS environment. You use them to tell MTS that your work is done and successful, that your work is done and was not successful, and to access component security settings. These will be covered in more detail later in this chapter.

Resource dispensers.   A resource dispenser does what its name says it does: dispenses resources such as database connections, network connections, objects, even blocks of memory. Its primary purpose is to manage resources by providing resource-pooling capabilities. MTS ships with two resource dispensers that you will use for most of your work: the ODBC Resource Dispenser and the Shared Property Manager.

The ODBC Resource Dispenser manages connections to databases. As components request database connections, the ODBC Resource Dispenser allocates them and hands them to the component that requested them. As soon as the component is done with the connection, it is returned to the connection pool managed by the resource dispenser. The ODBC Resource Dispenser can then allocate the component to another component or let it go. Using this mechanism, MTS can use a small number of connections to efficiently supply database resources to a much larger number of clients.

The Shared Property Manager provides safe access to what amounts to global data, stored as properties. If you need to maintain some sort of state between components, you can use the Shared Property Manager to do it. For example, you might want to create an ongoing count of the number of users accessing your application that any component could reference. The Shared Property Manager will do this for you.

You will probably not be creating your own resource dispensers. The two provided with MTS will accommodate most of your needs. You might consider creating your own resource dispenser if you need to create a resource pool of some sort wherein the resources being managed get allocated to components as requested and released when the component is done with them. This is similar to the way that the ODBC Resource Dispenser maintains a database connection pool. Microsoft recommends against creating a resource dispenser to create a pool of your application objects, because Microsoft itself will be providing this capability for your components in a future version of MTS.

Application components.   These are the components you write and snap in to MTS to do the work of your application. Your business logic and other server-based components built as MTS components can do just about anything you like as long as they comply with the MTS programming model. MTS manages the creation and execution of your components and their need for transactions without your intervention.

Because MTS is made up of several different components, it appears to be more complex than it really is. An understanding of each piece and its role makes the whole MTS concept much easier to grasp. At some point, as we cover MTS in more detail, the lightbulb will turn on and MTS will make sense. If it hasn't already, that is.

MTS Pros and Cons

MTS provides some excellent benefits for N-tier applications, even if they do not use transactions. However, MTS development is not all wine and roses. While the problems with MTS are not usually enough to deter you from using it, they are important to understand. You should not make the decision to use MTS in your application without examining the downsides first.

MTS forces you to use a specific architecture and programming model that dictates how you should allocate and use resources. If you don't subscribe to the MTS programming model, MTS won't work for you. MTS also requires that you build your components as COM DLLs. If you have a library of components built as DCOM components that you'd like to use in MTS, you'll have to rebuild them as DLLs. MTS is also a fairly new technology that you and your team will have to learn and gain experience with to use effectively. You will have to invest some time doing research on MTS usage and performance to find out how to use it to best fit your needs. MTS is also inherently component-based. If you are not planning a component-based architecture, MTS is not an option.

If you can handle these minor restrictions, then MTS provides many nice benefits to your application that are hard to pass up. As long as you follow the MTS programming paradigm, MTS will manage your transactions for you, ensuring that a transaction either succeeds or fails in its entirety. That is its primary purpose. MTS also helps you manage resources, allocating them from a resource pool and releasing them when they are no longer needed. This works for you even if you don't need transactions. If your service requests go through MTS, as is normal when using it, the creation and deletion of components and objects within components is handled for you automatically. As programmers, if you are already familiar with COM programming, MTS will be a breeze for you, because MTS components are just slightly different flavors of COM components. And, if you are planning a component-based architecture, the MTS Explorer makes it easy to install and manage the server-side components. If you've ever deployed a component-based application before, you know that any help in the area of server component installation is welcome.

If you are building an N-tier application, you really should consider using MTS. Unless you absolutely need to use DCOM EXE–based components, or if don't have the time to learn MTS, then it makes good sense to use it. It will allow you to concentrate on the business problem you are trying to solve with your software, rather than on the implementation architecture. MTS takes care of it for you.

The MTS Programming Model

MTS will work for you, managing transactions, dealing with threads, taking care of component creation and destruction, and handling security issues in your application. All it asks in return is that you subscribe to its programming model. This is not difficult, and is a small price to pay for the benefits it provides in return.

The basic premise behind the way MTS works is that you build components for your application as MTS components and install them into the MTS environment so that MTS can control their creation and execution. As a client application makes a request for the services provided by one of your components, it goes through MTS, which creates the component, starts a transaction, and allows it to process the client's request. If the component successfully completes the request, it tells MTS that everything went fine, and the transaction is completed and closed. All resources allocated, including any database connections and the component itself, are released. If the component encounters a problem during any phase of the transaction, it informs MTS that the transaction has failed. MTS then backs out anything that has been changed as a result of the processing that has occurred so far as part of the transaction, and it releases all allocated resources.

MTS components are simply COM components that follow a few rules and implement a few key interfaces. The primary points are as follows:

- MTS components are built as in-proc COM DLLs.
- MTS components are required to follow a basic programming and resource-allocation scheme.
- MTS components are required to communicate their status to MTS using the MTS API calls.

Each of these points is worth looking at in some detail, because they are integral to MTS programming.

MTS Components Are COM DLLs

When building MTS components, you build them as COM in-proc DLLs. In Visual Basic, this translates to ActiveX DLL projects. The implication is that DCOM components (or ActiveX EXEs) are not allowed to be MTS components. If you have a DCOM component you'd like to use as an MTS component, it must be rebuilt as a DLL. This is not a big deal, but is important to know when planning your components.

A Few Basic Rules

There are four primary tenets you must follow when building MTS components. They are the core of MTS component doctrine. Although you can create MTS components and still completely ignore these guidelines, you will not be building good MTS components. MTS relies on component builders such as yourself to follow these guidelines in order for the whole transaction system to work smoothly and efficiently. They trust you. To make sure you don't violate that trust, follow these tenets.

"Code for a single, standalone client." When you design and build an MTS component, build it as if only one client is talking to it at any given moment. Don't worry about multiple users, because MTS will handle that for you. Each instance of a component will only ever talk to one client at a time, so make sure you program that way.

"Acquire resources as late as possible." When you need a resource in your component, such as a database connection don't ask for it until the last possible moment. This allows MTS to manage resources more effectively, because resources are available more often. For example, don't grab hold of a database connection, and hold onto it because you are expecting a bunch of updates to come from the client. Ask for the connection only when you are absolutely ready to use it.

"Release resources as soon as possible." In order to keep as many resources available for all the requests coming into MTS, make sure you release any resources you are using, such as a database connection, as soon as you are done with them. Don't hang onto them in case you need them, because you are preventing others from using those resources.

"Components should not maintain state." While this is not an absolute, hard-and-fast rule, it is an extremely desirable goal. This means that an object should not hold onto intermediate data and settings, but instead should perform the services required of it and be done. The reason for this is that if a component maintains state, it cannot be deactivated or the state will be lost. Because one of the primary purposes of MTS is to efficiently manage resources, maintaining state is a no-no. It would prevent MTS from freeing up activated components in a timely fashion.

These guidelines exist so that everyone who participates in the MTS environment gets a fair shot at resources. Try your best to follow them in the cooperative manner that MTS defines, and your application will run more smoothly in a coordinated fashion.

The MTS API Calls

As we've mentioned, MTS components are COM components with a twist. The twist is the use of the MTS API calls, which allows your components to interact with MTS. They are fairly simple to use, as long as you plan ahead for them.

GetObjectContext. The first API call you will use is GetObjectContext. Every object created by MTS is accompanied by a context object that is created by MTS at the same time. The context object provides information about the component's runtime environment used by the MTS system. It gives the component a frame of reference. The context is part of the MTS concept of isolation, which helps keep a particular instance of an object separate from other concurrent instances. The practical part of contexts is that for your component to be an MTS component, you have to have one. You get a context by calling the GetObjectContext function. It's very straightforward to use. Code to implement it looks like this:

```
Dim x As ObjectContext
Set x = GetObjectContext()
```

Once you get an object context, you can use it to access the other MTS API calls. Note that to be able to call GetObjectContext, you need to add a reference in your Visual Basic ActiveX DLL project to the Microsoft Transaction Server Type Library. Do this by opening the Visual Basic Project menu item and selecting References. When the dialog appears, turn on the checkbox for the MTS type library.

SetComplete and SetAbort. MTS maintains efficient use of resources by way of a mechanism called *just-in-time (JIT) activation*, which is central to the MTS paradigm. JIT activation means that components are created, or activated, only when they are needed, at the last possible moment. This keeps resources available to as many applications as possible for as long as possible. The deactivation of components occurs as soon as possible. They can even be deactivated while clients are still using them. They will be reactivated by MTS as soon as the client needs them again. MTS also needs your help as programmers to make JIT activation work.

Your components participate in JIT activation by telling MTS when it has completed its work and when it encounters an error. You do this by using the SetComplete and SetAbort calls. If your component completes its work successfully and encounters no errors, you call Set-

Complete when the work is done. This tells MTS that everything is done and that this part of the transaction was successful. If your component encounters an error or a problem of some sort that prevents it from completing its work successfully, it should finish whatever cleanup or error recovery it needs to do and then call SetAbort. This tells MTS that this part of the transaction did not complete successfully. Whenever you call SetAbort, you are terminating the entire transaction in which you are participating. MTS will then take the steps necessary to end the transaction. A code sample that illustrates the use of these calls follows:

```
Dim oc As ObjectContext
Set oc = GetObjectContext()

' Do whatever your component needs to do. If an error occurs,
' jump to the ErrorHandler below.
...
' At this point, everything has completed successfully. Tell MTS
' we're done and all went well. Release the object context from
' memory when done.
oc.SetComplete
Set oc = Nothing
Exit Sub

ErrorHandler:
    ' An error has occurred. Tell MTS something went wrong
    ' and release the object context from memory.
    oc.SetAbort
    Set oc = Nothing
```

These are the primary calls you will use when building MTS components. Get to know them well, because they are your tickets to efficient and well-behaved MTS applications.

MTS Security

Security is an important aspect of running MTS component-based applications. You wouldn't want just anybody in the company to have access to the salaries of all the employees. MTS security allows you to define roles and security levels at the package level for any MTS components you create.

You need to understand three important aspects of MTS security: when security checks are performed, the two security models, and roles.

In MTS, security checks are performed when process boundaries are crossed. For example, when a call goes from a client to an MTS component, it crosses a process boundary, so a security check is performed. However, when a component is running in the same process as another client or component, a security check is not performed. A region of trust exists within a process, so components in the same process are assumed to be already checked. This can cause problems if you configure the components incorrectly. If two components are configured to run in-process with each other, but they require different security levels, no check is performed and the differing security levels are defeated. So the general recommendation is that application components not be configured to run together in the same process.

Two types of security models are used in MTS: declarative and programmatic. *Declarative security* means that you set up security outside of the program code using MTS Explorer. The code does not do any work on the security front and is handled entirely by MTS. *Programmatic security* means that you write code to perform security checks and act appropriately based on the results. The two methods are not exclusive; they can be used together if required.

Roles are central to MTS security. They are logical names that define groups of users with a specific set of access rights. For example, you might define two roles, one called WorkerBee and another called Overlord. They would both have access to the functionality of the Company-Benefits component, but only the Overlord role would have access to the Salaries component. Using the MTS Explorer, you can define roles for the various MTS packages you have created or installed. If you are using programmatic security, you'll want to define the roles your program will support before you build your components, because the code will have to refer to the roles by name.

A quick code fragment will illustrate how simple it is to perform a security check using programmatic security and the roles defined for an MTS component. The following listing shows code that first checks to see if security is enabled. If it is, then it checks to see if the client calling the component is in a role that the component allows to have access to its services. All the security API calls are accessed through the context object.

```
Dim oc As ObjectContext
Set oc = GetObjectContext()
If oc is Nothing Then
    Exit Sub
End If
```

```
' Check to see if security is enabled. If not, then get out
' since we're a secure component.
If Not oc.IsSecurityEnabled Then
    oc.SetAbort
    Set oc = Nothing
    Exit Sub
End If

' Because this is the Salaries component, make sure the caller
' is in the 'Overlord' role.
If Not oc.IsCallerInRole("Overlord") Then
    oc.SetAbort
    Set oc = Nothing
    Exit Sub
Else
    ' Everything is copacetic. Do whatever work we need to
    ' and get out.
    ...
    oc.SetComplete
    Set oc = Nothing
End If
```

MTS security is covered in more detail in Chapter 10, "Inside Transaction Server," when MTS is explored in a more extensive fashion with lots of nifty programming examples.

MTS Explorer

MTS Explorer is an integral part of MTS that allows you to install, maintain, and monitor MTS and the components and packages it contains. A bonus feature allows you to create installation programs that you run on client computers to tell them where the MTS components they need are located. It's a nice piece of work, and we're going to take you on a short tour to introduce its basic features. You'll learn more about it in Chapter 10 when we get into the implementation details of MTS.

If you don't have MTS installed on your Windows NT computer, you can install it from the Microsoft Windows NT Option Pack CD-ROM. You can also install MTS on Windows98 computers. It is part of the Personal Web Server installation (go figure). It looks a little different than the Windows NT version in that it has only one windowpane. We will be touring the Windows NT version.

Once installed, you can start the MTS Explorer by selecting it from your Start menu. It is located in the Windows NT Option Pack menu under the Microsoft Transaction Server submenu. Click the Transaction Server Explorer item to fire it up. When it opens, the main window looks like Figure 4.1.

Take a look at the main window. On the left, you'll see a collapsed tree that will allow us to view the objects we can interact with in MTS Explorer. On the right, you'll see a list of those items, depending on what is selected in the left pane. To expand your view, click on the following items in the left pane in the order specified:

1. Microsoft Transaction Server.
2. Computers.
3. My Computer.
4. Packages Installed.
5. Sample Bank.
6. Components.

Your view should look like Figure 4.2. Some minor variations may occur, depending on your system and the components installed, but you will at least see a group of packages and components. Now we can

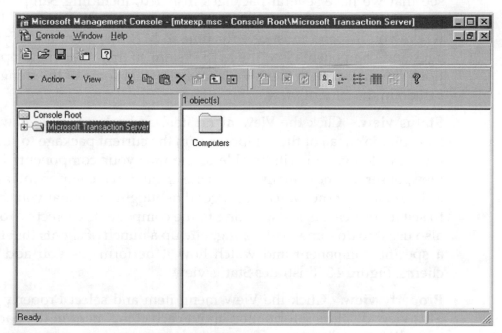

Figure 4.1 The MTS Explorer main window.

Figure 4.2 The MTS Main view, expanded.

see that we have several packages installed, including Sample Bank, each of which has a number of MTS components installed in it. This is where you'll spend most of your time in MTS Explorer, adding packages and components into the MTS system so that your client applications can make use of them. Let's take a look at some of the things you can do in the current view.

Status view. Click the View menu item and select Status view. This lets you look at all of the components in the current package to see how they are doing. You will be able to monitor your components in this view, observing how many objects are created in a component, as well as how many are activated. It's a good debugging tool that you can use to see if your clients are speaking to the components correctly. You can also use it to do some load testing. Fire up a bunch of clients that talk to a specific component and watch how it performs as you add more clients. Figure 4.3 illustrates Status view.

Property view. Click the View menu item and select Property view. This view displays information about each component in the package, including the following:

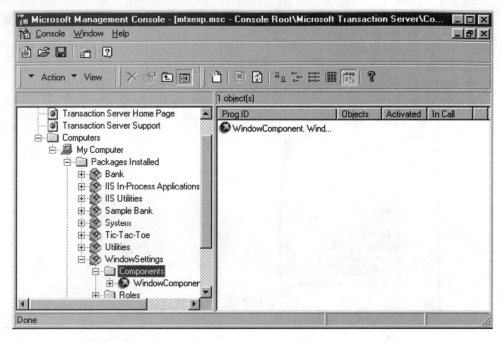

Figure 4.3   MTS Explorer Status view.

- *ProgID.*   This is the name of the component followed by the class name.
- *Transaction Setting.*   This can have various values that determine the nature of the object's need for transactions, including Required, Requires New, and Supported.
- *The DLL file.*   This contains the component code.
- *The CLSID.*   This uniquely identifies the component.
- *Threading Model.*   This tells you which threading model is in use by the component.
- *Security Setting.*   This shows whether security is enabled for the component.

You can use this view to obtain information about the components you have installed on the server. It's sort of a one-stop shop for component properties you'll need to know throughout your development cycle. This view is illustrated in Figure 4.4.

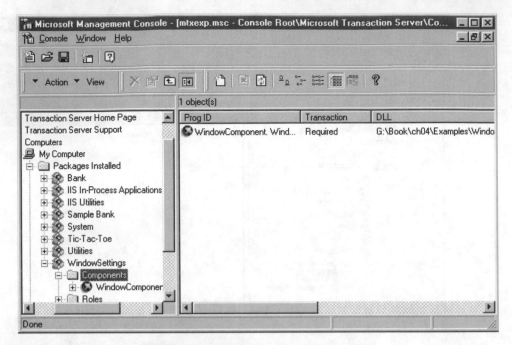

Figure 4.4   The MTS Explorer Property view.

Transaction Statistics view.   This is a quick, real-time view showing how many transactions are currently active, what the maximum number of active transactions has been, and a host of other statistics that you can use to monitor your components. This view is useful when you are testing your application. You can watch and see how many components your application loads at any given time. It's always a larger number than you think, especially when you start adding more clients to the system. Figure 4.5 shows what the Statistics view looks like.

Other capabilities.   There are other capabilities of the MTS Explorer that you'll be using off and on as you develop, set up, and manage components.

- *Adding packages and components.*   This is an important feature that you use to add packages and components to the MTS environment. We'll show you how this works in the example later in this chapter.

- *Security (roles and users).*   This feature allows you to configure the security settings for packages and components, including roles and

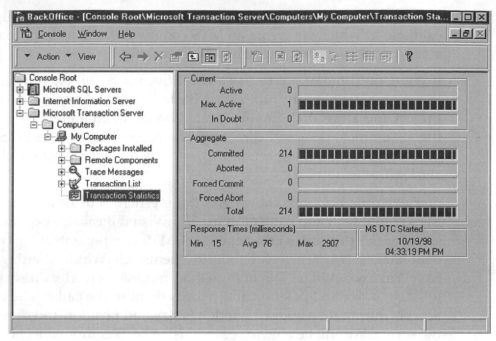

Figure 4.5 The MTS Explorer Transaction Statistics view.

users. This will be covered in more depth in Chapter 10, "Inside Microsoft Transaction Server."

- *Export capability.* Once you have your components installed in MTS, you need to tell the client software where to find the components. The Export feature of MTS Explorer creates installation packages that can be run on client machines to tell the client software where the components are located. We'll run through an example of this later in this chapter.

There is more to MTS Explorer that you can discover as you build components and use the Explorer more often. Remember that it's not only an installation tool, but also a maintenance and monitoring tool that you can use throughout the life cycle of your application and its components.

MTS and Visual Basic

You've already seen some of how MTS and Visual Basic work together. You can access MTS API calls from Visual Basic and use it to create MTS components. This section of the chapter will walk you through an example in which we create an MTS component and a client to use it, setting up the whole thing to function correctly.

If you would prefer not to risk a repetitive stress injury, you can load the example program into Visual Basic instead of typing it in. The project and all related files are located on the companion CD-ROM in the \examples\ch04ex01 directory. The project file for the MTS component is WindowComponent.vbp, and the project file for the client is ch04ex01.vbp.

Our example not only shows you the mechanics of how to build an MTS component and a client to use it in Visual Basic, it also illustrates some of the principles and benefits of MTS components. Our component makes two services public to clients: GetWindowSettings and SaveWindowSettings. The first method retrieves saved values about a window's size and position and returns them to the caller. The second accepts information about a window's size and position and saves it on the server. We will be able to see that using MTS components allows us to provide users with the capability to save settings on a server. In this way, they can go from one client computer to another, and their personal settings follow them around. Conversely, several users can run the client software from the same computer, and their own personal settings will be used.

We'll also take a look at error handling with MTS components and Visual Basic. Although we use the SetAbort and SetComplete methods to tell MTS when tasks have failed and succeeded, this does not communicate the error state to the client. We'll use the Visual Basic Err object and its Raise method to pass runtime errors on to the client, as well as to raise errors of our own invention. We even use the error mechanism to communicate the fact that no settings exist for a user.

Without further ado, let's head into Visual Basic and start our first MTS component. We're breaking this example into four stages: building the component, installing the component, building the client, and running the program.

Building the MTS Component

As we've mentioned, MTS components are COM DLLs. In Visual Basic, COM components are ActiveX DLL projects. For this stage, that's what we'll be building. Construction of the component is divided into the following steps:

1. Create and configure the project.
2. Add the code to the component.
3. Build the component into a DLL.

Begin by starting Visual Basic and creating a new ActiveX DLL project. In the project properties window, rename the project to Window-Component. In the project explorer window, select the class that Visual Basic created for us, and in its properties window, rename the class to WindowSettings.

Now, from the Project menu, select WindowComponent properties. When the dialog appears, select the Component tab. There is an option in this dialog called Version Compatibility. From the options there, select Binary Compatibility. This setting ensures that as you rebuild your component, it will be compatible with existing programs that make use of it (as long as you don't change the interface, of course). This setting is shown in Figure 4.6.

Last but far from least, select the References option from the Visual Basic Project menu. Find the reference to the Microsoft Transaction Server Type Library and check it on. This gives us access to the MTS library, and most important, the GetObjectContext function. We'll use this function as soon as we start writing code.

At this point, save the project. The class file should be saved as WindowSettings.cls, and the project is saved as WindowComponent.vbp.

What we're going to do here is give you the code to enter, and then we'll go over it a bit, explaining the high points. There are two public methods in this component. Open the code window for the class by double-clicking on it in the project explorer window in Visual Basic. Once the window opens, enter the following code:

```
Option Explicit

' The file extension to use for the saved settings file.
Const SETTINGS_EXT = ".WST"

' A few constants for error codes.
Const NoContextError = 9997
Const BadInputsError = 9998
Const FileError = 9999
```

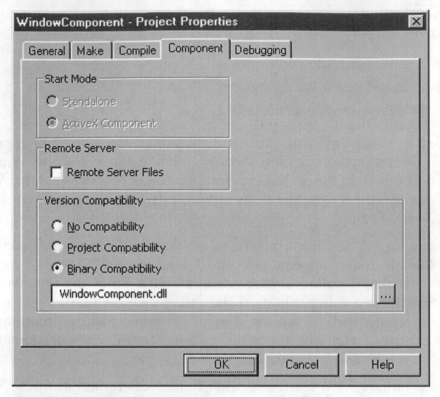

Figure 4.6 The Visual Basic Component Properties dialog.

```
' This method saves the window settings passed into it in a
' small binary flat file on the server.
Public Sub SaveWindowSettings(UserID As String, _
                            ByVal wTop As Integer, _
                            ByVal wLeft As Integer, _
                            ByVal wWidth As Integer, _
                            ByVal wHeight As Integer)
    ' Get the object context so we can cooperate with MTS. If this
    ' operation fails, then get out.
    Dim oc As ObjectContext
    Set oc = GetObjectContext()
    If oc Is Nothing Then
        Err.Raise NoContextError, , _
            "Could not establish an object context."
        Exit Sub
    End If

    ' Check our input parameters for valid data. For this example,
    ' we'll simply make sure that all our position values are
    ' positive.
```

```
        ' You could perform other checks in a real application
        ' component.
        If wTop < 0 Or wLeft < 0 Then
            oc.SetAbort
            Set oc = Nothing
            Err.Raise BadInputsError, , _
                "The top or left value was not valid."
            Exit Sub
        End If

        ' Turn on error handling so we can trap file errors.
        On Error GoTo SaveErrHandler

        ' We will be saving these settings to a simple binary flat file
        ' with the user's ID as the filename and .WST as an extension.
        Dim iFileNum As Integer
        Dim sFileName As String
        iFileNum = FreeFile
        sFileName = UserID + SETTINGS_EXT

        ' Open the file.
        Open sFileName For Random As #iFileNum Len = 2

        ' Write passed-in window settings to the file.
        Put #iFileNum, , wTop
        Put #iFileNum, , wLeft
        Put #iFileNum, , wWidth
        Put #iFileNum, , wHeight

        ' Close the file.
        Close #iFileNum

        ' Everything was successful if we got this far, so tell
        ' MTS it went well and free the memory used by the context
        ' object.
        oc.SetComplete
        Set oc = Nothing
        On Error GoTo 0
        Exit Sub

SaveErrHandler:
        ' You could place as extensive an error handler here as you
        ' like. For now, we'll assume that any error is a failure for
        ' the transaction.
        oc.SetAbort
        Err.Raise FileError, , "The file could not be replaced."
        Set oc = Nothing

End Sub

' This method retrieves window settings for a specific user.
Public Sub GetWindowSettings(UserID As String, _
                             wTop As Integer, _
```

```vb
                               wLeft As Integer, _
                               wWidth As Integer, _
                               wHeight As Integer)

' Get the object context so we can cooperate with MTS. If this
' operation fails, then get out.
Dim oc As ObjectContext
Set oc = GetObjectContext()
If oc Is Nothing Then
    Err.Raise NoContextError, , _
        "Could not establish an object context."
    Exit Sub
End If

' Turn on error handling so we can trap file errors.
On Error GoTo GetErrHandler

' We will be reading these settings from a simple binary flat
' file with the user's id as the filename and .WST as
' an extension.
Dim iFileNum As Integer
Dim sFileName As String
iFileNum = FreeFile
sFileName = UserID + SETTINGS_EXT

' See if the file exists. If it does not, then raise
' our own error.
If Dir(sFileName) = "" Then
    oc.SetAbort
    Err.Raise FileError
    Set oc = Nothing
    Exit Sub
End If

' Open the file.
Open sFileName For Random As #iFileNum Len = 2

' Read data from the settings file.
Get #iFileNum, , wTop
Get #iFileNum, , wLeft
Get #iFileNum, , wWidth
Get #iFileNum, , wHeight
' Close the file.
Close #iFileNum

' Everything was successful if we got this far, so tell
' MTS it went well and free the memory used by the context
' object.
oc.SetComplete
Set oc = Nothing
On Error GoTo 0
Exit Sub
```

```
GetErrHandler:
    ' You could place as extensive an error handler here as you
    ' like. For now, we'll assume that any error is a failure for
    ' the transaction.
    oc.SetAbort
    Err.Raise FileError
    Set oc = Nothing

End Sub
```

The first method is SaveWindowSettings. Its purpose in life is to accept some information about a window, specifically its size and position, as well as a user id, and save those window settings on the server for the specified user. This will allow a program to restore window settings for a particular user regardless of the computer he or she is using.

The first thing that this method does is to obtain a context object from MTS. This is the component's ticket to communication and cooperation with MTS. It is through the context object that calls to MTS are made. We get this context object by calling the GetObjectContext function. It returns a context object, which we can assign to an object variable of the ContextObject type (which we have named oc). If for some reason the GetContextObject function fails, we raise our own error to the client. This way, the client will know that something is wrong with MTS or the server.

TIP

Error handling with MTS components uses the standard Visual Basic error-handling mechanism. You use the Err object in your MTS component and its Raise method to pass errors back to the client. You can trap and pass back either normal Visual Basic runtime errors, or you can create your own errors. It's not complicated, but it is important. Clients need to know whether the component completed its work or if the transaction failed.

If you want to use constants for your own error codes, you can do so through a public enumerated type. Define it at the top of your component code, like this:

```
Enum MyComponentErrorsType
    FileError = 1000
    DatabaseError
    DivideByZeroError
    UnknownError
End Enum
```

As long as your client project has a reference to the MTS component, the client will have access to the enumerated type and the error codes that the component will raise.

The next interesting part is where we actually save the data. We use a simple random access flat file to write the data to the server. We turn on the Visual Basic error handler using the ON ERROR call, so that any file errors will be caught by our component. The file we are creating has the name of the user ID passed in to the method, with a .WST extension. The four data parameters are written to the file once it has been opened. Once the file is closed, we are done.

At this point we need to take care of two MTS-specific tasks. The first is to tell MTS that not only are we done, but that we have completed our task successfully. We do this by calling the SetComplete method in the context object. The second is that, now that we're done with the context object, we need to free the memory it occupies. This is accomplished by setting the object variable to Nothing.

If an error occurred during the file operations we just carried out, we need to handle it. Our error handler at the end of the method raises an error of our own if any file error occurred. This error will be communicated back to the client so that it can take action if necessary.

The second method in our component, GetWindowSettings, performs the opposite function of our first method. It retrieves window settings saved previously using the SaveWindowSettings method. It accepts a user ID, looks for a matching settings file, and if found, returns its contents to the caller. The only real differences from the first method are as follows:

- It checks to see if the file exists, and if it does not, raises an error and exits.
- It reads data instead of writing it.

Everything else is pretty much the same. It obtains an object context, tells MTS when it succeeds or fails using SetComplete and SetAbort, and handles any file errors that occur, passing them back to the client.

Was that pretty easy? We've just coded our first MTS component.

Now, let's build the component. Select the Make WindowComponent .dll from the Visual Basic File menu and tell it to build. The DLL that

Visual Basic creates is our MTS component, which will be hosted on a server.

Installing the Component

Actually, creating the component is the easy part. Now we have to install it on a server and make it available to client programs. To do this, we'll make heavy use of the MTS Explorer. Make sure you have a Windows NT Server somewhere with MTS installed on it, one that you will also be able to access from your development client machine. We'll run through the following steps to get this done:

1. Copy our component DLL into the MTS server.
2. Create a new package in MTS and add our component to it.
3. Adjust the settings of our component.
4. Create an Export utility to tell client machines where our component is.

To begin, copy the DLL you just built, which should be called Window-Component.dll, to either a floppy disk or a location on the network you can access from the MTS server machine. Walk over to the server. Create a directory somewhere on the server and copy the DLL into it. This is where the MTS component will live for the duration of its useful life.

Now we fire up MTS Explorer. It should be located off the Start menu under Programs, Windows NT Option Pack, Transaction Server, Transaction Explorer. Launch it now. When it comes up, we need to create a new package in which our component will reside and configure it to use transactions. Click on the following items in the left pane of the MTS Explorer window, expanding the tree until the Installed Packages branch is showing:

1. Microsoft Transaction Server.
2. Computers.
3. My Computer.
4. Packages Installed.

Once the tree is expanded and the Packages Installed item is highlighted, the MTS Explorer should look something like Figure 4.7. You

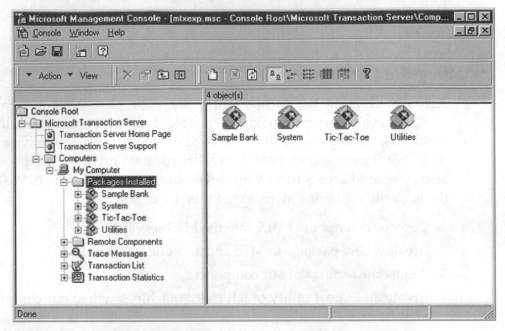

Figure 4.7 MTS Explorer with its tree expanded.

should see a few default packages in there. We're going to add a new one. Right-click on the Packages Installed item in the tree in the left pane of the Explorer, and from the context menu that appears, select New, Package. A new dialog will show up that will guide you through the creation of a new package, even though it is very simple. Click the large button labeled Create an Empty Package. When the next dialog appears, enter a name for our new package. In this case, enter WindowSettings. Click the Next button. In the last dialog, accept the defaults and click the Finish button.

Yea! We have a new package, even though it's empty. We'll add our component to the package by double-clicking on our WindowSettings package and then again on the Components folder. When you get there, the right pane of the window is empty, displaying the current contents of our package. To add our component to it, right-click on the Components item in the tree in the left pane, located right under our new package name. From the context menu that appears, select New, Component.

We have a new dialog that will walk us through the addition of a new component. Click the large button labeled Install New Component(s). A new dialog appears that lets us add whatever components we like. Click the Add Files button, locate and select the DLL we copied to the server using the Open dialog that appears, and click OK. Our component is added to the list, which looks like Figure 4.8.

Click the Finish button to complete the addition of our component. The MTS Explorer should now look like Figure 4.9, which proudly displays our component as a very cool icon.

To adjust the settings of our component, right-click on the component in the right pane and select Properties from the context menu. A dialog appears that displays the properties of our component. Select the Transaction tab, and then select the Requires Transaction setting. You can make other selections here, depending on the component needs. You can also use the Security tab to establish component-level security settings. For now, you can safely ignore them. Click the OK button to close the dialog.

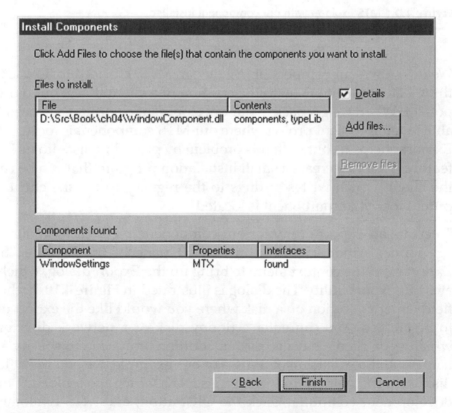

Figure 4.8 Our component being added to the package.

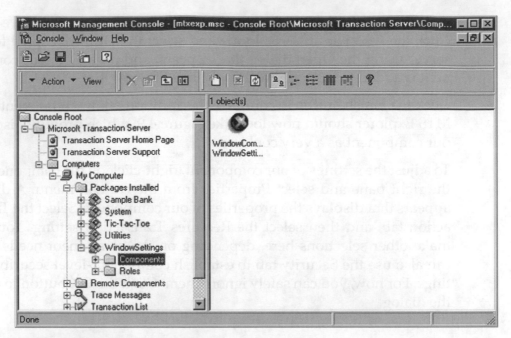

Figure 4.9 MTS Explorer with our component installed.

We now have our component installed in MTS. We need to do one more thing before we move on to the creation of a client to test out our component. When we get back to our development computer, we need to be able to tell the client project where our MTS component is located. MTS Explorer helps us out with this problem by providing us with its Export feature. This will create a small installation program that can be run on the client, which writes settings to the registry to tell the client computer where the component is located.

To create an Export utility for our component, right-click on our package name, WindowSettings, in the left pane of the Explorer. Select Export from the context menu to bring up the Export dialog, which creates our export utility. The dialog is illustrated in Figure 4.10. In the edit field, enter a location on a disk where you would like the export utility to be created. You can enter a floppy disk or a network directory to which your clients have access. In addition, you need to specify a filename with an extension of .PAK. For our example, we entered a floppy disk with the name WindowSettings.PAK, which we took back to our development computer. Click the OK button, and MTS Explorer will build the Export installation program for you. It created a directory in

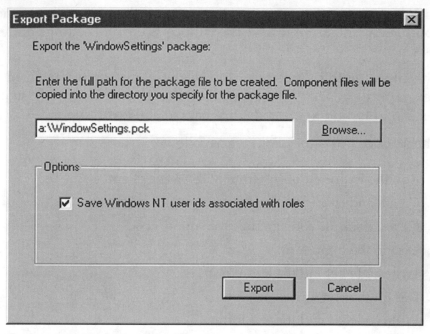

Figure 4.10 The MTS Export dialog.

the specified location called clients, which contains the installation EXE. You can now run it on any client machine to give it access to your MTS component.

Time to move on to the client test program. This is where it gets interesting, because we'll be able to see our MTS component in action. It's a great feeling when you see them working together for the first time!

Building the Client

Our test client program will allow the user to enter a user name, which will be used to key the correct window settings based on the user that saved them. When you fill in your name and click the OK button, the test program will connect with the MTS component and attempt to read window settings that you saved previously. If it finds them, it will then display a second test dialog in the size and position last saved. If not, it sticks the dialog in the upper-left corner of your screen. You can then play with the dialog in terms of its size and position on the window. Drag it around and resize it until you get tired of it. When you are done, click its Done button. The test program will then reconnect to the MTS component and ask it to save the window's current settings under your user name.

The code for this project is also on the companion CD-ROM in the \examples\ch04ex01 directory. Feel free to load it into Visual Basic instead of typing in the code. It is named ch04ex01.vbp.

The steps to build the client are as follows:

1. Run the Exported utility from MTS on the client.
2. Create and configure the project.
3. Create a simple code module for support code.
4. Design the login form.
5. Write code behind the login form.
6. Design the test form.
7. Write code behind the test form.
8. Build the project.

Client applications use MTS components just like they do any other COM or DCOM component, by creating an instance of it and then using it. The trick is to let the client computer know of the existence and location (in this case, on some other computer) of the components it wants to use. We will use the Export installation utility we just created to do this.

On your development computer, run the WindowSettings.exe program in the clients directory that was created by the MTS Explorer Export function. It runs very quickly, displaying its installation status dialog for only a second. It writes settings into your registry that make known the existence and location of our MTS component. It is now available to Visual Basic projects as a project reference.

To create and configure the project, start Visual Basic and use it to create a Standard EXE project. Name the project ch04ex01. To let this project know about our MTS component, select the References item from the Visual Basic Project menu. When it appears, select the reference to our component. It will be listed as WindowComponent.WindowSettings. Make sure when you select it that it refers to the instance of the component located in the Program Files\Remote Applications directory, as

Figure 4.11 illustrates. Now we can use it just like any other component, by creating an instance of it in our code.

TIP

If you rebuild your MTS component in Visual Basic after it has been used by a client project, you will have to reregister it using the Export program that was created by MTS Explorer. This is because rebuilding your component in Visual Basic overwrote the remote settings for the component with settings for the locally rebuilt version. When you run the Export installation program, it refers to the MTS version of your component and points to the stub in the Program Files\Remote Applications directory. When you rebuild the component locally, it will refer to the DLL you just built, which is in a local directory somewhere. If you want to test the MTS version, make sure your client project reference points to the Remote Applications version. If it doesn't, just run the Export utility again.

Next, create a simple code module for support code. Add a code module to the project by selecting Add Module from the Project menu. Name it Support, and add the following code to it:

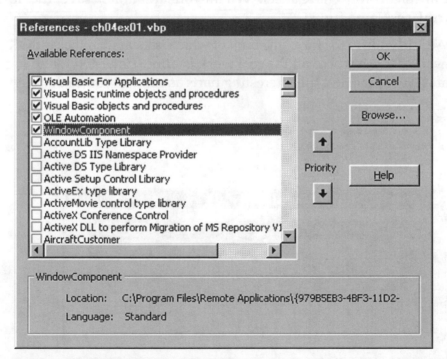

Figure 4.11   The References dialog.

```
Option Explicit

' This item is used to pass the user name entered on a
' form to some other form.
Global sUserName As String

' This public function centers a form on the screen.
Public Sub CenterForm(f As Form)

    f.Left = (Screen.Width - f.Width) \ 2
    f.Top = (Screen.Height - f.Height) \ 2

End Sub
```

The global string named sUserName will be used to pass the user's name to the second form. The CenterForm subroutine is a convenience routine we've created to center the first form on the computer screen. You can use the routine in a more general sense to center any form on any screen.

We need to construct a simple form that allows a user to enter his or her user name. Using the default form in the project, add controls to it until it resembles the form in Figure 4.12. Name the form frmUser-Name, the text box txtUserName, the OK button cmdOK, and the Cancel button cmdCancel. When you are done, save the form as frmUserName.frm.

We add code to the form, the bulk of which is located in the cmdOK_Click event. This is where all the real work is done. Enter the following code, and we'll point out the interesting parts as soon as you're done.

```
Option Explicit

' User decided to quit.
Private Sub cmdCancel_Click()
```

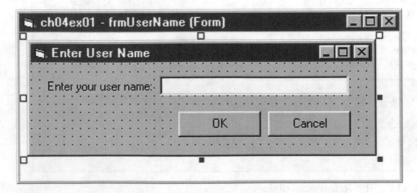

Figure 4.12   The User Name test form.

```
        Unload Me

End Sub

' When the user clicks OK, we need to show the new form that they
' can play around with, resizing and moving it. Before the form
' is displayed, we will get the last saved settings from the
' WindowComponent and use them to size and position the window.
Private Sub cmdOK_Click()

        ' Local data
        Dim wTop As Integer
        Dim wLeft As Integer
        Dim wWidth As Integer
        Dim wHeight As Integer

        ' This function performs the following steps:
        ' 1. Create an instance of the WindowComponent
        ' 2. Attempt to read the settings for the user
        ' 3. Position the window based on the saved settings
        Dim wc As Object
        Set wc = CreateObject("WindowComponent.WindowSettings")

        ' Turn on error handling so we can trap problems.
        On Error GoTo LoadError

        ' Attempt to read the settings for the user.
        wc.GetWindowSettings txtUserName.Text, wTop, wLeft, wWidth, _
wHeight
        Set wc = Nothing
        On Error GoTo 0
        ' Set the global user name variable to the name in the edit
        ' field, so the next form can read it.
        sUserName = Me.txtUserName.Text

        ' Load the next window and set its size and position based
        ' on the values we got back from the component.
        Load frmtest
        frmtest.Top = wTop
        frmtest.Left = wLeft
        frmtest.Width = wWidth
        frmtest.Height = wHeight

        ' Show the window
        frmtest.Show

        Exit Sub

LoadError:
        ' Probably no setting for this user yet, so just supply
        ' default values.
        wTop = 50
        wLeft = 100
        wWidth = 4000
```

```
        wHeight = 3000
        Resume Next

    End Sub

    Private Sub Form_Load()

        ' Center the form on the screen.
        CenterForm Me

    End Sub
```

In the cmdOK_Click function, we first create an instance of the MTS component. We use the familiar CreateObject function to accomplish this. Once we have access to the component, we can use all its methods just like any other object.

Next we make a call to the GetWindowSettings method of our MTS component. We send it the user name specified in the text box on the dialog and four parameters that the component will fill in with the window's top, left, width, and height settings. If the component cannot find any saved window settings for the specified user, it raises an error. Because we have turned on error handling, we can trap it. In this case, we handle the error by providing some valid default window settings, because the component couldn't find any. This is a great way to handle errors if possible, because the user does not have to get involved.

Next we set the global string sUserName to the value in the text box. It will be referenced by the second form we display and used to locate the correct window settings file on the server.

Now we load the form. Normally, you would load and display the form simultaneously, using the Show method. In this case, we want to tweak it a bit before we show it, so just use the Load function to get it into memory first. Then set its top, left, width, and height properties using the saved values returned by our MTS component. Then we show the form, and it comes up in the right place.

The second form in our test program demonstrates that the settings have been retrieved by using them to size the window. This form is also used to generate settings to save by allowing the user to move and resize the window, then telling the window to save its settings.

Add a new form to the project by selecting Add Form from the Project menu. Name it frmTest. Add controls to it until it looks like the form in

Figure 4.13. Configure the controls by adjusting their properties as listed in Table 4.1.

We need to add code to the form to accomplish two primary tasks: (1) updating the display when the window is resized and (2) saving its window settings using our MTS component. Enter the following code into the form's code window:

```
Option Explicit

' This code fires when the user is done resizing and moving the
' window and clicks the Done button.
Private Sub cmdDone_Click()

    ' Get an instance of our WindowSettings component.
    Dim wc As Object
    On Error GoTo SaveError
    Set wc = CreateObject("WindowComponent.WindowSettings")

    ' Save the current window settings to a small binary flat
    ' file on the server where the component lives. Unless we
    ' tell it otherwise, the file will be saved in
    ' the Winnt\System32 directory.
    wc.SaveWindowSettings sUserName, Me.Top, _
```

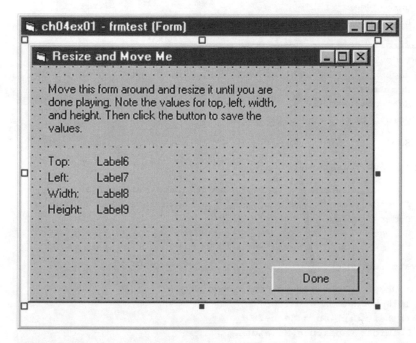

Figure 4.13   The second test form.

Table 4.1 The Test Form Controls and Their Settings

CONTROL	NAME	SETTINGS
Label	Label1	Caption = Instructions for use, as illustrated in Figure 4.13.
Label	Label2	Caption = Top
Label	Label3	Caption = Left
Label	Label4	Caption = Width
Label	Label5	Caption = Height
Label	lblTop	Caption = Label6
Label	lblLeft	Caption = Label7
Label	lblWidth	Caption = Label8
Label	lblHeight	Caption = Label9
Button	cmdDone	

```
      Me.Left, Me.Width, Me.Height
    On Error GoTo 0

    ' Get outta here, but not before we free the memory occupied by
    ' the WindowComponent object.
    Set wc = Nothing
    Unload Me
    Exit Sub

SaveError:
    ' Couldn't save for some reason, so tell the user.
    MsgBox Err.Description, vbOKOnly, "Could Not Save Settings"
    Err.Clear
    Set wc = Nothing
    Unload Me

End Sub

Private Sub Form_Load()

    ' Force an update of the window settings numbers, and
    ' reposition the Done button to a known location.
    UpdateDisplay

End Sub

Private Sub UpdateDisplay()

    ' Update the size and position display.
    lblTop.Caption = Me.Top
    lblLeft.Caption = Me.Left
    lblWidth.Caption = Me.Width
    lblheight.Caption = Me.Height
```

```
      ' Move the button to the right place.
      cmdDone.Top = Me.Height - cmdDone.Height - 450
      cmdDone.Left = Me.Width - cmdDone.Width - 200

End Sub

Private Sub Form_Resize()

      ' Force an update of the window settings numbers, and
      ' reposition the Done button to a known location.
      UpdateDisplay

End Sub
```

The cmdDone_Click event is where the most interesting code is located. It creates an instance of our MTS component and uses its SaveWindowSettings method to save the window's location and size values to a file on the server. If an error occurs in the component while attempting to save the values, the component raises an error and sends it back to our form. In this case, our form displays an error message to the user indicating the failure.

The rest of the code contains supporting functionality. If you resize the window, it moves the Done button around so that it is always located in the lower-right corner. It also displays the current location and size of the window so you can verify that settings were saved and later reloaded.

Finally, build the project. Select Make ch04ex01.exe from the Visual Basic File menu. The program will be built and ready to execute. The only thing left to do is run the program to see if we got everything right.

Running the Program

Run the program we just built, ch04ex01.exe. You should see a small window asking you to enter your user name. The form looks like Figure 4.14. Enter any user name you like and click the OK button.

The first time you run the program, there are no saved settings. When we call the MTS component and it does not find a settings file that matches your user name, it raises an error. Our test program handles it by providing default window values, positioning it in the upper-left corner of the screen. It looks just like Figure 4.15.

Move the window around and resize it a little. When you're done, click the Done button. The form uses the MTS component to save the current window settings. You can actually trot over to your MTS server and see the data file. It's located in your Winnt\System32 directory. The win-

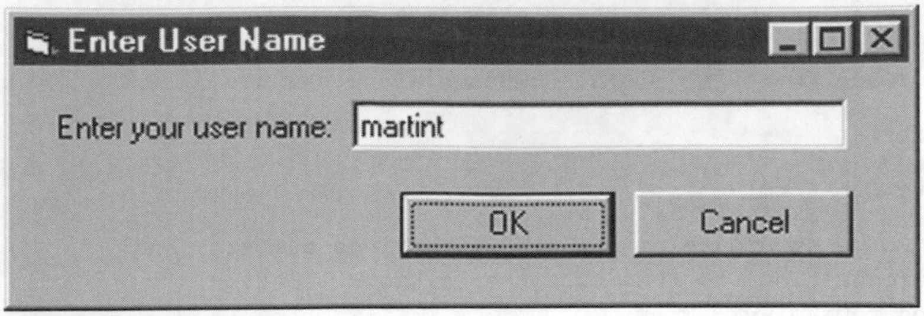

Figure 4.14   The user name dialog in action.

dow closes when the Done button is clicked. Try clicking the OK button on the user name dialog again, with the same name in it. The second dialog should come up in exactly the same place and at the same size you left it. Cool, huh?

Try using several different user names, and you'll see that it keeps the window settings for each user separate. For even more fun, install the client and the component references on another client computer and run it with a user name you have already used. The settings are still there, because they are stored on the server.

This test program has illustrated how to build, install, configure, and utilize MTS components in your own programs. Even though it was just an example, it actually has real-world usefulness. You might change it so that it saves the window settings in a database instead of separate data files, but otherwise, you can use it as is.

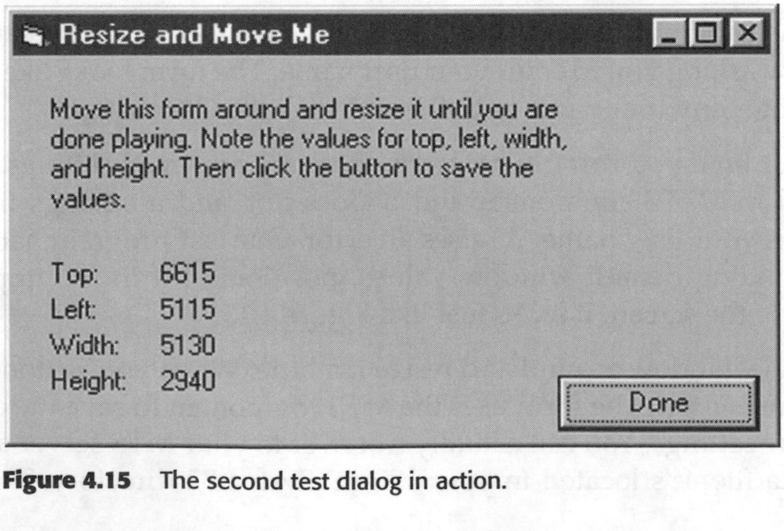

Figure 4.15   The second test dialog in action.

One Last MTS Explorer Feature

MTS and the MTS Explorer keep track of usage statistics for your components. This can be very useful for managing network loads and spotting bottlenecks in your component design. To see this feature in action, run our test application a few times, then leave it running. Then dash over to the MTS server and run MTS Explorer. Drill down until our WindowSettings component is exposed. Highlight it in the right pane, then select Transaction Statistics. It should be the last item in the left pane of the window. The right pane changes to look similar to Figure 4.16.

The Current section of the display shows what's going on in MTS at this very moment. It tells you what the current transaction count is and what the maximum has been. The Aggregate section shows some historical information. The Committed value displays how many transactions have terminated successfully (closed with SetComplete). The Aborted value tells you how many transactions ended unsuccessfully (closed with SetAbort). The Total is the sum of the Committed and Aborted transactions. The section at the bottom shows response times of transactions in milliseconds, including the average and the longest.

You can use these statistics to manage your design as you build your application. Do some periodic testing as you add components to the

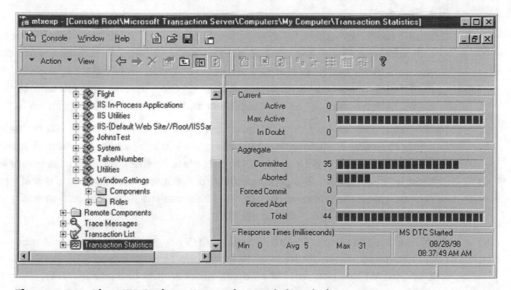

Figure 4.16   The MTS Explorer Transaction Statistics window.

system to see how they affect the load on the server. You may be able to get better performance by reorganizing your components into different packages. Besides, it's just plain fun to watch your creations working in real time.

COM+: The Future of COM, DCOM, and MTS

Microsoft is currently working on the next versions of COM, DCOM, and MTS, which we've covered in the last three chapters. Called COM+, it is part of Windows NT 5.0 and combines the capabilities of COM, DCOM, and MTS under a single umbrella. The purpose of COM+, to put it in the words of Microsoft, is to make it easier to write and utilize COM components regardless of the language in which they were implemented. It also adds some new capabilities and advancements that will make development and performance easier and better. Some of the new features being added include the following:

Language independence. COM+ is a binary specification that any language you use to build COM components must adhere to. This ensures that COM components will function together no matter which language was used to build them. This may open a wide market for third-party COM components.

The publish-subscribe event model. This allows components to make their events available to the public in general (the publish part) and for any number of components to act as "listeners" and respond to the same event (the subscribe part).

Dynamic load balancing. Currently, load balancing is done manually by the system administrator or the application development team. In MTS, you place components in various packages to achieve an optimum load balance. Under COM+, load balancing is done automatically. The COM+ system will allocate components to servers based on existing loads and try to achieve an optimum fit.

In-memory databases. A great buzzword, in-memory databases allow components to maintain state without requiring MTS to keep the component in an activated state. It should be able to save its state to the database in memory and then be deactivated. Once it is reactivated and needs its state back, it just yanks it back out of the in-memory database. Because the database is in memory and not on disk, access to it will be very fast.

All these COM+ features promise to make MTS programming easier and more convenient in the near future. And, according to Microsoft, your current COM, DCOM, and MTS components should still function just fine under COM+.

Winding Up

This is the last of our introductory chapters covering new technologies from Microsoft. All are important and critical to building successful N-tier applications with Visual Basic. And best of all, imagine how marvelous a conversationalist you'll be at parties from now on.

Now that the groundwork has been laid and you are COM-conversant, it's time to move on to the details of the N-tier application, including clients, the middle tier, and databases. The remaining chapters dig into the real details of building N-tier applications. Practical examples and lucid explanations will guide you through each tier until you are ready to build your own application.

CHAPTER 5

Creating Business Rules

E very business has rules that dictate how the business should be run. For example, if your company offers cable television service to the community, your business rules might include the following: not allowing customers to access premium stations unless they are subscribers, billing customers by the fifteenth of each month, and ensuring that the local utility tax is added to each bill. There are usually lots of rules, and they can get quite detailed. You will need software to help run the business—software that takes these rules into account. While your architecture dictates *how* your application should be built, the business rules tell you *what* to build.

This chapter will get you thinking about business rules in preparation for implementing them. We'll introduce you to the concept of business rules and even tell you how to develop them for your application. We'll be covering the following aspects of business rule and building them into your application:

- Defining business rules and why they are important

- Discovering and creating your own business rules

- Hosting your business rules

- Some basic tips for building and using your business rules

Understanding and implementing business rules is critical to making sure your application works correctly and does the job it was intended to do. Read on to learn how to make this happen.

What Are Business Rules?

At one level, business rules are actually rules or procedures to use when running a business, hence the name *business rules*. At another level—the software level—business rules define the job or jobs you want your program to perform. They dictate how your application should solve the problem it was built to address. Suppose you are creating a new program to help a junk-food distributor manage his delivery business. Some of his business rules might include the following:

- Automatically reorder if the stock of a particular item drops below 10 percent of a preset limit.

- Inspect all warehouse facilities on a monthly basis for health conditions and file reports with local authorities.

- File quarterly taxes for the business.

- Maintain availability schedules for all drivers. Do not schedule drivers when they are not available.

There are probably a zillion additional rules as well. Even if you are creating this application for internal use in your own company, you will still need a *complete* understanding of how the business works and all the details of the operation.

Business rules differ a little bit from product requirements. Requirements specify everything the program must do, whether it is directly related to the problem domain or not. They might include some data-backup functionality, compatibility with another existing system, or convenience features like cut and paste. While these are important requirements, they are not business rules. Features such as tax calculations, truck route planning, and employee scheduling are business requirements and are made up of business rules in order to function. For example, tax calculation formulas must be used to figure out the amount owed to the IRS or refunded to the company. Truck route planning might use a particular algorithm to devise a route that encounters the fewest traffic lights. An employee scheduling feature would have to account for holidays and vacations.

TIP

Remember the little guys. Business rules need not be complex. Even though calculating someone's health risk based on lifestyle might be complicated, you may need to incorporate simple things such as a list of available insurance rates into your business rules. This is important because lists of values can be part of the business rules a company lives by. You would need to decide if these list values are to reside on the client or on the server. If they change often, and we suspect that insurance rates would do so frequently, you'd rather update them once on the server than many times on each client.

Why are business rules important, especially to a software developer? Aside from supporting functionality such as utilities and user interface, business rules represent the major functionality you'll be building into your software that relates to the problem you are solving. This is the functionality your users are waiting for, the reason they are buying or using your software. We'll be talking about the discovery of business rules first, and then about building them into your software.

The Discovery of Business Rules

If your application is to have any chance of satisfying your users' needs, a detailed knowledge of the problem being solved is critical. The problem to solve is often referred to as the *problem domain*. If you don't know what the problem is, how can you write software to solve it? Therefore, you should endeavor to find out all you can about the customers' needs and the role the software will play in their businesses. Again, this is important even if you are creating software for use within your own company. You can accomplish this by reviewing the software requirements, interviewing your customers, observing them in their workplace, and conducting analysis sessions to consolidate your research.

After you have accumulated this information, you have to distill it in order to extract the relevant business rules. Usually, a small team of analysts familiar with the business does this. They peruse the studies and pull out concrete business rules that are relevant to the software you'll be writing. After this list is complete, it's time to move to the next level, which is to translate the business rules into functionality that you will be building into your software.

You can come up with your business rules in several different ways. If your project is very small, you may not need to do much beyond thinking about it for a while and making a list. If you are your own customer, you can make them up. If you have a project of any reasonable size, you'll need a process to make sure you don't miss anything. One of the primary techniques used to bring out the business rules is Object Modeling.

Object Modeling

Armed with a clear picture of the business problem you'll be solving with your software, you can begin developing your business rules. This is a process of research, analysis, and discovery. One of the more useful techniques for coming up with your business rules is *object modeling*. This is an analytical exercise that helps you extract not only business rules, but the objects in the system as well. To begin, you'll need a document that describes the requirements of the system. This can be a formal requirements document, a study of the workflow of your customer, or any type of listing of the functionality you'll be implementing.

The exercise of considering the entire problem domain through object modeling will help make the business rules for the application clear. While you're going through the object modeling exercise, watch for business rules and make a note of them. We'll give you the basic premise behind the process of object modeling, and you can research it further if you need to.

Step 1: Identify objects.   Start by getting a copy of your requirements document or whatever passes for it. Read through it, and as you do, make a list of all the nouns you run across. Remember, a noun is a person, place, or thing. Until you make a pass all the way through the document, don't try to weed them out, just make a complete list. Once that's done, you can refine the list. Throw out the obvious ones first. Then make a second pass through the list. This time, get rid of objects that are secondary or do not relate directly to the problem that you are trying to solve. You can iterate through the list as many times as you like, refining it until you have a list of objects that you feel completely represents the problem domain. The following list shows an example of some of the objects in the junk-food-distributor application we mentioned previously.

- Food Item
- Expiration Date
- Delivery Date

- Driver

- Customer

- Schedule

- Transaction

- Delivery

There is another technique, called *use cases,* that will help you discover objects in the system as well as properties and business rules. We'll cover this in more detail later in this chapter.

Step 2: Identify object properties. For each object in your list, create a list of properties. These are usually interesting attributes or data you want to know and/or store about the object. Take for example the Customer object from the preceding list. Some of the properties of the Customer object are company name, contact name, company address, phone number, credit limit, and order history. Doing this step now will help us with the next step, identifying relationships between objects, because we'll know a lot more about the objects we're analyzing.

Step 3: Identify object relationships. A whiteboard will help with this step. You need to define the relationships between the objects in the list you just created. By *relationship* we mean the following:

- Communication and data sharing between objects

- Services an object provides to others

- Containment of one object by another

For each object in your list, consider its relationship to all the others. Look for any of the relationships in the preceding list and connect the objects if one exists. Some examples using our junk-food-distributor application will serve to illustrate what we're talking about.

- A Delivery object has a Delivery Date

- A Customer object may contain one or more transactions or deliveries

- A Food Item has an Expiration Date

- A Delivery has one or more Food Items

You can make a quick sketch of the relationships as you go. Once you have a basic picture of your relationships, you should consider creating a formal diagram that would communicate your object model to others. Many notations are available, but one of the most popular is the Unified Modeling Language, or UML. In its most basic form, it is a diagramming notation for object models. Figure 5.1 is a sample UML diagram that shows part of our junk-food object model.

Step 4: Establish business rules and responsibilities. Finally, once your relationships have been defined, you can establish the responsibilities and functionality of each object. This is where business rules come in. Each object must perform the functionality related to it, and this means implementation of business rules. For example, a Delivery object has a Schedule and a Driver associated with it. A business prohibits scheduling a particular driver when that driver is not available. Therefore, you will be implementing a business rule in the Delivery object that checks to see when the Driver is available. It will then use an instance of the Schedule object to schedule the delivery. The business rule is implemented as part of the Delivery object and the Driver object.

A simpler example of using the business rule that prohibits scheduling unavailable drivers would be in the user interface. A user of the software wants to schedule a delivery and needs to select a driver to make

Logical View

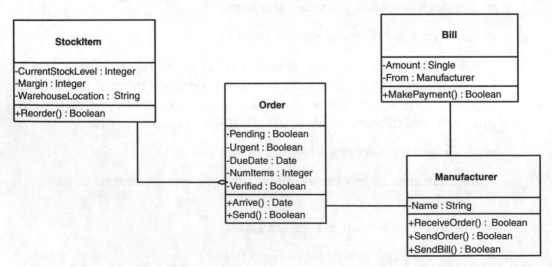

Figure 5.1 A sample UML diagram.

the delivery. The user interface would check the list of drivers and display only those who are available for the proposed delivery date.

Use Cases

One of the more useful techniques for discovering all of the objects, properties, business rules, and responsibilities is by creating *use cases*. A use case is like a scenario. Pick a single task that occurs as part of the business or process being modeled and walk through it, identifying the activities and the rules you use. Typically, use cases are developed by interviewing customers. Visit with them, talk about their business, and really probe deeply, forcing them to reveal the dark details of their day-to-day activities.

A simple example will help illustrate the use case. One of the tasks that occurs regularly in our junk-food-distributor example is the reordering of low-stock items. The process looks like this:

1. A stock item's current stock level is identified as being below its 10 percent margin.

2. The order clerk checks pending orders to make sure the current stock level can meet them. If it cannot, the stock item order is flagged as urgent.

3. An order clerk verifies that the item is placed on order with the appropriate manufacturer. If the order is flagged as urgent, this is communicated to the manufacturer.

4. When the due date of the order arrives, the order clerk verifies that the order has, in fact, shown up.

5. When the order arrives from the manufacturer, the receiving clerk makes sure that it matches what was ordered.

6. Once the order has been verified, the stock clerk places the items in the warehouse in the correct location.

7. Once the order has been verified, the receiving clerk informs the accountant that the bill can now be paid.

After walking through this task, we can examine the list of steps and extract the objects, properties, and business rules. Examine each item in the list for objects, then make a note of them in a table. Run through the list again looking for properties of the objects and add them to the list. Do the same thing again for the business rules. Table 5.1 lists the results of this analysis.

Unified Modeling Language

In the past, nobody did anything like object modeling. Programmers were busy getting their hands around exactly what objects were and how they worked. Since then, objects and object-oriented methodologies have proliferated like crazy. Each methodology had its own notation for creating diagrams to illustrate an object-oriented design, and each methodology had a different process for developing a design. You could choose the Booch method, the Coad method, the Rumbaugh method, or invent your own, which many people did in the face of too many options.

Then a few people in the object industry got together and decided that they should join forces and create one grand methodology and notation that would combine the best of all the available options. From this effort came the Unified Modeling Language, or UML, the result of years of experience in object modeling by some of the industry's best and brightest. It is a tool for creating, visualizing, and documenting object designs. It defines notations for several types of diagrams you can use to model different aspects of your object design, including class diagrams, object diagrams, interaction diagrams, state diagrams, and activity diagrams.

UML has some nice benefits that make it a good choice for documenting your business rules as objects and classes, as well as other parts of your system. First, it is process-independent. Regardless of the software development process you have chosen, UML can be used for your project. Second, UML is complete. Whether you are modeling business rules or database designs, UML can handle it. It's useful for all aspects of your software design process. Third, UML provides its own design process, the Unified Process, which is an iterative, use-case-oriented process that is easy to use and well documented. Fourth, UML is robust. It's been around for quite a while now, and it has been used successfully in many projects by many people. It's now up to version 1.2, which has been refined from a great deal of input.

If you have Visual Basic, Enterprise Edition, you'll find a cool Microsoft product on the CD-ROM called Visual Modeler. It is a tool that helps you design N-tier applications and create UML diagrams. Make sure you install it and try it out if you have any intention of diagramming your business rules as objects. Building a large software project without modeling is like building a suspension bridge without a blueprint. You can go to Home Depot, buy some girders and glue, and if you're really lucky, you might get a bridge in the end. But you're more likely to end up with nothing more than a pile of sticky girders. UML can do the job for you, whether you're using it for your entire system or just for the business rules. If you'd like to know more about UML, visit the UML Web site at www.rational.com/uml/index.shtml.

Table 5.1 Results of the Use Case Analysis

OBJECTS	PROPERTIES	BUSINESS RULES
Order	Pending, urgent, due date, items, verified	Is supposed to arrive by the due date.
Stock Clerk		Moves items from shipment to stock shelves in warehouse.
Order Clerk		Checks orders to make sure current stock level can meet them. Communicates urgency to manufacturer. Orders items from manufacturers. Verifies that orders arrive.
Receiving Clerk		Verifies that orders match shipment. Informs accountant that orders have arrived.
Stock Item	Margin, current stock level, warehouse location	Is reordered when stock level falls below 10 percent.
Accountant		Pays bills for ordered items.
Bill	Amount	Paid by accountant.
Manufacturer		Sends stock items. Sends bills.

Notice that there are some holes in the table. The stock clerk does not currently have any properties, for example. This is all right, because this use case did not uncover any. Additional use cases, which feature the stock clerk more prominently, might uncover some properties for him or her. At a minimum, the use case that covers the printing and distribution of employee paychecks will certainly add a name and address.

A Few More Examples

When it comes to creating business rules, practice is the best teacher. The more you go through the exercise of discovering them, the better you get at picking them out and deciding which are good ones and which are not so useful. To help out with this, we're providing you with some more examples of business rules that would be part of an application, and we'll show you how to use them.

Again, we're using the junk-food-distributor application. This software will help the Sweet Things Snacks Distributor, an imaginary company, run its business effectively.

Rules Governing Employees

1. Paychecks should be printed for all employees on the first and the fifteenth of each month.

2. All employees get three weeks of vacation every year. It needs to be tracked as it is used.

3. If vacation is not used by the end of the year, it must be carried into the next year.

4. Vacation can be accumulated to a total of no more than 120 hours.

5. Each employee is allotted 7 days of sick leave each year.

6. There is no limit to the amount of sick leave that can be accumulated.

7. Each employee's pay rate is to be increased by 4 percent on the anniversary of his or her employment.

8. The employee's pay rate increase can be lowered manually if performance is not adequate.

9. Social Security must be withheld from each employee's pay at the prevailing rate.

10. Taxes must be withheld from each employee's pay.

Rules Regarding Orders and Customers

1. Orders must be able to be taken 24 hours a day.

2. Orders must be packed and shipped within 12 hours of the time the order is taken.

3. Orders must be validated against stock on hand as they are entered, so the customer knows what's available and what isn't.

4. If an item is ordered but is not in stock, it should be backordered automatically.

5. As orders are entered, the total cost of the order to the customer must be checked against the customer's credit limit.

6. All customers are referenced by a customer number. All of the customer information and history is associated with this number.

7. If a customer requests a credit limit increase, the following ratio will determine whether it should be granted: number of orders divided by number of late payments. If this number is greater than 8, credit limit should be increased.

8. If customer is located in the state of Virginia, charge 1.45 percent sales tax in addition to the cost of the ordered items.

9. When new customers make their first order, their credit information must be routed through the credit department for approval.

Rules about Shipping

1. Returns of snack items are allowed, but an RMA number is required.

2. Unless otherwise specified, the shipping method will be via our own trucking fleet.

3. Other shipping methods are available for faster delivery, offered to the customer at actual cost.

4. If an order contains a request for refrigerated or frozen items, one of our freezer-equipped trucks must be scheduled.

5. All trucks in the fleet will have preventative maintenance performed every six months.

6. All drivers must be recertified every year.

7. Deliveries should be scheduled such that as many deliveries as possible can be made in the same area on a single trip.

Are you beginning to see why this is so important? Even a simple business like a distributor can have a complex set of business rules. Imagine carrying a single scenario (or use case) from order to delivery and writing code to handle all the rules. And the preceding list represents only a sampling of the rules in this business. It could get messy without some planning. This is why we evaluate a customer's business in detail, document all the business rules we uncover, and plan the implementation of those rules carefully.

Where Business Rules Live

As a software developer, you may or may not be involved in the discovery of the business rules. However, you will definitely be involved in implementing them. This means more than simply writing code to calculate an aerodynamic drag coefficient or to decide which breed of dog someone should buy. Just as important as implementing the functionality is deciding where it will reside.

The two most common choices for locating business rules in an N-tier architecture is in the client or in the middle tier on a server. Sometimes they are located in the database in the form of stored procedures. Base your decision on your needs and the individual business rules. Some rules work better in the client, while others provide more benefits when located on the server. The decision is based on one or more factors, including technological, performance, and maintenance factors.

The Case for the Client

There is one primary reason that you might want to locate your business logic on the client instead of the server, and that is performance. If it is critical that the business logic execute quickly and the results be presented to the user immediately, then building the business logic into the client could help. This technique will eliminate all requests to the server for the required functionality. If your business logic requires many complex calculations, yet still needs to be fast, try client-side business logic.

For example, if you are creating an application to monitor telemetry from a satellite, you might need many calculations and need the results quickly in order to make timely decisions. If your application reports on real-time events, you probably won't be able to afford the time to call to a server and wait for the results to come back.

The Case for the Server

There are several very good reasons to host your business logic on a server rather than on the client. Making the decision is easy if any of the following aspects of applications are important to you and your project.

Scalability.   Business rules implemented as server-side components can be shared among many clients. With the help of technology like Microsoft Transaction Server, business components can perform services for one client, then be released to perform services for another client. In this way, each client does not require its own instances of all the business components. The server might be running 10 instances of a particular business component at any one time, but be servicing over 100 clients.

If scalability is an important consideration for your application, then the server is probably the place for your business functionality.

Easy updates. Many applications require frequent updating of their business rules. If your application is updated often, especially if you have a large number of installed clients, it will be much easier to update those clients if most of the business functionality is located on the server. Instead of updating the software on 100 client machines, some of which might be remotely located, you can update it once on a server. The next time the clients use the software, the new functionality will be there.

A Web-based client. Clients that run in a Web browser are becoming popular and may soon become the preferred client technology. If your client is hosted in a Web browser, it can be more practical to host the business logic on the server. If it is included as part of the interface, it has to be downloaded over the Internet when it is accessed, which can take extra time.

Clearly, server-side business logic offers many benefits for your users. This is why N-tier architectures are becoming popular. It's not just a buzzword anymore.

On a Rule-by-Rule Basis

As with many things in life, it is difficult to make an absolute recommendation about where to host your business logic. Often you will find that it makes sense to host some of your logic on the client and the rest on the server. You can make the evaluation on a case-by-case basis or, in this instance, a rule-by-rule basis.

There are some types of business rules that make more sense to host on the *client*. Typically, you can place on the client logic that does not change or that needs to execute without the delays of network traffic. Some examples follow:

Abbreviations of states. This will only change if we add some new ones.

Calculation that converts Fahrenheit to centigrade. This has pretty much been decided on.

Basic quadratic equation formula. This has been around a while and is not likely to be updated.

Earth's gravitational constant. This is an example of the simplest business rule—a single value. Because this one won't change, it's located on the client.

Listing of all of Wolfgang Amadeus Mozart's works.   There are not likely to be any more.

Capturing a customer's signature from a signature pad.   Code that interfaces with client-side hardware may be much easier to write in the client. Recording the signature needs to happen very quickly.

Graphics display calculations.   Display operations typically need to be very fast, and the network traffic delays would probably be unacceptable.

Some of the preceding calculations typically will not change over time. It is worth noting that while the basic quadratic equation, for example, will not be changing, there is a possibility that your *implementation* of it will change. You might find a more efficient algorithm to calculate the result. If you think this sort of thing is likely to happen, then you might consider locating the functionality on the server instead of on the client. This might occur, for example, if your initial version was implemented in a big hurry.

The business rules you place on a *server* are those that are likely to change frequently or whose implementation might change.

Exchange rate to convert U.S. dollars to English pounds.   Another example of a single value acting as a business rule, this one could change frequently, so it is located on the server as a lookup method.

Listing of the known insect species.   This changes all the time, but is still a simple list lookup.

Calculations of customers' bills.   Your business may change this fairly frequently.

Income tax calculations.   Whether we like it or not, these change every year.

Lookup of your company's product's part numbers.   As you create new products, this list will change.

Theoretical scientific calculations.   Anything theoretical will be changing regularly.

Knowledge base.   Beyond simple information, this includes advanced cross-referencing algorithms that may change as they are improved. As new information is added to the knowledge base, you'll be glad it's located on the server instead of on 50 client machines.

Credit authorization routine. This functionality needs to talk directly to a database, and it will be faster for a server-side function to send back a TRUE value than to send back credit data that has to be evaluated.

It is unlikely that it will make sense for all your business rules to be located in one place. You will probably be placing some on the client and some on the server. However, experience shows that most of your rules make more sense on the server. This will, of course, depend on your application, but generally speaking, this will be the case.

Implementing Business Rules

Once you've defined all your business rules, you're ready to implement them. Typically, business rules are implemented as classes when built with Visual Basic. This makes it easier to keep the business rules packaged into coherent, maintainable units, makes them easier to replace when they need updating, and makes them easier to implement as COM components and (or initially build as) Microsoft Transaction Server components. This becomes very important as we scale our N-tier application up to more users.

If you are not familiar with Visual Basic classes, make sure you take a thorough tour of Chapter 2, "Introduction to COM." Because COM and Visual Basic classes are so closely related, they are both covered there. You'll see that COM and classes fit the business rule implementation model beautifully. For now, take a quick look at the following example to get a feel for how it is done.

A Business Rule Implementation Example

The following code implements a simple business rule for our junk-food-distributor company that determines whether or not a customer is allowed to have a credit limit increase. If the ratio of orders placed to the number of times their payments have been late is greater than or equal to 8, the increase will be allowed. The code implements a class that is constructed in the traditional fashion, with properties that are set, and then a method is called. In this case, after NumOrders and the Num-LatePayments properties are filled in, the AllowIncrease method can be called.

```
Option Explicit

Private iNumOrders As Integer
Private iNumLatePayments As Integer

' Set the number of orders the customer has made.
Public Property Let NumOrders(iNum As Integer)

    iNumOrders = iNum

End Property

' Set the number of times the customer has been
' late on their payments.
Public Property Let NumLatePayments(iNum As Integer)

    iNumLatePayments = iNum

End Property

' Calculate whether or not we should allow a
' requested credit limit increase.
Public Function AllowIncrease() As Boolean

    ' Handle a zero number of late payments
    ' to prevent a division by zero error.
    If iNumLatePayments = 0 Then
        If iNumOrders >= GoodStandingRatio() Then
            AllowIncrease = True
        Else
            AllowIncrease = False
        End If
        Exit Function
    End If

    ' If the number of orders divided by the
    ' number of times the customer has been late
    ' is greater than or equal to a predefined
    ' ratio, then allow the increase.
    If (iNumOrders \ iNumLatePayments) >= GoodStandingRatio() Then
        AllowIncrease = True
    Else
        AllowIncrease = False
    End If

End Function

' Return the ratio of orders to late payments
Public Function GoodStandingRatio() As Integer

    ' This value could be looked up in a database.
    ' For our purposes, a simple constant is fine.
    GoodStandingRatio = 8

End Function
```

Once the code for the class is filled in, it can be used in the client code. It might look like this:

```
Dim objCust As Object
Set objCust = New Customer

objCust.NumOrders = 10
objCust.NumLatePayments = 1

If objCust.AllowIncrease() Then
    ' Process the credit increase.
Else
    ' Inform order clerk that increase is not allowed.
End If
```

Suppose one little aspect of this business rule, the ratio that indicates whether the credit increase is allowed, changes. Regardless of where this class is located, we can change the class, recompile it, and distribute it without reinstalling the application and without affecting any other part of the program. If this class is located on the server, we can recompile it and install just this component in only *one place,* the server, and all users have access to the new ratio.

In Chapter 10, "Inside Microsoft Transaction Server," we'll learn how to convert a class like this into an ActiveX DLL component that can be used with Microsoft Transaction Server. However, the basic idea is the same. You will be building classes that implement your business logic and that will live on either the client or the server.

A Few Tips

After having created many different implementations of business rules, we'll pass along a few tips that might make your job a little easier. We will get into business logic implementation in detail later in this book, but the tips presented here will get you thinking about the process of building business rules into your application. If your impressed coworkers ask where you got this information, just answer smugly, "Isn't it obvious?"

Create composite methods in your server-side components. Try to organize your server-side business logic into as complete a package as possible, accomplishing as much work as possible in one call. These methods, called *composite methods,* accomplish multiple related tasks in a single call, often by simply calling several smaller methods. This will help eliminate multiple trips across the network. For example, instead of the following code:

```
Weather.GetTemperature
Weather.GetPressure
Weather.GetHumidity
```

create and call a method that does it all at one time:

```
Weather.GetReport
```

You might still want the individual methods GetTemperature, GetPressure, and GetHumidity, but you should also provide the composite method GetReport, which would just call the other three methods. The primary purpose of the GetReport function is to reduce network traffic. You can create these composite methods as they are needed by your client. Be careful, however, not to build server-side components that do so much work in one call that they create a huge delay for the user.

Lean toward a thinner client. Don't package too much business logic in your client. The more you do, the fatter the client gets, and the more difficult it will be to update remotely. Usually, fatter clients are desirable only when local performance on the client is of paramount importance. In this case, you can't afford any delays caused by network communication, so build your business logic into the client. Otherwise, a thinner client offers many more advantages, including easier functionality updates and better scalability.

Limit property references. If your components are located on the server, don't make use of their properties in the client too often. Each reference on a property generates another request to the components across the network. Instead of the following code:

```
If Date.Year > 1901 And Date.Year < 2000 _
    And Date.Year <> 1929 Then
    ...
End If
```

use this:

```
yr = Date.Year
If yr > 1901 And yr < 2000
    And yr <> 1929 Then
    ...
End If
```

You'll have only one reference to the property instead of three, one trip across the network instead of three.

Get rid of state. Server-side components, particularly running inside Microsoft Transaction Server, are better off if they do not maintain any sort of state. The reason for this is that, in order to be scalable, server-side components should be activated as late as possible and freed up as soon as possible. This ensures that a particular application holds onto the component's resources for as little time as possible. If a state is maintained in a component, it cannot be released until that state is no longer needed. The process of setting properties in a component establishes a state. As long as those properties are set, the object is remembering them and the component cannot tell when it is no longer needed.

In order to make server-side components handle loads more effectively, try not to design them with public properties that the client can manipulate. This will prevent them from setting a state in the object. Instead, make your components more service-oriented and less object-oriented. This sounds backward from what you have learned in the last few years—that object-oriented is the way of the future. However, in this case, it makes more sense to avoid it. Rather than setting properties and then calling a simple method, you will end up creating services that have large parameter lists. Consider the following simple, standard, object-oriented example, which sets the properties of a Rocket object and method to calculate its acceleration:

```
Rocket.IncreaseInVelocity = 125.0
Rocket.BurnTimeSecs = 30.0
dAccel = Rocket.Acceleration()
```

When writing a server-side component, you would simply pass the parameters into the Acceleration function instead of setting properties:

```
dAccel = Rocket.Acceleration(125.0, 30.0)
```

The benefits of this technique will allow your application to handle more users concurrently, because the server-side component will not have to hold resources while the properties are set and the function is called. Instead, it creates an object, makes a calculation, and releases the object. We'll talk more about this when we get to Chapter 9, "DCOM Details."

Winding Up

In order to fully appreciate the relevance and usefulness of the upcoming material, it is important to have a good grasp of what business rules are and why they are significant. As a result, when you cover the COM, DCOM, and MTS topics later in the book, your mind will be churning, thinking about how to implement all your own business logic.

While we've had a taste of code here, there's much more to follow. We'll be diving into the details of creating clients next, from how to make them thin and fast to how to implement them using Dynamic HTML. You've seen how business rules can affect your client code, so keep them in mind while we cover clients. Following closely on the client's heels will be the middle tier in our N-tier architecture, where this introduction to business rules will keep you awake and interested.

PART TWO

Digging Deeper

CHAPTER 6

Thin and Fast Clients

You are sitting in a meeting with your development manager, the vice president of sales, and the CEO of the company. The topic of discussion is the your shiny, new, N-tier, client/server software project, of which you are the technical project lead. It is the very beginning of this coveted new project. The conversation goes something like this:

VP OF SALES: We can't sell this product unless we have a thin client. Very thin.

CEO: Yes, I agree. I have it on good authority that thin clients are the way to go. Nobody wants a fat client these days. Thin clients are the way of the future. I read that somewhere on the Web.

VP OF SALES: That's what our customers tell us. When they call, they say our current client is too fat.

DEVELOPMENT MANAGER: I don't think that will be a problem. We have the best engineering team in the business. If anyone can make an excellent thin client, they can.

VP OF SALES: They want it fast, too. They're always complaining about speed problems.

CEO: Can we make it fast this time, Sam?

DEVELOPMENT MANAGER: You bet. We'll just allocate a couple weeks at the end of the schedule for some performance tuning. QA doesn't need all that time anyway.

CEO: Excellent! Now that we've settled that, let's move on to exactly what this product will do.

If this conversation makes you uncomfortable, that's a good thing. You should already be breaking out in a cold sweat. The VP of sales thinks a thin client is a customer that works out at the gym every day. The CEO is trying to hide the fact that he knows nothing about technology, and the development manager is a dedicated yes-man. The scariest part is that not one of them realizes that in a three-tier client/server application, both thin and fast have to be planned for and built in from day one.

The meeting attendees have no clue what thin means, what client means, or even why they want it, except that they think they should. The buzzwords are flying fast and furiously, like missiles fired by a loose cannon, and you are their most likely target. You need some ammunition of your own.

In this chapter we'll be covering the concepts you'll need to know to plan the development of your client software:

- What thin client means
- What tradeoffs are involved with thin clients
- How thin your client should be
- Important issues to keep in mind, such as fast code and client-side database access

If you are planning an N-tier application, then thin clients may well be in your future. We'll make sure you are able to make the right decisions about your client software, whether it's thin or not-so-thin.

What's Thin, Anyway?

When most people talk about thin clients, they immediately think of a small physical size, something that will transfer over the wire in a very short time frame. But thin has more than one definition, or it may mean several things at the same time. A thin client has one or more of the following attributes:

1. *A thin client is small in size.* It doesn't take up much disk space. The most common way to reduce the size of a client is to move functionality to the server. If your application is meant to be distributed across a network, smaller client size equates to faster transfer rates. If the client transfers faster, users will not have to endure long delays.

2. *A thin client does not do any processing beyond the user interface.* It has no brains of its own. Its purpose is to present an interface to the user that can be used to access the functionality of the program and to present processing results back to the user. All the real processing, including calculations and data retrieval, is done on a server.

3. *A thin client may be a Web browser.* With the evolution of the Internet, this is an important option. In this case, the Web browser acts as a container for the entire user interface. This provides many benefits, such as automatic software distribution and updates as well as an easy implementation of remote access to the functionality of your software. Technologies like Dynamic HTML and ActiveX Documents make this possible. It also appears that hosting your user interface in a Web browser will be a major trend in software development over the next few years, and you'll want to consider it as a serious option if leading-edge technology is important to you or your company.

All of these are important, and you may want your client to have one or all of these characteristics. The choice is not black and white, either. You can create light clients, thin clients, slightly underweight clients, and dangerously underweight clients. It's all a matter of degree, and you decide how far to go based on your needs. In general, though, you have to ask yourself, as the executives at the beginning of this chapter did not, why it is important to make a client thin, either in size or brains. There are good answers to this question.

Benefits

Having a trim client has some nice benefits. The smaller the client, the quicker it will download over a wire. Especially in this brave, new world of remote connectivity over the Internet, fewer bytes to send is a positive boon. A smaller client will also usually load faster (depending on what it does at startup, of course).

Why separate serious functionality from the client? You're removing from the client most of the functionality that could easily be implemented and placing it in more complicated components on a different machine. If you take this to its extreme, the client becomes nothing more than some simple forms that request the server to provide everything from financial calculations to the time of day. Why go to all that trouble? If the primary functionality of the entire application is hosted on a localized server, it is very easy to upgrade or replace defective components in one place, without having to reinstall anything on your client machines. You may have a thousand clients talking to a small handful of servers. Would you rather install a new calculation module on four servers or a thousand clients, some of which may be very remotely located? While we are not system administrators for such a program, we could still answer the question long before the coffee finishes brewing.

If you want extra convenience in your thin client, host it all in a Web browser. Not only can you replace server-side components easily, but components of the client are downloaded to the client machines automatically. Of course, this opens up a whole new can of worms regarding the way you build your client, which we'll talk about later in Chapter 7, "Web and Internet Clients," when we bring up Dynamic HTML.

Tradeoffs

Thin clients sound great. However, they have some drawbacks. You don't get faster clients with easily replaceable functionality on the server side without paying for it. There are some trade-offs to consider when deciding just how thin, functionality-wise, to make your clients.

The more functionality you remove from the client and place on the server, the more network traffic you will have as the client makes more frequent requests for services. The more requests that travel back and forth across the network, the slower your performance will be. Compared to the execution of typical code, network communication is much slower. There are techniques for minimizing this, however, such as limiting the number of requests to the server and getting as much work done as possible in a single request.

Server components take longer to create and test than does building functionality directly into the client. Because components are small pieces of software in and of themselves, you will need to spend more time planning ahead, orchestrating how they will all work together. Component interfaces and network communications add to your development time, because if you were to build the functionality directly into the client, you wouldn't need to implement them at all. These aspects of components add to the project complexity and can result in longer development times.

How Thin Should You Be?

Someone once said you can never be too thin or too rich. Who it was is not clear, but he or she obviously had no experience creating client software. When speaking of clients, it's important to remember that there are degrees of thin. You can simply put your client on a lightweight exercise program, moving a few of your heaviest pieces of functionality to a server, or go ultrathin, not allowing any serious functionality in the client. You can settle anywhere in between these two extremes.

It is easy to think that thinner is better and attempt to achieve this goal without regard for the costs and consequences. As we've seen, there are plenty of benefits that make this a worthwhile endeavor. However, there are costs associated with everything, and creating thin clients is no exception. We've also seen that there are tradeoffs to make when building a thin client. The key is to decide exactly how thin is right for you and your project.

The decision to "go thin," and just how thin to go, is based on the needs of both your users and your project. From your users' perspective, if you expect to have a large number of users utilizing the software simultaneously, thin clients become more important, because server-side functionality will be more able to handle large loads by brokering requests and connections. If your users are at the bottom of the technology scale, using low-end workstations, thinner clients could provide better performance by locating the primary functionality on one or more fast servers.

However, your project is important, too. It takes more time to build functionality into components than to build them into the client. With components come interfaces, client-to-component communication issues, component-to-component communication issues, and server-side resource management. You would be doing very little of this if your client contained most of the functionality.

As you can see, this is not a simple or straightforward decision. You will need to do some analysis of your users' needs and your project requirements. The issues become much clearer if you list them and then prioritize them. For example, you may have a need from your user's perspective to update the functionality of the software on a monthly basis due to changing government regulations. This means a thin client is important. However, you also have only eight months to implement a complete solution. This might require you to severely shorten your development cycle, and a thin client might take too long. If meeting your schedule is more important than the customer's need for easy updates, then you would make a fatter client, perhaps restricting server functionality to a minimum. On the other hand, if your client's need to change its business rules on a monthly basis is more important than the project end date, a thinner client would be a better decision.

The Client Questionnaire

In order to help you make the decision about how thin your client should be, we have created an informal questionnaire that will get you thinking in the right direction. Discuss these issues with your project team and you'll get a pretty good idea which direction is the right one for you.

Part 1: No Brains in the Client

1. *Do you expect to be updating the functionality of your software frequently?*
   You may have business components that change quarterly or monthly, in which case you'll be updating them often. Better to update just a few servers than many clients. If you have an application that requires regular updates (annual changes based on tax laws, for example), then this is an especially important reason to lean toward a thin client with little business functionality.

2. *Do you have a large number of client machines connected to your software?*
   Large is, of course, a relative number, which you'll have to judge for yourself. If you answered yes to this question, then a dumber client becomes important. Again, you would probably rather update four servers with new functionality than 150 clients. If you have an especially large number of clients, this is even more important.

3. *Do you have time in your schedule to build everything into components?*
   It will take more time to build your business logic into components. Not only does the functionality have to be built into a separate component, but interfaces also have to be designed, built, and maintained. The communications and performance will have to be tested. If you have time to do this, and the ability to update your logic on the server instead of on the clients is important to you, a brainless client is an important consideration. It is also important to

keep in mind that components are more difficult to deploy, troubleshoot, and debug. This can all add to the development schedule.

Part 2: Small Physical Size

1. *Will many of your users connect to your software from remote locations?* If your users are connecting to your software and servers over less-than-speedy lines, such as a modem connection or a busy ISDN line, you'll want to minimize the amount of traffic going back and forth. In this case you'll want a client and client components of small size, but fewer service requests. If this is the case, a small-size client is more important. If all or most of your users use your software over a remote or slower connections, then it's even more important. If you don't update your functionality very often, this may not be as much of a performance impact to your users, since components are downloaded only the first time they are used or when they are updated.

2. *Are your clients located on an already busy network?* If you need to install components over the network, then small size might be important to you so that the components transfer across the network quickly. In this case, you will want to lean more toward a small-size thin client.

Part 3: Web Browser?

1. *Do you have a large number of remote users?* Remote users need client software to talk to the server. If you have a large number of remote users, particularly traveling users, then the only software they need on their machines is the Web browser. They could point it to an address and be computing with your software in moments. If this is important to your customer, a browser-hosted client may be a good solution.

2. *Do you need easy software updates?* Those traveling users we just mentioned may need to get software updates without coming into the office. To receive new updates, all you have to do is post them on the server. The next time your clients connect from their motel rooms, they will automatically receive all the new updates. If this capability is appealing to your customer, a browser-hosted client could be just the ticket.

Issues to Consider

When planning the development of your client, there are a number of issues to consider. Should your client be hosted in a Web browser or be built as a standard Win32 application? Should you use database cursors? If so, which kind? Which type of client will provide you with the features and performance your users and your project needs? These issues—client weight, client speed, and type of client—are all important aspects of your client, and need to be thought out before you write the first line of code.

A Win32 Client

The traditional Win32 client is probably the type of client with which you are most familiar. When you create a Visual Basic Standard EXE project, you are creating a Win32 program. From your first "Hello, world" program to the document cataloging system you completed last week, the Visual Basic Win32 program has most likely been the core of your past and current development efforts.

Why a Win32 Client?

The Win32 client may seem pretty boring and lifeless in the face of all the new technologies appearing on the development scene these days. Why should you create a Win32 client when a Dynamic HTML client would look much better on your resume? Assuming that your project and your users are more important than your career development, there are plenty of reasons.

One of the clearest advantages to building a Win32 client is that you and your team already have the requisite experience to do the job. If you were to implement some other type of client, such as a Web browser–hosted client, your team members would require additional training before they could implement the client software. Even then, they still wouldn't have the same level of experience with the new technology as they do with developing Win32 clients. Their experience with Win32 clients will give you an edge in the following ways:

Development time. Your knowledge of the Visual Basic Win32 project type will allow you to code at top speed. If you were to use an unfamiliar technology, progress is typically more halting and involves ongoing research to figure out how to best utilize it.

Design. The design of your client software will lead to fewer dead ends because you know the technology well. When using new and unfamiliar technology, you do a lot of experimentation that can lead to unusable results, requiring you to backtrack.

Reliability.   You have experience with Visual Basic Win32 clients and are familiar with the traps and pitfalls of the environment and the project type. You have been down that road and know it well. Using new technology is like walking an unfamiliar path; you never know when you're going to run into a pitfall or quicksand.

Appropriateness.   Some applications do not lend themselves well to the Internet and are more appropriately built as Win32 clients. For example, programs that integrate tightly with the operating system, such as disk administration utilities, or with local hardware, such as a barcode scanner, will not function well (or at all in some cases) as a Web client.

Win32 clients are also typically easier to implement than other types of clients. The familiar Visual Basic development metaphor of dropping controls on a form, writing code behind them, and moving between forms is relatively easy to do and quick to implement. Formal builds of your project are also potentially less complex, because your client is wholly contained within the Visual Basic environment.

With other technologies, such as User Documents and Dynamic HTML, tasks you took for granted are suddenly bigger issues that you have to learn all over again. For example, with both of these alternative technologies, moving from one form (or page) to the next becomes more complicated. The Show method no longer applies, and we have to deal with navigation using other mechanisms that can be more involved. Communication of data between forms also becomes more difficult, requiring alternative mechanisms.

Win32 clients may also execute faster. While client performance is dependent on a large number of factors, such as the client machine, network traffic, and the job the client is performing, a Win32 client is a completely compiled executable application. It will typically run faster than a Web-based application, because the code behind Web-based applications is usually interpreted rather than compiled.

One of the disadvantages of a Win32 client is that it requires installation on the client machine. Usually, the administrator of the software will have to go from client to client to install the client software. Every time the client functionality is updated, the installation process will have to be repeated. Some tools, such as Microsoft's System Management Services (SMS), help out with this and perform the distribution of software to multiple users over a network, but they are complex and require setup by an expert user. If you plan to update your client functionality often, a Win32 client may not be the right choice.

While a Win32 client may be more difficult to update, it has a number of advantages that still make it an attractive option. Depending on how you design your architecture, it can still be a thin and fast client, communicating with server-side components to access business functionality and retrieve data. If your project and users require faster development time, fast execution, and do not require frequent updates, then a Win32 client may be right up your alley. Don't let the allure of new technologies blind you to the essential usefulness of the still lively Win32 client.

A Browser-Hosted Client

You can actually create your client so that it runs inside a Web browser. You've probably heard of this. Lots of people talk about it, but the industry hasn't seen much of it yet. The basic idea is that you fire up your Web browser, point to the right Web address (URL), and the application comes up in the browser.

Why Browser-Hosted?

There are several benefits to hosting your application in a Web browser. The most obvious one is that, beyond the browser itself (and most everyone has one already), you don't need to install anything on the client machine. Users come into the office one day and fire up their e-mail. A new message awaits them, stating that the new Financial Confabulator Software is on the network and ready for use. They click on the URL embedded in the e-mail message, which launches the browser and navigates to the application. That's about as easy as client installation gets. Another major benefit of a browser-hosted application is that remote connectivity is built into the browser and Internet architecture. If you can point to a URL from your office, you can dial into any Internet connection and point to the same URL and you'll have the same program you did in the office. Granted, you'll be limited by your connection speed, but your architecture can reduce delays related to this.

The third big bonus is that you can update the software for everyone by updating it once. All the components of the client reside on the Web server and can be replaced whenever an update occurs. The next time a client connects to the application, the Web server automatically sends any new components to the client. Picture, for example, remote insurance salespeople in the field getting all the latest daily insurance rate adjustments simply by using the browser-hosted program. No special steps required. You can change the content and functionality of the software as often as you like, up to the limits of your users' patience.

Technologies for Your Browser Client

There are several different techniques for creating user interfaces that work in a Web browser. The intricate details of how they work and how you create them are the subject of Chapter 7, "Web and Internet Clients," but when looking at options and planning your architecture, you should be aware of what's available, as well as the benefits and drawbacks for each option.

HTML and ASP

HTML is the basic page-description language used by Web pages. It is composed of the contents of the page and *tags* that tell the browser how to format it. It forms the basic structure and look of your Web page, and thus your user interface. If you create a browser-based user interface, you will probably be using HTML in one form or another, whether it involves Active Server Pages or Dynamic HTML.

Active Server Pages, or ASP, is a Microsoft hybrid that lets you use a combination of HTML, scripting, and controls to create a more interactive Web page. This option allows you to embed third-party and ActiveX controls into the Web page to make a page that is capable of more functionality. Active Server Pages have been around for a while now, and they are fairly stable. Lots of people out there understand them and know how to create them.

The problem with Active Server Pages is that the page is still mostly static. All the functionality occurs on the server, which does whatever processing is necessary and then generates a new static Web page that is sent back to the browser. If you need to change something about the page look or layout (such as incorporating data from a query), you have to go back to the server and get an updated page. ASPs are a good choice if you already know ASP and need to create a browser-hosted user interface in short order. However, newer and more capable options are available to help you create a more interactive client.

User Documents

User Documents, or ActiveX Documents, are complete Visual Basic forms that can run in a Web browser. You build them in Visual Basic, using standard Visual Basic form design and code. They are placed on a server or client and accessed by entering a URL in your browser, as with a regular Web site. When they are downloaded and executed, they look just like Visual Basic forms that fill the browser's client area. You have most of the capabilities of Visual Basic at your disposal while developing them. Visual Basic even has a conversion wizard that will convert existing forms to User Documents. User Documents have a lot of benefits. They look exactly like standard Win32 applications, but they are running in a browser. They are built almost like a standard Visual Basic application, with some minor modifications to the process of navigating from one form to the next. The full functionality of standard Windows controls and third-party controls are available to you while building them. You can even take control of the browser and turn off all the browser features such as toolbars and menus, if they don't suit your needs. User Documents are the easiest way to create a browser-hosted client if your primary expertise is in Visual Basic.

The major drawback here is that User Documents can be pretty big. In this section, we'll be using a simple User Document example to illustrate how they work. This example, which has no nonstandard controls on it, is a total of 34K. Remember that each User Document is a complete Visual Basic form, and large ones can take a while to download. User Documents might be a good choice if you need your program to look just like a regular application, if you need the full-featured user interface power of a regular application, and if you have a fast connection to the server. If you need to operate in a browser other than Internet Explorer, you'll want to choose another option.

We tossed together a simple example to illustrate what it takes to create a User Document and to show what they look like. The example, ch06ex01.exe on the CD-ROM, contains a few controls you can manipulate, then navigates to a second user document that shows the results of your selections. If you're interested in User Documents, this is a good place to start, because they don't work quite like normal forms. To run them from the CD-ROM, point Internet Explorer to the file udUserDocExample.vbd, making sure that the other files, ch06ex01.exe and udResults.vbd, are in the same directory. Figure 6.1 shows what the first user document, udUserDocExample, looks like.

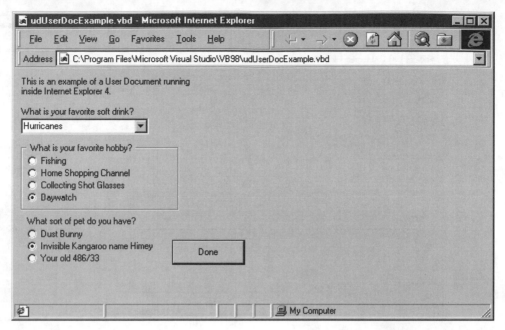

Figure 6.1 The first User Document, udUserDocExample.vbd. It's nosey, but fun.

By clicking the Done button in Figure 6.1, the browser navigates to the second User Document shown in Figure 6.2.

NOTE

User Documents do not use the Show method to display a new form. Each User Document has a Hyperlink object associated with it, which has a NavigateTo method. You use the NavigateTo method to display the new User Document. Point the URL parameter of the NavigateTo method to the appropriate VBD User Document file to load and display it.

While this sounds pretty easy, make sure you check out the code listing for the command button on the udUserDocExample User Document. It shows how to find the path to the new user document, whether it's on a Web site or a local machine.

Dynamic HTML

Dynamic HTML (DHTML), when used to build applications, is like Active Server Pages on steroids. Using HTML, you can create a page equivalent to a form in your user interface. You can also embed scripting and controls into the HTML, just as with ASP. However, in addition, you can change any portion of the display in any way you like, right on

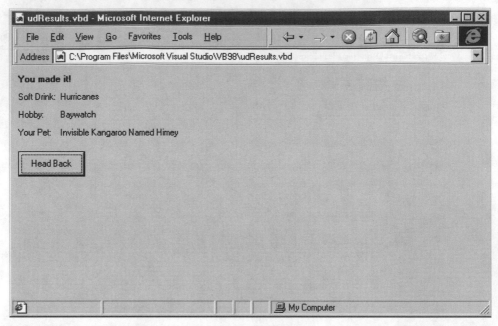

Figure 6.2 The second User Document, udResults.vbd.

the client, without a trip back to the server. You can also respond to any event that occurs on any part of the page, just as with a Visual Basic form. It promises to be very efficient. You even get an error-handling model, which is provided by the *Document Object Model* (DOM) in the form of an onerror event. The Document Object Model will be covered in more detail in Chapter 7, "Web and Internet Clients."

There are two ways to create the code portion behind the user interface. The first is the familiar embedded script, using VB Script or JavaScript. However, this exposes your code to the rest of the world. A very interesting alternative, which we'll cover in more detail in Chapter 7, is to put all your event-handling code into an ActiveX DLL. By embedding a reference to your ActiveX DLL in the HTML and referencing the page in your DLL code, you can write all your code in VB and respond to every event that occurs on the Web page, just as you would to any other event. This technique protects your code from prying eyes and allows you to compile the code for faster execution, and you can do all your work in the Visual Basic environment.

Does this method have any drawbacks? DHTML is being used in differing preliminary forms by Netscape Navigator and Internet Explorer

4.0. Because of this, creating browser-independent DHTML is currently a royal pain and a lot of work. The World Wide Web Consortium (W3C) committee, the group that creates the HTML standards, has not finished its work in DHTML and has not approved the standard as of this writing. If browser independence is important to you, you'll have to wait not only for W3C to complete its standard, but also for the browser folks to implement the standard. You will probably also have to invest in a little training time to get your teams up to speed. Because DHTML is a vast subject, it can take a while to learn it and become proficient.

Thin, or Maybe Not-So-Thin

At first, you'd think that a browser-hosted client would be superthin. The only software located on the client machines is the Web browser, so just send a bunch of Web pages to the client as they are needed. Well, the story is more complicated than that.

You're not just sending simple HTML. At best, you will be sending HTML with embedded script code (be it JavaScript or VB Script). You'll need significant script code to do anything meaningful. To create a usable interface that bears any real resemblance to software, you'll need to send down some additional software components, probably in the form of ActiveX controls. This can mean a control or two that gets downloaded once, or it can mean many controls, usually custom controls you create yourself that might change frequently. Imagine downloading four different 800K controls on a single page. One browser-hosted application we saw was comprised almost entirely of custom controls. They were fairly lightweight, but there were many of them. This architecture was beneficial, but there was a fair amount of network traffic, particularly when a segment of the program was run for the first time, and all the controls had to be downloaded and registered on the client machine.

Issues with Browser-Hosted Clients

Browser-hosted clients offer a lot of promise. However, these new rewards do not come free. You should be aware of the costs involved before deciding if the benefits are worth the price.

Creating a browser-hosted client involves using new technologies and architectures that are not yet familiar to most people. You may spend some time and money educating your development teams about how to do this. They will have to adjust to a new programming paradigm that focuses on different priorities, such as implementing basic user interface functionality (accelerator keys, toolbars) we normally take for granted. You will also need someone who understands page layout with HTML. This does not mean someone who just knows HTML, but a person who also knows how to make things appear on the page where you want them to be and how to design a decent page. In addition, because these are new technologies, they are evolving continuously. During your project development cycle, you may find that a technology has changed. As a result, you'll have some rework to do that may be minor or, unfortunately, may be substantial.

When designing and building a browser-hosted client, size does matter. Everything travels to the client over the wire (which, if you're unlucky, may be a 14.4 modem connection). This means that everything has to be built with small size in mind. You have to consider the size of the Web pages that get transmitted and the number and size of the controls used by the application. Keep your eyes open for ways to economize on size, such as reusing a type of control in several different screens to minimize downloads. You may also have to sacrifice some code speed for a bigger performance gain on download speed.

When creating your browser-hosted client, you will probably have to change the way you think about user interfaces. You will have to consider such things as navigation through your program, how to implement accelerator keys, and tabbing around the screen. For instance, if the user is looking at a data-entry screen and then clicks the browser's Back button, what does the program do? If the user then goes back to the data-entry screen after leaving an incomplete entry there, does it maintain state, remembering the partial data entered? If so, does the client store it temporarily, or is it stored on the server?

When considering whether a browser-hosted client is right for you, the maintenance of state is an important issue. A Win32 client can maintain state in a variety of ways, including through the system registry and data files. Currently, *cookies* are the only common mechanism to maintain state when your user interface is a Web page. Cookies are small data files that the Web page is allowed to create on the client machine. They have their own problems, such as limited size and the fact that the user can prevent them from being written to his or her computer. Internet Explorer 5.0 will be improving this situation by allowing you to save data name-value pairs without the limitations of cookies.

The real message here is that there is a lot to consider when deciding to create a browser-hosted client. You'll have to decide if the benefits are worth the tradeoffs. We'll go over browser-hosted clients in greater detail, including an example or two, in Chapter 7, "Web and Internet Clients." For now, understand that a browser-hosted client is an option in your quest to create a thinner client.

Client Performance

The client portion of your software is what your users see. To them, it's the whole program, and if any part of your system is slow, it will manifest at the client. Is your database design ineffective? It will be slow to retrieve data, and the user must wait until it's done. Is your architecture one that handles scaling well? If not, as more users start making demands on the system, it will bog down, and your users must wait until their requests are serviced. Is your client poorly coded? It will run slowly, and users will be frustrated, or even worse, they will not be able to do the work they need to get done.

There are two types of performance issues: real performance and perceived performance. *Real performance issues* are those that have effects on real things. For example, if your program is too slow to keep up with a data transmission rate and you experience data loss, you will have to speed up your program. This is a real performance issue. A *perceived performance issue* is one in which the user perceives delays in the program. In this case, the user might see a 15-second delay when loading a custom reports' module into memory. This really irritating to users when they click a menu item and then have to wait. They expect near-instantaneous response from the user interface.

Quite often, perceived delays are easier to deal with. The program has to be only fast enough or clever enough to make the user think there are no delays. If your program experiences a 15-second delay while waiting for a reporting module to load, the perceived performance issues can be eliminated if you preload the report module while the program is starting up, at which time the user is already expecting delays. Another 15 seconds during startup is not a big problem (unless your program crashes a lot). Later, when the user accesses the reporting module, the delay is not noticeable.

Keep this in mind while thinking about making your program faster. Where possible, work on the perceived performance problems, and then only until the user no longer perceives a time lag.

Database Access

Database access is one of the two biggest performance issues your software will have to deal with (the other being network traffic). Although creating fast database access has more to do with your database structure and query design, you can do some things on the client side to speed database access.

Database Alphabet Soup

One of your biggest decisions will be which data access mechanism to choose. Many are available, including OLE-DB direct, OLE-DB with Active Data Objects (ADO), Open Database Connectivity (ODBC), Remote Data Objects (RDO), and Data Access Objects (DAO). The newest mechanism from Microsoft is ActiveX Data Objects (ADO). In the absence of other information (such as your specific data requirements), we recommend using OLE-DB with ADO to get at your data. ADO is easy to use compared to the other choices. It's fast and works well over Internet connections. Also, all kinds of new controls and language features in Visual Basic 6 make this an easy choice, including new data-bound controls that work with ADO, such as the new Hierarchical FlexGrid, the DataGrid, the graph control, and the Data-Combo and DataList controls.

If you are writing a new application, ADO is your best bet as a general rule. It is Microsoft's new database application programming interface (API), and it will probably get the most development attention. ADO has lots of advantages:

- The ability to talk to all kinds of OLE-DB data sources using a single API
- Speed
- Support of server-side and client-side cursors of various types

- The ability to deal with both relational and nonrelational data sources at the same time

- Relatively easy to learn, especially compared to talking directly to OLE-DB or ODBC

- Especially good at Web-based data retrieval

If you are converting an existing application that uses Data Access Objects (DAO), you'll have some more work to do. DAO code will not convert automatically to ADO. You'll have to judge for yourself if the benefits of ADO are worth the effort it will take to rewrite the DAO sections of your code. If you have an existing DAO or RDO application that is working just fine, there is probably no need to rewrite it unless you specifically need the features of ADO. Existing RDO applications will also require rewriting, but will not, generally speaking, be as much work.

Cursors! Foiled Again!

Put simply, cursors hold data returned from a database query. They make it easy for programs to access a result set from a query in a sequential fashion, as records. In general, it is best to avoid using cursors because they can slow down your client. However, this is not always possible, and a knowledge of the types of cursors available will help you choose the one that will yield maximum performance and still suit your needs. There are many types of cursors—static, forward-only, keyset cursors, dynamic cursors—and each has its pros and cons. It's important to become familiar with them and understand when it is appropriate to use each one. You'll then be able to choose the right cursor for the job you need done. The key is to choose the cursor that provides you with the minimum necessary benefits in order to eliminate overhead. A brief summary of the available cursor types follows.

Dynamic. The Dynamic cursor has it all. It allows you to navigate all records in any direction, as well as to see all additions, deletions, and changes made to the records by other users. It is not as fast as the other cursors.

Keyset. If you don't need to see rows that were added or deleted by other users, but still want to see rows that have changed, Keyset cursors are a good choice. If the Keyset cursor is used on the client, it may not perform well with large Recordsets. Non-Keyset cursors used on the client send the entire Recordset from the query to the client all at once.

Static. If you need to navigate the records in any direction, but don't care about any updates to those records made by other users, then a Static cursor is a fairly fast and efficient one. If the Static cursor is used on the client, it may not perform well with large Recordsets.

Forward-Only. The Forward-Only cursor can view a given record only once before moving to the next record. If this suits your needs, it is a very fast and efficient cursor. It is ideal for retrieving lists of values from the database for the purpose of filling lists on the client.

Cursors can reside in one of two places: client side or server side. Client-side cursors always get all the data in a result set. Therefore, client-side cursors with a large number of rows in the result set may slow down your client. Once the data has been downloaded to the client, however, navigation through the data is very fast. And because the client now has the responsibility of dealing with the cursor, the server is less busy. This may result in a more scalable application. This is an especially good option if you expect your client to reside on faster or more capable computers.

Generally server-side cursors will yield better performance for an N-tier application. If you have lots of network traffic and high-powered servers, go with server-side cursors. In this case, the server manages the cursor, and sends only the data specifically requested by the client. If you expect to use only some of the data in a result set, server-side cursors will help reduce network traffic. However, this will put a heavier load on your servers. If you are using less-capable client computers, server-side cursors are a better option. Server-side cursors also support direct-positioned updates, which are fast and reduce the likelihood of a collision.

We'll further discuss cursors and the various types available later, but it's important to understand that the choice of cursor affects the performance of your client application.

Network Traffic

It is easy to fall into an unseen trap whereby your client unintentionally creates a huge amount of network traffic, bringing your application to its knees. Because communication across the network is one of the slowest activities your application will perform, it pays to reduce it to a minimum. This can be done by coding your client effectively and by designing your server-side components correctly.

Your client can reduce network traffic by staying off the highway. This is not always an easy thing to do, especially if you are designing a thin client. The thinner your client, the more often it has to hit the server for the functionality the user needs to run. Design the client such that it makes the fewest number of network requests possible, while keeping the amount of data transferred in each request to a minimum. You can reduce the number of requests by packaging as much work as possible into a single call. This requires a server component that can do all the required work in this one request.

Server components can be designed to reduce network traffic by providing services that accomplish as much work as possible in a single call. If the client has to make multiple requests to set up the component for the work it needs done and then has to issue several calls to the component to do the work in several steps, you've generated a large number of calls—all of which go across the network. If the client can instead make one call, passing all necessary parameters at once, then you accomplish the same thing in a single request.

Writing Fast Client Code

Performance problems in your program are most often caused by the database (its design or supporting code), or by excessive network traffic or data transfers. However, the actual code itself can cause trouble from time to time, particularly in routines that are called frequently, because a small delay in the code is magnified by the number of times the routine is called. Poor organization can also cause delays.

One of the most frustrating types of delays we encounter as users of software is when the client is poorly coded and delays are everywhere, even if they're small ones. For example, if you click on a button that pops open a new dialog, and it takes even 5 seconds to load and display, it's too long. User tolerances of interface latency (the time it takes to operate any part of the user interface) are very small, usually no more than 2 seconds. Any longer, and they think something is wrong and start to click again or work on other controls. This can lead to all kinds of problems, from a confused user to a returned product.

Usually, sloppy or inefficient coding causes these delays. The good news is that there are all kinds of coding techniques you can use to maximize performance of the client. Some of them are so easy that it's a simple matter of switching a coding habit. We'll let you in on the tricks we know if you promise to keep them to yourself.

Granted, the following information is detailed, even though the focus of this chapter is strategy and information to help you plan your project. However, it can be useful to know ahead of time that there are things you can do at the lowest level to speed things up. It can also help you define some Visual Basic coding guidelines your team can use from the very beginning of the project.

Select the Correct Data Type for the Job

The default data type in Visual Basic is Variant. While variants are vastly useful, they are also vastly slow. Save them for use only when you need to store a value that is of an unknown data type. By contrast, integer (and its bigger brother, long) is one of the fastest data types. And just to prove how much faster they are, we wrote a little test program, ch06ex02.exe. You can check it out on the accompanying CD-ROM if you want to see the complete code listing.

This program tested the relative speeds of these data types by executing a for...next loop through 10 million iterations, using the specified data type as the loop counter. It also does a simple increment of a variable of the specified data type in each iteration. The code for a given data type iteration looks like this:

```
Const ITERATIONS = 10000000   ' That's ten million.
Dim startTime as Single       ' The stopwatch time counters.
Dim endTime as Single

' Run the variant type first
Dim v     ' Creates a variant called v.
Dim v1    ' Use this to increment.
' Start the timer and begin counting.
startTime = Timer
For v = 1 To ITERATIONS
    v1 = v1 + 1
Next v
endTime = Timer
```

We repeated the code again for three additional data types: Long, Single, and Double. We would have used Integer, but our number of iterations, at 10 million, was way too high for poor little Integer to handle.

So Long stood in for Integer, even though it is a tad slower. We ran each of these data types through a similar code block, and we ended up with the results shown in Figure 6.3. Note that the tests were all run on a Pentium 100.

As you can see, Integer data types are far and away the fastest type. They are almost eight times faster than the next quickest, Single. In this case, they are over 36 times faster than Variant! Each time you type something like Dim x in your code, you are potentially slowing it down dramatically.

Use Constants

We all know named constants are much better to use than literal values. If you need to change them, you update the value in one spot and it is propagated to every place it is used. However, many people store these values in variables instead of actual constants. Why is this important? Constants are resolved at compile time, while variables are resolved at runtime.

During the compilation process, the Visual Basic compiler actually replaces occurrences of real constant names with the literal values they represent. The result is then compiled. When the code is executed, it is using the real value, and no extra time is used looking up a value. If a variable were used instead, the compiler would generate code to look up a reference and retrieve a value. Who needs that? Instead of the following code:

```
Global MaxAirSpeed as Single
MaxAirSpeed = 740.0
```

use this code:

```
Global Const MaxAirSpeed = 740.0
```

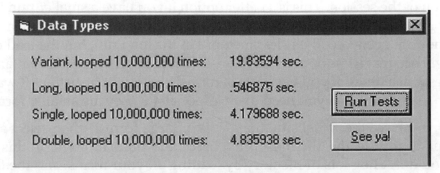

Figure 6.3 Data type speed comparisons. Smaller numbers are better.

In the latter case, the value 740.0 will be used by the compiler instead of the variable MaxAirSpeed, and the code will run faster.

Use Load and Show Correctly

In Visual Basic, forms come and go all the time. When most people need to show a form, they use the Show method. When calling the Show method on a form that has not yet been loaded, Show will load the form, then display it. When you are done with the form, you can either call the Hide method to make it go away or call Unload to do the same thing, which will remove the form from memory as well. The trick is to make the correct calls at the right times.

Loading a form takes time, and the bigger the form, the more time it takes. If you want to improve the performance of your application, reduce the time it takes forms to load. One way to do this is to preload all your forms when the client starts up, particularly if your forms are primarily small and simple. It might look something like this:

```
Sub frmMain_FormLoad()

    Load frmSearch
    Load frmReports
    Load frmCalc

End Sub
```

While this will slow down the initial loading of the program, further response times will be very quick. You can use Show and Hide to display and remove the forms as required. Remember that at startup, users are more willing to wait—they expect it to take a little time to load the program.

Of course, there are tradeoffs. Loading all your forms when the program first loads means they hang around eating lots of memory for the duration of the session. This is a better option if you have a smaller number of forms in your program. On the other hand, waiting to load them until they are needed will use less memory in the long run, but the load delay will occur at a less opportune time—when the users expect instantaneous response times. If you have lots of forms, you might be better off waiting to load them until you need them, especially if they are smaller forms.

If you have the worst situation—lots of large forms—then select a subset of your forms, the most often used, and preload them. In this way, you don't hog lots of memory by loading all your forms, and the forms used most often *are* loaded ahead of time. This is a perfect example of a tradeoff where you gain more in perceived performance than you lose timewise by preloading a few forms during program startup.

Bottom line: If you can afford the memory overhead and the extra delay at startup, preloading forms when the program begins is a good way to remove delays in the client. If you cannot afford the memory or initial wait time, then preloading may not be a good option.

TIP

If you are a clever programmer, you could use a timer to watch for idle time while the client is running. When the program has been idle for a specified time period, use the time to preload a form or two in the background. You could even predict which form would most likely be required next and load it. That's a job for those times at work when you're way ahead of schedule!

Watch Your Loops

By definition, loops do the same thing many times, so look for places to optimize inside loops. You may find one little tweak inside a loop, but the benefit of speeding it up is multiplied by the number of iterations. When you are planning where in your code to optimize, start with loops that have the most iterations or loops that get used most often.

The following code fragment is a very short piece of code and hence easy to overlook. However, not only does it iterate a gazillion times (well, 64,000 times—same thing), it also uses the unmercifully slow string concatenation (see following). Since the definition of the Const MAX_LINES may be separated from the loop by many lines of code (maybe in a completely different module), it would be easy to miss this when optimizing.

```
Const MAX_LINES = 64000
. . .
For i = 1 To MAX_LINES
    lines( i ) = verb( i ) & noun( i ) & prepPhrase( i )
Next i
```

A better way to do this might be to create each line of text as it's needed, rather than in a big loop all at once. This would split the single large delay into 64,000 tiny, imperceptible delays.

Keep It Simple, Sam

Another way to reduce form load time is to make forms smaller and less complex. When a form is loaded, everything about it is loaded at the same time, including all the code for it. If you can reduce the size of the form, load times will be quicker.

One technique for doing this is to move less frequently used form code into a module file. For example, you might have some large calculation routines encompassing several thousand lines of code used by the form. However, it is used only if the user presses a Calculate button on the form, which happens infrequently. If we move that code into a code module, it will not be loaded when the form is loaded, but rather when it is needed. We will not incur the load time penalty of the calculation routines unless the user clicks the Calculate button.

Another technique for reducing the size and load time of a form is to cut down on the number of controls it uses. Each visible control increases load time. Each control also uses memory, including a window handle and associated resources. You could move less frequently used functionality from a dialog into another dialog that is loaded only when necessary. This technique reduces the load time for everyone on the first dialog and spreads out the load time into two smaller time periods for those who use the secondary dialog, thus improving the perceived performance.

Remove Unused Code

During the development process, lots of functions and subs are written. Some become obsolete, and some are used for testing purposes. You may end up with a significant amount of code that never gets used. You may even have forms in your project that are left over from testing or old functionality and do not get used. There may even be duplicate code functions that do approximately the same thing and could be rewritten to use a common function. All this extra code actually stays in your program when it is compiled.

To make your program load faster and occupy less memory once it is loaded, make a pass through your code base and remove any unused code and forms. Refactor any code that performs similar functions into a single function that can be used throughout the program. Yes, it's a pain, but it make a significant improvement in the performance of your application.

Strings Good; Concatenation Bad

One of the most appealing things about the Basic language is how powerful and easy the string manipulation features are. You can do all sorts of nifty things with strings. One of our favorites is padding a string with leading zeros and ensuring that the string is only a certain length. For example, say you want a six-character string of digits with leading zeros, as in 000623. Here's how you get it in one statement:

```
s = Right("000000" & Trim(Str(iValue)), 6)
```

No matter what value is stored in iValue, this will work, and you'll always get a string that's six characters long. The problem is that this technique, and many others like it, uses string concatenation. While it's great that Visual Basic provides all this powerful dynamic string capability, string concatenation is slow. There's not much we can do about it except avoid using it. You would not want to do this for a large array of strings, for example. String tricks are a nice thing to have in your coding repertoire, but use them sparingly. They will slow down your code.

Who Needs Type Conversions?

We all need type conversions at one time or another. They are convenient, and we use them because they are there. You're coding along by the seat of your pants, and you find yourself in need of a value in a different type. Those type conversions are so easy and tempting to type in. Some you don't even have to worry about; Visual Basic does them automatically as implicit type conversions. They're seductive and addictive, like potato chips. You can't use just one.

However, like potato chips, use them too often and you (or your code) become slow and bloated. Type conversions are slow and costly. Use 10 of them in a function and you'll actually notice your code running slower (depending on the particular conversions used). Sometimes they are unavoidable, as when converting a numeric value to a string for display or formatting. Usually, a little planning will help you avoid type conversions.

Advanced Compiler Switches

Most people know that if you select Project Properties from the Visual Basic Project menu, you can get at the compiler settings on the Compile Tab. Make sure the Compile to Native Code and the Optimize for Fast Code options are selected. This is the default, so you shouldn't have to worry about it. However, there is also a button on this tab labeled Advanced. This button will display some advanced compiler options that will help you squeeze the last little bit of performance out of your program. Figure 6.4 shows what this dialog looks like. The help file in

Visual Basic can tell you all about them, but we'll tell you which ones we use. The others are usually too dangerous to mess with.

Remove Array Bounds Checks.   This option will cause crashes if you exceed an array boundary, but it speeds up array accesses.

Remove Safe Pentium FDIV Checks.   Use this option if your client will be running only on newer machines (less than two years old). Useful if you have lots of floating-point divisions.

Assume No Aliasing.   Use this only if you have checked your program carefully for aliasing. This means you don't refer to a variable later in a program by a different name. For example, you have a global variable named sPath and you pass it into a function as the name sFilePath and then use it in the function.

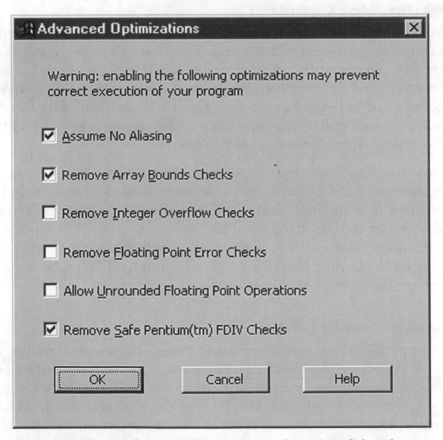

Figure 6.4   The Visual Basic 6.0 Advanced Compile Options dialog. They put that warning at the top for a good reason.

Note that these options should be used only for testing or for the final build of your software, after it has passed the entire quality assurance cycle. Otherwise, you're really asking for trouble! You could end up creating code that violates one of the settings during development and end up with a bug that could be very hard to find. The settings are turned off by default for the safety of your program, and they should only be turned on after a thorough review of the code to make sure the switches will not cause problems.

There is one more option available on the Compile tab called Favor Pentium Pro. If all your clients run on Pentium Pro machines, switch it on. This option can result in substantial performance gains. The resulting program code will still run on non–Pentium Pro machines, but will not perform very well.

While these compiler switches will result in faster code, they will probably also result in a larger EXE size. Try them one at a time and compare the program size with the size before the switch was turned on. If a thin, svelte client is more important to you than the performance gains these options will yield, then you might want to skip them altogether.

Make It Thin and Fast, Sam

As you can see, there are many factors that contribute to a thin and fast client. You'll be considering everything, from every aspect of the database and the architecture to the lowest bowels of the code. Almost all of these influences must be carefully contemplated at the beginning of the project, not at the end. Speed is not just a fine-tuning process that happens at the end of the project while the rest of the team is wrapping up the installation and final testing. You won't get a thin client in one meeting. And both of these important client characteristics are measured in degrees; they are not simply black-and-white issues. You'll have to decide for yourself just how much of each you need.

As a final treat, for having read every word of this treatise, we're going to rerun the meeting we encountered at the beginning of the chapter. This time, however, it will be a pleasant experience that you may have only dreamed about. And it will all be thanks to you.

VP OF SALES: We can't sell this product unless we have a thin client. Very thin.

CEO: Yes, I agree. I have it on good authority that thin clients are the way to go. Nobody wants a fat client these days. Thin clients are the way of the future. I read that somewhere on the Web.

VP OF SALES: That's what our customers tell us. When they call, they say our current client is too fat.

DEVELOPMENT MANAGER: I don't think that will be a problem. We have the best engineering team in the business. If anyone can make a competent thin client, they can.

YOU: You're right Sam, we do have an excellent team. And to help them create the best project possible, we need to consider carefully just how thin our client needs to be, and in which ways. I've written a white paper on the pros and cons of each option. It is sitting in all your mail boxes right now. I suggest you read it, and we'll meet again to go over exactly how we want to proceed. In this way, we'll get the best tradeoff for performance, schedule, cost, and maintainability.

CEO: That sounds like a great plan. Sam, would you make sure that this happens?

DEVELOPMENT MANAGER: Uh, sure. Um, good job there, uh [*whispering to you*] what was your name?

YOU: Nick.

DEVELOPMENT MANAGER: Right! [*Louder now*] Great job there, Nick!

VP OF SALES: Sounds like that will address our speed problems, too, right Nick?

YOU: That's right. We'll build in performance from day one, and we'll build in the right amount of performance based on the needs of our clients.

CEO: Super! This project is in great hands, eh Nick? I'm so confident, I'm taking next week off. Let's figure out what this product is going to do.

Later that same month, you are promoted to development manager.

Winding Up

The groundwork for your client has been laid, and you can plan your client strategy. Whether you need a thin or not-so-thin client is a decision you are ready to make. The only thing we can think of that could make this situation better is some heavy-duty detail about how to build this thin client.

Chapter 7, "Web and Internet Clients," does exactly this. If you have been itching to get your fingers into some code, then you're about to get your wish. We'll cover the creation of Web and Internet clients using the latest technologies, including User Documents and Dynamic HTML. Lots of useful information and entertaining examples will help make your client-building experience a rewarding one.

Web and Internet Clients

This chapter is one of the coolest in the book. It covers exciting technology, powerful client capabilities, and lots of programming. More than anything else, however, building Web clients is just plain fun. You get to play with graphics, Visual Basic, Web design, and programming all at once. It's like getting paid to play in your favorite sandbox.

There are a few prerequisites and requirements for this chapter. It is assumed that you have a basic understanding of HTML and Visual Basic. You will also need a copy of Visual Basic 6.0 or later, as well as Microsoft Internet Explorer version 4.0 or later. We will not be addressing other browsers, because there aren't any others that support the technology we'll be using. That's life on the cutting edge for you.

This is a hefty chapter. Plan to spend some time here, because we have a lot to cover:

- The various types of Internet functionality you're likely to run across, and why you'd want to implement them.

- How to use Visual Basic and the Internet Explorer browser ActiveX control in your Win32 client to add Web functionality to your application.

- How to use Visual Basic and User Documents to build a completely browser-hosted application.

- A few real-world issues you'll face when building a Web-based client.

Internet Functionality

Web-this, Internet-that, browser-the-other-thing. The Web and the Internet have all but subsumed the rest of the computing world. It's growing so fast that one can hardly keep up. Companies are scrambling to build Internet capabilities into their products, while developers are trying to learn the technologies required for the job. It's enough to make you think twice about turkey farming.

One of the biggest problems software companies face is not knowing exactly what they need to do to build Internet products. They know that they need Internet functionality to be competitive, but are unclear what this means or what to create. So they obfuscate, hoping someone else will figure it out. If we hear one more manager casually mention "Internet-enabled," there's going to be trouble.

It's not really their fault. There is a plethora of options when it comes to Internet-enabled, and finding clear information can often be difficult. Some of the possibilities follow:

Highly graphical content.   A Web-based user interface can take full advantage of the ease with which you can build colorful and professional graphics into the client. This provides tremendous flexibility in your user interface, as well as opening new frontiers in design possibilities.

Extension of your network.   In its purest form, the Internet is just a collection of many computers at different locations, connected to each other through various mechanisms. The vast expanse of the Internet means that you can reach just about everywhere from your computer, potentially giving your users unparalleled connectivity.

Internet-enabled features.   You can often easily make your product *Internet-enabled*, meaning at least one feature of the product makes use of the Internet. Some options include e-mailing reports, linking to the company Web site, linking to the company technical support Web site, or automatically updating software. This will allow you to put "Now Internet-Enabled!" on your product box.

A Web-based client.   Your entire user interface can be hosted in a Web browser. This has many benefits, including minimal or no client software installation, simple functionality updates, and free (well, almost free) remote connectivity.

You get the general idea of what is possible. The real meat of this chapter will tell you how to build this kind of functionality into your client using several different technologies. Of course, Visual Basic is at the heart of all of them.

A Browser in Your Application

One of the simplest ways to put some basic Web-oriented capabilities in your client is to shove a browser into it. When we first heard about this possibility, we asked ourselves, "What's the point? You've got a browser on your computer; just use that one." But the more we thought about it, the better the idea sounded. Having direct programmatic access to a browser in our client has potential. We could get the benefits of providing rich content using HTML as well as having access to the Web. And it will look like part of our software, not some separate program written by someone else. Some possible uses for the embedded browser follow:

Create a link to your company's Web site.   This is probably the simplest and most obvious thing to do with an embedded Web browser.

Create a link to your company's technical support Web site.   A variation on the previous example, it can be much more beneficial to your users.

Display HTML reports.   The graphical nature and automatic formatting of the HTML environment make it an ideal mechanism for displaying reports. Many reporting engines already output reports as HTML files. All you have to do is navigate the browser to the report file.

Control access to the Internet.   You can add the Web browser to your program without the standard browser navigation controls and instead provide buttons that go to fixed Web sites. In this way, only specific sites may be visited.

Host *part* of your client functionality in the embedded browser. Write a standard Win32 application that serves as your shell, with navigation controls and supplementary functionality. Host the rest in the browser window.

If this sounds appealing, you might like to know that it's also easy. You can get basic browser functionality into your client during your lunch break. Once the browser is in place, you can spend some time bending it to your will.

Using the Browser Control

Where did this browser control come from? It isn't advertised on the Visual Basic box. It's not on the control palette when you fire up Visual Basic with a new project. Perfectly valid question! The answer is that Microsoft invented it, disguising it as Internet Explorer. When Microsoft designed Internet Explorer, it split its functionality into many useful components. The result is that Internet Explorer can be used as an embedded object. An excellent example of this in a commercial product is HomeSite, an HTML editor that uses an embedded version of Internet Explorer to act as a viewer for the HTML you are editing. It looks just like part of the application. When designing a Visual Basic application, it acts as a third-party control.

Of course, for this to work, you must have Internet Explorer installed on your computer. This is an important consideration for the users of your software as well. If you use this functionality, users must also have Internet Explorer installed.

Finally, Some Action

One of the best ways to comprehend just how this works is to see it in action. We're ready to assemble a basic example of this browser control. We'll use a boot-camp approach. First you'll learn how to do it the hard way, and then we'll show you the slick shortcut. Doing it like this builds character. If you'd rather, you can load the example from the companion CD-ROM in the \examples\ch07ex01 directory. The steps are as follows:

1. Start a new Visual Basic project.
2. Add the browser control to the project.

3. Add an instance of the browser control to the main form.

4. Make it work.

5. Flesh it out.

Fire up Visual Basic and create a new project. The "Standard EXE" project type will do nicely.

Right-click on the Visual Basic control palette and select the Components option from the context menu. When the components dialog appears, check Microsoft Internet Controls. When you close the dialog, the controls will be added to the control palette. The Web browser control looks like a small globe. Figure 7.1 shows the Visual Basic components dialog with the correct option selected.

The browser control is a little disappointing when you first drop it onto a Visual Basic form. It literally looks like nothing. Who would make all this fuss over a gray rectangle? Figure 7.2 illustrates what it looks like. It really gets interesting when you actually give it something to do.

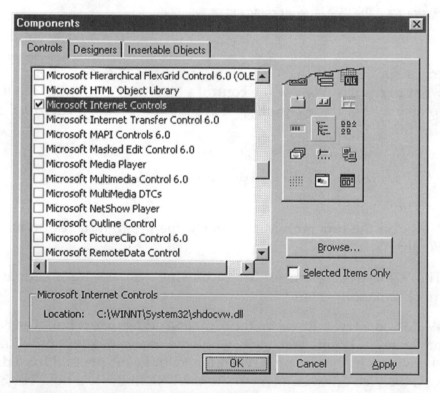

Figure 7.1 The Visual Basic components dialog.

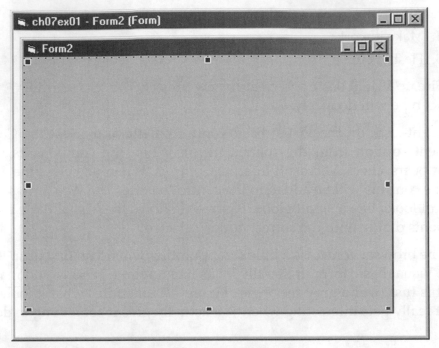

Figure 7.2 The Web browser control in design mode.

In its simplest, all the Web browser control needs is for us to tell it what to display. We use the control's Navigate method to tell it what to display. For this example, just put the code in the form's load event, like this:

```
Private Sub Form_Load()

    WebBrowser1.Navigate "http://www.wiley.com"

End Sub
```

Now run the program. Miraculously, the program takes on life, as in Figure 7.3.

That's the basic premise. Before moving on, let's do a couple other quick enhancements.

We tossed a few buttons on the form and added a text box. The buttons navigate to specific Web sites, while the user can enter any URL he or she wishes in the text box. When the Enter key is pressed from the text box, the Web browser navigates to the URL in the text box. The code is simple:

Figure 7.3 The Web browser control in action. It lives!

```
Private Sub txtURL_KeyPress(KeyAscii As Integer)

    If KeyAscii = vbKeyReturn Then
        WebBrowser1.Navigate txtURL.Text
        KeyAscii = 0
    End If
End Sub
```

Just make sure you set the multiline property of the text box to True so that the user can press the Enter key. To prevent the Enter key from actually creating a new line in the text box, eat the keystroke by setting the KeyAscii parameter to zero before leaving the KeyPress event function. Figure 7.4 illustrates the end result.

The Easier Way

You've had a little taste of the Web browser control and you understand the concept. Now that you've seen how to do it, we'll tell you the easy way. Start out by creating a new project, but instead of selecting Standard EXE, choose the VB Application Wizard. This will walk you through several steps to set up your project and, after a few screens, will

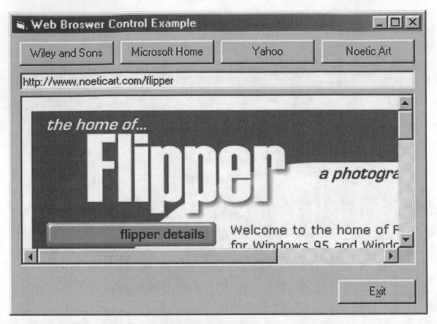

Figure 7.4 The Web browser control with some supporting controls.

ask if you would like Internet connectivity in your application. Figure 7.5 illustrates the dialog box. Select the Yes option.

When Visual Basic finishes generating your project, you'll have a complete Web browser as one of the forms. Figure 7.6 shows you how the browser form turns out. It has the basic functionality you would expect from a browser. The best part, however, is that now you can poke around in the code and see how everything is wired up. You'll get a good idea of some of the validations you should be doing if you want to build a browser into your own application.

The Web browser control has many other methods and properties available to you. Table 7.1 enumerates some of the more useful ones.

There are more properties, methods, and events available to you. You can find more information about them in the Internet Explorer Platform SDK documentation. Note that some of the items you'll find, such as the MenuBar and TheaterMode properties, apply only to Internet Explorer itself, not to the Web browser control. These properties are ignored by the browser control, so forget about them, even though they show up in the Visual Basic properties list for the control.

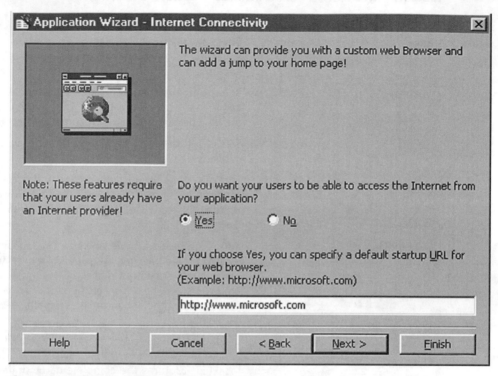

Figure 7.5 The Visual Basic Application Wizard.

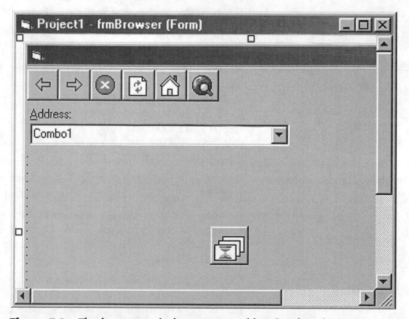

Figure 7.6 The browser window generated by Visual Basic.

Table 7.1 Web Browser Control Methods, Properties, and Events

NAME	TYPE	DESCRIPTION
Busy	Property	Boolean value that determines if the browser is engaged in downloads or navigation. Returns False if idle.
Document	Property	Returns an object reference to the document contained in the browser window. You can then access the document through the Document Object Model.
Height	Property	Sets or returns the height of the browser window in pixels.
Left	Property	Sets or returns the distance between the left edge of the browser control and its containing window. Units of measure are the same as the container control.
LocationName	Property	If the Web browser is viewing an HTML document located on the Internet, this property returns the name of the document (not the URL). If the browser is viewing a local file, it returns the complete name of the file, including the path.
LocationURL	Property	If the Web browser is viewing an HTML document located on the Internet, this property returns the URL of the document. If the browser is viewing a local file, it returns the complete name of the file, including the path.
Offline	Property	Boolean property that sets or returns whether the browser is operating in offline mode (that is, without an active connection to the Internet).
Parent	Property	Returns an object reference to the parent control that contains the Web browser control.
ReadyState	Property	Returns the ready state of the Web browser. Possible values: READYSTATE_UNINITIALIZED (0) READYSTATE_LOADING (1) READYSTATE_LOADED (2) READYSTATE_INTERACTIVE (3) READYSTATE_COMPLETE (4)
RegisterAsDropTarget	Property	If set to True, the browser control is registered as a potential target for a drag-and-drop operation.
Silent	Property	Boolean property that sets or returns whether the browser is allowed to show dialog boxes. If True, the browser is in Silent mode and cannot show dialog boxes.
Top	Property	Sets or returns the distance between the top edge of the Web browser control and its container control. Units of measure are the same as the container control.

NAME	TYPE	DESCRIPTION
Visible	Property	Boolean property that sets or returns whether the browser control is visible.
Width	Property	Sets or returns the width of the browser control, in pixels.
GoBack	Method	Navigates one location backward in the history list maintained by the browser control.
GoForward	Method	Navigates one location forward in the history list maintained by the browser control.
GoHome	Method	Navigates the browser to the start page specified by the Internet Explorer application settings.
GoSearch	Method	Navigates the browser to the default search page specified by the Internet Explorer application settings.
Navigate	Method	Navigates the browser control to the specified URL or file. There are lots of options on this method.
Refresh	Method	Forces a refresh of the currently displayed page.
Stop	Method	Stops the current navigation or load operation. Use in conjunction with the Busy property to see if you need to call Stop.
BeforeNavigate2	Event	Allows you to take some sort of action *after* the browser gets a command to navigate, but *before* the actual navigation takes place, including canceling the navigation.
DocumentComplete	Event	This event fires when the current document in the browser control has finished downloading completely.
DownloadBegin	Event	The DownloadBegin event fires right after the BeforeNavigate2 event.
DownloadComplete	Event	This event is fired when any navigate event stops, whether it is successful or not.
NavigateComplete2	Event	Occurs as soon as a navigate event has completed *successfully.* Even though the navigation has completed, items on the page may still be downloading.
NewWindow2	Event	Occurs when the browser control creates a new window.
ProgressChange	Event	This event occurs when the status of a download or navigation is changed. If your application shows status during a download, this event will tell you what and when to display it.

The Important Attributes

The API for the Web browser control is fairly complete, and it can be a little overwhelming. However, a handful of the properties, events, and methods of the Web browser control are going to be used far more often than others. Since they get the heaviest use, they bear closer scrutiny.

Navigate

The Navigate method is the most popular Web browser method in the whole school. It is used more often than any other, because without it the Web browser control sits on the screen like a lump of gray concrete. The Navigate method is fairly easy to use in its simplest form. Call it and specify a URL to navigate to. However, there are additional optional arguments that can be useful. The full syntax of the method follows:

```
WebBrowser1.Navigate URL, Flags, targetFrame, PostData, Headers
```

URL.   The Web page or file to navigate to.

Flags.   Specifies the options to use when navigating.

TargetFrame.   The name of the frame to send the navigation to.

PostData.   Data to send to the server during the POST.

Headers.   Additional headers to send to the server, if desired.

All parameters but the URL are optional. While the URL is clearly the most important parameter, the flags parameter can also be very useful. Flags lets you specify several options when navigating to the new page to give you finer control over the event. Options for the flags parameter are listed in Table 7.2. They can be combined using the logical OR operator. A call to Navigate using the flags parameter looks like the code that follows. It navigates to a URL, but the flags tell it not to read the information from a cache or save it to a cache. Perhaps the person who wrote it is a spy and wants no evidence of his or her work left on the computer.

```
WebBrowser1.Navigate "http://www.wiley.com", navNoReadFromCache Or _
   navNoWriteToCache
```

The rest of the parameters may be useful. But not today. If you want to explore them on your own, by all means, dive in.

Document

The Document property of the Web browser control gives you access to the actual page displayed in the browser control. Initially, this might not

Table 7.2 The Navigate Method's Flags Parameter Options

NAME	VALUE	DESCRIPTION
navOpenInNewWindow	1	When the navigation event occurs, the new page opens in a new browser window.
NavNoHistory	2	Will not add the page to which you are navigating to the browser's history list.
NavNoReadFromCache	4	Forces the browser to bypass the cache and read the page content from the URL's host server.
NavNoWriteToCache	8	Prevents the browser from saving the page you tell it to load in its cache. Possibly a good security measure.

seem very useful. However, it becomes important when Dynamic HTML (DHTML) comes into the picture. The five-cent explanation is that when you learn about DHTML later in this chapter, you'll be able to access and change any portion of the Web page displayed in the browser using the Document property as a starting point. The Document property represents the top-level object of the page hierarchy.

The Document object reference returned by this method makes the elements of the Web page available using the *Document Object Model*, or DOM. We'll cover the DOM in greater detail later, but here's a quick example of what it might look like in your Visual Basic code:

```
WebBrowser1.Document.alinkcolor = "#FF00FF"
```

This code fragment tells the Web browser control to change the color of all the active links on the page to bright purple. If you want a quick taste of what's available in the Document object, create a DHTML Application project in Visual Basic 6, open a code window, and type in "Document." When the period is entered, Visual Basic will display a list of all the methods and properties it supports. If you'd prefer to wait, we'll be covering it in detail later in this chapter.

The "Go" Methods

There are four Go methods associated with the Web Browser control: *GoForward, GoBack, GoHome,* and *GoSearch.* They all perform navigation functions and take no parameters. GoForward method moves the browser forward one in the navigation history, and GoBack method navigates back one in the browser history. GoHome moves the browser to the default home page defined in the Windows control panel Internet settings. GoSearch moves the browser to the default search page defined in the Windows control panel Internet settings. You can use these methods in response to user actions on your own interface controls. They're not exciting, but they get the job done.

LocationURL

This property simply returns the URL of the page currently displayed in the Web Browser control. You can use it to display the address of the visible page somewhere in your user interface. You can also use it to track your own history, perhaps loading it into a combo box like the browser support code that Visual Basic generates.

Stop and Busy

The Stop method tells the browser to stop what it's doing and return to an idle state. The Busy property is its complement, returning a value of True if the Web browser control is currently downloading anything. It's a good idea to check if the browser is busy before you call the Stop method. The following code fragment illustrates this.

```
Private Sub btnStop_Click()

    If WebBrowser1.Busy Then
        WebBrowser1.Stop
    End

End Sub
```

TIP

Here's a great idea for someday when you're bored. Create an MDI Visual Basic application. In each MDI child window, put an instance of the Web browser control. Build up the primary browser controls on the MDI parent window, so your application acts like a normal Web browser. Throw in some code to handle displaying and hiding the child windows. Voilà! You have an MDI Web browser that can view multiple Web sites at the same time. Why Microsoft hasn't done this yet in Internet Explorer is beyond us.

Armed with the knowledge of the Web browser control, you can now add Internet capabilities to your applications. It's even fairly easy. So go somewhere and code a new Internet feature real quick, and you can get those management types off your back. If you're not in a big hurry, read on to learn all about User Documents. They're good for what ails you.

The Wonder of User Documents

If you've never heard of User Documents before, we're not surprised. They don't seem to be very popular. Our guess is that Microsoft created User Documents and then got excited about Dynamic HTML. User Documents are still part of Visual Basic 6, but all we hear about is DHTML. It's almost as if User Documents are children who stay in their room all the time and won't socialize with anyone. It's unfortunate, because User Documents are a great technology, but low visibility will prevent many people from finding out about them. Well, we're going to make sure you know all about them, because they are a valuable addition to your collection of Internet programming tools.

User Documents, also known as ActiveX Documents, are programs that execute inside a Web browser. They look exactly like executable programs, not like Web pages. We saw an example of a User Document in Chapter 6, "Thin and Fast Clients" (see Figure 6.1). We'll walk through creating one in just a moment.

Some nice advantages of User Documents include the following:

- They look just like normal Win32 applications, but run inside a browser and can be accessed through the Internet.

- Because they run in a browser with a scrolling viewport, you can create forms that are longer than the screen itself. They are sometimes called *bottomless forms*, and they're especially useful for implementing long data entry forms.

- It's relatively easy to convert existing Win32 Visual Basic applications to User Documents.

One of the best things about User Documents is that they are very similar to standard Visual Basic applications. Your existing Visual Basic programs can usually be converted to User Documents by using a built-in conversion wizard. It will read forms in your project, convert them to User Documents, and optionally comment out any code that will no longer function correctly. While User Documents are similar to normal applications, they are not exactly the same, and some of your code may no longer function correctly. For example, forms do not access each other by loading and showing. They have to navigate to a new form. We'll discuss the details later.

A User Document Example

Let's take a look at how the process works. You can either follow along with us or open up the example project on the companion CD-ROM (ch07ex02). We'll walk you through using the example project.

Open Visual Basic and create a new project, selecting the VB ActiveX Document project type. Once the project is created, you can import any existing forms you like from your regular Visual Basic project. The way it works is a little odd, so bear with us. The conversion wizard will only work on forms that already exist in your project, so we have to add the existing form to the project first, then convert it to a User Document.

Add the form to our new Visual Basic project by right-clicking on the project name in the project tree, and select Add, Form from the context menu. If you have an existing form you'd like to try out, by all means use it. If not, select the file Form 1.frm from the \Examples\ch07ex02 directory on the companion CD-ROM. Figure 7.7 illustrates the form we'll be importing.

Now that the form is part of the project, we need to convert it to a User Document. Right-click on the project name in the project tree and select Add, User Document. When the Add User Document dialog comes up, select the VB ActiveX Document Wizard option. Figure 7.8 illustrates this dialog box and the option you will be selecting.

The wizard will walk you through the process of converting the form into a User Document. Skip the first screen and move on to the second. Here you specify which forms you want to convert to User Documents. You can check whichever forms you like, making it easier to convert an entire project at once. For now, select Form1 by checking it. Click Next to move on.

The next window asks you two questions. The important one is "Comment out invalid code?" Make sure you turn on this option. If the conversion wizard encounters code that will not work as a User Document (and it probably will), then it will comment it out for you. You can then cruise through the code after conversion and get a good idea of the kinds of code to avoid when creating User Documents. The other question—"Remove original forms after conversion?"—will remove the standard forms after they are converted. We usually turn this on to save

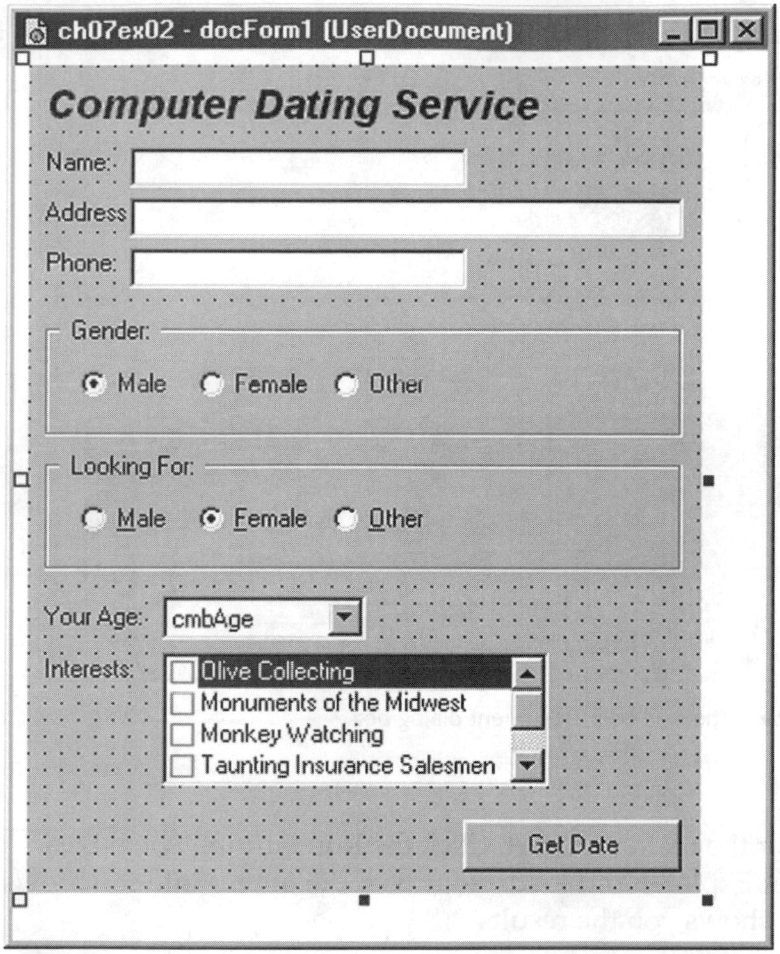

Figure 7.7 The standard Visual Basic form we are importing.

the step of having to remove the forms later, but it's up to you. Click Next to move on.

The next form asks if you would like to see a summary report regarding the results of the conversion process. Check it this time, because it's nice to see the first time. It tells you what to do next to get your program running. Click the Finish button, clear off any message boxes telling you the process is complete, and review the results. The project tree now shows a new User Document, the result of the conversion. Open it and take a look. Not much has changed. There is no window border or title bar, because the document container (in our case, Internet Explorer) controls them.

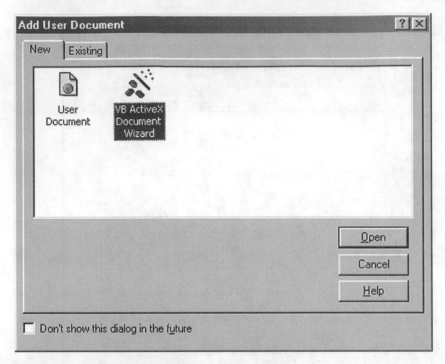

Figure 7.8 The Add User Document dialog box.

Now for the really fun part. Click the Run button. Visual Basic executes Internet Explorer and loads your user document into the browser. Figure 7.9 shows you the results.

You can see clearly that this looks nothing like a Web page. It more closely resembles a normal Win32 application. User Documents are an excellent mechanism to distribute an application across the Web while still retaining most of the capabilities and look of a normal application that your users may already be comfortable with. Build your application as a series of User Documents, post them on your Internet Information Server (IIS) Web server, and tell your users to point to the main Visual Basic Document (VBD) file, the compiled version of the User Document. Suddenly you have an application that can be run across the Internet.

One of the potential drawbacks with User Documents is that they can get fairly heavy, sizewise. Because they are ActiveX controls, they do not have the same level of efficiency as HTML pages. This can be a problem if network bandwidth is limited. However, if your users are all

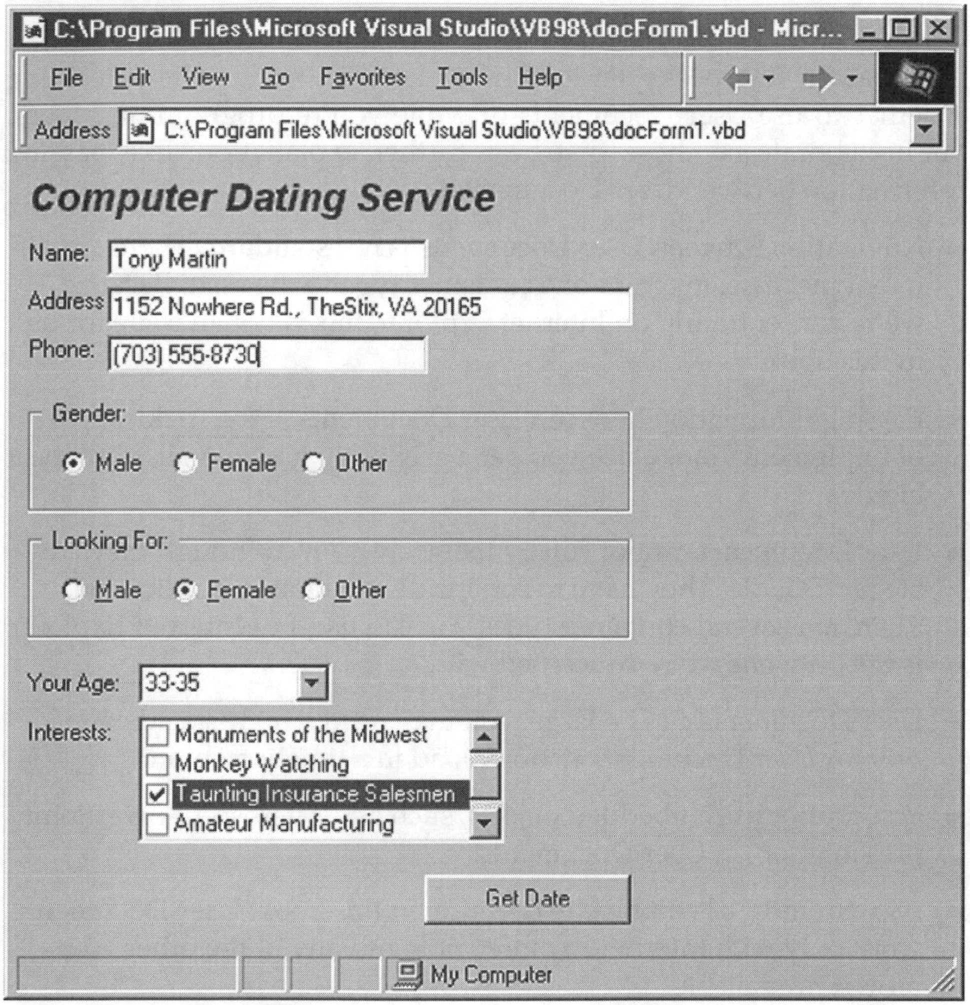

Figure 7.9 The completed User Document in Internet Explorer.

running on fast connections, then User Documents may be a good option for your application.

User Document Details

As we've said, User Documents are almost like regular form-based Visual Basic programs. They look pretty much the same, except that there's a browser wrapped around them. However, there are a number of differences and details about User Documents that you will need to know before diving headlong into them.

Limitations

There are a few pesky limitations to keep in mind when deciding whether to use User Documents or while you're programming them. We'll elaborate on those that bear further explanation, like passing information between User Documents:

■ Navigation between User Documents is not standard. There are different mechanisms from one container type to the next. Because we're concentrating on Internet Explorer, this is not an issue for us in this book.

■ Passing information between User Documents is the trickiest part of implementation. Once you get a grip on it, however, it won't be a big deal.

■ User Documents cannot run by themselves, even though they create an EXE file. They have to run inside a container application. There are several container types you can use, but Internet Explorer is the only one we're concerned with.

■ User Documents can be large. You may need a high-speed connection for User Documents to download in a timely fashion.

■ You cannot use embedded objects, such as a Microsoft PowerPoint presentation, in User Documents.

■ As with most of what we're covering in this book, User Documents work only with Internet Explorer, not with any of the other Web browsers available.

If you can live with these limitations, then User Documents hold some great potential for you. If you need a Win32-like application running remotely in a Web browser, then seriously consider User Documents. The limitations are fairly minor. Could be worse. Could be raining.

Navigation

Probably the first learned and most often used method in Visual Basic is Show. From the first day, we learned to use it to display another form from code. It's burned firmly into our brains and we use it at a subconscious level. When we switch to the world of User Documents, however, Show becomes less important. While we still use it to display regular forms from a User Document (see the next section, Implementing Menus, for more information), everything changes when navigating from one User Document to the next.

Moving from one User Document to another is accomplished using the Hyperlink object, which hangs off of the UserDocument object. It has a method called NavigateTo that navigates the browser to somewhere else. Somewhere else could be a Web site, or it could be another User Document in your application. The basic syntax looks like this:

```
UserDocument.Hyperlink.NavigateTo "http://www.test.com/nextDoc.vbd"
```

This code fragment would navigate from the current User Document to another one called nextDoc.vbd. When pointing the browser to a User Document, always provide it with the name of the VBD file associated with the document.

That's the easy part. The harder part is finding the location of the VBD file you want. In the previous example, the code knows the location of the VBD file: www.test.com. However, this is usually not the case, especially if you are creating a commercial product that many customers will be using. They will have their own servers and locations, so the code must figure out where to locate the document.

You may not be able to require your users to put the files of your product on a specific server with a fixed name, but you can require them to put the files all in the same location, whatever that location ends up being. As long as you can find the location of the first VBD file, you know the location of the rest of them. Fortunately, there is an object and property that provides this for us: Parent.LocationURL. All we have to do is get the value of this property, strip off the name of the file at the end, and save it. We've provided you with the code you'll need to do this. You can call it whenever you need to navigate to a specific User Document.

```
Private Sub NavigateToUserDoc (sUD as String)
    ' The parameter sUD receives the name of the User
    ' Document to navigate to, without a path.

    Dim iStringPos As Integer
    Dim iSlashPos As Integer
    Dim sChar As String

    ' Find the location of the LAST slash or backslash
    ' in the location URL of the current User Document.
    For iStringPos = Len(Parent.LocationURL) To 1 Step -1
```

```
        sChar = Mid(Parent.LocationURL, iStringPos, 1)
        If sChar = "/" Or sChar = "\" Then
            iSlashPos = iStringPos
            Exit For
        End If
    Next iStringPos

    ' Perform the actual navigation to the new
    ' User Document.
    If iSlashPos > 0 Then
        UserDocument.HyperLink.NavigateTo _
            Left(Parent.LocationURL, iSlashPos) & sUD
    End If

End Sub
```

There are two other navigation methods that can be useful: *GoForward* and *GoBack.* They navigate one page forward or one page backward in the history list maintained by the browser. Note, however, that these methods do not provide any error checking. If, for instance, you try to navigate using GoBack, but there is no prior page in the history list, a runtime error will result. It always looks *so* unprofessional when the application crashes, don't you think? Therefore, make sure you use error handling around these methods, as follows:

```
On Error Goto NavError
UserDocument.HyperLink.NavigateTo "CoolUserDoc.vbd"
On Error Goto 0
...
NavError:
MsgBox "No more history!", vbOkOnly
Resume Next
```

Navigation is fairly easy. Have you ever wanted to put a menu in your program? Sure you have. Everyone loves menus, especially beginning users. We'll show you how to add to the menus available in Internet Explorer that are specific to your User Document application.

Implementing Menus

You can add your own menus to a User Document, just as on a regular program. The difference is that they don't show up on the User Document itself, but as part of the container's menus. In our case, the menu options you add to your User Document will be added to the Internet Explorer menus. These menu items link to code in your User Document. For example, you can wire the Menu_Click event to a normal dialog box.

In fact, that sounds like a pretty good idea. Let's run through an example that illustrates adding a menu to a User Document, adding a normal form to a User Document project, and then displaying the form. We'll work with the previous example as a starting point, ch07ex02, located on the CD-ROM. Load it into Visual Basic to get started.

Adding a menu works similarly to the way you are used to. Make sure the User Document docForm1 is visible in design mode, and then select Menu Editor from the Tools menu. Add a top-level menu item called "Dating Options," and give it a name of mnuDatingOptions. Set the Negotiate Position option to something useful, like Right. This will dictate where in the list of existing menus our new menu is added. Now add a submenu item beneath it called "Set Options..." Make sure it is indented under Dating Options using the right-pointing arrow button. Give it a name of mnuSetOptions. The result should look like Figure 7.10.

Figure 7.10   The menu settings for our User Document menu example.

Now we need something for our menu to do. Add a new form to the project—a normal form, not a User Document—by right-clicking the project in the project tree and selecting Add, Form. Add some controls to the form until it resembles Figure 7.11. If you aren't a form designer kind of person, load the file frmOptions.frm from the \examples\ ch07ex02 directory on the companion CD-ROM.

All that remains is to wire the Dating Options form into the menu. Open the code window for the User Document and add the following code:

```
Private Sub mnuSetOptions_Click()

    frmOptions.Show vbModal

End Sub
```

You can now run your project. Click the Run button or hit F5, and Visual Basic will load your User Document into Internet Explorer. The result is shown in Figure 7.12. Notice that the new menu item has been added to the Internet Explorer menus, right before the Help menu.

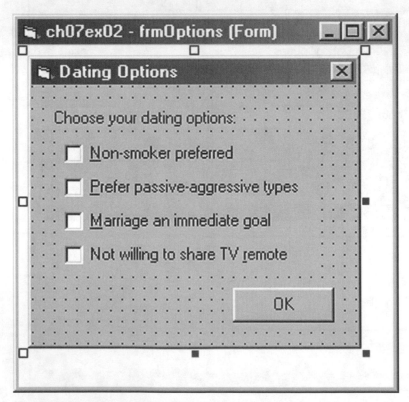

Figure 7.11 The Dating Options form.

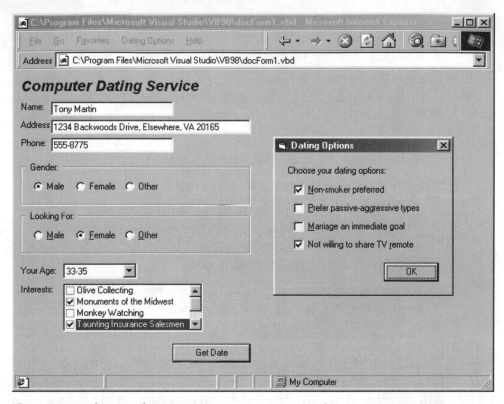

Figure 7.12   The complete User Document menu example.

Passing Data

Passing data sounds like something that could get you into trouble with the FBI. In our business as programmers, we do it every day. In Visual Basic, as with other languages, it's very easy to send data back and forth through functions. User Documents need some special handling, however, to make them talk to each other. Because they are effectively individual pages in the browser and may be navigated to out of sequence by unscrupulous users, we cannot use standard parameter-passing mechanisms. Besides, the NavigateTo method doesn't provide for parameter passing.

Here is the step-by-step overview of the process required to get two User Documents communicating. It's slightly complicated, but it's easier than counseling. Following the list of steps, we'll go through a complete example, showing you exactly how it works. Once you get the hang of it, it will be as easy as using regular Visual Basic forms.

1. Provide public properties in your first User Document that another User Document can use to read and write data to and from its caller (the first User Document).

2. Create a global reference to the first User Document that can be used by the second User Document to gain access to the Get and Set properties of the first User Document.

3. Before navigating to the second User Document from the first, set the global reference equal to the first User Document.

4. Navigate to the second user document.

5. In the Show method of the second User Document, check to see if the global reference to the first User Document is equal to Nothing. If it is, the user probably went to the second User Document before the first. You can do some error handling here.

6. You can now reference the public properties of the first User Document, setting or getting data as needed.

7. Free the memory allocated by our global reference.

User Document 1 is our starting point, the first User Document loaded. It will be navigating to User Document 2. The second User Document will be retrieving data from the first and displaying information based on the data. We'll be using our previous example, ch07ex02, and adding to it.

Before we begin, we need to add some code to the example to further our goals. Create a new module and add the following code to it:

```
Type OptionsType
    iNonSmoker As Integer
    iPassiveAggressive As Integer
    iMarriage As Integer
    iTVRemote As Integer
End Type

Global Const G_MALE = 1
Global Const G_FEMALE = 2
Global Const G_OTHER = 3
```

At the top of the code for the User Document docForm1, add the following line:

```
Dim Options As OptionsType
```

In the function mnuSetOptions_Click, which we added previously to handle the new menu item, replace all the code with the following code:

```
' Set the values on the options form in case
' the user has already specified some.
Load frmOptions
frmOptions.chkMarriage = Options.iMarriage
frmOptions.chkNonSmoker = Options.iNonSmoker
frmOptions.chkPassiveAggressive = Options.iPassiveAggressive
frmOptions.chkTVRemote = Options.iTVRemote

' Respond to the menu selection by
' loading the options dialog.
frmOptions.Show vbModal

' Collect the data from the dialog.
Options.iMarriage = frmOptions.chkMarriage
Options.iNonSmoker = frmOptions.chkNonSmoker
Options.iPassiveAggressive = frmOptions.chkPassiveAggressive
Options.iTVRemote = frmOptions.chkTVRemote

' Unload the form.
Unload frmOptions
```

Now we're all set. Let's get on with making two User Documents speak to each other.

We need to give the rest of the world, specifically the second User Document, access to the data that the first User Document contains. To do this, we create public Get and Set properties in the code. For our example, we'll need to provide only Get properties, because we're sending data one direction. Add properties to the code by double-clicking the User Document design window, and then entering the following property code:

```
Public Property Get NonSmoker() As Boolean

    If Options.iNonSmoker = 0 Then
        NonSmoker = False
    Else
        NonSmoker = True
    End If

End Property

Public Property Get Marriage() As Boolean

    If Options.iMarriage = 0 Then
        Marriage = False
    Else
        Marriage = True
    End If

End Property
```

```
Public Property Get PassiveAggressive() As Boolean

    If Options.iPassiveAggressive = 0 Then
        PassiveAggressive = False
    Else
        PassiveAggressive = True
    End If

End Property

Public Property Get TVRemote() As Boolean

    If Options.iTVRemote = 0 Then
        TVRemote = False
    Else
        TVRemote = True
    End If

End Property

Public Property Get LookingFor() As Integer

    If obLookingMale.Value Then
        LookingFor = G_MALE
    ElseIf obLookingFemale.Value Then
        LookingFor = G_FEMALE
    Else
        LookingFor = G_OTHER
    End If

End Property

Public Property Get Age() As String

    Age = cmbAge.Text

End Property

Public Property Get Interests() As String

    ' Append all the selected interests together
    ' into a single string for easy transport.
    Dim i As Integer
    Dim sI As String
    For i = 0 To 1stInterests.ListCount - 1
        If 1stInterests.Selected(i) Then
            sI = sI & 1stInterests.List(i)
        End If
    Next i

    Interests = sI

End Property
```

In order for our second User Document to be able to access the properties of the first, we need to create a global object reference that points to the first User Document. We need it to be global because there is no way to pass parameters to other User Documents. In step 0, we created a new module and added some code to it. Now we're going to add one more line to it, our global object reference:

```
Global gDoc1 As docForm1
```

This creates an object reference, gDoc1, of the type of our first User Document, docForm1. That was fairly painless. Will the rest of this process be this easy?

Next, we need to set the global reference equal to the first User Document. This occurs right before we navigate to the second User Document docForm2. We're going to add an event handler to the Get Date button at the bottom of the first User Document docForm1. We need to put in some code to find the path to the second User Document, as discussed previously in the section about Navigation, as well as the code to set the object reference. Enter the new function as follows.

```
Private Sub btnGetDate_Click()

    Dim iStringPos As Integer
    Dim iSlashPos As Integer
    Dim sChar As String

    ' Find the location of the LAST slash or backslash
    ' in the location URL of the current User Document.
    For iStringPos = Len(Parent.LocationURL) To 1 Step -1
        sChar = Mid(Parent.LocationURL, iStringPos, 1)
        If sChar = "/" Or sChar = "\" Then
            iSlashPos = iStringPos
            Exit For
        End If
    Next iStringPos

    ' Perform the actual navigation to the new
    ' User Document.
    If iSlashPos > 0 Then

        ' Before we navigate to the second User Document,
        ' set the global reference to ourself, so the
        ' second User Document can reference our properties.
        Set gDoc1 = Me

        ' Do the navigation.
        UserDocument.Hyperlink.NavigateTo _
            Left(Parent.LocationURL, iSlashPos) & "docForm2.vbd"
    End If

End Sub
```

To navigate to the second User Document, we have to add only a single line to the btnGetDate_Click function to perform the actual navigation operation. The listing that follows shows the last part of the function we just wrote, with the new code added in italics.

```
' Perform the actual navigation to the new
' User Document.
If iSlashPos > 0 Then

    ' Before we navigate to the second User Document,
    ' set the global reference to ourself, so the
    ' second User Document can reference our properties.
    Set gDoc1 = Me

    ' Do the navigation.
    UserDocument.Hyperlink.NavigateTo _
        Left(Parent.LocationURL, iSlashPos) & "docForm2.vbd"
End If
```

To make this work, we need a second user document. You can either load the form from the companion CD-ROM (\examples\ch07ex02\ docForm2.vbd) or create one that looks like Figure 7.13 (it takes only a minute).

In the second User Document we need to check the global object reference and make sure it has something in it. We do this in the document's Initialize event, which is analogous to a normal form's Load event. The code to do this follows.

```
Private Sub UserDocument_Initialize()

    ' Make sure the reference to the first User
    ' Document is valid.
    If gDoc1 Is Nothing Then
        ' Problems! You would normally do something
        ' more useful here.
        Exit Sub
    End If

End Sub
```

Now you can reference all those public properties you put in the first User Document by going through the global reference, gDoc1. Add some code in the second User Document to make use of the data from the first User Document. We added some code to generate a random date based loosely on the information provided by the user. We suspect that this is how real dating services work, anyway. We split the code into a second function called GenerateDate to fill in the fields on the sec-

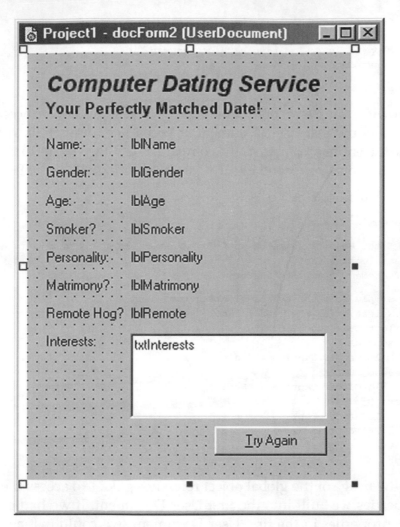

Figure 7.13 The second User Document.

ond User Document. Add the call to this function in the UserDocument_Initialize function, as shown by the italic text:.

```
Private Sub UserDocument_Initialize()

    ' Make sure the reference to the first User
    ' Document is valid.
    If gDoc1 Is Nothing Then
        ' Normally, you would do something more
        ' useful here.
        Exit Sub
    End If
```

```
' Generate a random date based on the data supplied
' by the user. We suspect that this is how it
' happens in real dating services anyway.
GenerateDate

End Sub
```

The following sample of some of the code demonstrates how to access the properties in the first User Document. If you'd like to see it all, you can examine the entire project from the companion CD-ROM (ch07ex02). Figure 7.14 illustrates the second User Document running in Internet Explorer.

```
Private Sub GenerateDate()

    Randomize Timer

    ' Name. Base the name on what gender the user
    ' is looking for.
    CreateName gDoc1.LookingFor

    ' Simply echo the user's "looking for" gender
    ' selection to the gender label.
    Select Case gDoc1.LookingFor
    Case G_MALE
        lblGender.Caption = "Male"
    Case G_FEMALE
        lblGender.Caption = "Female"
    Case G_OTHER
        lblGender.Caption = "Other"
    End Select
    ...
End Sub
```

Notice the usage of the global object reference gDoc1 to access the public properties we built into the first User Document. If we had created any Set properties in the first User Document, we could just as easily have sent data back to the first User Document.

This last step, even though simple, is important. The global reference to the first User Document must be set to Nothing so that the memory it occupies can be freed up. This code can be placed in the Terminate event of the second User Document. The Terminate event is similar to the Unload event of normal forms. The code looks like this:

```
Private Sub UserDocument_Terminate()

    ' This last step is important. Make sure we set
    ' the global reference to Nothing. If we don't,
    ' it stays in memory, even after IE shuts down.
    Set gDoc1 = Nothing

End Sub
```

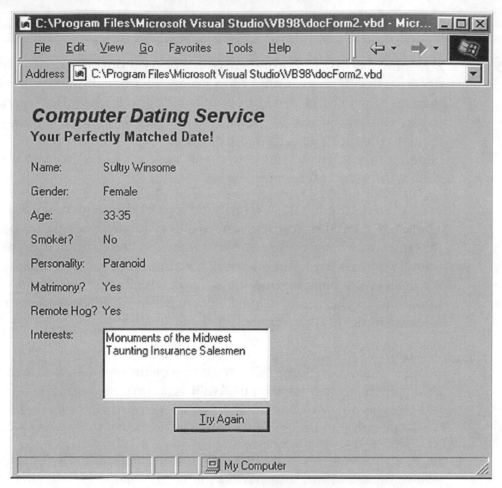

Figure 7.14 The second User Document in Internet Explorer.

That about winds up our coverage of User Documents. There are additional capabilities of User Documents you'll want to investigate, like Asynchronous Reading, but they are beyond the scope of this book. It is possible to write large, complete, and fully capable applications with User Documents. Because of their larger size, however, they are not as universally excellent as is Dynamic HTML for writing Web-based clients. If you want the light weight of HTML served with the power of Visual Basic, garnished with client-side dynamic flexibility, then read on.

Dynamic HTML

Dynamic HTML is raging all over the computing world. Brilliant designers and programmers are doing amazing things with it, and managers who just learned how to spell it think they ought to have it. If you've been wondering what it is or what it can do for you, you've come to the right place. Not only will you learn what it is and what its benefits are, but you'll also find out how to use it to start building clients for your N-tier applications.

First we're going to take a whirlwind tour of the elements of Dynamic. There is a great deal to cover, and we'll try to strike a balance between making sure you know enough to get the job done and getting through the rest of this chapter in a reasonable amount of time. We could easily write an entire book on this subject alone. We'll start with some definitions and explanations, then follow with more in-depth coverage of selected topics and examples.

Next, we'll be focusing on the construction of Dynamic HTML clients using Visual Basic. Some other tools will be involved as well, but Visual Basic will be the primary focus. We'll even provide you with a free tool to help you out with Dynamic HTML development, but you'll have to read through the chapter to find it!

Last, we'll show you some specific techniques to deal with situations you're bound to run into when building Dynamic HTML clients. This will include navigating between DHTML pages, client-side persistence, and even talking to a simple database.

What Is Dynamic HTML?

Traditional HTML is a page-definition language. It allows you to specify the structure of a document, as well as the look and layout in more recent times, so that a browser can interpret it and display it in a rich, graphical environment. This was a fantastic revolution for the presentation of online information. Anyone could create a Web page and make it available to the world.

Shortly thereafter, the world demanded interactivity from Web sites. Server-side CGI scripts started making this happen, but they are difficult to program and perform poorly. Netscape came up with JavaScript, a programming language that could run on the client side, however, it could operate only on form elements. Microsoft invented Active Server Pages (ASP) that allowed programmers to create server-side functionality more easily. But the basic problem remained—all the functionality was located on the server, and whenever the contents of the page needed to change, a trip back to the server was required.

Now Dynamic HTML (DHTML) has emerged, championed by Microsoft, Netscape, the World Wide Web Consortium, and others. The basic idea behind DHTML is that you can write code to manipulate *any portion* of the HTML page, not just form elements. DHTML provides a complete object model, a complete event model, and error handling to your code. Events can be fired by just about any element on the HTML page, and your code can respond to them. Your code is also able to change any part of the page without going back to the server. The page will automatically reflow as you change it, without any intervention of the server. You can even completely generate the visible elements of the page at runtime, should you need to.

DHTML promises to give the Web another order of magnitude of interactivity. However, it will be a while in coming. While DHTML exists today, it is not standardized. The current approved revision of the HTML specification is 3.2. The World Wide Web Consortium (W3C), the committee that standardizes HTML, is still working on version 4.0, which will cover DHTML. The result is that the various browser manufacturers currently have their own implementations of DHTML, and programming for more than one browser is a serious pain in the backside. Once the HTML 4.0 specification is complete, the browsers will catch up quickly, and the world will be safe again. For our purposes, however, we're sticking with Microsoft's version, because it is the most complete. As long as you're using Internet Explorer 4.0 or later, you'll be able to handle everything in this section.

The Components of Dynamic HTML

Dynamic HTML is really a combination of four primary elements:

HTML.   The latest version of the page-description language we all know and love provides the framework for the content we will be displaying.

Cascading style sheets (CSS). Style sheets allow us to define the attributes of the HTML tags used when building a Web page. They can also be used and manipulated using Dynamic HTML and code.

The Document Object Model (DOM). This is the object model we use to access the various parts of a Web page.

Script or compiled code. While style sheets and the DOM are integral to Dynamic HTML, code is the part that runs the show. It is the part that makes it *dynamic*.

One of the reasons that Dynamic HTML is viewed as complex is that these four components have to be used together to make DHTML effective. We'll be covering all of these elements in more detail. If you're anything like us, however, you're itching to see Dynamic HTML in action. So we're going to walk you through a quick example just to whet your appetite.

The following HTML code is available on the companion CD-ROM in the \examples\ch07ex03 directory, or you can enter it from the following listing. For short examples, we prefer typing it in manually because we tend to remember it better that way. If you're typing it in, you can use any editor, even the world's most popular HTML editor: Notepad. Save the file with any name you like, as long as it has an extension of .HTML or .HTM. Once it's entered we'll tell you what to do with it and then explain it briefly.

```
<HTML>
<HEAD>
    <TITLE>Chapter 4 DHTML Example</TITLE>
</HEAD>

<BODY>

<!-- Set up a few styles, just to show how it's done. -->
<STYLE TYPE="text/css">
H1
{
  color: blue;
  font-weight: bold;
  font-family: Verdana
}
SPAN
{
  font-weight: bold;
  font-family: Verdana;
  font-size: 10pt
}
```

```
P
{
  font-family: Verdana;
  font-size: 10pt
}
</STYLE>

<!-- All the code for this introductory DHTML example. -->
<SCRIPT LANGUAGE="VBScript">

Sub GetInfo()

    ' Fill in the information fields.
    S_URL.innerText = document.URL
    S_SIZE.innerText = document.fileSize + " bytes"
    S_TITLE.innerText = document.title
    S_UPDATE.innerText = document.fileModifiedDate

    ' If the domain comes back empty, it's most likely
    ' the file is located on a local machine.
    If document.domain = "" Then
        S_DOMAIN.innerText = "Local machine"
    Else
        S_DOMAIN.innerText = document.domain
    End If

End Sub

</SCRIPT>

<!-- The beginning of the stuff that gets displayed. -->

<H1>Dynamic HTML Example</H1>

<P>Click the "Get Info" button to have this page figure
    out the listed information.</P>

<!-- The information we want to display. Each part of the text we'll
     be updating with actual information is defined as a SPAN and
     given an ID we can refer to in the script code. -->
<P>
Title:        <SPAN ID=S_TITLE>Dunno yet</SPAN><BR>
File URL:     <SPAN ID=S_URL>Dunno yet</SPAN><BR>
File Size:    <SPAN ID=S_SIZE>Dunno yet</SPAN><BR>
Last update: <SPAN ID=S_UPDATE>Dunno yet</SPAN><BR>
Domain:       <SPAN ID=S_DOMAIN>Dunno yet</SPAN>
</P>

<!-- The button that fires the information collection. -->
<P>
<input id=GoBtn onclick="GetInfo" type="Submit" value="Get Info">
</P>

</BODY>
</HTML>
```

To see the results, open the file in Internet Explorer. It will load the page and display it for you. Once it's loaded, click the Get Info button. The page will change to look like Figure 7.15.

Let's take a brief look at what's going on in this DHTML page. The first part that may look unfamiliar is the <STYLE> tag. Everything between <STYLE> and </STYLE> tags is code to define styles. In this case, we're defining the look of three HTML tags: <H1>, <SPAN>, and <P>. For example, the <H1> tag is now defined to be blue and bold, using the Verdana font. Every time we use an <H1> tag from then on, these attributes will appear.

The next interesting bit is the <SCRIPT> tag. We have used VBScript instead of the more universally popular JavaScript mainly because this book is about Visual Basic. We also use it because we're sticking with Microsoft technology, namely, Internet Explorer. Our script tag defines one function called GetInfo. It uses the document object and its properties, such as URL and title, to get information about the Web page being displayed.

Moving to the actual part of the page that the user sees, you'll find five instances of the possibly unfamiliar <SPAN> tag. This tag defines a

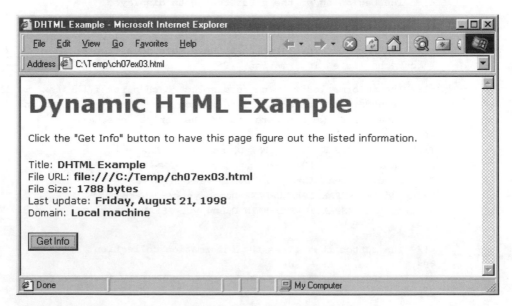

Figure 7.15 The DHTML example running in Internet Explorer.

section of text in the HTML that can be named and given an ID. We have created five spans, each with a different ID. If you look back to the script code, you'll see that we reference the SPAN IDs and use them as objects. This is an example of using script code to manipulate any portion of the Web page that we like. In this case, we're changing the text displayed in the SPANs to reflect the information we retrieve about the page using the document object and its properties. The InnerText property of the SPAN is used to change the text displayed within the SPAN.

Last, we define a button. The interesting attribute of the button is the onclick attribute. This allows us to assign code to run when the button is clicked. In this case, we are telling the button to run the GetInfo function we defined in the preceding script.

The sequence of events goes like this. The browser is told to load the page. As it's parsing the page, it loads the styles we defined so it can use them when the page is displayed. Once this is complete, the user can see the page before the button is clicked. Once the button is clicked, the onclick event fires and runs our function GetInfo. It uses the document object to retrieve information about the page and displays it by modifying the InnerHTML of the SPANs we defined. And it's done!

Granted, this is a simple example. However, we'll be covering all aspects of DHTML in more detail and you'll get a much more complete picture.

Cascading Style Sheets

Style sheets allow us to define the attributes of HTML tags. The attributes we can change are many and varied, and they give us a great deal of control over the *look* of Web pages. They were born out of the fact that HTML was never intended to define the look of Web pages, only the *structure*. All the tags in the original HTML specification are hierarchical. An H1 tag has higher priority than an H2 tag. An H3 tag was never meant to directly follow an H1 tag without an intervening H2. Over time, people started using the tags as formatting tools rather than structure tools.

With Dynamic HTML, the structure of the HTML document becomes important again, because accessing the document through code is based on its structure. We need another mechanism to control the appearance. Enter cascading style sheets. Their primary purpose is to give the page designer complete control over the appearance of the Web page while still being able to maintain the correct structure of the page.

Style sheets are pretty powerful. They let you change the fonts, spacing, borders, size, colors—almost everything about any part of your Web page. The preceding example shows the style definitions embedded directly in the HTML itself. However, a more useful way to use style sheets is to create them as a separate file and *link* them to all your Web pages. The HTML syntax for doing linking to a style sheet looks like this:

```
<HEAD>
    <LINK REL="stylesheet" TYPE="text/css" HREF="MyStyles.css">
</HEAD>
```

This code establishes a link to the style sheet called MyStyles.css. The style sheet must contain only style definitions, not any HTML code. It should not include the <STYLE> and </STYLE> tags.

The advantage of linking to a style sheet instead of embedding it in the HTML is that all your Web pages can make use of one or two style sheets. If you need to change the way the H1 tag looks throughout your entire site, you change it in one place and all your H1 headers are updated at the same time.

The Cascading Part

The basic idea of style sheets is fairly simple. They work very much like styles in a word processor. Define the style once, and everything with that style looks the same. But why is "cascading" in the title? Well, that's fairly simple, too. Cascading means that multiple style sheets can apply to the same page, and they are said to *cascade*, meaning that the style in both style sheets is in effect. You might use this capability if your company had an overall corporate look defined in one style sheet and you had some additional specific style you wanted to create for your group's Intranet site.

If two styles conflict, the style defined last generally has precedence over the previous definition. Make sure you put the most important style sheet last in the link order. If your own style sheet is more important than the corporate one, list it last.

Style Inheritance

HTML tags are frequently embedded within each other. When this is the case, and styles apply to both tags, the inner tag inherits the style of the outer tag and then adds its own style to it. Consider the following HTML fragment:

```
<STYLE>
UL { font-family: Verdana; }
A { font-weight: bold; }
</STYLE>

<UL>
<LI> Link 1: <A HREF="http://www.wiley.com ">Wiley Publishing</A>
<LI> Link 2: <A HREF="http://www.noeticart.com">Noetic Art</A>
</UL>
```

The anchor tag, <A>, is embedded within the unordered list tag, <UL>. We have defined a font style for the <UL> tag, setting it to the Verdana typeface. The <A> is defined such that whichever font it is displayed in will be bold. When loaded into a browser, the <A> tag, because it is embedded within the <UL> tag, inherits all the properties of the <UL> tag's style. One of the powerful implications of this is that an anchor can appear anywhere in the page, within any other style that may use other fonts, and it will always be bold. Figure 7.16 shows what the result looks like in Internet Explorer.

CSS and Dynamic HTML

Styles and Dynamic HTML work very well together. DHTML allows you to change the attributes of a style dynamically while a page is being displayed. This is done using the document object model to access the attributes of the style. For example, the following HTML and script code changes the font of the link to italic when the mouse moves over it, then back to normal when the mouse moves off of it.

```
<HTML>
<BODY>
```

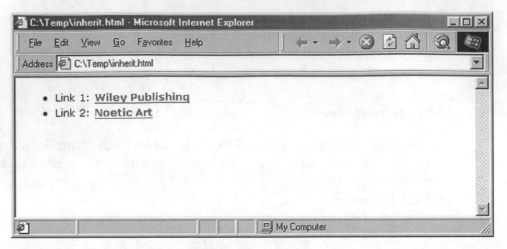

Figure 7.16 Style inheritance in action.

```
<SCRIPT Language="VBScript">

Sub OneAnchor_OnMouseOver()
    Me.Style.FontStyle = "italic"
End Sub

Sub OneAnchor_OnMouseOut()
    Me.Style.FontStyle = "normal"
End Sub

</SCRIPT>

<P>
Want to know about some other cool computer books?
</P>

<A ID=OneAnchor HREF="http://www.wiley.com">Wiley Website</A>

</BODY>
</HTML>
```

Notice a couple of things here. First, we have given the anchor a unique ID, OneAnchor, which we use to refer to that specific anchor on the page. Second, we have wired functions into two of the events that apply to the OneAnchor object, OnMouseOver and OnMouseOut. OnMouse-Over fires when the mouse is moved over the object, and the OnMouse-Out event fires when the mouse is moved off of the object. The code for these event functions does the font changing of the object's style using the document object model.

Type the code into a text file and load it into Internet Explorer to try it out. You'll find that the combination of style sheets and code can do wonders once you know the details of each.

Style Sheet Mechanics

You may not realize it yet, but style sheets give you a great deal of control over the look of your Web pages—and your Web clients—including new attributes you never had access to before. The purpose of this section is to give you an overview of the mechanics and syntax of style sheets, as well as the expanse of visual attributes available to you through styles. We'll cover styles thoroughly enough for you to make your Web clients so sharp that you'll never go back to a Win32 application.

Style Sheet Syntax

You've seen the basic layout of a style sheet, but we think it's important to provide you with the standard syntax. The most basic form of a style looks like this:

```
TAG { style-element: style-value; }
```

Tag is the HTML tag for which you are defining a style, such as A, UL, or P. Notice that they are entered in the style sheet without their HTML angled braces, < and >. It is important not to place any HTML syntax in your style sheet, or it will not function correctly.

The style-element is the aspect of the tag for which you are setting a value. Self-explanatory examples include font-size, color, and width. There are many style-elements, a large number of which will be detailed later in this section.

The style-value represents the value for the style-element you are setting. For example, if you were setting the font-weight style element, the available style-values are *normal* and *bold*. Each style-element has its own range of appropriate valid values.

The specification of a style begins with the tag itself, followed immediately by the open brace, then a series of as many style elements and values as you like, followed by a closing brace. A semicolon separates each style element-style value pair. The colon separates each style element and its associated style value or values. The actual layout is not relevant as long as the syntax is followed. For example, the following style listing:

```
A
{
    font-family: Verdana;
    font-weight: Bold;
}
```

is equivalent to:

```
A { font-family: Verdana; font-weight: Bold; }
```

Classes

Every tag in HTML can be assigned a Class Name that you designate. They are intended to allow you to reference arbitrary groups of tags, and they do not have to be unique. For example, you might want to distinguish between two different kinds of anchors: normal anchors and those contained in a sidebar. You could refer to normal anchors with no special class, but provide a class for the sidebar anchors. In HTML, it would look like this:

```
<A CLASS="Sidebar" HREF="about.html">About our site</A>
```

With style sheets, we can distinguish between the same tag with different classes. The syntax for this is the name of the tag, followed by a period and the name of the class. The following style sheet definition creates a style for normal anchors, and a second style for those with the Sidebar class.

```
A { font-family: Verdana; font-size: 10pt; }
A.Sidebar { font-family: Verdana; font-size: 8pt; color: #0000FF; }
```

All normal anchors appear in Verdana 10-point type, while anchors with the Sidebar class appear in bright blue Verdana 8-point type. We can also define a style for a class that has no specific tag associated with it, as follows:

```
.ReallyBig { font-size: 72pt; }
```

This style says that any tag with a class of ReallyBig should appear in 72-point type. We can assign it to any tag, be it an H1, a P, or an OL. This is a powerful concept, and it can go a long way toward making your pages more dynamic.

Style Sheet Elements

A large collection of styles is available to you. We recommend that you investigate them thoroughly so that you know what's available to you for designing your Web clients. We'll give you a basic list, but you can find more details at the W3C Web site, www.w3c.org. The elements and their values, along with a brief description, are listed in Table 7.3.

You now have a general overview of cascading style sheets. There are more features and subtleties of style sheets, and we encourage you to investigate them more fully. The complete specification for CSS can be found at the W3C Web site, www.w3c.org.

Bonus Software: CSS1 Stylesheet Designer

At the beginning of the Dynamic HTML section of this chapter, we promised you some bonus software that would make your life easier. We're not sure just how much easier it will make your existence, but it is fun, and we are providing it. We would never make a promise we couldn't keep.

So here it is, the CSS Stylesheet Designer. It's a simple utility that allows you to explore the possibilities of style sheets. Figure 7.17 gives you a glimpse of what it looks like. You can find the program on the companion CD-ROM in the \CSS directory.

This program sports the following features:

- Allows you to explore the styles available to you while you are creating style sheets. It will also tell you the valid values available for each element.

- Will save your style sheet to a file so you can embed it in or link it to any Web page you like.

- Will load existing style sheets. Granted, it works best with style sheets it has generated, but it will load some others as well. Check out the code for the style sheet loading functionality if you like—it features a simple style sheet parser you can extend or use in your own programs.

It does have a few limitations. It does not support style containment, IDs, shorthand tags, or pseudoclasses, if you're familiar with these. It performs best with style sheets it has created itself, but it will load a variety of layouts. It will generate and load the following layout:

Table 7.3 Available Style Elements and Values

STYLE ELEMENT	STYLE VALUES	DESCRIPTION
Width	numeric	Specifies the width of any tag with this style. Usually used with images.
Height	numeric	Specifies the height of any tag with this style. Usually used with images.
Background-color	HTML color string; named color; rgb() values	Specifies the background color of the object.
Background-image	url(url/filename)	Specifies the URL of an image to use for the background of the object.
Background-repeat	repeat, repeat-x, repeat-y, no-repeat	Specifies the direction(s) that a background image should be repeated underneath the object.
Background-attachment	scroll, fixed	Specifies whether a background image should scroll with the content on top of it or if it should remain fixed, causing the content on top to scroll over it.
Clear	none, left, right, both	Specifies on which sides of an object text should no longer be allowed to wrap when a left or right alignment has been specified.
Color	HTML color string; named color; rgb() values	Specifies the foreground color of the tag.
Cursor	auto, crosshair, default, hand, text, help, move, wait, e-resize, n-resize, s-resize, w-resize, ne-resize, nw-resize, se-resize, sw-resize	Specifies which mouse cursor to display when it is over the tag.
Display	block, inline, list-item, none	Specifies whether a tag is displayed and, if so, how.
Float	left, right, none	Specifies how content flows around the tag being styled.
Font-family	list of font names separated by commas	Specifies the fonts to use, in order of preference, for the tag.
Font-size	size in points, relative percentage, larger, smaller	Specifies the font size of the tag in either absolute or relative terms.
Font-style	normal, italic	Specifies the font style of the tag, either normal or italic.
Font-variant	normal, small-caps	Specifies the font variant of the tag, either normal or small caps.
Font-weight	normal, bold, bolder, lighter	Specifies the font weight of the tag.

STYLE ELEMENT	STYLE VALUES	DESCRIPTION
Letter-spacing	numeric spacing value	Specifies the space between the letters in the tag.
Line-height	numeric height value	Specifies the height of text lines for the tag.
List-style-image	url(url/imagefile)	Specifies an image file to use for list item bullets instead of the normal bullet character.
List-style-position	inside, outside	Specifies whether a wrapped line of a list item is indented level with the first line (inside) or is pulled back to the level of the bullet (outside).
List-style-type	disc, circle, square, decimal, lower-roman, upper-roman, lower-alpha, upper-alpha	Specifies the type of characters to use when bulleting or numbering lists.
Text-align	left, right, center, justified	Specifies how the text in the tag should be aligned.
Text-decoration	underline, overline, line-through, blink, none	Specifies what sort of text embellishment should be used for the tag. Use none on the anchor tag to remove underline from links.
Text-indent	numeric indent value	Specifies how far to indent the text of the tag.
Text-transform	capitalize, upper-case, lower-case, none	Specifies one of several text-modification functions for the tag.
Vertical-align	sub, super, top, text-top, middle, bottom, text-bottom	Specifies the vertical alignment of the contents of the tag.
White-space	normal, pre, nowrap	Specifies how white space is handled in the tag. Pre is handled like the HTML PRE tag; normal means collapse it like HTML normally does; and nowrap means don't break lines on spaces—only on the BR tag.
Word-spacing	numeric spacing value	Specifies how much space to place between words in the contents of the tag.
Margin-top, margin-right, margin-bottom, margin-left	numeric margin value	Specifies the margin spacing of borders on the tag or the spacing *outside* of the borders.
Padding-top, padding-right, padding-bottom, padding-left	numeric padding value	Specifies the padding spacing of border on the tag or the spacing between the border itself and the contents of the tag.
Border-top-width, border-right-width, border-bottom-width, border-left-width	thin, medium, thick, or width value	Specifies the width of border lines surrounding the contents of a tag. Make a value of zero to hide that side of the border.
Border-color	up to four color values	Specifies the color of the borders surrounding the contents of a tag. Can specify up to four color values.
Border-style	none, dotted, dashed, solid, double, groove, ridge, inset, outset	Specifies the line style of the border surrounding the contents of the tag.

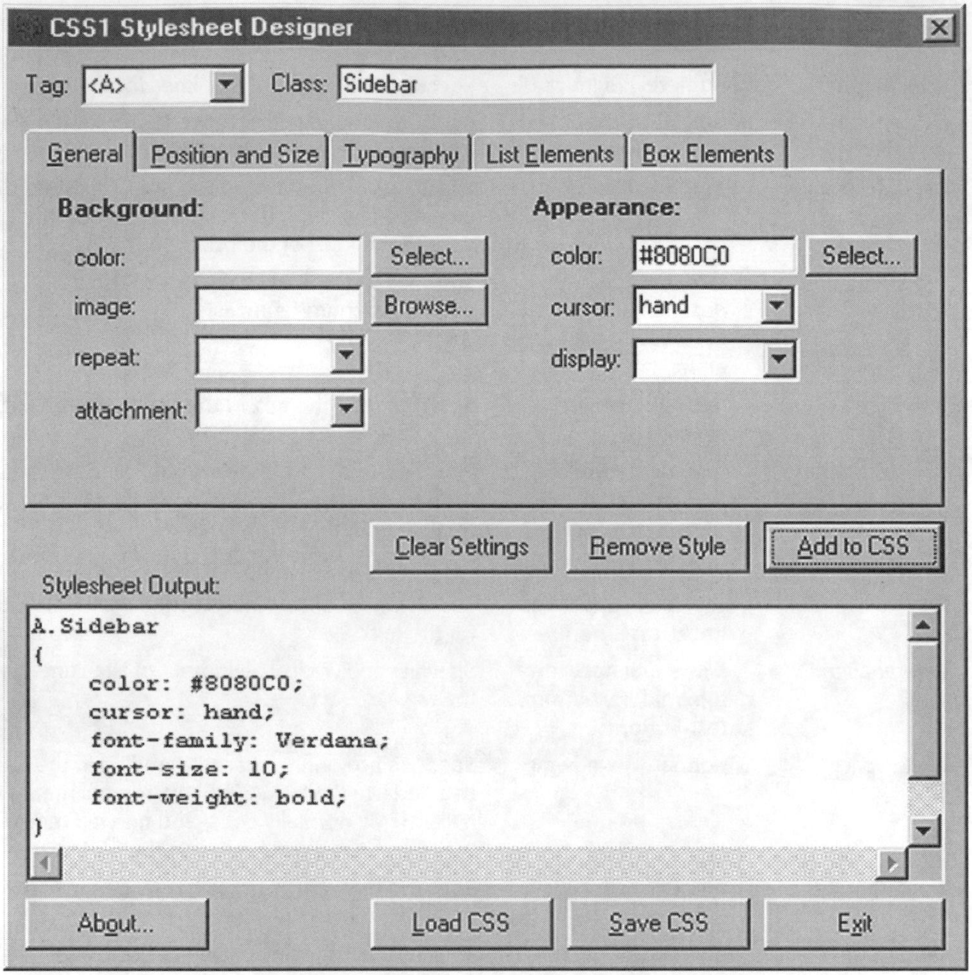

Figure 7.17 The CSS Stylesheet Designer: Our gift to you.

```
A
{
    cursor: hand;
}
```

However, it will just as easily load the following variation:

```
A { cursor: hand; }
```

Basic Usage Instructions

The general process for using this program is fairly straightforward. However, you should know about a few details.

To add a tag to the style sheet: Select the tag for which you'd like to create a style from the combo box at the top left corner of the dialog. Make any adjustments you like to the style by setting the properties on the various tabs. When you're done adjusting the settings, click the Add to CSS button.

To remove a style from the style sheet: Select the tag you'd like to remove from the combo box at the top left corner of the dialog. Click the Remove Style button to delete it from the style sheet.

To change an existing style: Select the tag you'd like to change from the combo box at the top left corner of the dialog. The program will load its settings into the style controls. Make any adjustments you'd like to the settings. Click the Add to CSS button to update the style.

To perform any of the previous operations on a tag with an associated class: Select the tag you'd like to operate on from the combo box at the top left corner of the dialog. Type the name of the class in the class field and hit Tab. If the tag already exists, its values will be loaded into the controls on the dialog.

If you'd like to clear all the settings on the dialog, including all the tabs, click the Clear Settings button.

When you're ready to save your style sheet, click the Save CSS button. If you'd like to load an existing style sheet into the designer, click the Load CSS button.

That's about it for the CSS Stylesheet Designer. Happy style-sheeting, and don't say we never gave you anything.

Extensible Markup Language

Extensible Markup Language, better known as XML, is a mystery to most people. When you throw it into the mix with HTML, CSS, DHTML, and DOM, you get quite a jumble of acronyms related to the Web and Web development. Because XML is the least known of all of them, questions arise: What is XML? How does it fit into the Web client picture?

What Is XML?

Like HTML and Dynamic HTML, XML finds its roots in the Standard Generalized Markup Language, or SGML. HTML allows you to define the structure and appearance of textual information, or documents. Dynamic HTML adds interactivity and browser-side modifiability to HTML. XML is similar, in that it uses tags to markup information, but XML is for use with data instead of documents (though we'll sort of retract this statement later).

XML is a markup language for defining data. Think of it as tags that you can use to define information as data fields. These data fields can then be read by data sources on Web pages, by components on a server, or even by another database. It can be used as a universal data exchange language as well. Imagine programs that can export data in XML format and others that can read it. You'd have almost unlimited data interchange possibilities.

Here's a quick example. You can display information using regular HTML, such as this partial listing from a dog breeder's stock:

```
<P>Dogs</P>
<TABLE>
    <THEAD>
        <TD>Breed</TD>
        <TD>Weight</TD>
        <TD>Color</TD>
    </THEAD>
    <TR>
        <TD>Border Terrier</TD>
        <TD>15 lb.s</TD>
        <TD>Brindle</TD>
    </TR>
    <TR>
        <TD>Rhodesian Ridgeback</TD>
        <TD>75 lb.s</TD>
        <TD>Wheaten</TD>
    </TR>
    <TR>
        <TD>Belgian Tervuren</TD>
        <TD>65 lb.s</TD>
        <TD>Fawn</TD>
    </TR>
</TABLE>
```

This HTML code will display the information about the dogs on the screen, but you can't do anything with it. It is good only for display in a browser. However, suppose we rewrite this code, using XML to describe the data rather than to display it. It might look like this:

```
<?XML VERSION="1.0"?>
<Dogs>
  <Dog>
    <breed>Border Terrier</breed>
    <weight>15 lb.s</weight>
    <color>Brindle</color>
  </Dog>
  <Dog>
    <breed> Rhodesian Ridgeback</breed>
    <weight>75 lb.s</weight>
    <color>Wheaten</color>
  </Dog>
  <Dog>
    <breed>Belgian Tervuren</breed>
    <weight>65 lb.s</weight>
    <color>Fawn</color>
  </Dog>
</Dogs>
```

We've defined a data set called Dogs, with three fields, Breed, Weight, and Color. There are three records in the data set. The XML we've used here has defined the data for us, but it has not displayed it. This data could be generated in this format by a server-side component that is built just for this purpose. This would allow the data to be sent just about anywhere: to another component, to another application, to another database, or to a Web browser that knows how to display XML-formatted data.

XML is infinitely extensible. You add whatever tags you like to describe your data. Typically, this will be in the form of data field names. However, you can also add attributes to the data fields, which can represent whatever you want, acting as properties of the field or even as additional data. In the preceding example, we invented the Dogs, Breed, Weight, and Color tags. If you are familiar with HTML, you will note that the Color tag is also used in HTML. XML allows you to use a tag name that exists in HTML, because the tag name is used in the XML context.

That's the short tour of the XML purpose and syntax. There are other details and possibilities, but you get the idea.

How Does XML Fit In?

If XML is all about data, why are we talking about it in a Web client's chapter? A fair question. The answer is that Web browsers, in conjunction with a *Data Source Object* (DSO), cannot only display XML data, but can manipulate it and format it in the browser without making a trip back to the server. You could create a Dynamic HTML Web page that displays XML data and allows the user to sort and filter it right in the browser—no server required. This has the potential to make N-tier browser-based applications fast and efficient by reducing trips to the server and operating in a universal and customizable data environment.

TIP

To find the latest information about the Microsoft implementation of XML, visit the dedicated Web site at www.microsoft.com/xml. You'll learn about the latest advances and features and have access to plenty of excellent examples. In addition, you can download the latest version of the Microsoft XML parser Java classes, which also includes examples. As of this writing, Microsoft is up to version 1.9, which contains many advances over the 1.0 version included with Internet Explorer 4.0.

The Data Source Object is an applet or an ActiveX control that you can embed in your Web page that understands how to deal with XML data. Once it's there, you can use the data as a regular data source and bind it to controls on your page or to HTML tables. Microsoft includes a Java applet with Internet Explorer 4.0 and later that does this. It provides only read capabilities, but it is ideal for displaying tabular or hierarchical data. Including the applet in your Web page is simple, and looks like this:

```
<APPLET
    Code=com.ms.xml.dso.XMLDSO.class
    id=DogsDSO
    height=0
    width=0
    MAYSCRIPT=true>
    <Param name="url" value="Dogs.xml">
</APPLET>
```

This tag defines the XML DSO applet provided by Microsoft. It assigns it an ID of DogsDSO, which will be used as the data source name when bound to a table. The only parameter sent to the applet is the URL that points to the XML data file. Once the applet is in place, you can bind it to a table, like this for instance:

```
<TABLE DataSrc=#DogsDSO>
    <THEAD>
        <TD>Breed</TD>
        <TD>Weight</TD>
        <TD>Color</TD>
    </THEAD>
```

```
     <TR>
         <TD><SPAN DataFld="breed">None</SPAN></TD>
         <TD><SPAN DataFld="weight">None</SPAN></TD>
         <TD><SPAN DataFld="color">None</SPAN></TD>
     </TR>
   </TABLE>
```

The previous code sets the data source of the table to our DSO defined in the applet. It creates a column in the table for each field in the XML data set. When the code is loaded into the browser, the applet runs and loads the data from the XML data set, which is then displayed in the table. If you'd like to see a complete, nicely formatted example of XML in action, check out sample ch07ex05.html on the companion CD-ROM (\examples\ch07ex05). Simply open it in Internet Explorer 4.0 or later.

In just a few minutes, we have displayed data in XML format in a Web page. As long as your database or server components can serve up data as XML, you'll be able to display just about anything. And because XML can come from many different data sources or databases, you'll be able to display data from anywhere. One last note about XML. Like most Internet technologies, it is evolving all the time. If you'd like to keep up on the latest developments, stop by the W3C Web site at www.w3c.org and read up on it.

The Document Object Model

The Document Object Model, or DOM, is an object hierarchy that defines every element that can possibly exist on a Web page. Using this object model, you can access and modify any element on a Web page from program code, be it embedded script or Visual Basic. By *define*, we mean that the object model encompasses all the elements as objects, the events that they generate or react to, the methods they expose that perform actions, and the properties that define them.

All these elements, the properties, objects, events, and methods, encompass the object model and can be referred to by the acronym POEM. That's not an industry standard term; we just made it up over lunch one day. We needed a few more acronyms for the book. The DOM fits into the Dynamic HTML picture, because everything in the Document Object Model is exposed to your code. You can read, adjust, execute, and react to just about any part of it. Figure 7.18 illustrates the Document Object Model hierarchy.

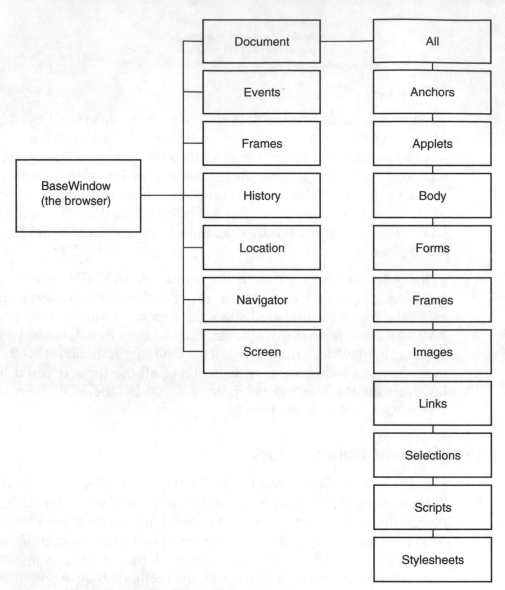

Figure 7.18 The Document Object Model hierarchy.

The best thing you can do to become proficient in Dynamic HTML is to review and know the DOM. It is the real key to what you can do to or with a Web page. One of the problems with this is that the DOM is evolving. It has not yet been standardized. When the HTML 4.0 specification comes out—someday—we'll all stand up and cheer because it will be stable, at least for a while. The best resource available at this time for the Document Object Model is the World Wide Web Consortium

Web site (www.w3c.org). It's a complete reference and is updated frequently by the W3C as things progress. We are not going to enumerate the entire DOM, because it's huge.

However, we can take a quick look at some of the object models in use, just to get the idea of what we're talking about. Back at the beginning of the section on Dynamic HTML, we demonstrated a sample program that displayed some information about the page being displayed. The following listing shows the code that did the real work:

```
S_URL.innerText = document.URL
S_SIZE.innerText = document.fileSize + " bytes"
S_TITLE.innerText = document.title
S_UPDATE.innerText = document.fileModifiedDate
```

This code illustrates two concepts in the DOM. The first is that there is a big, important object in the model called the document. It has properties, methods, and events associated with it. In this case, we are using some of its properties: title, URL, and fileSize. There are plenty more, too. Here's one more quick example:

```
Sub SwitchImages(sImg as String)
    theImage.src = sImg
    theImage.width = 320
    theImage.height = 240
    BaseWindow.open "http://www.wiley.com"
End Sub
```

Assuming that there is an image object on our Web page with an ID of theImage, we can manipulate many properties of the image, even which image is being displayed. The BaseWindow is another object in the DOM and refers to the browser itself. In the previous code, we tell it to open another instance of the browser and navigate to a specific URL.

The more you dig into the DOM, the more capabilities you'll have at your disposal. Make it your mission to become familiar with it.

Events

You've seen the basics of events and hooking them up to code. In the DHTML application using Visual Basic code, they look just like regular Visual Basic event routines. They are preceded by the name of the object and followed by an underscore and the event itself. For example, the following code:

```
Sub GotoButton_Click()
```

is a standard Visual Basic button hooked up to the click event. This you know. When we substitute form object for Web page objects (DOM objects), the events get replaced, too. If you create a DHTML Application project in Visual Basic (more on this in the next section) and put a button on the Web page with an ID of GotoButton, the function declaration now looks like this:

```
Function GotoButton_onclick() as Boolean
```

Ignoring the fact that it is now a function instead of a Sub, the only difference is the name of the event. When referring to a DOM object, you get the DOM event list instead of the Visual Basic event list. This allows you to access not only the elements on the Web page, but also their events.

Event Bubbling

This sounds silly, but that's really what it's called. The name comes from the fact that an event "bubbles up" the chain of objects until it finds one that will handle it. In Dynamic HTML, Web pages are organized as a hierarchy of elements. Earlier in this chapter we mentioned that HTML was originally intended to define document structure, not its content, and that with Dynamic HTML, this had become important again. The reason that it is important to create a correct document hierarchy is made clear here. If the structure of the document is not in good order, then the event bubbling sequence will not happen in the right order.

Take, for example, the following HTML fragment:

```
<BODY>
<UL>
<LI> <A HREF="http://www.wiley.com">Wiley's <B>cool</B> site</A>
<LI> <A HREF="http:/www.noeticart.com">Noetic Art (yawn)</A>
</UL>

</BODY>
```

If the user clicks on the word "cool," then the <B> tag is first to receive the event. If there is no code available to handle the onclick event for the <B> tag, the event bubbles up to the next tag in the hierarchy, in this case the <A> tag. If there is no event handler for onclick for the <A> tag, it bubbles up to the <LI> tag, and so on. This concept is important to understand because it can be put to good use. You can write high-level event handlers that process events from multiple objects. The BaseWindow.Event.SrcElement property will tell you which element caused the event.

There is one more aspect of event bubbling, and that is that you can cancel an event, which prevents it from bubbling up the chain of objects. This is also useful when writing a generic event handler. If you handle the event, you might not want to do anything with it, but you also do not want it to propagate any further. The BaseWindow.Event.Cancel-Bubble method will do this for you.

The event model in Dynamic HTML is pretty straightforward as long as you understand the bubbling part.

Building a Dynamic HTML Project

So far you've been introduced to the basic Dynamic HTML concepts you'll need to know to start building real client applications. You could probably do it on your own without the intervention of Visual Basic. However, including Visual Basic in the mix adds some significant benefits. What we'll be doing is replacing all the in-line script code you've seen so far with an ActiveX DLL. The benefits of this approach include the following:

- Your code is now compiled. It will run faster than interpreted script code, and it will not be available for others to see and perhaps "borrow."

- You are developing your code in the Visual Basic environment. This means you get the complete Visual Basic code editor and, more important, the debugger.

Visual Basic adds support for Dynamic HTML with version 6.0. You'll see, among other things, a new project type called DHTML Application. Basically, this new project type is a marriage of ActiveX DLLs with Dynamic HTML Web pages used as your user interface. Keeping in step with our Get-Your-Feet-Wet-Immediately program, let's do a walkthrough to illustrate the process of building a DHTML application with Visual Basic. Afterward, we'll talk about some of the specifics in more detail.

The DHTML Project Walkthrough

This guided tour will help you get started creating DHTML applications with Visual Basic quickly. You'll get a handle on the overall process, which looks like this:

1. Create a new DHTML Application project. Make sure the Apartment threading model is selected.

2. Design the pages of your application in the page designer.

3. Write any code you need, including event handlers tied to the elements of the HTML page.

4. Compile your project, fixing any errors encountered.

5. Test your application in Internet Explorer, debugging in Visual Basic.

We'll be stepping through each of these, working on a simple example application. If you'd like to bypass the actual work involved as you follow along, you can find the example project on the companion CD-ROM in the \examples\ch07ex04 directory. If you have any questions during the presentation, just raise your hand.

First, we need to create a new DHTML Application project. In Visual Basic, select New Project from the file menu. You'll notice a large number of additional project types you haven't seen in previous versions of Visual Basic. Select the one titled DHTML Application. You may have to scroll down the list to see it. This step is fairly easy. That's all there is to it. Visual Basic starts you off with one blank DHTML page and one code module.

One thing you might want to check is the threading model for the application. It should be set to Apartment Model. You can find this setting on the Project Properties dialog.

Next, we'll design the pages of your application. In the project viewer in Visual Basic, open the tree branch labeled Designers. This is where your HTML pages are located. Visual Basic created a blank page for you called DHTMLPage1. Double-click this item to open it. Visual Basic will load its page designer with your new blank page. Figure 7.19 shows the page designer window.

Our simple example will allow the user to select a restaurant from a list and have a brief review of it displayed. Our page will look like Figure 7.20 when complete.

Start by adding the title. Click in the empty page on the right and just start typing. You can format the size, font, and bold characteristics using the toolbar on the page designer. Enter the second line the same way, formatting it as displayed. Notice that as you add elements to the page, they are list in the object view of the page in a hierarchical format on the left. We'll discuss the page designer in depth later on.

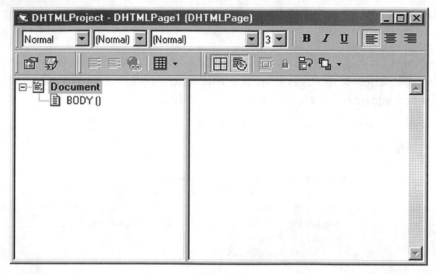

Figure 7.19   The Visual Basic DHTML page designer.

Add the select field (or combo box) by dragging it from the control palette to the page. Size it a little wider, then right-click on the combo box and select Properties from the context menu. In the resulting dialog, you can add items to the list. Add Purple Pete's, The Stunted Angus, and Too Much Spaghetti (or other restaurants you may be familiar with).

Last, add the button. Drag it from the control palette to the blank page. You can resize it, then change the caption by simply clicking on the but-

Figure 7.20   The restaurant page in the page designer.

ton and typing in a new one. Your page should now look similar to the one in Figure 7.20.

We need to add some event-handling code to the button on the screen. Double-click it and type in the following code, which will display the short restaurant reviews in a message box.

```
Private Function Button1_onclick() As Boolean

    Select Case Select1.Value
    Case "toomuch"
        MsgBox "Too Much Spaghetti is a marvelous " & _
            "place for the bottomless stomach. However, if " & _
            "you're looking for good Italian food, go " & _
            "somewhere else. The garlic bread is " & _
            "actually dangerous.", vbOKOnly, _
            "Too Much Spaghetti"
    Case "pete"
        MsgBox "Purple Pete's is easily the best seafood " & _
            "in entire beach area. Make sure you order the " & _
            "Groovy Groundhog, their own frozen mixed drink. " & _
            "It's spectacular!", vbOKOnly, _
            "Purple Pete's"
    Case "angus"
        MsgBox "The Stunted Angus is appropriately named. " & _
            "We've never seen such small portions in our " & _
            "lives. The food is good enough, but you'll have " & _
            "to order three entrees to get full. The house " & _
            "salad dressing is adequate.", vbOKOnly, _
            "The Stunted Angus"
    End Select

End Function
```

Notice that the normal Visual Basic button click event, called Click, has been replaced here with onclick. The name is different because it reflects the name of the event in HTML, not Visual Basic.

Next, let's compile your project. This step works just like it does when building a normal Visual Basic application. It will ask if you want to build DHTMLProject1.dll. Build it wherever you like. If you encounter errors, fix them. It may also ask you about creating an HTML file. Go ahead and do it for now.

Finally, click the Run button or press F5. Visual Basic will start Internet Explorer with your project. Play around with it. You'll see that it works as expected. Figure 7.21 shows the project running in Internet Explorer after one of the restaurants has been selected and the button pressed.

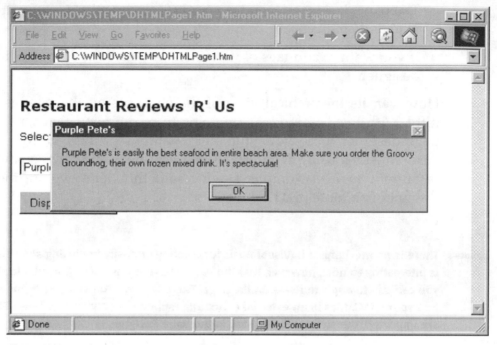

Figure 7.21   The restaurant example in Internet Explorer.

That's the low-budget tour of the DHTML project type. Next we will cover some of the aspects of the DHTML project in more detail, including the page designer and its limitations and the use of external HTML files.

The Page Designer

We're going to be frank with you right up front about the Page Designer. It's a very limited tool. Even Microsoft recommends using it for only simple projects. It supports only a small handful of tags; you can't edit the HTML directly in the editor; you can't create styles. Just about everything in it is limited. It was never intended to be a full HTML editor, even though that's exactly what we need. Some of the other limitations include the following:

- Some controls cannot be cut from the form and then pasted back. You'll have to re-create them.

- The tree view is static—it does not support drag and drop.

- You can't easily create or import a style sheet, even though the tool-bar lists styles.

- The page designer generates poor HTML code that is difficult to read and change.

- If you want to add tags of your own, forget about doing it with the designer.

However, its hierarchical view of the elements on the page is pretty nifty. With this is mind, we are going to recommend that you use the page designer to do your initial explorations of the DHTML project. Also consider using it for small projects, not much bigger than our restaurant review example. Having said this, let's explore the page designer in a more practical way.

TIP

There is no mechanism in Visual Basic for creating or easily importing style sheets. It is interesting to note, however, that the page designer has a list of available styles you can use to apply to items on the page. There is a way to get styles in the project. Edit your HTML files in an external editor and embed your styles in it. When the files are imported, the styles will be listed in the page designer.

For any serious DHTML project, the best way to use the page designer is to bypass it. Even though it has one or two nice features, it is essentially not appropriate for the kinds of projects we're talking about in this book. Fortunately, there is a fairly easy way to bypass the editor. You can create your Dynamic HTML project in Visual Basic and then import your externally created HTML files into the project.

This is a really good way to run your DHTML project. Create your pages in an editor outside of Visual Basic. You can use really slick HTML editors like Allaire's HomeSite to get into the page-creation task. They are built with one purpose in mind—helping you easily create HTML pages. You can create any tag supported by the standard, develop styles and apply them, and see exactly what they look like before you add them to the project. You also have better control over the layout of the actual HTML code. As programmers, we all know how important code formatting is to ensuring readability and maintainability.

NOTE

When creating DHTML pages for your client application, make sure you assign a unique ID to every element of the page that you intend to manipulate or reference with code. The ID is the mechanism through which Visual Basic refers to the page elements.

Once you have your pages and styles defined, you can import them into the DHTML project very easily. To do so, right-click on the Designers item in the Visual Basic project view. From the context menu, select Add, DHTML Page. When the dialog comes up, select "Save HTML in external file" and then click the Open button. Then you can select your HTML page and add it to the project. It will show up in the page designer, but don't do any editing there. It will, however, provide you with an interesting hierarchical view of your Web page. When looking at this view in the tree on the left side of the designer, note that any of the elements listed in bold have IDs designated for them, and thus can have code written for them.

Creating your pages outside Visual Basic is really the only practical way to go for a real development effort. However, while this technique is much better than using page designer, it is not without its own problems and quirks.

Dynamic HTML Project Tips

There are a few details you'll want to keep in mind while working on DHTML projects. Many of them are low-level details, but they'll probably make your development experience much more pleasant. They have helped us out, usually right after they have destroyed three days on our project.

Don't dynamically change IDs. Dynamic HTML allows you to change pretty much anything on the page, including the tags. However, your Visual Basic code is linked to the tags by the ID. Just make sure that when you use code to change the tags *you don't change the ID*. If you do, any code that is currently attached to it will no longer be attached to it. Your code will break, your user will be unhappy, and it will be incredibly hard to debug.

Write code in only one place. If you have script code in your HTML page assigned to a specific element and event, as well as code in Visual Basic responding to the same element and event, then both chunks of code will execute when the event fires. The Visual Basic code runs first, then the script code. It is important to remember this. It can happen easily when several people work on the same project.

Preserve your HTML formatting. As mentioned before, we recommend creating your HTML pages using a more capable external editor and then importing them into your Visual Basic DHTML project. However, when you import the page into the project, Visual Basic will dutifully load and then proceed to completely screw up your code formatting. If you import the page, then edit it externally after the fact, you will not recognize it. It might bear some passing resemblance to the original, but not enough to keep you from having to reformat it. Therefore, we recommend loading in a *copy* of the page. Then, if you need to change it, edit the original and import it again.

Use the same path everywhere.   One slightly annoying quirk of the Visual Basic DHTML project using external HTML files is that Visual Basic stores the reference to the file as a complete absolute path, drive included. The implication of this is that all developers on the project should store their code in the exact same path and drive to the external HTML files. Knowing this ahead of time will save your team some serious headaches.

More "gotchas" and shortcuts are bound to come up in the future. As the Visual Basic DHTML project type is around longer and more people work with it, more experience will be gained. Microsoft is sure to enhance the functionality of the page designer (or remove it altogether—that's happened before) and the project type itself. Keep your eyes open.

Dynamic HTML Topics

Once you understand the basics of creating Dynamic HTML clients, and you should by now, a few practical areas bear further discussion. They are topics we've had to deal with during our stint as programmers, and we thought we'd pass along what we've learned.

Navigating between Pages

If you've already read through the section on User Documents, you've seen that you can't just use the old tried-and-true Show method. Navigating between forms, or pages, in a DHTML client is about the same as it is for User Documents. Instead of using the NavigateTo method, which is part of the world of User Documents, you use the Navigate method. The following code fragment illustrates the call.

```
Private Sub BtnGo_onclick()

    BaseWindow.Navigate "next.html"

End Sub
```

Persistence on the Client

One of the nice things about using Web pages for your client is that you get security on the client side almost free. One of the biggest pains about using Web pages for your client is that security is always getting in your way. Security features prevent you from writing all but the most trivial information on the client's computer. Even then, the user can shut down security in the browser so you can't even do that much. What's a programmer to do?

Essentially, not much. The only disk activity you're allowed to do as a Web client is to write to and from *cookies*. You've probably heard of cookies before, though nobody can fathom where the name came from. They're small files that a Web page is allowed to write to a client machine. They are text files only, very much like old Windows INI files. They are very limited in size—a maximum of 4K each. Not very satisfactory for saving data in any quantity. Users can set up Internet Explorer so that you cannot save cookies to their machines, although it would seem a simple matter to tell your users not to do this. What's even worse, but less likely, is that your code could create a cookie, and before you have the opportunity to read it again, the user could delete it. You never can tell with users.

Still, even with these limitations, cookies can be useful. Tell your users to allow cookies through, and tell them not to wantonly delete them. Having established a safe haven for your cookies, you can use them to save small amounts of information for a number of purposes. The good news is that dealing with cookies in a Visual Basic DHTML application is fairly easy.

When you create a new DHTML Application project, Visual Basic adds a code module to your project. In this code module are two functions: PutProperty and GetProperty. They allow you to easily save (PutProperty) and read (GetProperty) values in the cookie file. A brief example code fragment follows:

```
PutProperty BaseWindow.Document, "LastURL", Document.LocationURL
```

This code saves the value of the current document's URL in a location in the cookie called LastURL. You can use cookies to pass information back and forth between pages or to remember the state between sessions of the application. The possibilities are wide and varied—as long as they fit into 4K, that is. The one exception is Internet Explorer 5.0. At the time of this writing, it has not been released, but it promises to make client-side persistence more flexible.

Prepare for the Next Tier

Unless you're a Web designer, you'll be creating DHTML clients with the next tier in mind. Without the ability to speak with the middle layer and adapt to its needs, the client sits there and looks good, but doesn't have much purpose. There are a few things that you can do while developing the client to make sure it will be ready for the middle layer.

Fill list boxes from code. Values that go into list boxes are typically fed to the client from the server in case they change. For example, if your client displays a list of products that your company offers, that list may change frequently. You'd probably rather change the list once on the database server and feed it to all the clients automatically. To accommodate this need, make sure such things as lists that change frequently are populated through code.

But not just through code. Make sure you put the population code in isolated functions that you can change easily. In this way, you can write code that fills the user interface with values using literal strings while the middle tier is being developed. Once the middle tier is working and feeding you real values from the database, you can change the code in that one function to fill the user interface with real data instead of canned data. In this way, the changes you'll have to make to the code are isolated to those functions that perform the population work.

If you have lots of elements on the user interface that will change on a regular basis, they can use the same technique. Any controls with labels that will be changing can be filled by population functions when they are fed from a database. In this way, your entire user database can be adjusted based on changing conditions, and the data can come from the server side.

Winding Up

You have a decent selection of options when building your client software. We generally prefer Dynamic HTML, because it is leaner, very capable, and gaining wide support. However, User Documents can be an excellent choice when you need to "Webify" an existing Visual Basic application or when you need a Web client with a Win32 look. If you just need a few Internet capabilities for that "Internet-enabled" check mark, the Web Browser control is worth considering.

You can create a killer client using these newfound skills and knowledge. You can choose the technology that's right for your project. Your development teams can start building the client while you move on to the middle tier. You're about to dig into COM, business rules, Microsoft Transaction Server, and a host of other fascinating topics that will make your product fast, scalable, and secure.

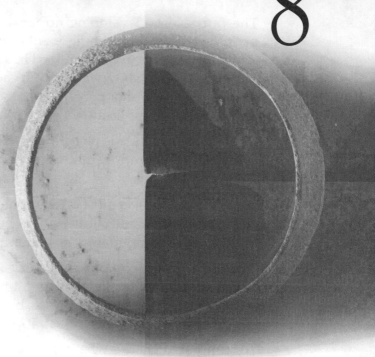

Understanding COM Internals

C hapter 2, "Introduction to COM," covered several of the basic COM concepts. We discussed the benefits of building COM components as well as how to build these components using Visual Basic classes. We also looked at tools that helped us build these components, such as the Class Builder; how to use these COM components; and how to manipulate the components with Visual Basic.

So far we have been looking at COM from the outside, with some peeks here and there into little pieces inside. This chapter looks deeper into COM components to help you understand how they work internally and how they interact with other COM components.

Because an N-tier application is composed of several COM components working together and interacting over a distributed environment, you will be writing all your application's business logic in COM components and communicating with other COM components through interfaces. Although Visual Basic makes the inner workings of COM interfaces transparent, it is important to understand how interfaces work so that you can effectively develop your classes and class behaviors. Understanding interfaces and how they work will help you in designing robust COM business components. We'll cover that in this chapter.

The purpose of developing applications with COM is to allow other people to reuse your components. In order to do this, though, your application needs to be organized in a way that makes finding the interfaces easy. We'll show you how to achieve this by creating an object model—the view that people outside your application see and interact with—for your application.

COM also brings some object-oriented techniques to Visual Basic. We'll show you how to apply these techniques to facilitate the construction of COM components.

And finally, because most of your business components will be dealing with data and communicating data between components, we will look at how COM components can communicate data using ADO.

These are fairly complex but very important topics to understand. Don't get discouraged if they aren't totally clear at first pass. You may need to go over them a few times, but once you completely grasp these concepts, building robust N-tier application will become second nature.

To summarize, here's what's covered in this chapter:

- How COM interfaces work
- Creating object models for your application
- Using object-oriented techniques with VB
- Accessing data with COM and ADO

Let's get started!

COM Interfaces

We mentioned in Chapter 2, "Introduction to COM," that COM is a binary standard for creating software components. It does not specify what particular programming language to use. COM does not even specify what a component is or prevent the use of objects to implement components. The one thing COM does do is define interfaces.

A COM interface allows applications and other components to communicate with the functions of COM components. The functions of a component are accessed through a virtual function table, also known as a *vtable* or VTBL. The vtable does not contain the actual functions. Instead, it contains a set of pointers to the functions of the component. A component that wants to access a function of another component needs to go through the vtable.

Clients can't access the vtable directly. A pointer, called an interface pointer, adds an extra level of indirection to the interface that makes implementing this interface possible. So a client will see a pointer to a pointer in the vtable. Figure 8.1 shows the structure of a COM interface.

The only requirement for the vtable of a COM interface is that the first field of the table be a pointer to IUnknown. IUnknown is the only interface any component must implement to become a COM component. It's basically the door to all other interfaces, because all other interfaces inherit from IUnknown. When it comes to creating COM components in Visual Basic, you really don't have to do anything other than create an ActiveX component; the rest is done for you transparently. We'll talk about IUnknown in more detail later in this chapter.

How does the COM interface work? To understand, we have to look at COM's calling convention. Methods of an object have one additional parameter: the object they belong to. This self-parameter is called "Me." A self-parameter to any of the interface's operations is passed to the interface pointer, which passes it to the vtable. Passing the parameter allows operations in a COM interface to exhibit true characteristics of object calling.

A COM component is free to contain implementations for any number of interfaces. The entire implementation can be a single class, but it does not have to be. Because a component can contain many classes, these classes can instantiate as many objects of as many kinds as they require. These objects then collectively provide the implementation of the interfaces provided by the component.

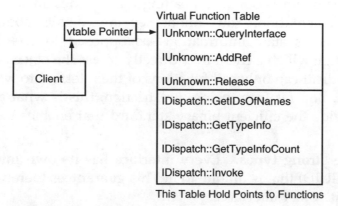

Figure 8.1   A COM interface.

Components depend on interfaces to communicate. If the interfaces don't exist any longer or if they have been changed, then the communication lines are broken. When you decide to create and publish an interface to your components, you are signing a contract on behalf of your components. You can't just change your interface—if you do, the components that depend upon it won't be able to communicate. Once an interface is created, it cannot be altered. Because of this immutability, it is important for you as a Visual Basic developer to put some thought into your interfaces before creating them.

Interface Characteristics

The good thing is that Visual Basic hides all the inner workings of COM interfaces from you. But because interfaces are essential for communicating with your components, it is very important to understand the characteristics of interfaces and to be aware of how they work when you code your applications.

There are four points to note when working with interfaces:

An interface is not a class. An interface is not a class in the normal definition of a Visual Basic class. An object is created from a class, but an interface cannot be instantiated because the object carries no implementation. An object must implement the interface, and that object must be instantiated for there to be an interface.

An interface is not an object. An interface is just a related set of functions and the method by which clients and objects communicate. When a client has access to an object, it has nothing more than an interface pointer through which it can access the functions in the interface. The pointer is opaque, meaning that it hides all aspects of internal implementation. You cannot see any details about the object—such as its state information—as opposed to C++ object pointers through which a client may directly access the object's data. In COM, the client can only call functions of the interface to which it has a pointer. But, far from being a restriction, this is what allows COM to provide the efficient binary standard that enables location transparency.

Interfaces have strong types. Every interface has its own interface identifier (a GUID) that is unique to it. This guarantees there will be no conflict with other interfaces.

Interfaces are immutable.   Interfaces are never versioned, thus avoiding versioning problems. A new version of an interface, created by adding or removing functions or changing semantics, is an entirely new interface and is assigned a new unique identifier. Therefore a new interface does not conflict with an old interface even if all that changed is the implementation.

If you are going to provide services through interfaces, it is important that your interface have these characteristics to ensure that the services being provided match the expectations of the users. Understanding these characteristics will help you design better interfaces for your components.

Guidelines for Creating Interfaces

As mentioned earlier, interfaces are implemented inside a class in VB. In order to create better interfaces, we need to learn how we can design these classes. We also need to understand the impact of these interfaces on our class.

If a class supports one interface, there is no requirement that it should support any other, because interfaces are independent of one another. If you write a class that implements an interface, your class must implement all the functions defined by that interface.

The encapsulation of functionality into objects accessed through interfaces makes COM an open, extensible system. It is open in the sense that anyone can provide an implementation of a defined interface and anyone can develop an application that uses these interfaces, and extensible in the sense that new or extended interfaces can be defined without changing existing applications and that those applications that understand the new interfaces can exploit them while continuing to interoperate with older applications through the old interfaces.

Types of Interfaces

There are several types of interfaces. We will outline these types here.

IUnknown

All ActiveX objects must implement the IUnknown interface, because it manages all the other interfaces supported by the object. IUnknown is the most significant interface: Every COM component must implement it. The IUnknown interface contains three methods developed for the C++ programmer: QueryInterface, Addref, and Release. In C++, Query-Interface is used to find out about all the available interfaces an object exposes. When you want to use one of these interfaces, Addref is called. When finished with that particular interface, you call Release.

NOTE

Visual Basic doesn't deal directly with the IUnknown interface. When we want to call an interface using VB, we create an object and type a period after the object name to get all the exposed interfaces. We use the object and then, when we're done with it, we set it to Nothing, which is equivalent to using the Release method.

IDispatch

This interface derives from the IUnknown interface. It consists of functions that allow access to the methods and properties of ActiveX objects. IDispatch enables VB to manipulate the properties and methods of an object. IDispatch has two important methods: Invoke and GetIDOf-Names. GetIDOfNames receives the ID of an element to manipulate and Invoke gets the job done. For example, if you want to change the BackColor property on a label control, in VB you would call that label control, or write some code to search for that control, and then invoke the BackColor property on it. If you were a C++ developer, invoking this function would take several lines; VB only uses two.

Dual Interface

This occurs when you implement both an IDispatch and a vtable interface for an automation object. All VB components support dual interfaces, and you don't have to do additional work—or any work at all, for that matter.

It is important to note that interfaces are not classes. An interface is an abstract base class, so it is not instantiable. It is merely a template for the correct vtable structure for that interface, providing names and function signatures for each entry in the vtable—an interface definition carries no implementation. It must be implemented in order to be usable.

As mentioned earlier in this chapter, the vtable points to the addresses of all the properties and methods that are members of an object, including the member functions of the interfaces it supports. The first three entries of the vtable are the members of the IUnknown interface. The remaining entries are members of other supported interfaces. Figure 8.2 shows the vtable for an object that supports the IUnknown and IDispatch interfaces.

Microsoft strongly recommends that you provide a dual interface when exposing an object for automation. In a dual interface, the first three entries in the vtable are the members of IUnknown, the next four entries are the members of IDispatch, and the subsequent entries are the addresses of the members of the dual interface. Again, your VB components are all dual-interface components, so you are safe.

Figure 8.3 shows the vtable for an object that supports a dual interface named IMyInterface.

In addition to providing access to objects, automation also provides information about exposed objects. By using IDispatch or a type library, an ActiveX client or programming tool can determine which interfaces an object supports, as well as the names of its members. Type libraries, which are files or parts of files that describe the type of one or more ActiveX objects, are especially useful because they can be accessed at compile time. In Visual Basic, type libraries are combined into the same binary file.

Client and Object Interaction

So, how exactly do clients get access to your objects and interfaces? There are two ways:

- Use the IDispatch interface.
- Call one of the member functions in the object's virtual function table (vtable or VTBL) directly.

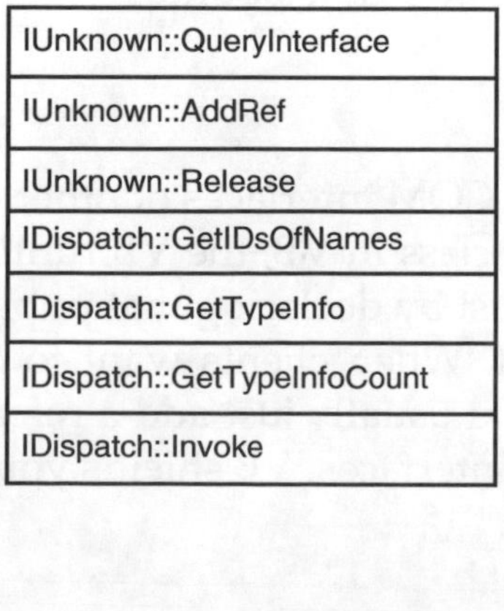

IUnknown::QueryInterface
IUnknown::AddRef
IUnknown::Release
IDispatch::GetIDsOfNames
IDispatch::GetTypeInfo
IDispatch::GetTypeInfoCount
IDispatch::Invoke

Figure 8.2 A conceptual view of an object with vtable.

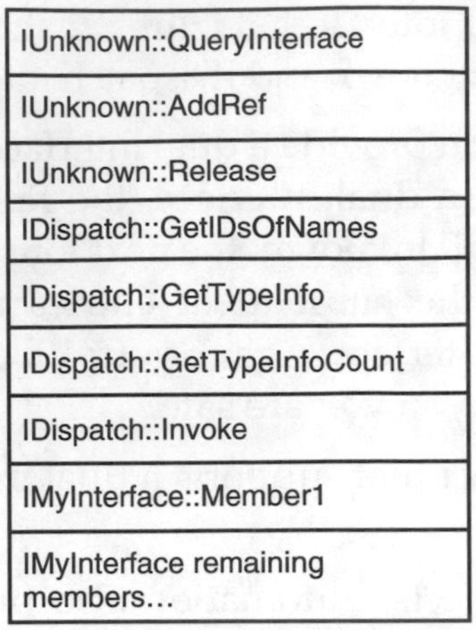

IUnknown::QueryInterface
IUnknown::AddRef
IUnknown::Release
IDispatch::GetIDsOfNames
IDispatch::GetTypeInfo
IDispatch::GetTypeInfoCount
IDispatch::Invoke
IMyInterface::Member1
IMyInterface remaining members…

Figure 8.3 A conceptual view of an object with a dual interface.

The IDispatch interface provides the tools some developers need to work between C/C++ applications and Microsoft Visual Basic applications. This interface essentially provides an indirect way to expose object methods and properties. The IDispatch method provides information about what methods an object supports, provides identifiers for those methods, and executes the methods on the caller's behalf if needed. Many objects built on OLE expose the IDispatch interface to support OLE Automation. Server applications must support the IDispatch interface for this purpose. When creating COM components in VB, you don't have to implement IDispatch: VB does this for you automatically.

The member function is called in the vtable directly when Visual Basic uses an offset into the vtable. Visual Basic uses vtable binding whenever possible. As a VB programmer, you don't have control over choosing the type of binding to perform. However, when you design your objects, if client applications declare variables using explicit class names, Visual Basic objects will always be vtable bound.

COM Activation

So how do clients activate and call the COM interfaces of other components? Well, when you create a public class in VB, the VB runtime creates a default interface for that class. Just by declaring that public class, you make your class COM compliant. When clients want to create a COM object in a server component, you usually just add a reference to the server to your project and call the interfaces. VB shields you from a lot of activation that happens behind the scenes. Let's take a look at what happens when you invoke a COM object.

There is a COM service called the Service Control Manager (SCM). When clients first request a server COM object, they pass the Object ID to SCM. SCM will go out to find and load the server by getting this information from the registry. SCM will then ask the server component to create the requested object, after which it takes the reference to the interface of the object and returns it to the client. Once SCM returns the reference to the client, SCM's job is complete. The client and server are now ready to interact. Of course, as mentioned earlier, as a VB developer you don't have to worry about SCM and the details of how COM works in VB. However, you should know about this as a COM developer.

There is an additional piece of detailed information you should be familiar with although you won't have to worry about implementing or calling it. It is something that happens behind the scenes every time you declare an object as New. When SCM asks the server component to create a new object, it is actually asking something called a Class Factory to create an uninitialized instance of the object class. Although this might sound interesting enough to watch it work, as a VB programmer you have no direct access to the Class Factory, and you don't have to implement it or work directly with it. However, it is important to know that it is there and how it works.

Object Models

As mentioned earlier in this chapter, the whole point of COM is to allow for reuse. In order to do this, your application needs to be organized in a way that makes it easy for people to find your COM interfaces. A VB application can have hundreds of classes and interfaces. Using your COM interfaces, you can group these and categorize them in a hierarchy in a way that makes it easier for people to find what they're looking for. Additionally, organizing your application allows you to expand your application's functionality and flexibility without disrupting other services.

An application consists of two things: content and functionality. Content refers to the forms the application contains and the data in the forms. Functionality refers to all the ways you can work with the content in the application. Before you can programmatically gain access to an application's content and functionality, it's important to understand how the content and functionality of the application are organized. Object models help us do this.

The content and functionality in an application are broken down into discrete units of related content and functionality called objects. You're already familiar with some of these objects—for example, Microsoft Word Documents and sections—as elements of the user interface.

The top-level object in an application is usually the Application object, which is the application itself. For example, Microsoft Word itself is the Application object in the Microsoft Word object model. The Application object contains other objects that you have access to only when the Application object is active. For example, the Word Application object contains Document objects. Because the Document object depends on the existence of the Word Application object for its own existence, the Document object is said to be the child of the Application object. A parent object can have multiple children; for example, the Word Window object has as children the Panes, Selection, and View objects. Likewise, a child object can have multiple parents; for example, the Word Windows collection object is the child of both the Application object and the Document object.

The way the objects that make up an application are arranged relative to each other, together with the way the content and functionality are divided among the objects, is called the object hierarchy or the object model. Object models represent the road map to your application. In addition to containing lower-level objects, each object in the hierarchy contains content and functionality that apply both to the object itself and to all objects below it in the hierarchy. The higher an object is in the hierarchy, the wider the scope of its content and functionality. You often don't get to what you think of as the contents of a file (such as the values on a Microsoft Excel worksheet or the text in a Word document) until you've navigated through quite a few levels in the object hierarchy, because this specific information belongs to a very specific part of the application. The content and functionality stored in an object are thus intrinsically appropriate to the scope of the object.

In summary, the content and functionality in an application are divided among the objects in the application's object model. Together, the objects in the hierarchy contain all the content and functionality in the application. Separately, the objects provide access to very specific areas of content and functionality.

Creating Object Models

The process of creating an object model for your application is not random. It requires a deep understanding of how your application functions and how it is architected. It will take some time to come up with a coherent object relationship. The way to get to this point is by carefully designing your classes and your class behaviors and identifying the appropriate interfaces to expose.

Once you've defined a class by creating a class module and giving it properties and methods, you can create any number of objects from that class. How do you keep track of the objects you create? The simplest way is to declare an object variable for each object you plan to create. Of course, this places a limit on the number of objects you can create.

In the beginning, you'll probably locate object variables, arrays, and collections in forms or standard modules, as you do with ordinary variables. As you add more classes, though, you'll probably discover that the objects you're using have clear relationships to each other.

Creating Containment Relationships

Containment occurs when an outer object behaves like a client to the inner object it contains. When the outer object wants to use the services of the inner object, it delegates implementation to the inner object's interfaces and uses the inner objects like its own functionality.

Object models give structure to an object-based program. By defining relationships between the objects you use in your program, an object model organizes your objects in a way that makes programming easier. Typically, an object model expresses the fact that some objects are "bigger" or more important than others. These objects can be thought of as containing other objects or as being made up of other objects.

For example, you might create a MyApplication object as the core of your program. You might want the MyApplication object to have other types of objects, such as Customer and Vendor objects, associated with it. You can define three classes, named MyApplication, Vendor and Customer, then give each appropriate properties and methods.

So far we've created just the objects without any relationship. Now we need to create the relationship and the model. You can create this relationship using the Object properties and the Collection object. Let's see what the code that establishes the hierarchy might look like.

```
' Place in the Declarations section of the MyApplication class
Public Name as String
Public Vendors As New Collection
Public Customers As New Collection
```

The following code will create and set the name and Credit Limit of the MyApplication object's Vendor object.

```
'Public myApp As New MyApplication
Sub Main
 myApp.Name = "MySoftware Company"
myApp.Vendor.Name = "My Favorite Vendor"
myApp.Vendor.CreditLimit = 50000

End Sub
```

NOTE Implementing an object property with public variables is sloppy. You could inadvertently destroy the Vendor object by setting the property to Nothing somewhere in your code. It's better to create object properties as read-only properties like this:

```
' Code for a more robust object property. Storage for
' the property is private, so it can't be set to
' Nothing from outside the object.

Private mVendort As New Vendor

Property Get Vendor() As Vendor
   ' The first time this property is called, mVendor
   ' contains Nothing, so Visual Basic will create a
   ' Vendor object.
   Set Vendor = mVendor
End If
```

In this section we discussed how to create some pieces of the object models using containment and delegation. This technique helps us simplify our object model. It is very critical to have a comprehensive object model that can explain what our application functionality is. However, it is even more important to make this object model simple. Containment and delegation is the way to accomplish this simplicity. Of course containment and delegation might not always work or be appropriate, so there will be cases where the hierarchy of objects is a pure one-to-one relationship.

Object Relationships

Object properties work well when the relationship between objects is one-to-one. It frequently happens, however, that an object of one type contains a number of objects of another type. In the MyApplication object model, the Vendors property is implemented as a Collection object, so that the MyApplication object can contain multiple Vendor objects. The following code fragment shows how new Vendor objects might be added to this collection.

```
Public Function NewVendor(Name, AcctNumber,CreditLimit) As Vendor
    Dim nVendor As New Vendor
  nVendor.Name = Name
  nVendor.Salary = AcctNumber
  nVendor.HireDate = CreditLimit
    ' Add to the collection, using the AcctNumber as a key.
myApp.Vendors.Add nVendor, CStr(AcctNumber)
    ' Return a reference to the new Vendor
    Set NewVendor = nVendor
End Function
```

The NewVendor function can be called as many times as necessary to create vendors for the business represented by the MyApplication object. The existing vendor can be listed at any time by iterating over the collection.

NOTE

Once again, this is not a very robust implementation. A better practice is to create your own collection classes and expose them as read-only properties. As you can see, the process of creating object models can be a tedious one, but the Class Builder utility included in the Professional and Enterprise editions of Visual Basic can generate much of the code you need to implement an object model. Class Builder creates robust object properties and collection classes and allows you to rearrange your model easily.

Implementing object relationships is sometimes confusing. It depends on how you want your object model to look and how you want others to use it. You will have to try different types of relationships until you decide on the optimum approach.

Parent Properties

When you have a reference to an object, you can get to the objects it contains by using its object properties and collections. It's also very useful to be able to navigate up the hierarchy to get to the object that contains the object you have a reference to. Navigating upward is usually done with Parent properties. The Parent property returns a reference to the object's container.

TIP

When you assign a Parent property to an object in a collection, don't use a reference to the Collection object. The real parent of the object is the object that contains the collection. If the Parent property points to the collection, you'll have to use two levels of indirection to get to the real parent—that is, obj.Parent.Parent instead of obj.Parent.

As mentioned before, there are several ways to present your object model. It is very difficult to suggest a cookie-cutter approach to developing application object models: You must study your application behavior and decide how you are going to present services in an easy-to-understand model. Don't get discouraged if it takes a while to complete; your clients will thank you for it.

Designing Your Application Object Model

It's important to understand an object's place in the object model, because before you can work with an object you have to navigate through the object model to get to it. This usually means you have to step down through all the higher objects in the object hierarchy to get to your desired object. The challenge is to create an object model that is simple enough and descriptive enough for clients to use. You want to make the objects that are most commonly used high-level objects and drive the next level of children from them. It is very confusing for clients when you spread objects that do the same thing all over your object model, or worse yet, bury them in deep hierarchies. Clients need to be able to get to your objects easily without having to type long descriptive locations and navigate up and down the hierarchical trees.

Designing good application object models comes with experience. The more applications you build and the more you understand how your users are going to be using your applications, the better your object models are going to get. The best advice we can give you is to follow the KISS (Keep It Simple, Stupid) approach. If you look at ADO's Object Model, which we will be examining later, you will find that it is very simple yet very powerful, and allows you to get to any interface very easily.

Object-Oriented Techniques

So, what do object-oriented techniques have to do with COM? On the face of it, nothing. There is nothing inherent in object-oriented techniques that would make COM function better. However, these techniques can help us concentrate on the business problems and come up with solutions in the form of objects that we can implement as COM components. Object-oriented systems have four attributes: encapsulation, abstraction, polymorphism, and inheritance.

The subject of object orientation and VB has long been discussed extensively. We are not here to argue whether Visual Basic is a pure object-oriented language or not. There are some areas where Visual Basic has no support for object-oriented features, but there are also others where it does.

In the following discussion of object orientation, we will be looking at how Visual Basic specifically implements some of the object-oriented techniques and how we can take advantage of these features to build well-designed COM-based N-tier applications.

Before we delve into some of the object-oriented techniques, let's get a quick overview of the four major concepts of OO. These concepts are not related to COM, because COM is new, but if we understand them in their pure forms, we will be able to discuss later how they relate to COM and how COM helps us implement these techniques.

Encapsulation. Encapsulation is the concept of containing properties and behavior together and only exposing interfaces to use these properties and behaviors.

Abstraction. Abstraction is the concept behind information hiding and black box routines. Abstraction helps in achieving improved representation of real world objects as compared to functions.

Polymorphism. Polymorphism is the concept of using an interface to perform different functions in different situations.

Inheritance. Inheritance is the concept of reusing functionality without having to reimplement it.

Let's take a look at each of these in more detail.

Encapsulation

Encapsulation is the idea behind the black box approach to building objects. The concept is that objects should separate their implementation details from their interfaces, so that when you examine an object and view it, you know what the object can do but you can't tell how it does it. This means that an object should completely contain any data it needs and it should also contain the code it needs to manipulate that data. COM interfaces hide this implementation detail, so when you examine an object all you see are interfaces and not implementation.

As discussed earlier, programs interact with objects through interfaces, using properties and methods. Clients wanting to use your objects and components will never work directly with the data owned by the object. This interaction between clients and objects is done by sending requests to the object. These requests are sent by other objects. The object reacts to these requests through methods and properties.

Visual Basic 6.0, as well as some earlier versions, provides full support for encapsulation through class modules, discussed in Chapter 2, "Introduction to COM." This means we can create classes that entirely hide their internal data and code, providing a well-established interface of properties and methods to the outside world.

For example, let's create a class with two properties.

```
Option Explicit

Private iDistance As Integer
Private iConsumption As Integer

Public Property Let Distance(D As Single)
   iDistance = D
End Property

Public Property Let Consumption(C As Single)
   iConsumption = C
End Property
```

In this class we have created two properties, one called Distance and the other called Consumption. Notice that these names are generic. You could rename them Miles and Gallons, but that would limit you from using your program in countries where kilometers and liters are used. The point of these properties is not that they are generic in their description, but rather that they hide the implementation of how the efficiency of the car is calculated. For example, if you have a method that divides the two properties to give back miles per gallon or kilometers per liter, the client using these interfaces would never know if you decided to change the way you calculated the car's efficiency. Clients will continue to set these properties and invoke the methods, and the result will change, based on the implementation.

Abstraction

Abstraction is the technique of isolating complexities and focusing on the necessary. It is a methodology for understanding complex issues without focusing on details, in much the same manner as a map. A map gives you direction by pointing out the major areas you need to look for. It does not give you all the details of the street—for instance, the cars parked on it or the pedestrians. COM concepts help in bringing the concept of abstraction to life. You could say that COM makes abstraction real.

Abstraction is a guideline. Let's explain what we mean here. We said that encapsulation provides the explicit boundary between an object's interface and its implementation details. Encapsulation puts these details into a "capsule," providing developers of abstraction the freedom to implement the abstraction in any way consistent with the interface. Abstraction provides business value; encapsulation protects abstractions.

If you provide good abstraction, users won't be tempted to peek at the object implementation. There is nothing more frustrating than a poorly developed abstraction that is encapsulated. When a developer encapsulates a bad abstraction, users will continually attempt to violate the abstraction barrier.

Providing good abstraction is the key to software reuse. You simply can't reuse something that is bad.

Polymorphism

Polymorphism is the feature that allows programmers to use the same method name for many different objects. Each object can have its own method of any given name. When a method is called, the method code in the invoked object will be used.

Each method is a part of an object. It is possible to have the same method available in different objects. For example, if the method Get-Balance is part of the General Account class, every checking account and savings account will have this method.

It is possible, and often desirable and necessary, to write a program that uses accounts (checking, savings, loans, IRAs) without knowing which particular class each account belongs to. The ability to write general code like this, calling a method without knowing in advance which object is being called, is what polymorphism is all about.

COM interfaces can be derived from other COM interfaces using single interface inheritance. In fact, all COM interfaces directly or indirectly inherit from IUnknown. Besides IUnknown, there are only two other important base interfaces that are commonly inherited from: IDispatch and IPersist. Otherwise, interface inheritance in COM is rarely used. Surprisingly, interface inheritance in COM has nothing to do with the polymorphism COM supports.

For example, assume a client holds a reference to an interface called IDispatch. In reality, the interface the client refers to can be of any subtype of IDispatch. In other words, the vtable may contain additional methods over and above those required by IDispatch. However, there is no way for the client to find this out. If the client wants a more specific interface, it has to use QueryInterface, the mechanism that clients use to find out about the features the object supports. However, in VB we don't explicitly call QueryInterface. It is all done behind the scenes when we do an object assignment.

If you are using a language such as C++, you will have to write code such as the following line to query for object interfaces. We promise this is the only C++ line of code in this book. The reason we include it is to demonstrate how Visual Basic spoils its programmers.

```
HRESULT QueryInterface(REFIID riid, void **ppvObject);
```

In VB you don't need to write any code to query for object interfaces, because VB automatically and transparently to you calls QueryInterface when you do an object assignment. The following VB code provides an example:

```
Dim IMyNewObject as ItheMotherObject
Set IMyNewObject = Something
IMyNewObject.Method
```

Why is it important to know this? Because QueryInterface is how versioning happens in COM. When you create interfaces for your components and start evolving them over time, whether by adding or removing interfaces, clients will always get these changes the next time they query the component.

Polymorphism and Late Binding

We've discussed binding when calling a polymorphic method, which is just another way of referring to methods that mean the same thing but to different object. Let's say we created a class with methods such as a Save, Delete, and Update and called it CDataManipulation. Different objects such as a customer, vendor, or product would react to these methods in different ways because the implementation for each of these methods is different.

Let's examine the following routine.

```
Public Sub Save(AnyObject As Object)
  AnyObject.Save Me
End Sub
```

This code will run whether you pass it to the Customer, Vendor, or Product object simply because it accepts the Object parameter and will figure out which object's Save it should call. This mechanism is referred to as Late Binding or IDispatch binding. With IDispatch, the client has no pre-existing information about the object. During compilation it assumes the code you are calling is correct. It then attempts to execute the code at run-time and trap for runtime errors. This is a step backward from the familiar syntax and type checking we have come to expect from Visual Basic.

An IDispatch binding also requires both the client and the server to marshal their arguments into a consistent form that is understood by both. In most cases, this means that arguments are copied into and out of variants. This not only slows down IDispatch, but it also limits the data types that can be passed using this technique.

Polymorphism and Early Binding

We called the methods in our previous CDataManipulation class using the Late Binding technique. We also said this was not efficient. There is another technique, called interface inheritance using early binding, that is much more efficient. We mentioned earlier that we can have access to interfaces either through IDispatch or directly through the vtable. If Visual Basic can tell at compile time what object a property or method belongs to, it can look up the vtable address of the member in the type library. Type information provided in the form of a type library is required to perform early binding. This type information allows VB to perform compile-time syntax and type checking. At runtime, this type of binding is faster, because the entry points for the objects are already known and the data types and syntax have already been verified. The key to using this technique is a keyword in Visual Basic called Implements. We will see an example when we discuss interface inheritance in the next section.

Inheritance

Inheritance has always been associated with reuse. Most developers who want to reuse some piece of functionality and have worked with pure object-oriented languages usually think of inheritance in the form of implementation inheritance, meaning including the one class implementation into their own class implementation. Visual Basic does not support implementation inheritance. However, COM VB supports a different type of inheritance called interface inheritance.

Inheriting Interfaces

The Implements keyword—the key to interface inheritance—causes the class to accept COM QueryInterface calls for the specified interface ID. Visual Basic does not implement derived classes or interfaces. When you implement an interface, you must include all the public procedures involved. A missing member in an implementation of an interface or class can cause an error. If you don't place code in one of the procedures in a class you are implementing, you can raise the appropriate error (Const E_NOTIMPL = &H80004001) so a user of the implementation understands that a member is not implemented.

Interface inheritance lets us inherit the interface of one class into a new class, not the implementation of the object. Although this is a great feature, one of the disadvantages of interface inheritance is that COM does not allow you to extend that interface.

Maybe in the future, when VB supports full inheritance, we will be able to inherit implementation as we do in other object-oriented languages, in addition to inheriting interfaces via COM. Until that happens, we have to live with interface inheritance.

Let's see how we apply the Implements keyword and inherit the interfaces of a component called Account. If we look at an Account class, we'll find an interface that includes elements appropriate for any type of account. So let's design a class with an interface we can use in different types of accounts, such as checking accounts, saving accounts, and any other types of accounts we add to the system.

```
Option Explicit

Public Property Get AccountBalance() As Long

End Property

Public Property Get AccountStatus() As String

End Property

Public Property Get AccountRating() As Integer

End Property
```

Notice we did not add any implementation code inside these properties, meaning we did not specify what happens when the AccountBalance property is called. We don't need to, because we are inheriting the interface.

Now we can create a new class, Checking, and inherit the interface from the Account class by using the Implements keyword.

```
Option Explicit

Implements Account

Private Property Get Account_AccountBalance() As Long
 Account_AccountBalance = 1235
End Property

Private Property Get Account_AccountStatus() As String
 Account_AccountStatus = "Active"
End Property

Private Property Get Account_AccountRating() As Integer
 Account_AccountRating = 3
End Property
```

Instead of declaring AccountBalance, AccountStatus, and AccountRating directly, we need to make them private in scope and put Account_ in front of each name so Visual Basic knows these routines belong to the Account interface.

We might also create a Saving class, again based on the Account interface:

```
Option Explicit

Implements Account
```

TIP

When you add the word **Implements** followed by the class name, and then go to the object combo box in your code window, you will see the class name you've implemented. We mentioned earlier that you will have to place that class name in front of your properties manually. However, in the Interface class (although there is no code in it), if you place just a comment line, VB will automatically add the class interface prefix to all your properties without your manual intervention.

```
Private Property Get Account_AccountBalance () As Long
 Account_AccountBalance = 15986
End Property

Private Property Get Account_AccountStatus () As String
 Account_AccountStatus = "Active"
End Property
```

```
Private Property Get Account_AccountRating () As Integer
  Account_AccountRating = 5
End Property
```

You can now write code that will use these two classes in this nice elegant way, accepting two types of accounts and summing them up:

```
Public Function GetTotalBalance(Checking As Account, Savings As _
Account)
  GetTotalBalance = Checking.AccountBalance + Savings.AccountBalance
End Function
```

What we've created here is different classes that have both inherited the same interface from Account. This technique allows us to write client code that treats all the objects the same—even though they have different implementations.

Delegation and Aggregation

The way to attain reusability in Visual Basic is through a process called delegation, also referred to as containment. Many object-oriented design books talk about reuse as two different kinds of relationships:

- is-a relationships, where a class is an enhanced version of another class
- has-a relationships, where one class has features of another class

Because Visual Basic doesn't support inheritance, it forces you to define both kinds of relationships with delegation. Although delegation accomplishes the same thing as inheritance, inheritance is automatic while delegation is usually manual. When using inheritance to model is-a relationships, you have to write code for the new features only. When using delegation for is-a relationships, you delegate everything; even the methods and properties that don't change.

COM supports another reuse technique called aggregation. Aggregation means combining several inner objects so that they appear to be part of an outer object. This is a collective rather than a hierarchical organization. If you tried to combine a checking account, a savings account, and a loan using this method, you'd end up duplicating your code and efforts, and it would be very difficult for your users to know which object to use. Although Visual Basic doesn't directly support this feature, you can get some of the advantages of it with the new Implements statement.

ADO COM Components

No system is complete without data access. Moving data between components is referred to as data marshaling. The mechanism recommended by Microsoft to manipulate and use data in your application is called Active Data Objects (ADO). ADO was designed to be the only data access method for working with local as well as remote databases.

Through COM, ADO exposes some interfaces that make communicating data between components easy. In the following sections we will explain the ADO object model and how components use ADO to ask for, receive, and change data from other components. We will also discuss the different techniques used by client components and server components.

To gain access to ADO 2.0 objects in Visual Basic, set a reference to the appropriate ADO type library. There are two ADO type libraries. One is called ADODB and is contained in MSADO15.DLL. It appears in the References dialog box (available from the Project menu) as Microsoft ActiveX Data Objects 2.0 Library. The other is called ADOR and is contained in MSADOR15.DLL. It appears in the References dialog as Microsoft ActiveX Data Objects Recordset 2.0 Library.

ADODB is the more feature rich of the two; it contains the main ADO objects and is the library you'll probably want to use in most circumstances—we will discuss where and when later in the chapter. ADOR is a lightweight subset of the ADODB type library that supports only Recordsets. We will also explain when and how to use ADOR later in the chapter.

The ADO Object Model

Now that you are familiar with what object models are, let's examine the ADO 2.0 object model. Understanding the object model will make your task easier when trying to dig up the appropriate function to use in ADO.

TIP

You can learn more about the features and parameters of the ADO objects by examining them using Visual Basic's Object Browser by pressing F2 while inside VB.

The ADO object model is composed of eight objects:

Command object. Holds information about different types of command (these commands are discussed in detail in Chapter 11, "The Database Server").

Connection object. Holds information about a data provider. The Connection object contains the information on schemas as well as some functionality such as transaction control.

Error object. Holds extended information when an error occurs.

Field object. Holds information about a single column of data in a Recordset.

Parameter object. Holds a single parameter for a parameterized Command object. The Command object has a Parameters collection to contain all of its Parameter objects.

Property object. Holds a provider-defined characteristic of an ADO object. ADO objects can have two kinds of properties: built-in properties that are native to ADO and dynamic properties that are not native to ADO and are defined by the underlying data provider. These appear in the Properties collection of the appropriate ADO object.

Recordset object. Holds records returned from a query as well as a cursor into those records.

You will be using most of these objects frequently, but when talking about moving data between components we need to focus on the Recordset object. This object is the placeholder for the data. Let's look more closely at how Recordsets are constructed and how we can manipulate them.

Understanding Recordsets

The Recordset object provides methods for manipulating result sets. It allows you to add, update, delete, and scroll through records in the Recordset. Each record can be retrieved and updated using the Fields collection and the Field objects. Updates on the Recordset object can be in an immediate or batch mode. When a Recordset object is created, a cursor is automatically opened.

The Recordset object allows you to specify the cursor type and cursor location for fetching the result set. With the CursorType property, you can specify whether the cursor is forward-only, static, keyset-driven, or dynamic. The cursor type determines whether a Recordset object can be scrolled forward and backward or updated. The cursor type also affects the visibility of changed records.

By default, the cursor type is read-only and forward-only. If you only need to read the data once in a forward fashion, you do not have to change the default cursor type. Otherwise, you can choose one of the cursors to suit your needs.

You can also specify whether to use the server or client cursor with the CursorLocation property. The cursor location plays a big role in disconnected Recordsets, as discussed in Chapter 9, "DCOM Details." A Recordset object can be created through the Execute method of the Connection or Command object, as we discuss in detail in Chapter 11, "The Database Server."

Using ADODB

Now let's look at how components exchange data using ADO. When data is requested in an N-tier application, a client component asks a server component to retrieve a set of records from a database and return the records to the client component. The server component needs to make the call to the database using ADO and retrieve the records to the client. This sounds like something that happens frequently with applications. In such a scenario, ADO is the most efficient way to send data back and forth between clients and server because the client and the server components happen to be on the same physical machine, although they are logically separate.

There are alternative methods for passing data back and forth between clients and servers when they are not located on the same machine. We'll talk about these methods in Chapter 9, "DCOM Details."

Let's look at an example that shows how to use the Recordset object to open a connection and retrieve records from a table.

On the server we have created a function called GetInfo, which will return an ADO Recordset object. Notice that in order to have full control of all the ADO objects we need to use the ADODB version of ADO. You will see this in the declaration line of the code that follows. This function accepts the name of the customer to retrieve security information for that customer. The first thing we need to do is to declare a Recordset object, a Connection object, and an Error object. We then set our connection string to the database that we are going to be working with.

```
Public Function GetInfo (ByVal CustName As String) As ADODB.Recordset
Dim rsset As ADODB.Recordset
Dim cn As ADODB.Connection
Dim connectstring As String
Dim anerror As ADODB.Error
Dim Sql1 As String
Dim Sql2 As String
Dim sSecurityAccess As String
```

Next we need to set the ADO connection string and cursor location and invoke the Open method on the connection. The final step is to execute the SQL statement by calling the Execute method and setting the result of our Resultset object. The final line of code sets the return value of the function to the Recordset.

```
'setup connect string
 connectstring = "Provider=Microsoft.Jet.OLEDB.3.51;Persist Security
Info=False;Data Source=C:\MyApp\Application.mdb"

    'SQL statement for Recordset
    Sql1 = "Select AccessType FROM tlbSecurity where _
CustomerName='" & CustName & "'"

    'create connection object
    Set cn = New ADODB.Connection

    'assign connectstring to connection object
    cn.ConnectionString = connectstring

    'specify client side cursor
    cn.CursorLocation = adUseClient

    'open connection
    cn.Open

    Set rsset = cn.Execute(Sql1)
Set GetInfo = rsset
    End Function
```

That's all it takes to have a server component get the results back from the database when passed a request from the client. We have explained the server side component before looking at the client because the client's code is even simpler.

Now let's move on to the client implementation and see how we can use the lighter-weight ADO object to collect the data coming back from the server. You will be surprised how simple the implementation is and how efficient moving data back and forth between clients and server can be.

Using ADOR

The client side of the previous example uses ADOR. This is the lighter-weight ADO object. ADOR is great to use on clients when all they need to see and manipulate are Recordsets. The clients simply request data and can browse and display it when they receive it. In our example the client passes the server component a customer name and the server component retrieves the customer security information.

Let's walk through the code to see how it is done. The first thing you need to do to the client is declare an ADO Recordset object. This is different than what we did on the server component, where we declared the full-blown ADO object. On the client you choose the ADOR.Recordset declaration.

```
Dim rsset As ADOR.Recordset
Dim sCustName As String
Dim oCustInfo As CCustomerInformation
```

Next you call the GetInfo function (which we wrote earlier) on the server, passing it the customer name you are interested in. Remember we said the server component would return a Recordset. On the client we need to declare an object that will hold this Recordset. Once the function call returns from the server, we now have a Recordset that we can browse.

```
sCustName = List1.Text
    Set oCustInfo = New CCustomerInformation
    Set rsset = oCustInfo.GetInfo(sCustName)
    'Show and populate the form with the customer information
```

Because the Fields collection is part of the Recordset, all we have to do is call the Fields method, passing it the name of the database field we are interested in and populating the UI with this information. Finally, if the Recordset being returned contained more than one record, we could easily navigate through it using the MoveNext and MovePrevious methods.

```
frmSecurity.Show
frmSecurity.Text1.Text = rsset.Fields("SecurityLevel")
frmSecurity.Text2.Text = rsset.Fields("AccessRight")
```

As mentioned earlier, had the client and the server been on separate machines, we would have evaluated the situation and determined whether or not ADO was the most efficient way of sending data back and forth. Until the next chapter, you can safely use ADO in most scenarios.

Winding Up

As you can see, COM is not an easy or limited technology to use. COM will continue to grow and expand. As we speak, COM+ is making its way out to the world, and this is not the end—there will undoubtedly be more enhancements, features, and changes. In this chapter we looked closely at how COM works and how you can start architecting your application based on a foundation that will allow you to grow as these technologies grow.

It is very important to understand the reasoning behind the concepts implemented in this chapter. These concepts can be expanded and enhanced as you get deeper into COM, but it is very important to first understand them by rereading them and reapplying them into small prototypes before you jump into implementing them in large-scale systems.

DCOM is coming up next. Most of the concepts discussed in this chapter will be carried over and expanded upon in the next chapter. So be prepared to discuss marshaling and security, among other things.

CHAPTER 9

DCOM Details

D COM is similar to COM in terms of how components are built. The challenge in building DCOM components is how the components are designed. Two important issues face DCOM developers: how to secure DCOM components and how to optimize their use. Because DCOM components can run on any distributed environment regardless of location, the servers that run these components can be situated across the hall or across the country. Finding the proper technique for sending data across networks or across the Internet is most of the battle with DCOM.

In this chapter we look at how DCOM works under the hood and explain the mechanism DCOM uses to communicate. We also discuss some of the techniques used to design efficient DCOM components. Because DCOM components run on the server, we look at a new type of Visual Basic project that generates remote components that run under Microsoft Internet Information Server (IIS).

In Chapter 8, "Understanding COM Internals," we talked about using ADO to send data back and forth between components located on the same machine. We also mentioned that we would suggest some alternatives to marshaling data with remote components, such as using disconnected Recordsets, creating your own Recordsets, and using user-defined types. In this chapter we explore these alternatives.

Another added complexity in designing remote components is the concept of error handling. This chapter explores some of the more effective error-handling techniques and explores how to communicate errors back to the clients. Finally, we discuss security considerations and how security works to authenticate clients using DCOM components.

Here are the areas that we cover in detail in this chapter:

- DCOM internals
- DCOM design guidelines
- IIS applications
- Recordsets and other techniques
- Remote error handling
- DCOM and NT security

Let's get started!

Inside DCOM

Recall from Chapter 3, "Introduction to DCOM," that marshaling is necessary for out-of-proc components to communicate. This involves using a proxy and a stub. Let's take a look at how this process works and who makes it happen. DCOM is entirely dependent on Microsoft Remote Procedure Call (RPC) to provide its distributed capabilities. In fact, it is RPC that turns COM into DCOM. Grasping what this key service does is essential to understanding the inner workings of DCOM.

RPC is a procedure that, when called by clients, executes a function on a remote machine and then returns with results from that function when completed. RPC is the mechanism DCOM components use to communicate. Distributed processes pass controls and data between application processes just as they do for local procedure calls. There is an obvious difference between the way distributed applications and single-processor systems pass data. Single-processor systems can pass data between procedures by passing only the address or the name of the data item. Because these systems run in the same execution environment, storage formats and data structures are usually the same, and the data is effectively shared. The data in this case may be in shared memory. If an application is distributed, the data must actually be packaged and moved across the network with the call in order for it to be used by the called process. In this sense, RPC can be regarded as middleware. RPC can be used without DCOM to support distributed processing. In other words, a developer could build distributed applications only with RPC. In the DCOM context, Microsoft uses RPC to support remote function calls across the network, and RPC becomes invisible to the application developer. Thus, in the context of DCOM, RPC is enabling middleware used by Microsoft.

RPC's prime duty is to ensure that requests for a function with its parameter and the resulting reply are transmitted across the network. The RPC runtime environment reduces the data structures passed into a buffer for transmission, converts the individual data elements to a format used during transmission, and then makes calls to the network interface using the appropriate network protocol to coordinate the sending of the packaged data to the called process.

So how does all of this relate to DCOM? What happens to turn a method call into an RPC? When a programmer uses DCOM, he or she invokes a method on an interface using certain arguments. The method call is translated within DCOM into a call to a remote procedure call. The procedure in this case is equivalent to a method found within a component. Similarly, when a DCOM service is invoked using a method call on a DCOM interface, this too is translated internally into a remote procedure call on a method within a DCOM service component. This translation is easy because the paradigm used for component invocation and that used for remote procedure calls are so similar. When the programmer uses components, he or she is actually looking at a group of methods described by an interface. When the programmer uses a remote procedure call, he or she is looking at only one of those methods. As procedures are also defined by interfaces, the similarities between RPCs and component invocations are obvious. In fact, the difference is that the interfaces used for component invocation group methods together around the concept of the class, whereas with RPC interfaces no grouping takes place and each method has one interface.

We have looked at what RPC is and how it relates to DCOM. Now let's take a look at the steps that RPC goes through to accomplish its task:

1. Pack and unpack the data in the message.
2. Perform data format conversion.
3. Pack and unpack the data into buffers ready for transmission.

4. Establish session.

5. Handle network calls.

6. Coordinate transmission.

7. Handle faults.

These steps make up the general approach taken by RPC to support DCOM. As a programmer, you rarely see the effects of what RPC does. Sessions, network synchronization, network calls, and data format translation are all handled automatically for you by this piece of technology, and you get the results of its error-handling services. Only when dealing with error-handling do you actually communicate with RPC and use its services directly, and only with error-handling is the service not automatic.

Running COM Components Remotely

There is one more piece of detail about DCOM that is worth mentioning. Although DCOM components run as out-of-process servers, the steps taken to build and implement these components are not entirely different from those for building and implementing COM components. However, there are cases where you will need to build DCOM components as DLLs and make them run remotely. To do this, you will use a surrogate process that runs on the remote machine. In Chapter 10, "Inside Microsoft Transaction Server," we refer to MTS as a surrogate process. If you have to run your COM components under MTS, there is a system called a surrogate that can work in a similar manner to MTS by allowing COM objects to be activated on remote machines. This system allows clients to create and invoke the methods of objects on other machines. These components can be activated remotely using the system surrogate support (D11Surrogate) in DCOM for Windows95 and Window NT 4.0 with SP2 or SP3.

In order to accomplish this you will need to make some changes to the Windows registry as follows:

```
HKEY_LOCAL_MACHINE\SOFTWARE\Classes\APPID\
{AppID_value}\D11surrogate = surrogate_path
```

If an empty string is specified in the entry of the D11Surrogate, the system-supplied surrogate is used; otherwise the value specifies the path of the surrogate to be used.

The Difference between COM and DCOM

The purpose of this chapter is to help you fully understand the impact of utilizing previously used techniques on local components and enable you to apply these techniques to remote components. Although the design of DCOM and COM components is the same in terms of how to create and compile them, there is a major difference in how you effectively use these components once they are moved to a remote location. The main themes of this chapter are efficiency and security.

So, with these two themes in mind, let's dig into some of the guidelines that can help us design DCOM components without suffering great performance degradation.

Marshaling Revisited

A client and an in-process component share the same address space, so calls to the methods of an in-process component can use the client's stack to pass arguments. This is not possible for an out-of-process component. Instead, the method arguments must be moved across the boundary between the two processes. This is called marshaling.

A client and an out-of-process component communicate via a proxy/stub mechanism, as shown in Figure 9.1. The proxy and stub handle the marshaling and unmarshaling of arguments passed to methods of the component; they are completely transparent to the client.

Marshaling is slower than passing parameters within a process, especially when parameters are passed by reference. It's not possible to pass a pointer to another address space, so a copy must be marshaled to the component's address space. When the method is finished, the data must be copied back.

Referencing Objects

When you declare methods for objects provided by an out-of-process component, always use the ByVal method argument to declare arguments that contain object references. The reason for this is that cross-process marshaling of object references requires significantly less overhead if it's one-way. Declaring an argument ByRef means that the

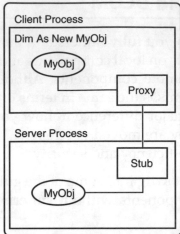

Figure 9.1 A client communicating to an out-of-process component.

object reference must be marshaled to your component, and then back to the client when the method is finished.

However, you will need to use the ByRef method argument if the method replaces the client's object reference with a reference to another object.

If the method you declare requires a property value supplied by an object that belongs to the client, declare the argument with the data type of the property rather than the object's class. Marshaling an object reference requires significantly more overhead than marshaling a simple data type.

Data Types

It's common practice to declare parameters in Visual Basic procedures with ByRef if they are used to pass large strings and Variant arrays, even if the procedure doesn't make any changes to the parameter. It's much faster to pass a four-byte pointer to the data than to make a copy of the entire string or array and pass a pointer to the copy.

This practice works within the address space of your own process—that is, within your own program or with an in-process component—because the method to which you pass the parameter can use the pointer to access the data directly. Cross-process marshaling reverses this practice. Data for a ByRef method argument is copied into the component's address space, and the method is passed a pointer to the local copy of the data.

The method uses the pointer to modify the copy. When the method ends, the data for any ByRef parameters is copied back into the client's address space. Thus a parameter declared ByRef is passed cross-process twice per method call. If you expect users to pass large strings or Variant arrays to a method of your component, and the method does not modify the data, declare the parameter ByVal for an out-of-process component and ByRef for an in-process component.

If you declare a parameter of a method ByRef in an out-of-process component, developers using the component cannot avoid the effects of marshaling by putting parentheses around the parameter or by using the ByVal keyword when they call the method. Visual Basic creates a copy of the data in this situation, but since Automation has no way of knowing the data is just a copy, it marshals the copy back and forth between processes. The data is thus copied a total of three times.

Parameter Passing

Properties make objects easy to use, but setting properties for an out-of-process component can be slow, as we will see in the section on Record-sets later in this chapter. When a client uses an out-of-process component, the extra overhead of cross-process marshaling makes it faster to call one method with five parameters than to set five properties and then call a method.

In cases where users of your component frequently set a group of properties before calling a particular method, you can add a group of optional parameters to the method, one for each property. If one of these parameters is supplied, the method sets the corresponding property before proceeding. If you give the optional parameters the names of the properties they are used to set, they can be used as named parameters—also known as named arguments.

New Types of VB Applications

With the increasing popularity of the Web, Microsoft has loaded Visual Basic 6 with tons of new features that support component-based Web development. In Visual Basic 6 there is a new type of application called the IIS application. Because DCOM components can reside on any remote servers, including Web servers, communication with these DCOM components is critical. We wanted to give you a perspective on how to build DCOM components for Web servers, how clients communicate with them, and how data exchange happens.

IIS Applications

IIS applications run on the Web server. They respond to requests sent by the browser. An IIS application's user interface is based on HTML. This may include DHTML, DHTML projects, ActiveX controls, or any other browser-supported technology (see Figure 9.2). The user does not interact directly with an IIS application. Instead, by clicking on a link, the user interacts with the HTML page inside the browser, which sends a request to the IIS application on the server. The application receives this request and sends a response. The browser then receives this response and displays a new page. *IIS applications are browser independent.* Figure 9.3 shows the architecture of a VB IIS application.

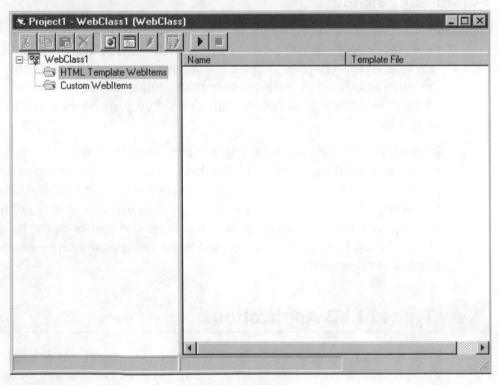

Figure 9.2 An IIS application with a default Webclass.

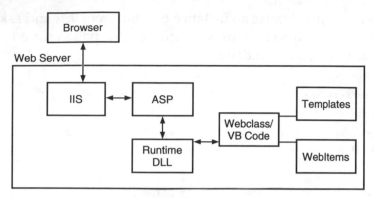

Figure 9.3   The anatomy of an IIS application.

Webclasses

Webclasses are VB components exposed by the IIS application DLL that you build. They live on the server and respond to browser requests. An IIS application must have one or more Webclasses. You add a Webclass by adding a Webclass designer to your project. A Webclass is associated with one and only one client for its entire life cycle. Webclasses typically contain Webitems and the code that delivers Webitems to a client. A Webitem is generally an HTML page, but it can be a MIME-type file, such as an image or a .wav file.

Visual Basic creates a logical instance of the Webclass for each client that accesses it. However, for each client, the Webclass is capable of maintaining state between requests. So, if you want, you can tell your Webclass to stay active for the duration of the client's session, or you can tell it to shut down as soon as it sends a response to the client's request. You do this by setting the StateManagement property of the Webclass to either wcNoState or wcRetainInstance.

If your Webclass is set to stay alive between requests, the end user must have a browser that supports cookies and cookies must be enabled.

Invoking Webclasses

For each Webclass you create, VB creates an ASP page. The client (the browser) starts your Webclass by requesting this ASP page using a URL such as http://www.company.com/directory1/page1.asp.

The ASP page in turn creates an instance of your Webclass and asks it to process the user's request. Here is a sample ASP page created by VB with manually added comments:

```
<%
Response.Buffer=True
Response.Expires=0

If (VarType(Application("~WC~WebclassManager")) = 0) Then
'If there is not already a Webclass Manager created, create one
    Application.Lock
    If (VarType(Application("~WC~WebclassManager")) = 0) Then
    Set Application("~WC~WebclassManager") = _
Server.CreateObject("WebclassRuntime.WebclassManager") _
'create Webclass Manager object
    End If
    Application.UnLock
End If

Application("~WC~WebclassManager").ProcessNoStateWebclass _
"VSlice1.CHomePage", _
'Ask the Manager to run your Webclass(VSlice1.CHomePage)
        Server, _
'Pass required objects to provide context for request processing
        Application, _
        Session, _
        Request, _
        Response
%>
```

Figure 9.4 shows the relationship between ASP pages, Webclasses, and Webitems. Note that each Webclass is associated with an ASP page.

Working with Templates

Let's say the client sends a request asking for the home page. Your Webclass then has to send back an HTML page with the following user-specific information:

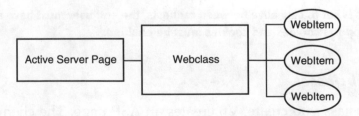

Figure 9.4   Relationship between ASP and Webclasses.

- User name
- List of companies the user is interested in
- List of most recent events under each company
- List of tasks for the user

One way to do this is to gather this information, then put some HTML tags around it and send it to the user. This is simple to implement but requires that the HTML tags be hard coded as strings or string constants inside your code. Can you imagine what it would be like to maintain the HTML for the home page? The simplest things, like adding a GIF, would require change to VB code and recompilation—bad! A better way is to put all the HTML in a separate text file and call it a template, with placeholders for the data. The placeholders can be tags that you invent, for example $$USERNAME$$ or PUTUSERNAMEHERE, and so on. Then you can write a routine that opens this template file, reads a line in, and examines it for placeholders. If it finds a placeholder, it will replace it with actual data (for instance, the actual user name), then simply send the entire line to the browser as part of the response (HTML page). This is certainly much better, because now you can change the template without affecting the VB code. We have separated data from formatting.

DCOM templates are like other types of templates, with one big plus: You do not need to write your own code to read from the template file and scan for placeholders! Instead, you use a prefix of your choice for all your placeholders, such as WC@ or PLACEHOLDER. Then, by calling the WriteTemplate method on your template object, the Webclass Manager will scan the template looking for placeholders and fire the event:

```
templatename_ProcessTag(ByVal TagName As String, TagContents As _
String, SendTags As Boolean)
```

This event lets you know which placeholder needs to be processed (TagName). You can then place relevant data (for example, the actual user name) in TagContents; this data will be sent to the browser. This makes dynamic HTML pages easy to implement and maintain.

The following is a sample ProcessTag event used for the GroupView page. The code sets a different view of the groups based on a supplied tag.

```
Select Case TagName
    Case "WC@GROUPS"
        GetGroupList TagContents, URLFor("TplGrpView")
    Case "WC@DATA"
        GetRecords g_strSelectedGroup, TagContents, _
CLng(Session("CurrentPage"))
    Case "WC@NEXT"
        SetupPaging 1, TagContents, CInt(Session("CurrentPage")), _
URLFor("TplGrpView")
    Case "WC@PREV"
        SetupPaging 2, TagContents, CInt(Session("CurrentPage")), _
URLFor("TplGrpView")
    Case "WC@PAGENUM"
        DisplayPageNum CLng(Session("CurrentPage")), TagContents
End Select
```

Templates are the key to separating data and format. You can use any HTML editor, for example HomeSite, to create templates. Once you add a template—say, mytemplate.htm—VB makes a copy of it and calls it mytemplate1.htm. This copy gets added to your project. If you want to go back and edit the file outside of VB, make sure you edit the copy, not the original.

Custom WebItems

You can add custom Webitems rather than files to your Webclass program resources. Custom Webitems are containers that group a set of code procedures you want the Webclass to be able to access from multiple places in the application. Custom Webitems can provide a good way to encapsulate code in an IIS application that produces a frequently used HTML response, such as a standard header or a table. Custom Webitems can allow you to send a response to the browser when a template is not available. They can also help you produce more modular or structured code.

To make an element invoke a custom event, use the URLFor function to create the URL to that event, as in the following example:

```
Response.Write "<A HREF=""" &
URLFor(CustomWebItem1,"CustomEventName") & """></A>"
```

IIS Applications and VB Forms

Although IIS applications are a type of a VB application, they cannot contain VB forms. Even if you did have forms, where would you display them? This is a server app that can run unattended, so there is no point in displaying forms on the server. As far as the user interface goes, you have to send HTML in responses to the browser's requests. You can, however, include DHTML pages in your IIS application.

Communicating with DCOM Components

In Chapter 8, "Understanding COM Internals," we exclusively used ADO Recordsets to send and receive data from clients to server components. We also mentioned that this technique is fine when servers reside on the same machine as the client and we use COM rather than DCOM to communicate, and we referred to another technique that might work better when DCOM is used. Well, here we are, ready to introduce you to a few concepts that make data marshaling more efficient. Remember what we said earlier in this chapter about using previously learned techniques more efficiently.

When marshaling data between processes, you need to keep two guidelines in mind. Let's look at them:

Connect as late as you can and break as early as you can.   When you communicate with remote components, make your connection as late as you can and break the connection as early as you can. The objective is to minimize the number of resources on the server. Connections are considered valuable resources, so don't take them for granted and hold on to them forever.

Minimize network trips.   One of the reasons remote applications occasionally do not perform well is that they are designed as local applications. The techniques used to communicate data back and forth between clients and server are performed using property setting. Remember, every time you write a piece of code that refers to an object dot property (Object.Name), that dot is a flag indicating that you will make a call to the object. If your server component sits on a machine in Hong Kong and you call it from Los Angeles, you make a trip to Hong Kong and back every single time. The objective is to package your data all at once and send it.

In the following sections we give examples of how to apply these guidelines.

Disconnected Recordsets

A disconnected Recordset, wherein the connection is removed from a populated Recordset, is one of the powerful features of ADO. This Recordset can be manipulated and again connected to the database for updating. Remote Data Services (RDS) uses this feature to send Recordsets via either HTTP or DCOM protocols to a remote computer. Because RDS is used for Internet-based applications, we don't discuss it for the purposes of this book. Instead we use ADO to create disconnected Recordsets.

One of the primary requisites for a Recordset to become a disconnected Recordset is that it must use client-side cursors. That is, the CursorLocation should be initialized to adUseClient.

In Visual Basic, disconnecting a Recordset can be done by setting the ActiveConnection property to Nothing.

```
Let's take a look at some code:Dim Conn As ADODB.Connection
        Dim Rs As ADODB.Recordset

        ' Create instance of connection object and then open the
        ' connection.
        Set Conn = New ADODB.Connection
        Conn.Open "DSN=SQLServer", "sa", ""

        ' Create instance of recordset object and open the
        ' Recordset object against a table.
        Set Rs = New ADODB.Recordset

        ' Setting the cursor location to client side is important
        ' to get a disconnected Recordset.
        Rs.CursorLocation = adUseClient
        Rs.Open "Select * from Table1", _
                Conn, _
                ADODB.adOpenForwardOnly, _
                ADODB.adLockOptimistic

        ' Disconnect the recordset.
        Set Rs.ActiveConnection = Nothing
        ' Get the value of one of the fields from the Recordset
        ' after disconnection.
        Text1.Text = Rs.Fields(0).Value

        Conn.Close

        ' Get the value of one of the fields from the Recordset
        ' after closing the connection to ensure that you have a
        ' disconnected Recordset.
        Text2.text = Rs.Fields(0).Value

        ' Now edit the value and save it.
        Rs.Fields("au_lname").Value = "NewValue"
```

```
' Now reopen the connection and attach it to the Recordset.
Set Conn = New ADODB.Connection
Conn.Open "DSN=DBSq1", "sa", ""
Rs.ActiveConnection = Conn
Rs.UpdateBatch

Rs.Close
Conn.Close
Set Rs = Nothing
Set Conn = Nothing
```

This example should be familiar to you. We discussed it in Chapter 8, "Understanding COM Internals," when we talked about using ADO Recordsets. However, the only difference here is that when we executed the SQL statement and got our Recordset, we immediately closed the connection. It's important not to hold on to connections when working with remote components. We can then change our fields' values, establish the connection again, update the fields in the batch, close the connection again, and finally destroy the ADO connection object to release the memory.

Creating Your Own Recordsets

Sure, you can create ADO Recordsets in VB pretty easily. Grab a DB connection, attach it to a Recordset object, slap a SQL command in there, and you've got it. Recordsets also make it simple to navigate through the records, display them in your UI, and even create your own data control. Recordsets are convenient to pass back to client applications from server-side DCOM components as well. Passing them to a client is easy. Using the ADOR Recordset on the client, we request a Recordset from the server component. The server component will return us the Recordset.

```
' Code is in the client side. x.LoadHomePageSettings returns a
    ' Recordset. Notice that we are using the lighter ADOR
    ' Recordset on the client. It does not
    ' need all the functionality of the complete ADODB Recordset.
    Dim rs As ADOR.Recordset

    Dim x As Object
    Set x = CreateObject("CustomizationComponent.Customization")
    Set rs = x.LoadHomePageSettings("martint")

    ' In the server-side component, create a Recordset and pass it
    ' back as the function return type.
    Public Function LoadHomePageSettings(ByVal sUserID As String) As _
ADODB.Recordset
```

```
Dim rs As New ADODB.Recordset

' ... Build your Recordset here.

Set LoadHomePageSettings = rs

End Function
```

One of the principles of programming server-side, out-of-process components is that you should pass arguments using ByVal when possible, because the marshaling mechanism for ByRef parameters is very slow. It has to create a new address that is compatible with the target address space of the DCOM component. It also has to maintain a connection across the network to the component until the component has completed its work and finishes with the ByRef parameter. Another DCOM programming principle states that your server-side components should be service oriented instead of the more common property oriented. The reason for this is that every time you access a property of a server-side component, you generate a round trip across the network. Instead, components should package up as much data as possible and send it back to the client in a single network trip as the result of a single service call from the client.

Recordsets are a very attractive option for passing data back from DCOM components to a client-side application. Large amounts of data can be stuffed into Recordset and passed back all at once, significantly reducing network traffic. The problem is that you'd think Recordsets, by their very nature, would need access to a database in order to populate themselves. As it turns out, you can build your own Recordsets manually, with no database in the loop at all. Building your own Recordset involves:

1. Creating the Recordset object.
2. Setting up the fields you want it to contain.
3. Opening the Recordset.
4. Adding records to the Recordset.
5. Sending the Recordset back to the client.

Here's an example that illustrates how this works.

Create a function that will load the user homepage setting, then declare a Recordset object. Set up the fields you want to contain in the Recordset, then open the Recordset. At this point you can start adding records to the Recordset using the Addnew methods; when you finish, you'll be ready to send the entire Recordset back to the client.

```
' This code is in a DCOM out-of-process component.
Public Function LoadHomePageSettings(ByVal sUserID As String) As _
ADODB.Recordset

    ' 1. Create our Recordset object.
    Dim rs As New ADODB.Recordset

    ' 2. Set up the fields you want the Recordset to contain.
    ' We have only two in this case.
    rs.Fields.Append "SettingName", adChar, 32
    rs.Fields.Append "SettingValue", adChar, 255

    ' 3. Open the Recordset. Note that this must be done AFTER
    ' the fields have been defined for the Recordset.
    rs.Open

    ' 4. Add records to the Recordset. Here we are adding 4 rows
    ' to the Recordset.
    rs.AddNew
    rs!SettingName = "BodyFont"
    rs!SettingValue = "Verdana"

    rs.AddNew
    rs!SettingName = "TitleFont"
    rs!SettingValue = "Rictus"

    rs.AddNew
    rs!SettingName = "RecentOnOff"
    rs!SettingValue = "1"

    rs.AddNew
    rs!SettingName = "BodyFontColor"
    rs!SettingValue = Str(RGB(100, 120, 140))

    ' 5. Send the Recordset back to the client.
    Set LoadHomePageSettings = rs

End Function
```

That's really all there is to it. You can stuff anything you like into the Recordset, and if you use a technique similar to the one used here, which uses name-value pairs, the client can adapt to varying data returned.

Problems with ADO Recordsets

While developing the example, we encountered a bug with ADO marshaling from MTS. When an ADO object is passed by reference to a method living in an MTS server and an error is raised by that method, the error message gets destroyed somewhere on its way back to the client. Rather than the proper error number and message, the client receives the notorious "Method '~' of object '~' failed," with some incomprehensible error number tagging along. The following function would return the error to the client successfully.

```
Public Function TestThis(rst as ADODB.Recordset) as String
Error.Raise vbObjectError + 105, 'Oh oh', 'Now you've done it'
End Function
```

This function would not:

```
Public Function TestThis(CompanyID as integer, rst as _
ADODB.Recordset) as Boolean
    Error.Raise vbObjectError + 105, 'Oh oh', 'Now you've done it'
End Function
```

To duplicate this error you must have an additional parameter sent before the ADO object, and the return type must be Boolean. It is simple to work around this bug. If you have a multi-parameter method, one parameter of which is an ADO Recordset, and the method returns a Boolean value, declare the ADO object as the first parameter, and your method can return an error unhindered by the ADO marshaler.

User-Defined Types

Remoting is the process of passing parameters between two different processes, usually across a network. For example, imagine a three-tier system on the client machine. The application makes a call for data, passing several parameters as the criteria. On the middle-tier machine, an ActiveX EXE accepts the call and uses the criteria for retrieving the data.

Passing a UDT as a Parameter of a Public Sub

While passing parameters has always been possible in previous versions of Visual Basic, passing user-defined types (UDTs) as parameters of public subs has not. This is now possible and a very welcomed enhancement. This feature allows you to look at alternative ways of passing data between remote components. Let's check out the technique used to accomplish this.

For example, code on business components that reside on one of the tiers might look like this:

```
Option Explicit
' This code is in a code module.
Public Type udtMyType ' Definition of a Public UDT
    lastName As String
    firstName As String
```

```
        address As String
    End Type

    Public Function passUDT(myrec As udtMyType) As udtMyType
        ' Modify the data somehow.
        passUDT = myrec ' Return the UDT.
    End Function
```

While code on the client machine that calls the function would be:

```
    Option Explicit
    Private myrec As udtMyType

    Private Sub Command1_Click()
        Dim x As udtMyType
        x = passUDT(myrec)
        ' Do something with the UDT data.
    End Sub
```

As you've seen, there are several ways to marshal data between components. With every release of Visual Basic we are acquiring new features and new ways of efficiently communicating data. Examine each technique to determine the best approach to your needs and the most effective ways of mixing techniques based on the scenario.

Performance Considerations

The cost of passing parameters out-of-process is far higher than passing them in-process. When passing a parameter, the data must be marshaled and passed to the external process. The code to accomplish this action can be expensive, but Visual Basic conceals this cost. The advantage of remoting data, however, is that easily comprehensible code can be created. Depending on the size of the UDT, it may also be easier to maintain than an ADO Recordset object.

Error Handling

Error handling is an important part of a robust application, and it should not be overlooked or left until the end of a project. It needs to be planned carefully from day one until the end of a project. When you introduce components, especially server-side components, the error-handling issue can get complicated. For example, suppose you have a client application that makes a service request from a server-side DCOM component. That DCOM component in turn uses the services of another server-side component to get its work done. If an error occurs in the last component, who handles the error—the component itself? If it is not handled, does it propagate to the next component? If it is not handled there, does the error get raised to the client? All good questions. Fortunately, they all have answers. Let's take a look at some of the techniques used to solve some of these issues.

Server-to-Client Error Handling

The general rule about component error handling is that a component should handle all errors if possible. If a component has an internal error, it should do its best to handle it if this is appropriate. If it receives an error that was generated in another component, it should attempt to handle that as well. However, this is not always appropriate or possible. For example, if the error requires user notification of intervention, it must be passed along to the client software. If a component attempts to display even a simple message box, the message appears on the server, not the client, which may be (geographically speaking) several states away.

You could invent your own mechanism for error handling from the component to the client. For example, if an error occurs in a component, it could set an internal data item called iLastError to a known error code, and the client could call a public property called LastError. A simplified version might look something like this:

```
' This code is located in a server-side DCOM component.
Dim iLastError As Integer
...
Public Property get LastError() As Integer

    LastError = iLastError
    iLastError = 0    ' Clear the error code once it has been retrieved.
End Function
```

The problem with this is that the client has to check the error code after every call to the component. This may generate a lot of code on the client side. It also generates a network round trip every time the client checks the code.

A better solution would be to use the Visual Basic Err.Raise capability. This will allow you to raise your own errors in the component; these will automatically be propagated to the client when they occur if they are not handled by the component. The VB mechanism gives us the same functionality as the custom solution, plus more. It only generates a one-way network trip, and then only if an actual error occurs. The custom solution creates a round trip every time anyone checks for an error.

Using the Err.Raise mechanism is pretty easy. The component can raise the error, and the client can handle it. VB even provides a simple mechanism for the client error handler code to determine whether the error was generated locally or by a component. Here's how it works:

1. In the component, raise the error, whether it is the result of a VB-generated error or one that you have detected in your own component code.

2. Add the value of the constant vbObjectError to your error code before you raise the error.

3. If the error is a VB error, leave the description alone. If it is your own error code, change the description to suit your own needs.

4. In the client, set up a standard VB error handler using ON ERROR.

5. In your error handler code, subtract the value of vbObjectError from the code. If it is still in the range of 0 to 65,355, it is a component error and not a local one.

6. Handle the error as you see fit.

The following code is the server code. It has a public enumeration that client components can use, as well as a public function that accepts two numbers and divides them. It has error checking code to ensure that we are not attempting a division by zero operation. If it encounters the error, it needs to raise the error back to the client.

```
' This public Enum type is in the DCOM component. To access it in
' the client, add a project reference to the component.
Public Enum CustErrorType
    UserNotFoundErr = 1000
    DatabaseErr
    UnknownErr
    DivideByZeroErr
End Enum

' This public function is in the DCOM component.
Public Function IntDivide( iNum As Integer, iDivisor As Integer) As _
Integer

    ' Check to make sure the divisor is not zero. If it is, then
    ' raise an error.
    If iDivisor = 0 Then
        IntDivide = 0
        Err.Description = "Attempt to divide by zero."
```

```
            Err.Number = DivideByZeroErr
            Err.Raise
        Else
            IntDivide = iNum \ iDivisor
        End If

    End Function
```

This code practices safe parameter passing and checks for validity before performing its work. If it detects an invalid value coming in, it uses the Raise mechanism to raise an error to the client. The following code illustrates how the client handles the error. In order to access the enumerated error codes defined in the component, we have added a reference to that component in the VB client project, which, in combination with the fact that the Enum type is public, makes the enumerated values part of the global name space.

```
' Client-side code.
Private Sub btnDivide_Click()

    Dim RealError As Long
    Dim iResult As Integer
    Dim x As New MathComponent

    On Error Goto HandleErr
    iResult = x.IntDivide( CInt( txtNum.Text ), CInt( _
txtDivisor.Text ))
    On Error Goto 0

    Exit Sub

HandleErr:

    ' Strip off the constant added by the component to indicate one
    ' of its own errors.
    RealError = Err.Number - vbObjectError

    If RealError > 0 And RealError < 65535 Then
        Select Case RealError
        Case DivideByZeroErr
            MsgBox "Math Problem: & vbCrLf & vbCrLf & _
Err.Description, vbOKOnly, "Math Component Error"
        Case UnknownErr
            MsgBox "An unknown error was detected.", vbOKOnly, _
"Customization Component Error"
        End Select
        Err.Clear
    Else
        ' Local error, not in component. Do something to handle it.
        Err.Clear
    End If

End Sub
```

As you can see, handling errors can be a complicated problem. Not planning for it in advance can be detrimental. Error-handling mechanisms have to be outlined in your architecture document in order for developers to implement them. Writing test cases to test possible error scenarios can help you tremendously in finding the optimal error-handling method. Here we have shown you the concept: The detailed implementation is up to you, because no two applications are alike. Your application might have additional requirements for handling errors, such as error localization, that you will need to factor into your design. How will a client in Germany using your component get an error in German, while another in France, using the same component, gets the error in French? The bottom line is planning, planning, planning.

DCOM Configuration Utility

In Chapter 3, "Introduction to DCOM," we glanced over the DCOM Configuration Utility and all the services it provides for configuring DCOM components. Now let's take a look at this service from a security configuration perspective. The tab responsible for setting the security is the Default Security tab, shown in Figure 9.5.

This tab is used to specify default permissions for objects on the system. The tab has three sections: Access, Launch, and Configuration.

Access Rights.   In the Access tab you can set user accounts by selecting the groups and users to whom you will allow or deny access to the application on this computer. This is a systemwide default that applies to all applications installed on the computer. The default security setting determines whether or not you can override this option for individual applications. The access dialog used by this utility is NT user/ groups permissions, which should make it easy for you to create systemwide groups and assign specific users to the groups based on an access control list.

Launch Rights.   This right is very similar to the Access right in how it is configured; but, as the name implies, it is used to configure who is allowed to launch the application. This is a higher-level right than the Access right, because some users might be able to launch an application but will be denied access to some parts of the application. Denying this right to groups or users prevents them from even launching the application.

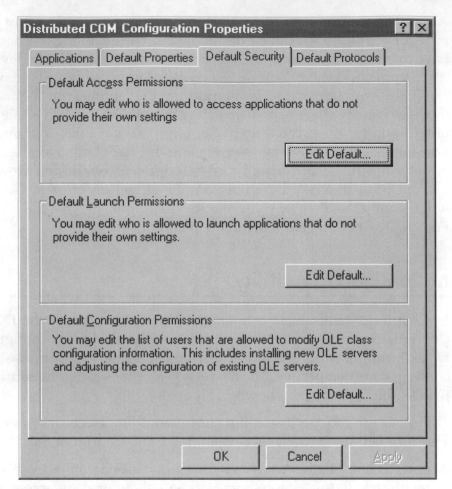

Figure 9.5 Security tab for the DCOM Configuration Utility.

Configuration Rights. By enabling this right to groups and users, you are allowing them to modify OLE class configuration information, which includes installing new servers as well as adjusting the configuration of existing OLE servers. This right is usually granted to system administrators and configuration managers and should not be granted to users of the components.

To change a section's defaults, click the corresponding Edit Default button. These default security settings are stored in the registry under HKEY_LOCAL_MACHINE\Software\Microsoft\OLE.

In the following section we discuss DCOM machine configuration security as well as security related to NT and components interaction.

DCOM and Windows NT Security

One of the more difficult aspects associated with designing and implementing distributed applications is ensuring security against theft or malicious damage to the resulting application. Whenever you build a distributed application, you are not only vulnerable to the normal risks associated with functions and data resident on machines, but a new set of risks as well: those associated with data passing over the network. These threats can include any of the following:

- Removal of the message while being transmitted
- Corruption of the data while being transmitted
- Tampering with the data while be transmitted
- Loss of the data while being transmitted
- Diversion of the message while being transmitted

To decide which mechanism you should use to protect yourself, you need to take a first step and decide which services or functions you need. We will examine four of the more popular functions used to protect the distributed main function from the risks just described.

Authentication

This mechanism ensures that the users requesting access to the system are who they claim to be. Authentication is a test of proof of identity. You can enforce this concept by using NT's integrated security utilizing User Names and passwords. This option is fairly safe and saves the system administrator effort.

The second approach for authentication is to provide Digital Certificates—electronic proof of identity using cryptographic keys—which are then used to sign the message. This technique has the advantage that both the sender and the recipient can be asked to prove their identity, thus providing some assurance to the client that the server is also who/what it says it is. Digital Certificates in this case are issued by a third party called the Trusted Third Party (TTP) or Digital Certificate Authority.

Authorizations

This is a service that ensures that the user or process, once proven to be authentic, is allowed to request a specific service or resource. Therefore, authorization establishes whether an authenticated principal is entitled to use a service or to access defined information. Most authorization is implemented in practice using Access Control Lists (ACLs). But access control lists can differ quite markedly in their level of sophistication—from exceptionally weak to nearly foolproof.

NOTE

Implementing an ACL component that makes use of the NT users and groups can be very complex, because it involves knowledge of the Windows NT network API and the ability to resolve complex data structures. On the companion CD-ROM we provide an NT Access Control List (ACL) that we built in VB with a sample application that is ready for you to use as you wish, thereby saving you several days of development implementation and testing.

Encryption

Public key encryption is based on the Digital Certificates mentioned in the previous section, in which a message gets encrypted from one process to another. However, the sender uses the public key of the recipient to encrypt the message. In this way only the recipient is able to decrypt the message, because only the recipient has the private key. The sender first gets the public key of the recipient from the directory of public keys. The public key is then used by the sender to encrypt the message. It is then sent and decrypted by the recipient using its private key.

Encryption is a very sophisticated approach that might prove to be overkill for the type of security you would like to implement. This is a technique you might not want to implement yourself in your application; you might instead want to consider integrating a third-party software component that might help you accomplish this task.

Integrity Checking

One of the most frequently used methods of checking integrity is the checksum. The contents are summed using a specific algorithm on sending the message and the checksum is added to the message. On receipt, the message is again summed using the same algorithm to see whether the checksum on the message and the one obtained on the reply are the same.

Another way of checking integrity is to apply a hash function. In this case, a variable-length input string (the message) is converted by hashing algorithms to a fixed-length (smaller) output string. Both the sender and receiver create the hash value. The check on integrity value can be achieved either by sending the hash value with the message or by comparing sender and receiver hash values.

As you can see, there is more than one methodology with which to approach security implementation. Each of these security alternatives can be used individually or in conjunction with other approaches. You are the only person who can answer the question: How much security is too little and how much is paranoid?

Winding Up

As you can see, this chapter is filled with techniques on everything from how to design DCOM components and how to pass data across a distributed environment to how to provide security for your application. There is no single technique that works with every single possible scenario. In order to discover what works for you, you have to test and prototype each of the techniques explained in this chapter. What worked for one component may not work for another.

It is very common when designing and implementing complex systems to use more than one technique and approach to solve a problem. Don't worry if you have to adopt a few data access methods that best fit your application behavior and the type and size of data marshaled.

Next we will dig into Microsoft Transaction Server (MTS) and learn more about components and transactions.

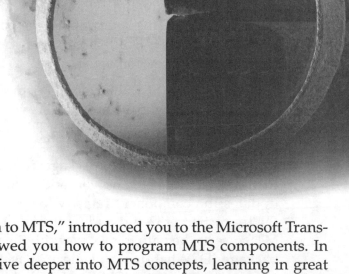

Inside Microsoft Transaction Server

C hapter 4, "Introduction to MTS," introduced you to the Microsoft Transaction Server and showed you how to program MTS components. In this chapter we will dive deeper into MTS concepts, learning in great detail about topics such as distributed transactions and security. This chapter takes you further into the world of MTS, building on the knowledge you have accumulated so far about MTS, COM, and DCOM. In this chapter subjects covered include:

- Transactions—what they are and why they are important
- Microsoft's solution to the transaction issue
- MTS pros and cons
- The MTS programming model
- MTS security
- MTS Explorer
- MTS and Visual Basic, including a quick example program

Even though transactions and MTS seem complicated at first, they will readily become clear as you read this chapter. A little background on transactions and what they are will start us off on the right foot.

How MTS Components Work

In Chapter 4, "Introduction to MTS," you learned how to add components to MTS using MTS Explorer. Now let's examine what happens when a component is added to MTS. First consider an ActiveX DLL before it is added. As you know, when you register this DLL using REGSVR32.EXE, you get a new key in the registry pointing to the DLL, as shown in Figure 10.1. Under the CLSID key, you see a key called InprocServer32. This key contains the path of the ActiveX DLL for the case of in-process (DLL) servers. As you can see from the figure, the InprocServer32 key contains the path to the DLL file.

If we now add this DLL to MTS using MTS Explorer, an interesting thing happens to the registry key. As you can see in Figure 10.2, there is now a key called LocalServer32. This key contains the EXE path for local ActiveX Exes—out-of-process servers. How did we get this key? When you create an MTS package, it is assigned a unique package ID that is a GUID. Then, as you add components to this package, MTS updates the component registry key by removing the DLL path from the InprocServer32 and adding the key LocalServer32. In this new key, MTS inserts the path to mtx.exe with the parameter /p: followed by the package ID. What does this mean? Basically, MTS is saying that when someone requests the CLSID provided by your component, MTS runs and invokes the package where your component resides. This is how MTS intercepts requests to create your components and puts itself between the base client and your components. This extra layer introduced by MTS is the context wrapper that enables most MTS features.

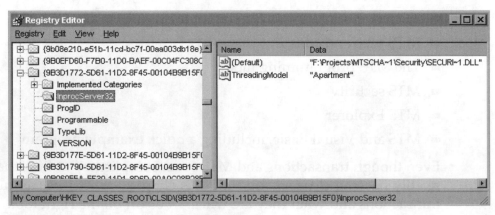

Figure 10.1   Registry entry for an ActiveX DLL.

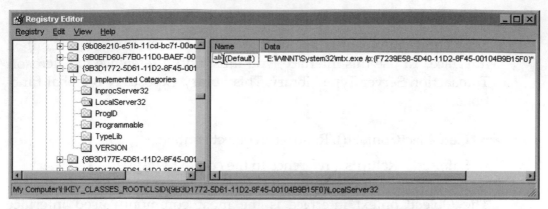

Figure 10.2 Registry entry for an ActiveX DLL installed as an MTS component.

Figure 10.3 shows what a typical MTS process looks like. The context wrapper is your gateway to communicating with MTS. Chapter 4, "Introduction to MTS," introduced you to the ObjectContext interface. This interface provides access to the object's context wrapper, from which you get most MTS functionality.

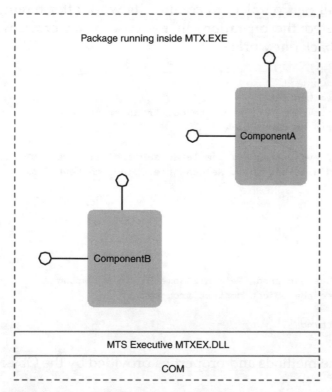

Figure 10.3 Component running inside an MTS process.

The ObjectContext

Your component can communicate with MTS via the ObjectContext interface. To use this interface, you must add a reference to Microsoft Transaction Server Type Library. This library exposes two global functions:

- GetObjectContext(). Returns an object context.
- SafeRef(). Returns a reference to the context wrapper.

The ObjectContext interface is the most commonly used interface within an MTS component. You can use the ObjectContext for things such as transactions, security, and creating other objects. You'll see this object used throughout this chapter for creating objects, committing or aborting transactions, and retrieving information about the user's identity. Chapter 4, "Introduction to MTS," introduced you to the SetAbort and SetComplete members of the ObjectContext interface. The example used in that chapter is repeated here for convenience. Note how we call SetComplete to commit its work after having successfully completed the operation. In the case of an error, we call SetAbort to roll back our work:

```
Dim oc As ObjectContext
Set oc = GetObjectContext()
' Do whatever your component needs to do. If an error occurs,
' jump to the ErrorHandler below.
...
' At this point, everything has completed successfully. Tell MTS
' we're done and all went well. Release the object context from
' memory when done.
oc.SetComplete
Set oc = Nothing
Exit Sub


ErrorHandler:
    ' An error has occurred. Tell MTS something went wrong
    ' and release the object context from memory.
    oc.SetAbort
    Set oc = Nothing
```

Table 10.1 lists the methods and properties provided by the ObjectContext interface:

Table 10.1 Methods and Properties Provided by ObjectContext Interface

METHOD/PROPERTY	DESCRIPTION
Count	Gives the number of context object properties.
CreateInstance	Instantiates another MTS object. Use this method to include the other objects' work within your object's transaction.
DisableCommit	Disables committing of current transaction and keeps the object alive.
EnableCommit	Enables committing of current transaction and keeps the object alive.
IsCallerInRole	Checks whether the direct caller is in a specified role.
IsInTransaction	Lets you find out whether the object is executing inside a transaction.
IsSecurityEnabled	Determines whether security has been enabled.
Item	Returns a context object property from the collection of properties.
Security	Returns a reference to the object's SecurityProperty object.
SetAbort	Tells MTS that the object is done with its work and the transaction should be aborted.
SetComplete	Tells MTS that the object is done with its work and the transaction should be committed.

We discuss Security, SetAbort, and SetComplete in more detail later in this chapter.

The Life and Death of an MTS Component

As you know, a Visual Basic class has two basic events: Class_Initialize() and Class_Terminate(). If you've programmed in C++ or Java, these events are similar to the constructor and destructor methods. When you instantiate an object from a Visual Basic class, the class's Class_Initialize() event is called automatically. Traditionally, this is where you would put initialization code such as setting values of member variables. Similarly, when you destroy the object, the class's Class_Terminate() event is called. Again, this is where you put cleanup code such as releasing references to objects and so on.

Visual Basic classes that run as MTS components add two additional phases to these events: activation and deactivation. The sequence of events for an MTS object is:

1. Creation
2. Activation
3. Deactivation
4. Destruction

When a client creates an object, MTS creates the object but does not activate it. An MTS object is activated on the first method call. The timing of object deactivation depends on whether the object supports transactions. If a transactional object calls SetAbort or SetComplete (see the section on distributed transactions), the object is deactivated as soon as the method call is complete, even if the client still has a reference to the object. The next time the client calls this object, MTS will automatically reactivate it without the client even knowing about it. On the other hand, nontransactional objects remain active until the client releases all references to the object. MTS lets you know when your component is being activated and deactivated by firing special events provided by an interface called the ObjectControl interface.

The ObjectControl Interface

MTS programming requires you to forget about the Class_Initialize() and Class_Terminate() events. The ObjectControl interface is another useful interface exposed by MTS. This interface provides the following Activate and Deactivate events:

- ObjectControl_Activate. This event is fired when an object is being activated by MTS.

- ObjectControl_Deactivate. This event is fired when an object is being deactivated by MTS.

Use these events to perform initialization and cleanup work such as initializing variable values or reading some registry entries (avoid performing lengthy tasks in either events). Again, how these events are called depends on whether a component is transactional and whether it calls any of the object context's transaction methods.

TIP

The ObjectControl interface provides a method called ObjectControl_CanBePooled. A future version of MTS will rely on this method to determine whether your object may be pooled (reused by others). Because this feature is not yet implemented, you should return FALSE in this method.

Examples

Here is some sample code to help you explore the life cycle of an MTS object. The first sample (\samples\ch10exla) is implemented in a class that does not support transactions. In the General section of the class module, we use the keyword Implements to specify that this class implements the ObjectControl interface. As a result, we get the events ObjectControl_Activate() and ObjectControl_Deactivate(). As you can see from the code, we pop up message boxes each time one of these events is called. This is a simple way for us to see the sequence of these events.

```
Option Explicit
Private gSessionID As Long 'this is where we keep our state
Implements ObjectControl 'this class implements the ObjectControl
                         'interface

Private Sub Class_Initialize()
    'this is the standard Class_Initialize() event
    MsgBox "Stateful Component being initialized"
End Sub

Private Sub Class_Terminate()
    'this is the standard Class_Terminate() event
    MsgBox "Stateful Component being terminated"
End Sub

Private Sub ObjectControl_Activate()
    'The ObjectControl_Activate event is called by MTS when object
    'is activated
    MsgBox "Stateful Component has been activated"
End Sub

Private Function ObjectControl_CanBePooled() As Boolean
'The ObjectControl_CanBePooled function is called by MTS before an
'object is deactivated
MsgBox "Stateful Component: Can I be pooled? I think not"
    ObjectControl_CanBePooled = False
End Function

Private Sub ObjectControl_Deactivate()
'The ObjectControl_Deactivate event is called by MTS when object is
'deactivated
    MsgBox "Stateful Component has been Deactivated"
End Sub

Public Property Get SessionID() As Long
    SessionID = gSessionID
    'not calling SetComplete means I won't be deactivated
End Property
```

```
Public Property Let SessionID(ByVal NewID As Long)
    gSessionID = NewID
    'not calling SetComplete means I won't be deactivated
End Property
```

The second example is implemented in a class that requires transactions:

```
Option Explicit
Private gSessionID As Long 'this is where we keep our state
Implements ObjectControl

Private Sub Class_Initialize()
    'this is the standard Class_Initialize() event
    MsgBox "Stateless Component being initialized"
End Sub

Private Sub Class_Terminate()
    'this is the standard Class_Terminate() event
    MsgBox "Stateless Component being terminated"
End Sub

Private Sub ObjectControl_Activate()
'The ObjectControl_Activate event is called by MTS when object is
    MsgBox "Stateless Component has been activated"
End Sub

Private Function ObjectControl_CanBePooled() As Boolean
'The ObjectControl_CanBePooled function is called by MTS before an
'object is deactivated
MsgBox "Stateless Component: Can I be pooled? I think not"
    ObjectControl_CanBePooled = False
End Function

Private Sub ObjectControl_Deactivate()
'The ObjectControl_Deactivate event is called by MTS when object is
'deactivated
    MsgBox "Stateless Component has been Deactivated"
End Sub

Public Property Get SessionID() As Long
    SessionID = gSessionID
    'calling setcomplete tells MTS its OK to deactivate
    GetObjectContext.SetComplete
End Property

Public Property Let SessionID(ByVal NewID As Long)
    gSessionID = NewID
    'calling setcomplete tells MTS its OK to deactivate
    GetObjectContext.SetComplete
End Property
```

As you can see, the main difference between this listing and the previous one is that we call SetComplete at the end of the SessionID property

Let and Set procedures. This tells MTS that we are done with our work and it is now okay to deactivate the object.

The following listing shows a sample client that can be used to test these components. The client lets you call each of the SessionID property Let and property Get procedures for both the stateful and stateless components.

```
Option Explicit
Private oStateFul As Ch10Ex1a.CCh10Ex1a
Private oStateLess As Ch10Ex1b.CCh10Ex1b

Private Sub cmdGetSF_Click()
    txtSessIDSF = CStr(oStateFul.SessionID)
End Sub

Private Sub cmdGetSL_Click()
    txtSessIDSL = CStr(oStateLess.SessionID)
End Sub

Private Sub cmdSetSF_Click()
    oStateFul.SessionID = CLng(txtSessIDSF)
    txtSessIDSF = ""
End Sub

Private Sub cmdSetSL_Click()
    oStateLess.SessionID = CLng(txtSessIDSL)
    txtSessIDSL = ""
End Sub
Private Sub Form_Load()
    'initialize components
    Set oStateFul - New Ch10Ex1a.CCh10Ex1a
    Set oStateLess = New Ch10Ex1b.CCh10Ex1b
End Sub
```

NOTE
For the client to work properly, both ch10ex1a.dll and ch10ex1b.dll must be installed in MTS in a package set to run as the interactive user. This is necessary because the components popup message boxes (something you would never do in a real production MTS component).

When you run the sample client, you will get the dialog shown in Figure 10.4.

When you start the client, you should get a few message boxes indicating that the various components are being initialized, terminated, and initialized again! To test the nontransactional component, follow these steps:

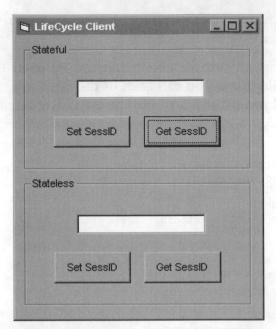

Figure 10.4   Sample client's dialog.

1. Enter a number (an integer) in the top text box, located under Stateful.

2. Click on the Set SessID button.

3. When a message box from the stateless component appears saying it is being activated, click OK.

4. Next, click the Get SessID button.

The number you entered is returned, without a message box this time. This demonstrates two things:

- A nontransactional component is not deactivated until all references to it are set to Nothing. We do not see the message box indicating that the object is being deactivated until we set the object reference to Nothing.

- You can hold state in a nontransactional component (the number you entered is considered state). You set the object's SessionID property to an integer value; then, when you read the object's SessionID property, you get the same value you set earlier. This illustrates that the object holds on to that value between calls.

Repeat these steps using the transactional component (the text box under Stateless). When you click the SetSessID button, you get a series of message boxes indicating that the object is being activated, deactivated, and terminated. When you click on Get SessID, another series of message boxes appears, indicating that the object is being initialized, activated, deactivated, and terminated. You will not get back the number you typed.

TIP

The MS DTC must be started for the transactional component to work properly. The section on managing DTC, later in this chapter, explains how to start the MS DTC service.

This illustrates two things:

- A transactional component is destroyed after it calls SetComplete/SetAbort and exits.
- You cannot hold state in a transactional component after it calls SetComplete/SetAbort.

We'll talk about state in more detail later in this chapter.

MTS Activities

MTS manages concurrent access through the use of activities. An activity is a logical group of objects running for a client. When a client calls an MTS object, an activity is created. If the called object in turn calls other MTS objects, they join the same activity.

Objects within an activity may be distributed across multiple processes executing on one or more machines. Because of the distributed nature of activities, MTS maintains a logical thread of execution throughout the activity. MTS allows only a single logical thread of execution within a given activity. MTS allows multiple objects to execute only if they are in different activities, even if they are in the same component. This means we do not need to worry about concurrency issues. Keep one thing in mind, though: MTS blocks all calls to an activity until the currently executing call completes, even if the blocked calls are from the same client. This can happen if you have a multithreaded client with different threads calling the same object instance (this is bad design anyway!).

Using Components within MTS

How do you create objects in VB? You probably use one of the following methods:

```
Dim obj as new MyObject
'Do something with obj
Or
Dim obj as MyObj
Set obj=New MyObj
'Do something with obj
Or
Dim obj as MyObj
Set obj=CreateObject("MyDLL.MyObj")
'Do something with obj
```

Let's see what happens with each of these methods when they are used inside an MTS component to create an object from another MTS component.

The first two methods are similar: The only difference is when the object gets created. If you call one of the first two methods in MTS, MyObj is created without MTS intercepting it. MyObj will not run as an MTS component because there is no context wrapper. Calling the CreateObject function, as in the third method, is a somewhat better choice. It allows MTS to intercept the request, and MyObj runs as an MTS component. The bad news is that the new object does not inherit your object's context wrapper. This means it will run in a new activity, which may lead to issues with multiobject transactions.

The correct way to instantiate MTS objects from within other MTS objects is to use the ObjectContext's CreateInstance method. Take a look at the following code:

```
'Dim the object context
Dim objCtxt As MTxAS.ObjectContext
Dim obj as MyObj
'obtain a reference to my object context
Set objCtxt = GetObjectContext()
'create object using CreateInstance
Set MyObj=objCtxt.CreateInstance("MyDLL.MyObj")
'release context
Set objCtxt = Nothing
```

As you can see from this code, we use the CreateInstance method to instantiate an object of type MyDLL.MyObj.

You may also use the shorthand technique:

```
Dim obj as MyObj
'obtain a reference to my object context and call CreateInstance
Set MyObj=GetObjectContext.CreateInstance("MyDLL.MyObj")
```

The ObjectContext's CreateInstance method is used to create the new MTS object. MTS creates the object with a context wrapper that inherits the current object's context wrapper and runs it in the same activity.

TIP Never create MTS objects from within MTS components using anything but the CreateInstance method.

SafeRef

Suppose an MTS object, called A, creates another MTS object, called B. Now suppose that, for some reason, B needs a reference to A in order to call A later. How is this reference passed? It is tempting to simply pass in the reference Me (VB's equivalent of the "this" pointer in C++). Do this and you are in for a disaster. Passing references in this way is like sneaking up behind MTS's back and calling its objects. Recall that MTS provides a context wrapper around an object that intercepts all calls to the object. MTS has no way of providing the proper context for objects called directly using their references. Instead, the reference needs to be passed to the context wrapper. Do this by using the SafeRef function provided by the MtxAS DLL.

The SafeRef function takes in one parameter: a reference to the calling object (i.e., Me). It returns a reference to the object's context wrapper that can be safely passed to and used by other objects. The following sample code demonstrates how to use the SafeRef function:

```
'create the object to which we will pass the safe reference
Dim obj as MyObj
Set MyObj=GetObjectContext.CreateInstance("MyDLL.MyObj")
MyObj.SetReference(SafeRef(Me))
```

First you must create the object that will receive a reference to the current object. To do this, use CreateInstance as discussed previously. Next, call a method on MyObj that takes in a reference to the current object. To pass this reference, use the SafeRef function as discussed previously.

This sample listing shows how you can pass a reference to an MTS object. You should never use Me to pass a reference to an MTS object; use SafeRef instead.

Distributed Transactions

Chapter 4, "Introduction to MTS," introduced the concept of transactions. As you'll recall, a transaction is a task or unit of work that is either completed in total or canceled entirely. In this section, we take transactions a step further and discuss distributed transactions involving heterogeneous databases on multiple servers. We'll start by exploring the Microsoft Distributed Transaction Coordinator, then go into MTS-specific technologies.

MS DTC Overview

As we all know, new technologies tend to give rise to new sets of IT issues. Well, distributed applications are no exception. In many cases, a distributed application finds itself updating multiple databases residing on different platforms and being managed by different Database Management Systems (DBMSs). For example, consider a sophisticated order entry application for a large, multinational construction equipment manufacturer. The order comes in from the customer and is entered by the salesperson. The application must then update the local branch's sales database so that sales records are accurate for purposes of calculating salesperson commissions, branch sales figures, and so on. The application must also update the central order-tracking database, which is used to instruct assembly plants to start assembling the ordered equipment. This central database may not be in the same branch; it may not even be in the same country; and it is almost certainly a different type of DBMS.

Let's assume the application first updates the central database, which returns a new unique order number. The application then attempts to use this order number to update the local database, only to find that the DBMS is not available because the server decided to take a rest. What do you do now? Wouldn't it be great if you could combine the remote and local database operations into one transaction and not have to worry about the locations and semantics of different DBMSs? The need for distributed transaction management should now be obvious.

Microsoft Distributed Transaction Coordinator (MS DTC) is a necessary piece of the Windows DNA. It provides scalable, robust distributed transaction management services. MS DTC coordinates transactions spanning multiple DMBSs, allowing your application to commit or abort such transactions by simply calling SetAbort and SetComplete as discussed earlier. MS DTC shields your application from the complexities of handling distributed transactions by allowing you to treat them as simple nondistributed transactions.

We as MTS application developers do not have to talk to MS DTC directly. MTS transactions used by your components will go through

MS DTC behind the scenes. Let's take a look at how MS DTC works. This will help you to better design and manage transaction processing applications.

Managing MS DTC

By now you are probably wondering: Where is this MS DTC and how can I manage it? MS DTC runs as a Windows NT Service. Therefore, it can be started and stopped from the Control Panel Services applet shown in Figure 10.5. It is recommended that you set MS DTC to start automatically with server startup. To do this using the Services applet:

1. Open the Services applet from inside the Control Panel.
2. Find and select the MS DTC service.
3. Click on Startup.
4. Set the Startup Type to Automatic.
5. Click OK to save your changes.

If you prefer, you can also start or stop the MS DTC service directly from the Services applet. To do this, change the Startup Type to Manual. In addition, MTS Explorer allows you start or stop the MS DTC service by selecting the appropriate menu option from the Actions menu.

When programming transactions, make sure MS DTC is running. If your transactional component fails, check the NT Event Viewer to see if the problem is DTC related.

How MS DTC Does It

There's no magic to how MS DTC is able to commit or roll back distributed transactions. MS DTC coordinates writing activities between distributed DBMSs by using a two-phase commit protocol. Each DBMS must provide a transaction manager. MS DTC talks to these transaction managers to coordinate the overall transaction. Each transaction manager must support a protocol called OLE Transactions in order for MS DTC to be able to communicate with it. MS DTC also supports the X/Open protocol, which is a more generic equivalent of OLE Transactions.

What this means is that in order for you to use MS DTC as your distributed transaction coordinator, all DBMSs involved must provide trans-

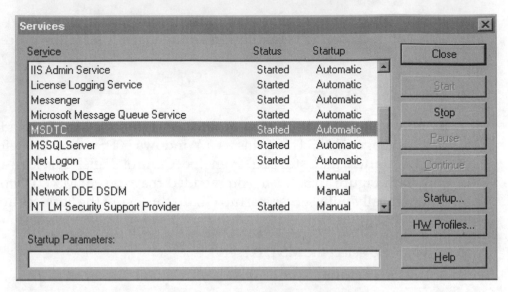

Figure 10.5 Using Control Panel Services applet to start MS DTC.

action managers that know how to communicate with MS DTC. Currently, SQL Server 6.5 (SP2) and 7.0, Oracle (through ODBC), and MSMQ all provide transaction managers compatible with MS DTC. This list is expected to grow as more and more people build transactional MTS applications.

How MTS Transactions Work

We talked about the Microsoft Distributed Transaction Coordinator (MS DTC) and how it can manage your distributed transactions. But how does this apply to MTS? And how do you program the MS DTC?

The answer is, you don't! MTS provides its own wrapper around MS DTC transactions in the form of MTS transactions. This means that in your code you never explicitly start, commit, or abort the physical MS DTC transaction. Instead, you tell MTS what it should do to a particular transaction by setting a transaction property. When an object is created from a transactional component, MTS automatically creates an MTS transaction. When the object is activated—that is, when a method is called—MTS creates a physical MS DTC transaction. When the object is deactivated, MTS calls Commit or Abort on the physical transaction, depending on what your object told it to do. To influence the transaction's outcome, you call SetComplete or SetAbort on the MTS Object-Context within your method execution.

TIP The default transaction timeout value is 60 seconds. You can change that from the computer properties inside MTS Explorer. Set it to 0 if you do not want to impose a timeout.

Before we go any further, it is worth explaining how you can control transaction creation. When you install a component in MTS, you have the option to set its transaction property to one of the following four settings:

Requires transaction.   This component must be run within a transaction. If the calling object already has a transaction, this object inherits the same transaction. Otherwise, MTS creates a new transaction.

Requires new transaction.   This component must be run in a transaction by itself. MTS always creates a new transaction.

Supports transaction.   This component may be run within or outside of a transaction. If the calling object has a transaction, this object inherits the same transaction. Otherwise, this object will not have a transaction.

Does not support transactions.   This object cannot be run inside a transaction. If the calling object has a transaction, MTS runs this object outside the context of that transaction.

TIP An object may find out whether it's in a transaction by calling IsInTransaction on the MTS ObjectContext.

Let's take a look at an example of how these settings can be used. Suppose you have three objects A, B, and C with the following settings:

Object A.   Requires Transaction

Object B.   Requires New Transaction

Object C.   Supports Transaction

Now, assume the client calls object A, which in turn calls object B and object C. The transaction layout will be as shown in Figure 10.6.

As you can see from the figure, MTS creates a transaction for object A because it is set to Requires Transaction. A separate transaction is created for object B because it is set to Requires New Transaction. Object C is activated within the same transaction as object A. In this scenario, object A is referred to as the root object. Objects B and C are called secondary objects.

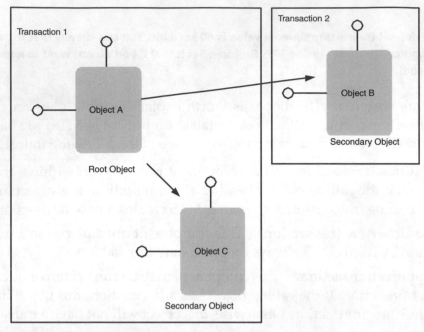

Figure 10.6   Multiobject transaction.

To understand how multiobject transactions work, let's walk through a scenario. When a client calls component object A, MTS starts a new transaction with A being the root object. Next A calls B, which requires that a new transaction be created. If B succeeds, it calls SetComplete and exits. MTS deactivates object B and commits its transaction. Next, object A calls object C. If object C encounters some major difficulties while performing its work, it calls SetAbort and exits with a return code indicating that an error occurred. Because object A is still running, MTS simply takes note of the fact that object C called SetAbort. Note, however, that the physical (MS DTC) transaction is not yet aborted. Execution is returned to object A, which detects that C failed and decides to return an error to the client and exit. MTS deactivates A. Because A is the transaction's root object, MTS now aborts the physical transaction. This mechanism, called a voting mechanism, means that any secondary object may affect the overall outcome of the transaction.

TIP   When programming multiobject transactions, make return codes from secondary objects calls to determine whether they succeeded. Never call SetComplete in the root object after a secondary object has called SetAbort. This will cause a runtime error.

The Shared Property Manager

If you've programmed multithreaded systems in C or C++, you know the issues of sharing global data in concurrent applications. MTS application development is subject to the same issues. For example, how do you share a vital piece of information across multiple objects? How do you lock access to this piece of information so that only one object may update it at any time? Traditionally, you would have to use global variables and critical sections, mutexes, or some other synchronization mechanism. But isn't the reason we program in VB to avoid doing this kind of stuff?

Fortunately, we no longer have to worry about it—MTS provides a resource dispenser called the Shared Property Manager (SPM). The SPM provides a way to share global data across multiple objects running within the same process. It also provides ways for you to lock access to a property.

The SPM may be used to share global data or to hold data in memory for future reference. For example, suppose you want to be able to generate a unique, sequential ID for each new employee added to an HR database. You could store the last used key in a database and retrieve it, increment it, then resave it to the database each time a new employee is added. But this is a lot of database I/O. Instead, you can choose to keep the last used employee ID in a shared property. Your components can get the next available employee ID by reading the value of this shared property and then incrementing it.

To use the SPM, you need to add a reference to mtxspm.dll to your project. Start by creating a SharedPropertyGroupManager object. This is the root of the SPM object hierarchy. It manages property groups and is used to create new property groups and access existing ones. Next, use the SharedPropertyGroupManager to create a SharedPropertyGroup. You can specify a group name and a locking method. If a group already exists with the same name, you get a reference to the existing group and the bExists flag is set to TRUE. The locking parameter lets you specify how property locking behaves. Setting it to LockSetGet causes a property to be locked only while you are reading or setting its value. Setting it to LockMethod causes a property to be locked for the duration of your method's execution. Let's look at a specific example of how to do this. The following function listing, which can be found in the \samples\ch10ex2a directory, shows how to use the SPM. We start by creating the SPM object called oSPMgr. Next, we call CreatePropertyGroup to create a group called EmployeeGroup. Then we call CreateProperty to create the EmpID property. We then increment the value of the EmpID property and call SetComplete to indicate that we have successfully finished.

```
Public Function GetEmpID() As Long

On Error GoTo EH
Dim oSPMgr As MTxSpm.SharedPropertyGroupManager
Dim oSPGrp As MTxSpm.SharedPropertyGroup
Dim oSP As MTxSpm.SharedProperty
Dim bExists As Boolean
'create the Shared Property Manager object
'Set oSPMgr = CreateObject("MTxSpm.SharedPropertyGroupManager.1")
'create a group or get a reference to the existing EmployeeGroup
group
Set oSPGrp = oSPMgr.CreatePropertyGroup("EmployeeGroup", LockMethod, _
Process, bExists)
'Create the EmpID property or get a reference to the existing one
Set oSP = oSPGrp.CreateProperty("EmpID", bExists)
'Initialize the property if it didn't exist (it is initialized to 0
'by default)
If bExists = False Then
    oSP.Value = 0
End If
increment the value of the shared property
oSP.Value = oSP.Value + 1
GetEmpID = oSP.Value
'we completed successfully
GetObjectContext.SetComplete
Exit Function

EH:
'we ran into a problem
GetObjectContext.SetAbort
GetEmpID = 0
Err.Raise Err.Number, "GetEmpID", Err.Description
End Function
```

TIP

Set the Package Server Process Shutdown property to Leave running when idle to keep your shared properties alive. Otherwise, MTS will shut down your package after a preset timeout and all shared properties will be lost!

The following code listing is a sample client that uses the preceding component to demonstrate the use of the SPM. This sample client can be found in the \samples\ch10ex2b directory.

```
option Explicit

Private Sub cmdNextEmpID_Click()
On Error GoTo EH
Dim oUseSPM As Ch10Ex2a.SPMTest
Set oUseSPM = New Ch10Ex2a.SPMTest
txtEmpID.Text = CStr(oUseSPM.GetEmpID())
Exit Sub
EH:
MsgBox Err.Description
End Sub
```

State or No State

Traditional server components are mostly stateful. What does that mean? Well, consider the example of a Human Resources Client/Server application. The client creates an Employee object on the server passing it the EmployeeID. The Employee server object uses the EmployeeID to read various employee information from the database (e.g., Name, Address and Date of Hire). Suppose the client then keeps this Employee object alive and uses it to perform operations on the employee data. For example, the client may call the ChangeAddress method, which changes the employee's address, then the IncreaseSalary method, which gives the employee a raise (this is a nice client!). In this case the server component is said to maintain state.

Suppose the client is designed such that the Employee object is kept alive for the duration of the client's session with the server. Only when the client ends its session does the Employee object get unloaded from memory. This scenario is not all that uncommon; however, it is dangerous, to say the least. To understand why, think big. Imagine having 50 users of this application, each of which handles 100 employees. That is 5000 Employee objects to be created and maintained concurrently on the server. If each object takes up 5 KB of memory, that's 25 MB of memory just for the Employee objects! As you can see, this figure will increase as the number of users and/or employees increases. Not very scalable, is it?

There are two problems with this scenario:

1. All information pertaining to the employee(s) being handled by each client is maintained at the server.

2. All information is retained for the duration of the client's session, which is defined as the time from when the client application starts until it exits.

To make this application more scalable, we need to cut down on the resources required per user. We start by eliminating the concept of a persistent session. Instead, when the client calls a method on the Employee object, the server creates an instance of the Employee component to serve the client's request. When the method call is completed, the server destroys the newly created Employee object. So the Employee object exists only for the duration of the method call. In this case, the server component is said to be stateless. Obviously, this reduces the amount of resources required for each client, but it also introduces interesting issues.

Using this new paradigm, a client cannot rely on information previously communicated to the server. So a client can't pass the EmployeeID to the server component in a method call (e.g., SetEmployeeID), then later decide to increase the salary of this employee while assuming the server knows which employee the client is talking about. Instead, the client needs to pass the EmployeeID with each method call. For example, to change an employee's address, the client would have to pass the EmployeeID as well as the new address. The client cannot make any assumptions about the state of an object.

It is up to you to decide whether your component will be stateless or stateful. However, be forewarned that stateful components have many drawbacks, as we will see in a minute. Just remember that when a transactional component calls SetComplete or SetAbort, MTS automatically deactivates the object and therefore destroys its state.

Pros and Cons of State

Stateful components are like all other things in life: They have a good side and a bad side. The good side is easier client programming. Because stateful components are familiar to most of us, it is more natural to program a client calling stateful components. On the other hand, there are the following drawbacks:

- Use of stateful components usually implies setting and reading multiple properties one at a time. This is one sure way to burn network bandwidth and slow down your application.

- Stateful components live on the server for an extended period of time. This means higher consumption of resources such as memory and database connections.

- A transactional component calling SetComplete or SetAbort is automatically deactivated by MTS. This may cause problems for a client expecting the component to hold state. For example, consider the following code snippet:

```
Dim oHRServer as HRServer
Dim sAddress as String
Set oHRServer=New HRServer
oHRServer.EmployeeID=12345678
oHRServer.IncreaseSalary 0.05
sAddress=oHRServer.GetAddress()
```

This seemingly innocent code may not work properly. When the client calls IncreaseSalary, the HRServer component saves the change to the database and calls SetComplete to commit the transaction. MTS deactivates the object and cleans up any state information (such as the EmployeeID, i.e., 12345678). The next method call (sAddress=oHRServer .GetAddress()) causes MTS to reactivate the object with a fresh new state. This new object does not know which Employee ID the client is talking about, so the GetAddress() method fails. Such problems are common when clients expect transactional objects to maintain state information.

How to Maintain State

So how do you maintain state? First, you must decide whether you need to maintain state within or beyond transaction boundaries. To maintain state within transaction boundaries, simply call EnableCommit or DisableCommit at the end of your method execution. This tells MTS to keep the current transaction alive and not deactivate your object, thereby allowing it to keep state.

Holding state beyond the boundaries of a transaction requires a little bit more work. By definition, an object is deactivated and state is lost at the end of a transaction. You must find a way to persist state information beyond transactions. How you do this depends on the amount of data involved, the required state durability, and the frequency with which the stored state is referenced. You can persist state information by storing it in a database or a file of some kind. You can also use the Shared Property Manager to persist state, although this is more volatile because the SPM stores properties in memory and destroys them when the owner process exits.

Transactions and Stateful Objects

When maintaining state in an object, transactions can become problematic because calling SetAbort or SetComplete causes MTS to deactivate your object when the method exits. Therefore you cannot maintain state after calling SetAbort or SetComplete. However, the ObjectContext interface provides two methods for stateful transactional objects: DisableCommit and EnableCommit. If your object is happy (method execution was successful) and you want it to maintain its state, you can call EnableCommit. This tells MTS that database changes *could* be committed in their current state, but it should not deactivate your object. Conversely, if method execution fails, your object may call DisableCommit. Now MTS knows that database changes cannot be committed in their current state but that the transaction should not be rolled back either. In addition, your object remains active and retains its state. These methods come in handy when you are developing a special component that requires state and transactions.

MTS and Security

Chapter 4, "Introduction to MTS," introduced you to the MTS security model and MTS roles. This section takes a closer look at MTS security and the implications of calling MTS components from other tiers such as a Web application running in IIS.

Types of Security

Security is a general word that can take on many meanings. When designing N-tier applications, it is necessary to define what is meant by security and your application's security requirements. There are generally three distinct types of security:

Authentication.   When a user attempts to access a secure system, his or her identity must be confirmed, or authenticated, before access is allowed. For example, when you attempt to access a Windows NT workstation, you must first log on by supplying your user name and password. When the correct password is supplied, NT assumes that you are really who you claim to be. This is NT's way of authenticating users. Similarly, a secure application must authenticate a user before allowing access. Note that authentication does not necessarily involve typing in your user name and password. For example, with NT's integrated security model, you only have to log on once; after this, all applications can authenticate you without reprompting for your user name or password.

Access control.   Once a user is admitted into a secure system, he or she requests access to resources and/or functions. Depending on the system, some users may have different access privileges than others. Because the system has already authenticated the user, it knows who he or she is; therefore it can find out whether that particular user is allowed access to the requested function. An example of access control is security in the NT File System (NTFS). Just because you have logged on to an NT workstation does not necessarily mean that you have access to all files on the local machine. An administrator may use NTFS security to lock you out of certain directories and/or files. Access control on resources is usually implemented in levels rather than as an all-or-nothing case. For example, you may have read-only access to certain NTFS directories, read/write access to other directories, and full control over a third set of directories. The sets of privileges that can be granted or denied to users are defined by the application itself.

Data encryption.   In some applications, the information being transmitted over network wires is valuable enough for someone to go through the trouble of intercepting it. An example of this would be your credit card information being transmitted over the telephone lines to some Internet shopping site. Someone could potentially listen in on the connection and steal this information, enabling him or her to charge all sorts of items on your credit card. To protect data traveling over communication links, it is necessary to use encryption. Encrypted data is basically the original data transformed in such a way that it becomes nonfeasible to hack it. Note that encrypted data is—at least theoretically—not impossible to decode. Breaking the code is just too expensive in that it requires very fast computers to work at it for a very long time (many years). This discourages hackers by making the task not feasible.

Data encryption is not required by all applications. In fact, very few business applications use data encryption when both client and server are on an enterprise LAN (if you have hackers on your LAN, you have bigger things to worry about than MTS!).

Impersonation

We talked about controlling a user's access to the resources and functions of a system. What about applications that a user runs? A Windows application or a process takes on the identity of the user that runs it, a process that is referred to as impersonation. By impersonating the calling user, the application can be treated as a user by the access control system. So if you have read-only access to a directory, any application that you run will not be able to write to that directory, because it impersonates you. The process of impersonation is key to understanding N-tier application security. An MTS package runs in its own process and therefore takes on the identity of (impersonates) some NT user.

Package Identity

An MTS package signifies a process. All Windows NT processes must have an identity, that is, they must run as some user. Similarly, a package takes on the identity of (impersonates) some user. You can specify the identity of a package from the Identity tab on the package's properties dialog available within the MTS Explorer. Although you can choose to run a package as the interactive user, this is not recommended because it requires that someone be logged on to the server at all times. However, this is a very powerful feature for troubleshooting component problems because it lets your component interact with the desktop, thereby bringing up message boxes. In most cases you'll want to define a specific user account with limited rights and use that as the package's identity. Remember that when a process *impersonates* a user, it has all the privileges of that user. Therefore, it is not a good idea to let a package run as the system administrator. On the other hand, it is necessary that the package identity be set to a user account that has sufficient permissions to allow the package to do its work. For example, if the package needs to open a file with read/write access, then it must be impersonating a user who has read/write access to that file.

Another Look at Roles

As we mentioned in Chapter 4, "Introduction to MTS," MTS uses the concept of roles to implement security. Roles are simply another way of grouping users. By allowing some roles access to certain functions and denying others, you are effectively exercising access control.

Recall that authorization checking is performed at process boundaries. To understand the implications, consider the following example: A user logged in as Bob is running a client application that calls the MTS component A. Component A checks whether Bob is in the Admin or User roles and finds out that he is in the User role. So it starts performing the necessary tasks for someone in the User role. Then it calls component B, which happens to be in a different package because it runs in a different process. Assume that component A is configured to run as the Administrator account, which happens to be a member of the Manager role—that is, the package identity is set to Administrator. If component B now calls IsCallerInRole("Manager"), the call returns TRUE. So how did Bob suddenly get in the Manager role? He didn't. When component A calls the out-of-process component B, MTS performs authorization checking. Because component A is running as Administrator, this is the user that B recognizes as the direct caller. Therefore the call to IsCallerInRole("Manager") succeeds. The morale of the story is: If your component is going to call components in other packages, be careful about checking roles, because they apply only to the direct caller—that is, the calling component's identity, not the client's identity.

How to Program Security

Chapter 4, "Introduction to MTS," discussed Declarative versus Programmatic MTS security. In most cases, you will need to use a little of each. Keep in mind that declarative security requires careful planning of your components and interfaces because access control is exercised at the component and interface levels. Programmatic security lets you control access within your code. To do this, you need three key elements:

- Knowledge of what application resources and functions need to be secured

- Knowledge of the privileges each user or role is granted

- Knowledge of who the user is or at least what role he or she is in

Once you have this information, programmatic access control becomes a matter of checking the requesting user name or role versus a list of allowed users for the requested function/resource. The first two items are up to you. You need to design your application in such a way that you can maintain records of who has access to what. The third item must be queried at runtime.

Obviously, you do not need to authenticate the user yourself (we VB developers would never do such a thing). Instead, you can find out the user's name and role if the user is the direct caller of your component by asking MTS. The Object Context has a property called the Security-Property. This is actually an extremely useful MTS object. Using the SecurityProperty you can get information such as:

- The original creator
- The original caller
- The direct creator
- The direct caller

The difference between original and direct becomes evident when you consider a multiple-package example like the one just discussed. In this example, the direct caller of component B is Administrator, while its original caller is Bob. So, although component B cannot find out which role Bob is in, it can find out that it was Bob that started this call chain.

To use the SecurityProperty, you first get a reference to it by calling the Security property of the object context:

```
Dim cs As MTxAS.SecurityProperty
Set cs = GetObjectContext.Security
```

Having done that, you then call methods on the SecurityProperty object to retrieve caller name, creator name, and so on.

```
sCaller = cs.GetDirectCallerName()
sOrigCaller = cs.GetOriginalCallerName()
```

To demonstrate how this works, we have put together three sample projects: two MTS components and a client. These projects let you examine the difference between Caller and OriginalCaller. They also demonstrate how role checking works. To run the projects, perform the following steps:

1. Build the Ch10Ex3a component and install it in MTS package A.
2. Build the Ch10Ex3b component that needs to reference Ch10Ex3a and install it in MTS package B. Configure the identity of this package to run as a different account than the one you are using (e.g., Administrator).
3. Build the Ch10Ex3c client that needs to reference both components.
4. Run the client and test both components.

Let's walk through the code to see how it works. The SecurityInfo component has three methods: GetSecurityInfo, IsInRole, and GetUserID.

GetSecurityInfo returns the original caller name, the creator name, and the original creator name. To do this, it gets the SecurityProperty object by calling GetObjectContext.Security. Then it calls the four methods GetDirectCallerName, GetDirectCreatorName, GetOriginalCaller-Name, and GetOriginalCreatorName.

The next function, IsInRole, takes in a role name and returns TRUE if the caller is in the specified role, and FALSE otherwise. To do this, the function calls the GetObjectContext.IsCallerInRole, passing to it the specified role name.

The third function, GetUserID, returns the original caller name by calling GetObjectContext.GetOriginalCallerName().

```
Option Explicit

Public Sub GetSecurityInfo(ByRef sOrigCreator, ByRef sOrigCaller, _
ByRef sCreator, ByRef sCaller)
    Dim cs As MTxAS.SecurityProperty
    Set cs = GetObjectContext.Security
    sCaller = cs.GetDirectCallerName()
    sCreator = cs.GetDirectCreatorName()
    sOrigCaller = cs.GetOriginalCallerName()
    sOrigCreator = cs.GetOriginalCreatorName()
    Set cs = Nothing
End Sub
Public Function IsInRole(sRole As String) As Boolean
On Error GoTo ErrorHandler
IsInRole = GetObjectContext.IsCallerInRole(sRole)
Exit Function
ErrorHandler:
IsInRole = False
End Function
Public Function GetUserID() As String
  Dim cs As MTxAS.SecurityProperty
  Set cs = GetObjectContext.Security
  GetUserID = cs.GetOriginalCallerName()
  Set cs = Nothing
End Function
```

The Indirect Caller component has one method, GetSecurityInfo, which acts as a wrapper around the SecurityInfo component. The key here is to have the Indirect Caller and the SecurityInfo components run in different packages with different identities. This method simply creates an instance of the SecurityInfo component and calls GetSecurityInfo on it.

```
Option Explicit
Public Sub GetSecurityInfo(ByRef sOrigCreator, ByRef sOrigCaller, _
ByRef sCreator, ByRef sCaller)
```

```
Dim csec As CSecurityInfo
Set csec =
GetObjectContext.CreateInstance("SecurityInfo.CSecurityInfo")
csec.GetSecurityInfo sOrigCreator, sOrigCaller, sCreator, sCaller
Set csec = Nothing
End Sub
```

To drive the above two components, we built the SecurityInfo client. This client has four buttons. The first button, cmdCalldirect, is used to instantiate the SecurityInfo component and call the method GetSecurityInfo on it. The returned information is displayed in a message box.

The second button, cmdCallIndirect, is used to call the GetSecurityInfo method of an IndirectCaller object. Again, returned information is displayed in a message box.

The last two buttons, cmdIsInrole and cmdUserName, are used to retrieve and display role information and user name. CmdIsInrole checks to see whether the user belongs to the role specified in the text box called txtRole. For example, to test whether the user belongs to a role called Manager, type Manager into the text box, then click on IsInrole.

```
Option Explicit

Private Sub cmdCalldirect_Click()
Dim oSec As SecurityInfo.CSecurityInfo
Set oSec = New CSecurityInfo
Dim sOrigCreator As String
Dim sOrigCaller As String
Dim sCreator As String
Dim sCaller As String
oSec.GetSecurityInfo sOrigCreator, sOrigCaller, sCreator, sCaller
MsgBox "Orig Caller: " & sOrigCaller & vbCrLf & _
       "Orig Creator: " & sOrigCreator & vbCrLf & _
       "Caller: " & sCaller & vbCrLf & _
       "Creator: " & sCreator
Set oSec = Nothing
End Sub

Private Sub cmdCallIndirect_Click()
Dim oIndirect As IndirectCaller.CIndirectCaller
Set oIndirect = New CIndirectCaller
Dim sOrigCreator As String
Dim sOrigCaller As String
Dim sCreator As String
Dim sCaller As String
oIndirect.GetSecurityInfo sOrigCreator, sOrigCaller, sCreator, _
sCaller
MsgBox "Orig Caller: " & sOrigCaller & vbCrLf & _
       "Orig Creator: " & sOrigCreator & vbCrLf & _
```

```
            "Caller: " & sCaller & vbCrLf & _
            "Creator: " & sCreator
    Set oIndirect = Nothing
    End Sub

    Private Sub cmdIsInRole_Click()
    Dim oSec As SecurityInfo.CSecurityInfo
    Dim bIsInRole As Boolean
    Set oSec = New CSecurityInfo
    bIsInRole = oSec.IsInRole(txtRole)
    If bIsInRole = True Then
        MsgBox "Caller is in role", vbInformation
    Else
        MsgBox "Caller is NOT in role", vbCritical
    End If
    Set oSec = Nothing
    End Sub

    Private Sub cmdUserName_Click()
    Dim oSec As SecurityInfo.CSecurityInfo
    Set oSec = New CSecurityInfo
    MsgBox oSec.GetUserID()
    Set oSec = Nothing
    End Sub
```

Security and Database Access

When developing applications for a database system such as MicroSoft SQL Server, you need to think about controlling access to the database. In traditional client/server applications, the application connects to the database using a user name and password supplied by the end user. Or, in the case of SQL Server with integrated security, this is all done automatically without having to prompt for a user name and password. It is tempting to carry the same model over to MTS components where we get the user name and password and use those components to connect to SQL Server. Don't do it! There are at least two good reasons why you shouldn't.

First, relying on database access control requires that the database administrator (DBA) define who has access to what resources within the database. This can be a very tedious process and adds extra administrative overhead. The second, more important reason has to do with performance. We've talked about database connection pooling and how that does all sorts of wonders for your application's performance. Well, if you use the user's name to log on to SQL Server, you can kiss connection pooling goodbye. A database connection is a secured resource: It can be accessed only by the user that created it. So if an object connects to the database as Bob, another object attempting to connect as Sandy cannot reuse the same connection. This is clearly an inefficient use of database connections and defeats the purpose of resource pooling.

A better way to manage database access control is to configure SQL Server so that database access is provided only to the user account used as the package identity, in addition to other users such as developers and administrators. You then exercise access control on your components and interfaces using either declarative access or programmatic access. This way, database connections used by all objects will be properly pooled, which boosts your application's performance.

Debugging MTS Components

Soon after you start developing MTS components, you will find yourself asking, "How do I debug my application?" Debugging MTS components is not as easy as debugging regular applications. The main reason is that an MTS component runs inside a special context wrapper provided by MTS. However, there are several ways to debug the application by stepping through your source code. This section provides an overview of these methods and gives the steps necessary to implement each.

Conditional Compilation

One of the issues of debugging MTS components is the fact that while outside of MTS, you do not have access to many of the MTS services such as GetCallerName. To work around that, you can employ the use of conditional compilation constants (constants used to control how an application is compiled) to include or exclude some of your code on the basis of whether you built a debug or release version.

To define a conditional compilation constant, go to Project Properties and select the Make tab, shown in Figure 10.7. In the Conditional Compilation Arguments field, type in the name and value of the constant. Note that TRUE is –1 in Visual Basic.

You can then test on the values of these constants using #If Then #Else constructs to include or exclude parts of the code. For example, the following code listing shows a function that returns the original caller name if compiled as release and some constant (hard coded) user name if compiled as debug.

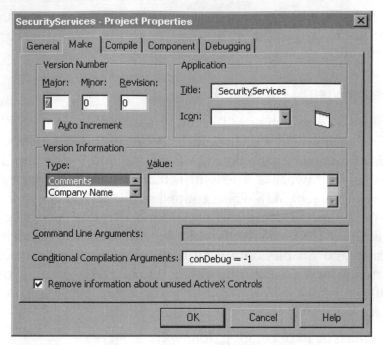

Figure 10.7 Defining conditional compilation arguments.

```
Public Function GetUserID() As String
#If conDebug Then
    GetUserID = DebugUserId
    Exit Function
#End If
  Dim objCtxt As ObjectContext
  Dim objCtxtSecur As MTXAS.SecurityProperty
  On Error GoTo ErrHandler
  Set objCtxt = MTXAS.GetObjectContext()
  Set objCtxtSecur = objCtxt.Security
  GetUserID = objCtxtSecur.GetOriginalCallerName()
  Set objCtxtSecur = Nothing
  Set objCtxt = Nothing
  Exit Function
ErrHandler:
  Set objCtxtSecur = Nothing
  Set objCtxt = Nothing
  Err.Clear
  Err.Raise 1510, "Security Server", "Error in getting UserID"
End Function
```

TIP

Don't forget to set all your compilation arguments so that you compile a release version before putting your component in MTS.

By using compilation arguments you can build and debug a non-MTS version of your component with no code modification. This can be a very useful tool for debugging MTS components.

Debugging Using Visual Basic IDE

The simplest way to debug MTS components is by using the Visual Basic IDE the same way you would to debug non-MTS components. While this approach has the benefit of putting you in the familiar VB IDE, it has some drawbacks. The issue is that with this approach you do not get any of the real MTS object context services. You can still get an object context; however, this is a special kind that does not behave the same as within MTS. Specifically, calls to SetAbort, SetComplete, DisableCommit, and EnableCommit all have no effect. Similarly, calls to IsInTransaction and IsSecurityEnabled return FALSE, while calls to IsCallerInRole return TRUE. Although this is not perfect, it is sometimes better than not getting a context object at all.

To enable this type of debugging, follow these steps:

1. Using Regedit, add the following key to the registry.

   ```
   HKEY_LOCAL_MACHINE\SOFTWARE\Microsoft\Transaction _
   Server\Debug\RunWithoutContext
   ```

2. In your MTS component project, go to the Project menu, select Properties, and click on the Debugging tab, shown in Figure 10.8. Select Wait for components to be created.

3. Place break points in your MTS component project and start it.

4. Bring up another instance of the VB IDE and run the test client.

5. When the client calls your MTS component, processing will stop where you placed the break point and you can resume normal debugging from there. Figure 10.9 shows the VB IDE while debugging an MTS component.

Using the Visual Basic IDE to debug MTS components is very similar to debugging non-MTS components. Just keep in mind that the component is not really running inside MTS and therefore most MTS functionality is not available to your component while it is being debugged.

Debugging Using Visual Studio IDE

The second debugging method is to use Visual Studio IDE. This is somewhat cumbersome, but a lot more powerful because it lets you

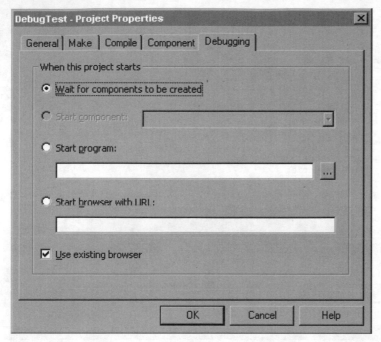

Figure 10.8 Setting the project debugging properties.

debug your component while it runs in MTS. With this approach, you can step through the code while fully utilizing the MTS environment. Here is how to implement this approach:

1. In the Project Properties dialog, click on the Compile tab.

2. Choose Compile to Native Code, No Optimization, and Create Symbolic Debug Info.

3. Build your DLL.

4. Add your component to MTS using the MTS explorer.

5. Start Visual Studio.

6. From the file menu, choose File Open.

7. Open the .DLL file that you built in Step 3.

8. From the file menu, choose Open again.

9. Open all Visual Basic .cls files included in your component.

10. Go to Project, Settings Dialog, and click on the Debug Tab.

11. Under Executable for Debug Session, type in the path to mtx.exe (\winnt\system32\mtx.exe).

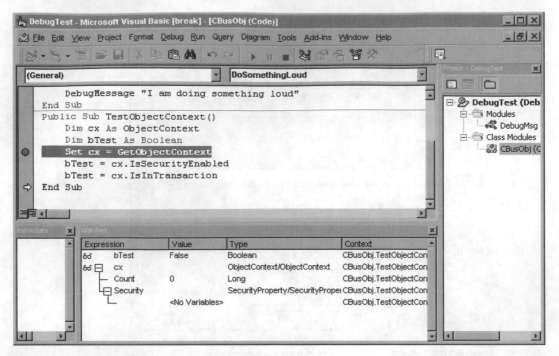

Figure 10.9 VB IDE debugging an MTS component.

12. Under Program Arguments, type in /p: followed by the name of your MTS package, as shown in Figure 10.10. Don't confuse the package name and the component name. Click OK.

13. In the Tools, Options dialog, check Display Unicode Strings.

14. Place break points where you want execution to stop in your .cls files.

15. Shut down the package using MTS explorer.

16. From the Build menu, choose Start Debug and Go.

17. Start your test client and call the component; execution will stop when a break point is encountered.

Now you can step through the code using F10 or F11 while maintaining all MTS functionality. In addition, you can view debug output by going to the View menu and selecting Output. If you want your component to generate debug output, or trace messages, check out the topic "Debugging Visual Basic MTS Components" in the MTS Programmer's Guide. This topic shows you how you can use the OutputDebugStringA API to display messages in the output window for tracing execution or for displaying assertion results, and so on.

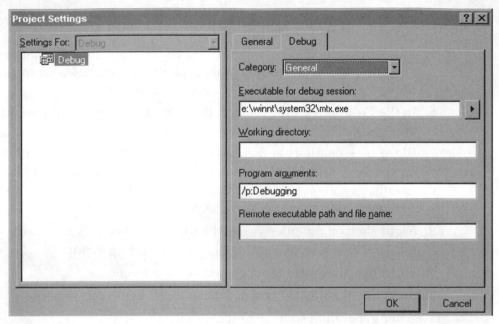

Figure 10.10   Setting the debug properties inside VS IDE.

Visual Studio Analyzer

Let's say you have a fairly complex N-tier application with dozens of components. If the application starts acting up (e.g., performing slower than usual) all of a sudden, how do you narrow down the possible cause? Visual Studio Analyzer (VSA) provides a bird's-eye view of your application where you can drill down to extreme detail. VSA relies on special events to do its work. Many operating-system-level components, as well as other systems, raise VSA events. For example, COM and ADO raise VSA events that you can monitor. To get the most out of VSA, you need to install Windows NT 4 Service Pack 4.

While you cannot use VSA to step through your code, you can narrow down the possible problem source to a component or method. Here is how to use VSA:

1. Make sure you have the VSA server components installed.
2. Make sure you are running at least NT4 SP4, so you will be able to view COM events.
3. Under the Visual Studio 6.0 Enterprise Tools group, click on the Visual Studio Analyzer icon.

4. Choose Analyzer Project and type in the project name in the text field below, as shown in Figure 10.11.

5. In the Project Explorer, expand the project, right click on Machines and choose Connect to Machine. Type in the name of your machine or browse and choose a server machine to connect to.

6. In the Project Explorer, expand the project, right click on Event Logs, and choose Add Event Log.

7. Right click on filters and choose Add Filter. The Edit Filter dialog comes up. Select All Machines, All Components, and All Regular Events, as shown in Figure 10.12 (this is a lot, but it's helpful for demonstration purposes). Click OK.

8. Right click on the filter you just added and choose Set Recording Filter. This tells VSA to use this filter for recording events.

9. From the Analyzer menu, choose Record Events.

10. Switch to your test client and make it call your component(s).

11. After generating some activities, switch back to VSA.

12. Double click on the event log you added in the project explorer.

13. You will see a grid, similar to that shown in Figure 10.13, showing all VSA events that were fired as a result of running your component.

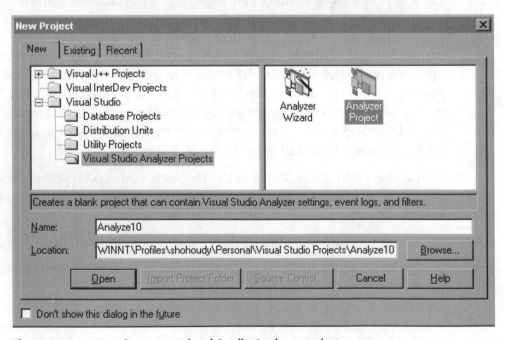

Figure 10.11   Creating a new Visual Studio Analyzer project.

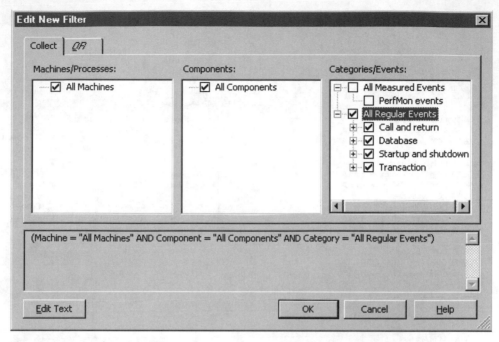

Figure 10.12   Choosing filter options.

14. You can view a timeline of events by going to the View menu and choosing Analyzer, Chart. This brings up a list of recorded events next to a timeline showing you the duration of each event as shown in Figure 10.14.

15. You can also view the interactions of your application components by playing back recorded VSA events using the event player (we think this is really cool). You can play back events in several views including component view and machine view (all accessible from View, Analyzer). You can also control the speed of playback and you can zoom in and out to display more or fewer components. Figure 10.15 shows how VSA replays events.

Visual Studio Analyzer can provide the missing link for debugging N-tier applications by providing a system-level view of your application. Through event recording, timing, and playback, you can narrow down the possible source of a problem to a specific component and then debug that component following these steps. Although Visual Studio Analyzer is not a debugger per se, it can certainly be a powerful tool in your debugging suite. To learn more about Visual Studio Analyzer, consult the Visual Studio Analyzer Reference.

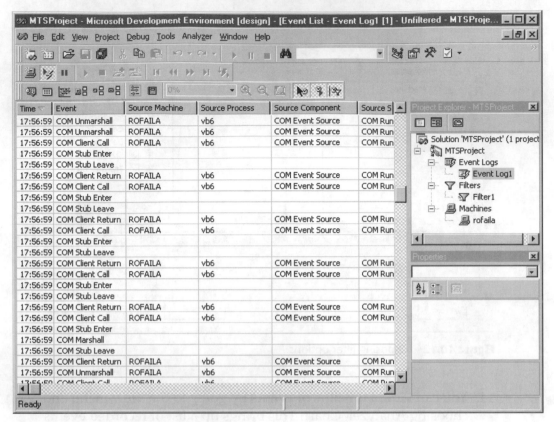

Figure 10.13 Events recorded by VSA.

Automating MTS Configuration

So you wrote this great MTS application and you want to roll it out. Unfortunately, your customers—unlike you—are not MTS gurus; they would not be able to install and configure MTS packages. Don't despair: MTS provides an object-oriented programming interface that allows you to fully automate administration tasks such as adding packages and components and setting security. MTS Administration Objects can be easily used from a variety of languages including Visual Basic.

The MTS Administration Objects navigation model is shown in Figure 10.16. As you can see, it is a fairly rich, hierarchical model. Your program needs to follow this navigation model in order to access the desired object(s). For example, to get hold of the Packages collection, you will need to first get the Catalog object, then use it to get the Packages collection by calling the GetCollection Catalog method.

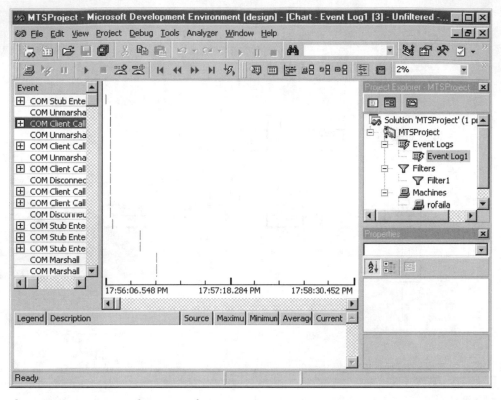

Figure 10.14 VSA performance chart.

Overview

The concept behind automating MTS configuration is simple: You navigate to a collection of objects, then use the collection to add, remove, and modify objects. For example, to add a new package, first get the Catalog object, then get the Packages collection from the Catalog object. Next, call the Add method on the Packages collection. When you are finished adding the new package, simply call SaveChanges to commit the changes you've made. See the following section for more information.

It is worth pointing out that certain tasks, such as adding components, are performed in a slightly different manner. In some cases, you will have to get a UtilityInterface that exposes the methods necessary to accomplish your tasks. This is explained in more detail later in this chapter.

The rest of the chapter walks you through the steps necessary to programmatically add a package, add a component, configure package roles, and remove a package.

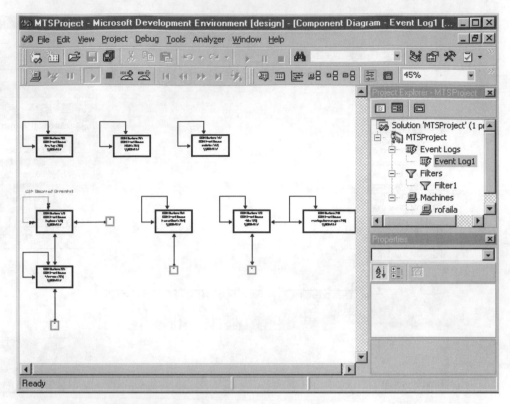

Figure 10.15 VSA event replay in component view.

Adding a New Package

Let's start by learning how to add packages. This can be used as part of a setup program to configure your application on a customer's server. The following code sample adds a package called Vacation Package. Let's examine this in detail.

```
Public Sub AddPackage()
'Adds a new Package to the Local MTS server
On Error GoTo ErrorHandler
Dim oCatalog As MTSAdmin.Catalog
Dim oPackages As Object
Dim oNewPack As Object
Dim sNewPackID As String
'create catalog
Set oCatalog = CreateObject("MTSAdmin.Catalog.1")
'get Packages collection
Set oPackages = oCatalog.GetCollection("Packages")
'Add new package
Set oNewPack = oPackages.Add
```

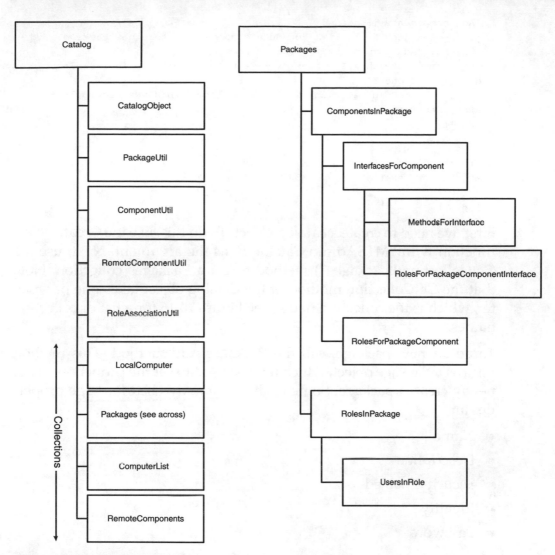

Figure 10.16 MTS Admin Objects Navigation Model overview.

```
'Set package properties
oNewPack.Value("Name") = "Vacation Package"
oNewPack.Value("Description") = "Used for the vacation reservation _
app"
'Get ID assigned to Package
sNewPackID = oNewPack.Key
'Remember to save changes otherwise they're gone!
oPackages.SaveChanges

Set oPackages = Nothing
Set oCatalog = Nothing
```

```
'Add components if needed
If (MsgBox("Would you like to add a component to this new package?", _
vbYesNo, "Add Component?") = vbYes) Then
    sComponentPath = InputBox("Please type component path", "Select _
desired Component")
    If (Len(sComponentPath) > 0) Then AddComponents sNewPackID, _
sComponentPath
End If
Exit Sub

ErrorHandler:
MsgBox Err.Description, vbOKOnly, "Error"
Err.Clear
End Sub
```

First, we need to create a catalog object. To do this, use the CreateObject function with "MTSAdmin.Catalog.1" as the argument. Next, use the GetCollection("Packages") method to get a Packages collection. Note that the GetCollection method of the Catalog object takes one parameter, which is the collection name. See Figure 10.16 for a list of collection names.

To add a new package, call the Packages.Add method. This method returns a Package object, which may be used to set the properties of the newly created package. Some of the commonly used Package properties are:

- Name
- Description
- SecurityEnabled
- Identity
- Password

Next, set the new package name and description. Because we are planning on adding components to this package, we need to know the package ID. When you add a new package it is automatically assigned a unique identifier in the form of a GUID. You can specify your own unique ID as part of the Add method. To get this new unique ID, use the package's Key property.

So far we've added a new package and given it a name and a description. However, all these changes are not committed to the MTS Catalog until you call SaveChanges on the specific collection that you changed—in this case the Packages collection. Forgetting to do this will cost you all your changes!

Finish off by calling AddComponents and passing it the new package ID. The code for adding packages as well as all sample code for this section can be found under samples\ch10ex4.

Retrieving a Package ID

In many cases you will find yourself with a package name when you really need its ID. To get a package's ID you open the Packages collection, tell it to read the catalog information (using Populate), then enumerate through all packages until you find the one you're looking for. The following code snippet shows how to do it:

```
Public Function GetPackageID(sPackName As String) As String
'returns the Key of the specified package
Dim oCatalog As MTSAdmin.Catalog
Dim oPackages As Object
Dim oPackage As Object
Dim iCount As Integer
Dim i As Integer
On Error GoTo ErrorHandler
'create catalog
Set oCatalog = CreateObject("MTSAdmin.Catalog.1")
'get Packages collection
Set oPackages = oCatalog.GetCollection("Packages")
oPackages.Populate
iCount = oPackages.Count
For i = 0 To iCount - 1
    Set oPackage = oPackages.Item(i)
    If oPackage.Name = sPackName Then
        GetPackageID = oPackage.Key
        Exit For
    End If
Next
Set oPackage = Nothing
Set oPackages = Nothing
Set oCatalog = Nothing

Exit Function
ErrorHandler:
MsgBox Err.Description, vbOKOnly, "Error"
Err.Clear

End Function
```

First we get the Packages collection using the GetCollection method of the MTS Catalog object. The For loop iterates through all packages in the collection looking for the package we want. Once we find our package, we read its ID using the Key property. We then free the objects we allocated and exit.

OK, so we've learned how to add packages: now what? Well, unless we add some components to our new package it won't be much use. Let's look at some code that does this.

```
Public Sub AddComponents(sPackID As String, sComponentPath As _
String)
'Adds components to specified package
On Error GoTo ErrorHandler
Dim oCatalog As MTSAdmin.Catalog
Dim oPackages As Object
Dim oCompsInPack As Object
Dim oCompsUtil As Object
'create catalog
Set oCatalog = CreateObject("MTSAdmin.Catalog.1")
'get Packages collection
Set oPackages = oCatalog.GetCollection("Packages")
'get the ComponentsInPackage collection
'note that we need to use the PackageID
Set oCompsInPack = oPackages.GetCollection("ComponentsInPackage", _
sPackID)
'Now get the component utility interface
Set oCompsUtil = oCompsInPack.GetUtilInterface
'install the component
'note that the typelib is embedded in the dll and we do not have a
'custom proxy/stub
oCompsUtil.InstallComponent sComponentPath,"",""
'No need to save, components are written to the catalog directly!

Set oCompsUtil = Nothing
Set oCompsInPack = Nothing
Set oPackages = Nothing
Set oCatalog = Nothing

Exit Sub

ErrorHandler:
MsgBox Err.Description, vbOKOnly, "Error"
Err.Clear
End Sub
```

Again, we go through the steps necessary to get the Catalog and the Packages collection. This time, we need to get the ComponentsInPackage collection for the newly added package. This is where we use the package ID. Unfortunately, the ComponentsInPackage collection does not allow adding new components using the Add method. Instead, we need to get the ComponentUtil object by calling GetUtilInterface on the ComponentsInPackage collection. Next, install a component by calling InstallComponent on the ComponentUtil object. This method takes three parameters: DLL Path, TypeLib Path, and Proxy/Stub Path. Because our component has the type library embedded in it, and because we are not using a proxy/stub DLL, use empty strings for the second and third parameters.

Interestingly, components are added directly to the catalog. Therefore, you do not need to call SaveChanges as in the case of packages.

Configuring Roles

Configuring roles is very similar to adding components and packages. A code example will help us understand how to configure roles.

```
Public Sub AddRoles(sPackID As String)
'Adds a role to the Vacation package
On Error GoTo ErrorHandler
Dim oCatalog As MTSAdmin.Catalog
Dim oPackages As Object
Dim oRolesInPack As Object
Dim oNewRole As Object
Dim oUsersInRole As Object
Dim oNewUser As Object
Dim oCompsInPack As Object
Dim oComp As Object
Dim oRolesForComp As Object
Dim oRoleUtil As Object
'create catalog
Set oCatalog = CreateObject("MTSAdmin.Catalog.1")
'get Packages collection
Set oPackages = oCatalog.GetCollection("Packages")
'Get RolesInPackage collection
Set oRolesInPack = oPackages.GetCollection("RolesInPackage", _
sPackID)
'Add a new role to the RolesInPackage collection
Set oNewRole = oRolesInPack.Add
'set the new Role's name
oNewRole.Value("Name") = "King Of The Jungle"
'Save changes we made
oRolesInPack.SaveChanges
'Get UsersInRole collection for the new Role
Set oUsersInRole = oRolesInPack.GetCollection("UsersInRole", _
oNewRole.Key)
'Add a new user to the collection
Set oNewUser = oUsersInRole.Add
'Set the new user's name (this must be an already existing NT
'Account)
oNewUser.Value("User") = "Administrator"
'Save changes
oUsersInRole.SaveChanges
```

```
'Now we need to loop through all components in this package and
'associate the new role
Set oCompsInPack = oPackages.GetCollection("ComponentsInPackage", _
sPackID)
'Read configuration from MTS catalog
oCompsInPack.Populate
'Enumerate all components
For Each oComp In oCompsInPack
    'Get the collection of Roles for this component
    Set oRolesForComp =
oCompsInPack.GetCollection("RolesForPackageComponent", oComp.Key)
    'Get the RoleAssociationUtil object
    Set oRoleUtil = oRolesForComp.GetUtilInterface
    'Associate the New Role with this component
    oRoleUtil.AssociateRole oNewRole.Key
    'No need to save changes
    Set oRolesForComp = Nothing
    Set oRoleUtil = Nothing
Next oComp
'cleanup
Set oCatalog = Nothing
Set oPackages = Nothing
Set oRolesInPack = Nothing
Set oNewRole = Nothing
Set oUsersInRole = Nothing
Set oNewUser = Nothing
Set oCompsInPack = Nothing
Set oComp = Nothing
Exit Sub

ErrorHandler:
MsgBox Err.Description, vbOKOnly, "Error"
Err.Clear

End Sub
```

First you get the Packages collection. Next you get the RolesInPackage collection using the package ID. If you know the package's name but not its ID, you can call Populate on the Packages collection and then enumerate through all packages, examining their names. Once you find your package, get its ID using the Package.Key property.

To add a new role, simply call the Add method on the RolesInPackage collection. Next, set the new role's name (and optionally its description). Like packages, roles get assigned a unique ID used as the key in the collection. Remember to save the changes by calling the SaveChanges method.

We still haven't assigned users to this new role. To do this we need to get the UsersInRole collection from the RolesInPackage collection (are you dizzy yet?). Then add a new user, specifying the user's name (note that this must be an already existing NT account). You may use a user name or a group name. To use a domain account, simply use the domain\account syntax.

One more thing to do: Assign roles to the components under our package. In this case, we will assign the new role to all components in our package. So we get the ComponentsInPackage collection and enumerate through all components. For each component, we get the RolesForPackageComponent collection, then get from it the RoleAssociationUtil interface. We use this interface to add the new role (we'll need to use the new role's ID). Finally, we clean up and we're done!

Removing Packages

If you add packages as part of a setup program, then you should consider removing them as part of the uninstall (of course no one will ever uninstall your product, but just in case). Examine the code sample shown here, which demonstrates how to remove an MTS package.

```
Public Sub DeletePackage(sPackID As String)
'This sub deletes a package and its components
Dim iCount As Integer
Dim i As Integer
Dim oCatalog As MTSAdmin.Catalog
Dim oPackages As Object
Dim varCLSID(0) As Variant
On Error GoTo ErrorHandler
'Delete all components under this package
DeleteComps sPackID

'create catalog
Set oCatalog = CreateObject("MTSAdmin.Catalog.1")
'get Packages collection
Set oPackages = oCatalog.GetCollection("Packages")
'Read catalog information for specified package
varCLSID(0) = sPackID
oPackages.PopulateByKey varCLSID
'remove specified package
'note that it will be at index 0 since its the only one we read from
'the catalog
oPackages.Remove 0
'save changes
oPackages.SaveChanges
'cleanup
Set oPackages = Nothing
Set oCatalog = Nothing
```

```
Exit Sub
ErrorHandler:
MsgBox Err.Description, vbOKOnly, "Error"
Err.Clear

End Sub
```

To remove a package, simply get the Packages collection, tell it to read the package information from the catalog, and then remove the package and save your changes. Although it is not necessary, the following sample code removes all components inside a package before removing the package. The sub DeleteComps shown next handles deleting MTS components by iterating through the ComponentsInPackage collection and calling the Remove method on for each component in the collection. Note that after each call to Remove, you must call SaveChanges to commit your changes.

```
Public Sub DeleteComps(sPackID As String)
'This sub deletes all components in a package
On Error GoTo ErrorHandler
Dim iCount As Integer
Dim i As Integer
Dim oCatalog As MTSAdmin.Catalog
Dim oPackages As Object
Dim oCompsInPack As Object

'create catalog
Set oCatalog = CreateObject("MTSAdmin.Catalog.1")
'get Packages collection
Set oPackages = oCatalog.GetCollection("Packages")
'Get the ComponentsInPackage collection
Set oCompsInPack = oPackages.GetCollection("ComponentsInPackage", _
sPackID)
'Read catalog information into the ComponentsInPackage collection
oCompsInPack.Populate
'Get number of components in this package
iCount = oCompsInPack.Count()
'loop through and delete all components
For i = iCount - 1 To 0 Step -1
    oCompsInPack.Remove i
    oCompsInPack.SaveChanges
Next
'cleanup
Set oCompsInPack = Nothing
Set oPackages = Nothing
Set oCatalog = Nothing
Exit Sub

ErrorHandler:
MsgBox Err.Description, vbOKOnly, "Error"
Err.Clear

End Sub
```

Managing Remote Servers

Managing remote servers is identical to managing the local server, with one exception: You need to use the Connect method of the Catalog object to specify which server you want to manage. Let's see how this is done through a code example. This sub adds a package to the server called Doofis:

```
Public Sub AddRemotePackage()
'Adds a new Package to the Local MTS server
On Error GoTo ErrorHandler
Dim oCatalog As MTSAdmin.Catalog
Dim oRoot as Object
Dim oPackages As Object
Dim oNewPack As Object
Dim sNewPackID As String
'create catalog
Set oCatalog = CreateObject("MTSAdmin.Catalog.1")
Set oRoot = catalog.Connect("Doofis")

'get Packages collection
Set oPackages = oRoot.GetCollection("Packages")
'Add new package
.
.
.
Code the same as for local machine
```

After we get the MTS catalog object, we call the Connect method, which returns a Root collection object. We use this object to get access to lower-level collections (this is equivalent to the Catalog object on the local machine). From that point on, the code is the same as the example for adding a package.

Winding Up

In this chapter we learned how to effectively use MTS as a solution for many of the middle-tier problems, such as transaction management and scalability. We started by looking inside MTS to see how it runs your components. We talked about passing parameters to MTS components and MTS transactions. We then discussed stateful and stateless components and learned how to use the Shared Property Manager (SPM) to hold state. Next we looked at security and learned how to use MTS roles as well as program security within MTS components. We also learned how to use Visual Studio tools to debug multitier MTS applications. Finally, we learned how to automate MTS administration in order to create installation programs to help roll out our MTS applications.

CHAPTER 11

The Database Server

I n this chapter we look at the database tier of our N-tier application. Designing the database tier is an important step in developing N-tier applications. In fact, ignoring database design issues will void all your hard work developing and architecting your application. A poor database design can hinder your application salability and performance. All along we've been discussing how to make our distributed applications robust and efficient, and the database is no exception. We want to ensure a well-designed database that will enhance our design and implementation. Here is what we will cover in this chapter:

- Database design considerations
- Client design issues
- The COM in SQL Server
- Optimization and security

Database Design Considerations

Database design is one of the most critical elements of a client/server solution. A well-planned database design contributes tremendously to the performance of your application. Poor or unplanned design affects not only performance, but your application's overall quality as well. Poorly designed databases can create bottlenecks and logjams. Not thinking ahead about how your tables and their relationships are laid out can cause unnecessary delays in running your in-line queries and stored procedures. Additionally, a poorly planned database can make it very difficult for external applications to communicate or run queries against your table. This isolates your application from participating with other applications' requests.

Database design begins when you design your components to ensure that the system is balanced in all areas. It is important to keep the database in mind while designing your components, anticipating that the database will participate in some of the activities performed by the components. Most developers tend to ignore the database side of things, believing that it's okay to just write the code first, then design the database to match it. This is not entirely accurate, nor is it recommended.

The database is a reflection of your application's business functionality. For the most part, the table relationships model how your components interact; therefore it is very important to model your design to accurately describe your business. There are several questions you should ask yourself when designing your database:

- *What are the security requirements for the database?* Understanding security requirements helps you to choose the proper security approach. For example, would NT's integrated security be sufficient to secure the database, or are there additional security requirements?

- *What are some of the database normalization rules that need to be enforced?* Understanding the requirements for normalization helps you balance your application. Consider, for example, the ease of querying your tables (in a highly normalized database) versus obtaining the maximum performance benefit (in the case of a denormalized database).

- *What are the application performance requirements?* This knowledge serves as a guideline for how your application should perform. Performance requirements are usually measured either against your previous version of your product, if you are trying either to improve or be consistent with previous performance, or even against your competitor product where you want to exceed it.

- *How can I design the tables so that they can be easily maintained?* This requirement can have a tremendous effect on your overall application maintenance. You will need to understand up front how you can minimize the frequency of schema changes. Schema changes also impact component design. If you need to update your component every time your table schema changes, then understanding how to make tables easily maintained will pay off on the long run.

- *What are the concurrent multiuser requirements for the database?* It is highly recommended that you understand how your application and database will be used, and that you be able to accurately predict the concurrent number of users in order to make appropriate decisions without overdesigning your application. For example, you might not need to spend time designing your application to accommodate thousands of users if only 20 people will be logged on at the same time. You might be spending too much time solving a problem that does not exist.

- *How can I design the database so users can use their own ad hoc query tools to retrieve data?* This question is important to answer if your application is going to provide a mechanism for third-party tools and applications to query your database. If this is the case, then you will need to consider how you can make the integration process easy for these applications.

- *How do I guarantee the data integrity in the database?* Answering this question will clarify whether you should be resorting to triggers and stored procedures to help you in maintaining your database integrity, or whether you should be looking at other methods to guarantee the integrity of your application.

These are just a few of the questions you should consider. While this book is not about data modeling and normalization, we feel it is important to understand the importance of these issues when developing your N-tier application.

Our mission when designing a robust distributed N-tier application is very precise and clear: Keep the balance. We want to be sure that we are making sound decisions in every tier and that tiers and servers are not overloaded. Our responsibility in the database tier is to ensure that we are able to do the following:

1. Properly design and normalize the database.

2. Consider the multiuser requirements by not holding on to old habits.

3. Understand how we can take advantage of server features such as stored procedures.

4. Use the most efficient ways to access the data.

5. Understand how to design better clients.

If you follow these guidelines, you are on the right track to developing a very scalable system that is now ready to service thousands of users.

Normalizing Your Database Design

Database normalization, in a nutshell, is the process by which you design your database to minimize the duplication of information. Database normalization is a very tricky issue: Developers often disagree on how far to go to achieve it. There is no right or wrong answer to this question. Remember, a database design should represent the application's functionality. Therefore, how you go about normalizing a database is dependent on your application's functionality.

It is easy to determine how normalized a database is by examining the tables. A greater number of narrow tables is characteristic of a normalized database. On the other hand, a lesser number of wide tables is characteristic of a denormalized database. A highly normalized database is always associated with complex relational joins, which can hurt performance. Every time you run a query, you jump between tables instead of staying within one table. The process of jumping and joining tables is very costly. However, the benefits of normalization cannot be ignored. There are several benefits to a reasonably normalized database:

- More tables results in more clustered indexes. When clustered indexes exist, the optimization engine will always attempt to use them, thereby enhancing performance.

- Narrower tables result in faster sorting and index creation. Because the optimizer does not have to move large sets of data into temporary tables for sorting, records are copied and sorted more quickly.

- The indexes are more compact. Compact indexes help the optimizer select the best optimization plan to execute with your query.

- Fewer indexes per table allows our UPDATE statements to perform better. There are several rules that come in play on how exactly the update should be performed. If your tables have less to index, then inserts are faster because the optimizer does not have to check every index for validation.

- Fewer NULLs and less redundant data makes the overall database more compact. Allowing nulls in your database will overinflate it and increase fragmentation. Keeping the database compact means your tables are better positioned to execute your search queries much faster than they could if they had to sift through null records.

The important issue to keep track of is the level of normalization you are willing to adopt. A database that is very normalized will have to perform several joins between tables, thereby affecting performance. At the other extreme, very wide and few tables can be difficult to use if users are attempting to query these tables by means of external tools.

The new enhancement in SQL Server 7, combined with reasonable normalization, will help boost performance. As normalization increases, so does the number and complexity of joins required to retrieve data. A reasonable normalization is one that does not exceed four joins to retrieve a complex query.

Getting Rid of Old Habits

When moving from a single-user environment or a nondistributed environment to an N-tier environment, we unfortunately bring with us lots of bad habits that can affect the performance of our system. Some of these habits are easy to get rid of, while others need some work and practice.

Network trips are one of the most critical factors that slow down performance. The number of trips your application makes over a network to send and receive data impacts performance. There are choices that need to be made in order to optimize performance, and bad choices will lead to excessive network round trips. To improve performance, you will need to use different approaches to getting your data back from the database:

1. Stop browsing tables

2. Choose your Recordset wisely

3. Think of your operations in terms of batches

Although the techniques we are about to discuss will help boost your application's performance, you will find that as a result of adopting them your application will scale better, serving multiple concurrent users. This is because operations performed using these techniques cause fewer table locks and enable quick in and out operations on your tables. Users will not have to wait to start while other operations finish.

Stop Browsing Tables

Loosely using Select * from a table to view hundreds if not thousands of records at a time is a common habit. This approach is fine for a single-user application that runs on a desktop. You don't have to worry about database locks or network traffic and resources. However, opening up multiple tables and allowing users to browse as many records as they want is not something you want to continue to do. These types of operations can bring your system to its knees and make your application unusable because SQL Server will place a lock on the tables that are used so that they cannot be changed by other users. What is a designer to do?

The solution is to carefully calculate the number of records that users absolutely must see. For example, if your users are accustomed to viewing a list of all inventory items in a system in order to perform a physical count, offer them an alternative, such as an alphabetical or a quantitative list. This makes use of the WHERE clause of the select statement. Users will never be able to work with 10,000 records at the same time, so why present all these records?

You might notice a performance bottleneck when testing your application over the network using one or two users sending back lots of records. When you deploy your application for use by many concurrent users, you will start realizing these bottlenecks occur when your application is not scaling well. So don't be deceived by your initial simple tests.

So you ask, "What can I do if I narrow down my criteria as much as possible and still get thousands of records?" This is a valid argument. Sometimes there is no escape from having to deal with large numbers of records. A solution to this problem is to replicate the table records on a local database from your SQL Server database. SQL Server 7 allows you to install desktop versions of the database instead of using an access database. This way you don't have to change data access methods for each database type.

When you replicate the most frequently used tables, you avoid network traffic. For example, if you are developing a human resource system, and you want to query employees, you can just bring down the employees' table locally and decide how often you are going to replicate this table from the server. It is safe to do something like this simply because the chances of your company adding new employees every day of the year are small, so you can decide on the replication strategy based on the frequency with which your database records change. You can even make this frequency customizable by the client. For example, users can choose to check for new records every time they log on, or you can even schedule this activity to happen transparently at night.

Choose Your Recordset Wisely

One of the most common mistakes in designing a single-user application is to use the default setting of the database and disregard the Recordset types that are being used. There are two types of Recordsets: Snapshot and Dynaset.

The Snapshot Recordset downloads all of the data immediately. You can use a Snapshot Recordset type if you do not need to update the server tables or if the table contains relatively few columns. Under these two conditions, the Recordset opens faster. You can also use a Snapshot Recordset for combo boxes and list boxes, to keep the number of records as small as possible.

The Dynaset Recordset downloads a small number of records, then downloads pointers to the rest of the data. You can use this Recordset when you don't want to suffer the overhead of having to bring all the records down to the client.

Your choice of Recordset type will depend on the situation. The important thing is to understand how each type works and what its consequences are. You must evaluate each operation carefully and select the type that is most appropriate and that results in faster execution.

Think in Terms of Batches

As we discussed earlier, among the most important considerations of a distributed system are network traffic and network round trips. Most of the systems that show slow performance are those that migrate from a single-user environment to a distributed environment. Network round trips occur in a single-user environment, where single records are manipulated and sent back to the database one at a time. For a distributed environment, a better approach is to batch records and package them together to send all at once over the network.

There are two ways to do this. The first option for batching records is to reevaluate your in-line SQL statements. Instead of using a single SQL statement to update one record at a time, such as:

```
UPDATE Employee SET BonusPercentage = 4 WHERE EmployeeID = RD456
```

you can rewrite your statement like this:

```
UPDATE Employee SET BonusPercentage = 4 WHERE EmployeeID = RD456 OR _
RD984
```

In the second statement we appended all the records that needed updating to the WHERE clause using the OR. This will cause the changes to be written to all the records that meet the criteria without having to come back to the client, pick up the next record, and repeat the process again.

If you run this query, you'll find that it is at least twice as fast as the original query.

The second approach is to use stored procedures where you pass all your record parameters and let the stored procedure execute the query on the server for all the records. We discuss this in detail in the next section.

Understanding Stored Procedures

Stored procedures are one of those things that developers either use excessively or not at all. It is important to understand stored procedures and how they work in order to make wise decisions on how and when to use them. Before we go into when to use them, let's first understand how stored procedures work.

When stored procedures are created, they go through the parsing and normalization steps that SQL Server performs on any SQL statement. The stored procedure is then saved to disk in the parsed, normalized form of a query tree. When stored procedures are executed for the first time, SQL Server retrieves the saved query tree and optimizes the execution of the SQL statement based on the values of parameters passed in, such as:

```
CREATE  PROC sp_EmpBonus
(@EmployeeID Char(10), @BonusPercentage INT)
AS
UPDATE Employee (EmployeeID, BonusPercentage)
    VALUES(@EmployeeID,@BonusPercentage)
```

and the available statistics of the tables and their indexes used in the statement. When the stored procedure is called again by any user, SQL Server first looks to the procedure cache to see if a matching optimized execution plan is available for use with a new set of parameters. If it finds a plan, it uses it. This process is shown in Figure 11.1. SQL statements compiled into stored procedures can thus save a significant amount of processing at execution time; because the system has already determined the most efficient way to execute the statement, it will not waste time trying to figure out how the statement should be run.

TIP

Because SQL Server looks at the statistics of the stored procedure to get the execution plan, it is important to update these statistics if your table and index designs change. This tells SQL Server to find a better way to execute the stored procedure in light of the new plan. You can update statistics using a SQL DMO command, discussed later in this chapter.

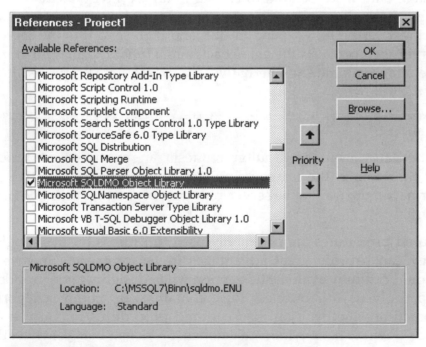

Figure 11.1   Calling a stored procedure by a client.

Stored procedures are an all-or-nothing deal for lots of developers; they either love them or don't use them. This should not be the case. It is important to understand stored procedures and to know how and when to use them effectively, not blindly.

When to Use Stored Procedures

All well-designed distributed applications should always use stored procedures. True or false?

The answer is both. Stored procedures are very powerful, but they do come with a price. As mentioned in the preceding tip, stored procedures require some maintenance overhead. They also expose your application's functionality if they contain business logic. And they don't fit the seamless upgrade that logic in a component benefits from. They still need to be updated manually or via dropping a script; then the new logic must be created and the statistics updated and checked.

However, stored procedures do come in handy and can provide tremendous benefits in several areas: for example, in the use of images. Suppose your application needs to insert a large binary value into an image data field. Sending this data in an INSERT statement requires some work; the application must convert the binary value to a character string, causing it to expand in size, and then send it to the server. The server then converts the value back into a binary format for storage in the image column. An alternative is to create a stored procedure, such as the following:

```
CREATE PROCEDURE sp_StoreImage(@picture1 image) AS INSERT N VALUES _
  (@picture1)
```

When the client application requests an execution of procedure sp_StoreImage, the image parameter value stays in its native binary format all the way to the server, reducing processing time and network traffic.

Stored procedures are commonly used to process business logic, and they can provide great advantages in performance. However, you should carefully evaluate this option when designing your application, especially if your business logic contains very complex algorithms. Sometimes the decision to use stored procedures for business logic boils down to having more developers proficient in SQL syntax than in using VB.

Using ADO to Call Stored Procedures from VB

In previous chapters we have been using ADO and passing a SQL statement directly into the Execute method of the ADO object. This approach works great when using in-line SQL statements. But in order to call stored procedures, we need to change the implementation slightly and create a new type of ADO object.

The ADO object model is very simple and straightforward. So far we have been using the Connection, Recordset, and Error objects. Now we are adding another object called the Command object. The Command object allows you to specifically invoke certain command types such as stored procedures. Table 11.1 show what all these command types are.

The only change from our previous ADO examples in Chapter 8, "Understanding COM Internals," is that we are not invoking the SQL statement in line and passing it to the ADO Execute method. Instead, we create a Command object first, then pass the SQL statement—in this case it happens to be a stored procedure name—into the command text, then call the Execute method. This technique gives us the flexibility of invoking different types of commands, including in-line SQL statements, through one mechanism. Table 11.1 shows all the command types available in ADO and when they should be used.

We still need to create a connection, and then execute the command and return the result into the Recordset. That's it. There are no tricks involved in executing a SQL stored procedure.

Table 11.1   ADO Command Types

COMMAND NAME	USAGE
AdCmdText	Used to execute SQL statements or textual statements that the engine would know how to evaluate.
AdCmdTable	Causes ADO to generate a SQL query to return all the data from the specified table.
AdCmdTableDirect	Causes ADO to return all the data directly from the table.
AdCmdStoredProc	Causes ADO to run the named stored procedure.
AdCmdFetchAsync	Indicates that the remaining data after the quantity specified in the cache size should be fetched.
AdCmdExecuteAsyn	Causes the command to execute asynchronously.

The following is the stored procedure that we are going to call from the Command object. This stored procedure returns the author ID, author first name, and author last name from the Pubs database in SQL Server. We are not suggesting that you should build stored procedures to perform this type of functionality: We're just using this as an example to demonstrate how to use and call a stored procedure.

```
CREATE   PROCEDURE getauthorinfo AS SELECT
au_id,au_lname,au_fname,phone from Authors

    Dim rsset As ADODB.Recordset
    Dim cn As ADODB.Connection
    Dim cmdStoredProc As New ADODB.Command
    Dim anerror As ADODB.Error

    Dim connectstring As String
    Dim Sql As String

    cmdStoredProc.Prepared = False
    cmdStoredProc.CommandText = "getauthorinfo"
    cmdStoredProc.CommandType = adCmdStoredProc

    connectstring = "Driver=SQL
Server;Server=FASDEVSPHINX;Database=pubs;UID=sa;"

    Set cn = New ADODB.Connection
    cn.ConnectionString = connectstring

    cn.CursorLocation = adUseClient

    cn.Open

    Set cmdStoredProc.ActiveConnection = cn
    Set rsset = cmdStoredProc.Execute
```

In this example we executed a stored procedure that we created to retrieve the author ID, last name, first name, and phone number. We then created our ADO Command object and told it the name of the stored procedure to execute. We collected the result set of the stored procedure, and now we can perform any operation on it.

So far we have learned how we can directly call stored procedures from ADO clients and get the data back into the client. Next we discuss other techniques that can give us some flexibility and control over the execution and maintenance of these stored procedures.

Wrapping Stored Procedures in COM Components

Stored procedures are scalable and powerful enough to perform and exist as a standalone tier. However, you may need to be able to isolate the user from accessing the stored procedure directly from the client and creating an abstraction layer between the client and the database server. To do this, we need to create a COM component that can live in the business tier and be the communication link between the client and the database server. The steps are as follows:

1. Reuse the stored procedure we created earlier.
2. Create a server component to talk to the stored procedure.
3. Create a client that will call the server component and ask for specific operations.

Creating a component that abstracts the client from communicating with the database tier can be a benefit if we want to scale the application to other database servers without asking the clients to change their implementation and the way they call the stored procedure, especially if the stored procedure names change. Additionally, the COM component that we build might perform other data manipulation logic that the client does not need to know about, such as masking and formatting the data in a specific way to match a business need, concatenating data items together to make up one field, and so on.

The concept of creating a COM abstraction component is very simple. We need to expand the code we just wrote in the previous section that was calling the stored procedure and move it to a separate ActiveX DLL. Let's create a new ActiveX DLL and add a function called Retrieve-Recordset. Inside the function, we place the code we wrote in the previous section and add two new lines of code:

1. The first line is the return value of the function, which we declare as ADODB.Recordset. This declaration causes the function to return a Recordset object to the caller.
2. The second line is added at the end of the function as follows:

```
Set RetrieveRecordset = rsset
```

This causes the function to set the Recordset of the result of the stored procedure that will be returned.

That's all we need to do to our ActiveX DLL server component. We now have a COM wrapper that isolates the stored procedure call and implementation from clients.

```
Function RetrieveRecordset() As ADODB.Recordset
    Dim rsset As ADODB.Recordset
```

```
     Dim cn As ADODB.Connection
     Dim connectstring As String
     Dim anerror As ADODB.Error
     Dim Sql As String

     Dim cmdStoredProc As New ADODB.Command
     cmdStoredProc.Prepared = False
     cmdStoredProc.CommandText = "getauthorinfo"
     cmdStoredProc.CommandType = adCmdStoredProc

     connectstring = "Driver=SQL
Server;Server=FASDEVSPHINX;Database=pubs;UID=sa;"

     Set cn = New ADODB.Connection

     cn.ConnectionString = connectstring

     cn.CursorLocation = adUseClient

     cn.Open

     Set cmdStoredProc.ActiveConnection = cn
     Set rsset = cmdStoredProc.Execute
     Set RetrieveRecordset = rsset
End Function
```

Now let's examine the code that goes in the client and see how simple it is. The objective of this model is to create isolation from the client. We are successful if we don't implement any logic in our client, but rather make the client responsible for simple navigation.

The first task is to create a disconnected Recordset to hold the Recordset being sent back from our wrapper component. We do this by declaring a global Recordset variable such as the following:

```
Global rsset As ADOR.Recordset
```

Next we set the return Recordset from the COM wrapper to our disconnected Recordset. We can perform this step in the Form Load event of the form for simplicity.

Insert the following code in the Form Load:

```
Dim x As CStoredProcWrapper
Set x = New CStoredProcWrapper
        Set rsset = x.RetrieveRecordset
```

The next step is to create navigational command button of the form, so that it would look like Figure 11.2. The navigational button scrolls through the Recordset performing the standard MoveFirst, MoveNext, MovePrevious, and MoveLast methods. To do this, we use navigational code that uses the disconnected Recordset to navigate:

```
rsset.MoveFirst
```

The final step is to populate the text fields on the form with the fields from the result set by creating a procedure called Populate_Fields. This procedure moves the database fields into the appropriate text boxes as follows:

```
Text1.Text = rsset.Fields("au_id")
Text2.Text = rsset.Fields("au_lname")
Text3.Text = rsset.Fields("au_fname")
Text4.Text = rsset.Fields("phone")
```

That's how simple it is to create the client. As you can see, the client code is very pure from business logic and is isolated from the database and the stored procedure. If you choose, you can change the logic of the stored procedure by adding WHERE clauses; the client will still function. Additionally you can completely change the stored procedure and even the entire SQL Server engine, and the client will still continue to work, provided of course that you stick with ADO as the data access method.

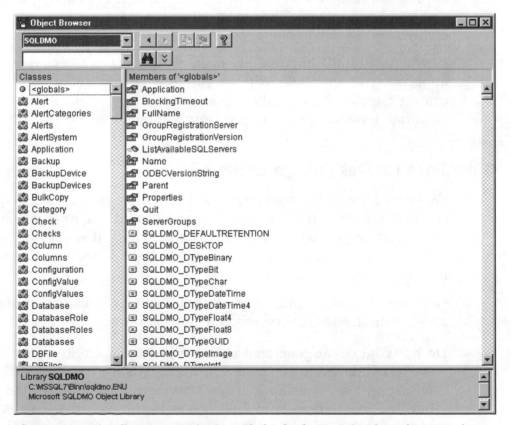

Figure 11.2 The client communicating with the database engine through a COM abstraction layer.

The SQL Servant

SQL Server is not magic. The reason we say this is that we see a lot of developers making bad design decisions and counting on SQL Server to save them. Application design plays a very important role in SQL Server performance as well as successful implementation of a distributed system. The key to better understanding the role the database engine plays is to picture the server as the servant, not the master. The client plays the role of the boss, and the server is the worker. The boss tells the workers what they need to do, how they are going to do it, and when they are going to do it. Most companies that fail can be traced back to bad management: The boss is counting on the workers without giving them any direction; then, when the company goes down, the boss goes around blaming the workers for not doing their jobs.

Designing applications is no different. A lot of developers count on SQL Server to save their bad design and to solve their problems when the application does not scale well because the client is making bad calls and bad assumptions. They blame the server for not being powerful enough and go looking for a faster and stronger server.

For this reason it's important to make the correct decisions during the application design phase. With a well-designed application, SQL Server can do a great job supporting thousands of concurrent users. On the other hand, with a poorly designed application the server has no chance.

Guidelines for Designing a Better Client

We know it might seem strange to talk about the client in the database section, but now that you know how to build clients and have an understanding of database design fundamentals, it is very important to fine-tune your knowledge of clients in light of the better database understanding you now possess.

Here are some of the most important guidelines to follow in designing a well-optimized SQL Server–based application:

Do not take client-generated code for granted. Control clients that are programmed to generate SQL statements dynamically are based on an object relationship. You don't have control over generated code, but you must know how this code is being executed. This is very common with legacy applications that use abstraction layers to communicate to SQL Server, or applications that are migrating from other database servers and are now adding support to SQL Server. Equally important are applications that rely on wizards (including wizards that come with Visual Basic) to generate code. Make sure to examine this client code and change it to fit your application architecture and model.

Prompt for sufficient input.   It's better to design the client application to prompt the user for sufficient input so that queries are submitted that generate low result sets. By prompting for sufficient input, you narrow your search criteria. The more input you can provide, the better your query will perform and the better your client will run. Use client design techniques such as limiting the number of wildcards when building queries and prohibiting ad hoc queries.

Give the users the option to cancel out of a query in process gracefully.   Do not force the user to soft boot to cancel a query, because this may cause orphaned and wasted connections.

Implement a time out limit on query processing.   Do not allow queries to run forever. When developing an application you should have an idea of the acceptable time it should take to process a query, so set the timeout accordingly.

You now know how queries are executed on the server and how the database design helps us increase performance. We also discussed how to avoid excessive and unnecessary network round trips. By understanding the guidelines for building clients that help make these things happen and do not hinder them, we are ensuring that our system is balanced and that all aspects of the system are cooperating and working together toward a common objective.

The COM in SQL Server 7

So far we have been creating our own objects and components and making them available to our own programs as well as allowing the outside world to take advantage of them. We have learned a lot about COM- and interface-based programming as well as how to program for reuse. We'll turn the tables a little bit now by asking for things for free. Instead of having to write every component ourselves, we will demand to be able to use someone else's components for a change.

SQL Server provides us services in a form of COM components that we would otherwise have to code from scratch ourselves. It also provides two methods for reusing some of its components. The first is known as SQL Distributed Management Objects (SQL DMO). The second method is a new feature added to SQL Server 7 called the SQL NameSpace or SQL NS (don't blame us for the name). Let's take a look at these two approaches in detail. We will provide you with code samples to help you utilize their services.

What Is SQL DMO?

SQL DMO is a COM layer that communicates with the internal functionality of the SQL Server engine. It exposes some of the elements you can manipulate via a COM-enabled language such as VB. You can write VB code that controls and manages some of the objects inside SQL Server, such as tables and stored procedures.

Using SQL DMO is no different than using a COM server. However, you need to understand the object model hierarchy and the available properties and methods in that model. The process of using SQL DMO can be explained in three easy steps:

1. Add a reference to the SQL DMO server to your VB project (Figure 11.3).
2. View the VB Object Browser to get a quick overview of all the available properties and methods (Figure 11.4).
3. Start writing VB code against these objects.

SQL DMO provides an excellent alternative to building your own system utilities. One of the disadvantages of a client/server system is the number of utilities that surround the system. Reusing some SQL Server services via SQL DMO is a more robust and time-saving technique.

Two examples of these features are the pager and e-mail notification processes that are built into Microsoft SQL Server. These services hardly require you to do anything at all other than program their objects.

The process of using DMO is very straightforward. Here are the high-level steps you need to perform:

1. Create a DMO object.
2. Call methods on this object.
3. Enumerate through result collection.

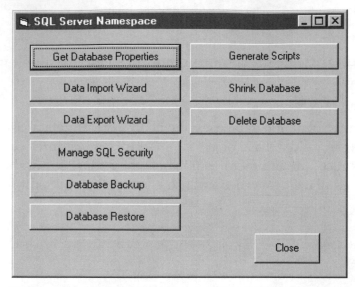

Figure 11.3 The COM reference to the SQL DMO Object Library.

Now let's take a look at how to use the SQL DMO objects to retrieve data from SQL Server. Start by declaring two SQL Server DMO objects, the Database object and the SQLServer object.

```
Dim oDatabase As SQLDMO.Database
Dim nDatabase As Integer
Dim oSQLServer As New SQLDMO.SQLServer
```

Next we need to establish a connection to the database server by calling the Connect object.

```
'List the Databases
oSQLServer.Connect "YourSQLServerName", "sa", ""
```

Using these objects, we first get the count of how many databases we have stored in SQL Server, then loop that count to retrieve the names of these databases.

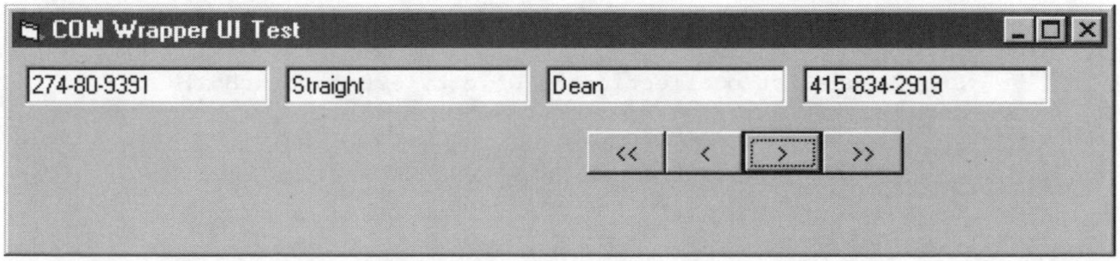

Figure 11.4 The Object Browser exposes all the properties and methods of the SQL DMO.

```
For nDatabase = 1 To oSQLServer.Databases.Count
    Combo1.AddItem oSQLServer.Databases(nDatabase).Name
Next nDatabase
```

Now we need to disable the command button so that we don't invoke the object again.

```
Command1.Enabled = False
```

After we get a list of all the databases, we need to get the database information by passing a database object to a GetInfo procedure we wrote. The GetInfo procedure enumerates through the properties of the database. It retrieves all the properties and lists them in the multiedit Textbox.

```
Sub GetInfo(oInfo As Object)

    Dim oProperty As Object
    With Form1.Text1
        .Text = ""
        For Each oProperty In oInfo.Properties
            .Text = .Text & oProperty.Name & ": "
            .Text = .Text & oProperty.Value
            .Text = .Text & Chr$(13) & Chr$(10)
        Next
    End With

    Exit Sub
End Sub
```

The final step is to retrieve the table names of the specified database. To do this, call two functions: GetCollection, which that retrieves the table number count, and CreateList, which retrieves the names of the tables in the database.

```
Sub GetCollection(oCollection As Object, strName As String)

    With Form1.Text1
        .Text = "Properties for: " & strName
        .Text = .Text & Chr$(13) & Chr$(10)

        .Text = .Text & "Count: " & oCollection.Count
        .Text = .Text & Chr$(13) & Chr$(10)
    End With
    Exit Sub

End Sub

Sub CreateList(oCollection As Object, 1st As ListBox)

    Dim oObject As Object
    For Each oObject In oCollection
        List1.AddItem oObject.Name
    Next

End Sub
```

That's it. A few procedures and calls to the SQL DMO objects lets us retrieve lots of information about our database and tables. This definitely beats coding these functions against the very low-level SQL API. The next few lines show how to invoke the functions we just created.

```
Set oDatabase = oSQLServer.Databases(Combo1.Text)
        GetInfo oDatabase
Command2.Enabled = False

'Get all the tables in the Database
     GetCollection oDatabase.Tables, "Tables"
CreateList oDatabase.Tables, List1
```

TIP

When running the code, place a break point on the List1.AddItem oObject.Name in the CreateList procedure, right click the oObject to display the menu, then select Add Watch. When the Add Watch window comes up, examine all the available properties besides the Name property for a list of other very useful properties, such as getting the primary keys, clustered index, and much more.

One SQL DMO Limitation

What limitation? Isn't SQL DMO the best thing since SQL Server itself? Well, yes; however, with the popularity and growth of COM and what we can do with it, our eyes are bigger than our stomachs. In the discussion of SQL DMO having properties and methods, we started comparing the SQL DMO object with VB objects such as TextBoxes and command buttons. It is nice not to have to code the functionality that SQL DMO provides us, but what about the user interface?

In the SQL DMO example provided in this chapter, we coded our own user interface. SQL Server does not give us access to its user interfaces in addition to SQL DMO. It provides us with all these objects, but we still have to create our own UI.

What Is SQL NameSpace?

SQL NameSpace is a different breed of the SQL DMO. It represents the solution to the problem of coding your own user interface. SQL NameSpace allows you to invoke SQL Server Enterprise Manager user interface components. Unlike in SQL DMO, you don't have to create the user interface yourself. When you invoke a SQL NS command, the entire user interface is invoked. This is a truly great feature of enabling COM-based user interfaces.

SQL NS gives you direct access to all the wizards that ship with SQL Server 7. You don't need to reinvent the wheel by redesigning the user interface and ensuring that you have covered all the functionalities and tested all the possible uses of the wizard. When you invoke a command with SQL NS, you get the real thing—tested, debugged, and ready to go. In addition, the users of your application won't have to learn two different UI styles if they are using the wizards directly from SQL Server, because the exact same UI is included in your application. This feature alone cuts a tremendous amount of development time from your schedule and allows you to concentrate on other critical tasks of your application.

Using SQL NS is not a whole lot different from using SQL DMO. You still need to add a reference to the SQL NS Object Library, then call methods and properties on these libraries. One of the main differences between SQL NS and SQL DMO is the hierarchical location of the components inside the name space.

In order to get to the components provided in SQL Server 7, you will need to perform four simple steps

1. Create a SQL Namespace object.
2. Get to the root object of the hierarchy.
3. Start with the first element in the hierarchy.
4. Navigate and invoke the elements you need from the object hierarchy.

The first step in using SQL NS is to initialize a name space environment. You do that by creating a SQLNameSpace object and calling the Initialize method on it. This object needs to know the server information. This is no different than connecting to a server using ADO or ODBC.

```
Dim oSQLNameSpace As SQLNamespace
Dim arSQLArray(10) As Long

'In the Form Load Event

' initialize SQL Namespace
    Set oSQLNameSpace = New SQLNamespace
    oSQLNameSpace.Initialize "SQL Name Space Tester", _
SQLNSRootType_Server, "Server=.;UID=sa;pwd=;", hWnd
```

The next step is to get to the root object or node. Because the information is stored in a hierarchical fashion, we need to start from the top of the hierarchy and then go down the branches.

```
' get a root object of type Server then drill down into the
' hierarchy
    arSQLArray(0) = oSQLNameSpace.GetRootItem
```

Once you get to this point, the rest is simple. Just go down the tree querying for children items using the GetFirstChildItem of the SQL-NameSpace object (see Figure 11.5):

```
'Behind a button

    ' get first level server->databases
    arSQLArray(1) = oSQLNameSpace.GetFirstChildItem(arSQLArray(0), _
SQLNSOBJECTTYPE_DATABASES)
    ' get second level server->databases->database('pubs')
    arSQLArray(2) = oSQLNameSpace.GetFirstChildItem(arSQLArray(1), _
SQLNSOBJECTTYPE_DATABASE, "pubs")

    ' get a SQLNamespaceObject to execute commands against on the
    ' wanted level
    Set oSQLNS = oSQLNameSpace.GetSQLNamespaceObject(arSQLArray(2))
```

Once you get the child items you can then execute the command by name, where the name is the actual dialog name returned from the SQL NameSpace child item.

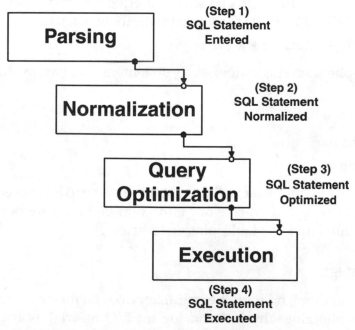

Figure 11.5   A VB program calling SQL NS components.

```
' execute the command by Name
    oSQLNS.ExecuteCommandByName ("Properties")
```

That's all you need to do. It really can't get any simpler. Can you imagine what you would have to do if you didn't have access to the SQL Server COM components? You would be spending days if not weeks reconstructing all the UI needed to perform a backup and restore any of the administrative tools exposed by SQL server.

SQL Server Optimization

In order to know how to take full advantage of SQL Server and gain the performance users demand, it is very important to understand how SQL Server Optimizer works. SQL Server Optimizer is the engine that makes SQL Server perform its tasks efficiently. Understanding how the optimizer works will guide you to the areas you should be investigating to make sure they are designed properly and effectively.

The SQL Server database engine uses a cost-based query optimizer to optimize queries that are submitted to the engine. This cost-based query optimizer produces cost estimates for a SQL clause based on statistical information. The SQL clauses or queries are those that have a WHERE or HAVING criteria associated with them, such as:

```
Select CustId from Cust WHERE CustID >12
```

When the optimizer encounters such statements, it has to do three things:

1. Query analysis
2. Index selection
3. Join selection

Knowing what the optimizer will do is half the battle. All we need to do is figure out how to concentrate our efforts on making sure our index choices are sound and our table joins are efficient.

Smart Query Design

Now that we understand how the optimizer does its magic, we need to help it by minimizing physical and logical I/O as well as balancing processor and I/O time. What this means is that we should design queries that result in the use of indexes and the fewest disk reads and writes. So let's look at some of the guidelines that will help us accomplish this task:

Rule 1. This should be a rule of thumb: Data conversions and string manipulations are resource intensive, especially when applied to large data sets. Use them very wisely and scarcely.

Rule 2. The WHERE clause can be very costly if used randomly. WHERE clauses that contain (OR or IN) can affect performance from a data access perspective. Therefore, the optimizer may choose to use the OR strategy. This results in the creation of a worktable that contains row IDs for each possible matching row. The optimizer will then scan through the worktable, getting each row ID and retrieving the corresponding rows from the data table. So the OR criteria will cost you. Exclusive rather than inclusive criteria, such as clauses that contain NOT, <>, or !=, will also cost you, because the optimizer will have to scan the entire table to determine the selection.

Rule 3. Be aware of the clauses that cause the optimizer to create worktables. Worktables are a necessary evil: There is nothing you can do about them. However, you need to know under what conditions they are created so that you can try to avoid them whenever possible. Table 11.2 lists the clauses that will force the creation of a worktable and explains why this will happen.

Table 11.2 The Most Commonly Used Clauses and How Their Use Affects Performance

CLAUSE	ACTION
DISTINCT	This is one of the most common mistakes made in SQL statements. The trick is that if you only need to get distinct records, there is no need to use DISTINCT for columns that are covered by a unique index.
ORDER BY	A worktable will be created if an index is not available for index ordering or if the available indexes are in conflict with the sort order.
GROUP BY	This action always causes the optimizer to create a worktable.
SELECT INTO	This clause causes the optimizer to build a worktable in your database and not the Tempdb, unless you explicitly specify otherwise.
JOINS	This is very costly if there are no indexes found that cover the JOIN clause. In this case a worktable is built to hold the rows from the smallest table in the join, and then a clustered index is created on this table in order to perform the join.

Optimizing SQL Server, or any database for that matter, is no easy task. In most cases it is a trial-and-error technique. It is also time consuming. In order to effectively optimize your database, you need to balance the activities you are performing. Sometimes making certain changes to gain speed in one area can cause performance degradation in other areas. The key to an efficient optimization is to study and follow the rules we've outlined and then monitor your application behavior to determine your tradeoffs.

Smart Index Design

There are three main operations that are affected by indexes: INSERT, UPDATE, and DELETE. Balancing indexes can cause what is referred to as a direct or indirect action. A direct action is what we want to accomplish. A direct action on INSERT, UPDATE, or DELETE will cause just the required data to be changed and not the entire record, as in the case of the INSERT clause for example. Let's discuss some of the guidelines that can help us create effective indexing selection.

Rule 1. Indexes should be kept narrow to be more efficient. Narrow indexes result in more index rows per page and fewer index levels, causing them to be cached and resulting in fewer I/Os. Narrow indexes provide the optimizer with more index selection. On the other hand, although this is a positive result, do not get carried away creating unused indexes that add maintenance overhead.

Rule 2. Large numbers of indexes on a table will affect INSERT, UPDATE, and DELETE operation performance.

Rule 3. The SQL Server Optimizer only maintains distribution statistics on the most significant column of a compound, composite, or multicolumn index. Therefore, selectivity should be great for the first column of the index. Do not index a column that is updated frequently, for this will affect performance.

Rule 4. It is advisable to create indexes on the columns that participate in a WHERE clause, because the optimizer is primarily focused on this clause.

As you can see, there are many index combinations and scenarios you can use. Balancing indexes is not an easy task. It is mostly a trial-and-error exercise in the areas where the optimizer may not be clear or consistent on how it performs. One approach is to calculate the number of index rows per page and analyze the worst-case scenario with respect to the number of reads required to obtain the solution set. You should also run the SQL Server Profiler and other enterprise tools to view some of the plans and statistics and make your decisions accordingly.

Security

SQL Server 7.0 includes a better Windows NT integrated security architecture, which provides increased flexibility. You can now assign database permissions directly to Windows NT users. You can also define SQL Server roles to include Windows NT users and groups and SQL Server users and roles.

SQL Server user can now be a member of multiple SQL Server roles. This allows database administrators to manage and control SQL Server permissions as Windows NT groups or SQL Server roles rather than as individual user accounts. You can also now manage database access and permissions using Windows NT groups. New fixed server and database roles such as dbcreator, diskadmin, and sysadmin provide more flexibility and improved security than the system administrator login.

Discussing security in detail is beyond the scope of this chapter, but it is very important to understand the new security changes and enhancements in SQL Server 7 when designing your application. Refer to Chapter 9, "DCOM Details," where we talked about how to handle security from DCOM components.

Winding Up

In this chapter we have explained the importance of a well-designed database and the normalization process and rules. We have also discussed the importance of a well-designed client that can make efficient use of the database without overloading it. We have looked at some of the new COM dialogs in SQL Server 7 that save us coding time, and have discussed how and when to use stored procedures and how you can isolate clients from learning implementation details. There is a lot more to learn about SQL Server 7 that is beyond the scope of the book and the chapter. But we encourage you to dig into some of the wizards and enterprise tools that can help you debug and better optimize your data access.

The next chapter discusses the tools and wizards that VB6 provided us to quickly build data-aware clients, as well as the various designers that shipped with VB6 and the benefits of architecting these clients using the data designers.

CHAPTER 12

Data Access with Visual Basic 6

This is the chapter you've been waiting for. We promised that things would get easier and that VB could provide some help in getting started with the data portions of COM. Although there is only a small, direct COM relationship in this chapter, you can think of it as the easier side of N-tier development: easier because of all the ready-to-run database support that comes with VB6. Although Visual Basic is widely known as the leader in Rapid Application Development (RAD) for visual user interfaces, it has lacked support for database prototyping since its inception. That changes with the release of version 6, however. In this chapter we explore all the new tools and wizards that make working with database sources effortless. We will look at the wizards and designers that come with Visual Basic 6 and how they can help us automate some of the tedious tasks associated with developing data-aware clients. We also explore how to create data-bound ActiveX controls that encapsulate certain business functionalities as well as some of the new designers that come with VB6. Before we get started, let's see what kinds of goodies await us and look at a brief description of what they do.

- *Data Projects.* The Data Project is a new type of project added to VB6 that allows you to build data-aware clients by providing a Form and Report Designer and a Data Environment Designer.

- *Data View.* The Data View window allows you to link to any database using OLE DB providers and gives you access to the data in the database as well as the ability to use database elements such as tables, views, and stored procedures to design your client access to the specific database.

- *Data Environment Designer (DED).* This designer is one of the more powerful tools in VB6. It allows you to visually create the hierarchy and commands of your data model by including stored procedures and assigning ActiveX controls to data field elements, then seamlessly dragging your design into a blank form to create your client with the needed code and data access links.

- *Data Object Wizard.* This wizard allows you to create data classes based on the hierarchy you developed in your data environment, or even to bind a user ActiveX control to a data environment element.

- *Data Form Wizard.* This wizard helps you generate complete functional forms that are based on table relationships. You can select the type of form you wish to create (i.e., master/detail, grid, and so on). You can also choose to use a bound or unbound format, which will then generate all the necessary ADO code.

In addition to these tools, here's what we cover in this chapter:

- The ADO Data control
- How to create a front-end database application
- How to create a data-bound ActiveX control
- A reusable user interface

We must place a disclaimer here. There are many details behind the concepts covered in this chapter. We try to explain everything in a clear and precise manner; however, this is not exclusively a database book and it is hard to justify bloating this chapter with database basics. Our goal is to present the information that will help you design better N-tier applications.

Designers and Wizards

Visual Basic 6 comes loaded with new designers and wizards to facilitate the tedious task of developing data-aware applications. Unlike their ancestors, some of these designers and wizards are capable of creating robust clients quickly and effectively. They are worth studying and looking into, whether or not you are planning on using them to create functional prototypes of mission-critical clients. Most of these wizards and designers work together, with results from one feeding into another. So all you need to do is figure out the sequence in which to use them and choose the right wizard for the right job. In the following sections we look closely at how each data wizard and designer works by providing examples and walking you through the gray and undocumented features.

Data Project

VB6 offers a new type of project, called the Data Project, that provides a head start in the development of data-centric applications. Because we want to build a tiered system, there is no doubt we will need to develop presentation layers that are very data heavy. If you've worked with previous versions of Visual Basic, you already know how tedious database work can be. It used to be that outside of the data controls, you received no other assistance from VB, and developers had to rely on third-party add-ons. Now you can safely throw away most of these add-ons and start looking at what VB6 has to offer to make your data-centric forms development a snap. A word of caution here—don't get carried away by developing the entire application using all the wizards that come with VB6. We still want to maintain the solid framework of components that we built. You should only use the techniques offered in this chapter for rapid prototyping, or those forms that won't need to change or be dependent on other parts of the project.

When you select a new project type with Data Project, VB builds a project framework that has a Form, a Data Environment Designer, and a Data Report. In the next section we discuss how the Data View helps us build the Data Environment, and how we can use the Data Environment Designer to build fully functional data-aware clients.

Data View

The Data View is the topmost window when working with Data Projects. It enables you to view your database layout as if you were looking at it from Access or SQL Server. Of course the value here is that it is not just a view but rather an environment that you use to start building the look and feel of your data environment. The Data View is basically a one-stop shopping place for all your data needs. From the Data View you can create data environments—discussed later in this chapter—as well as add multiple database connections. You can have multiple data represented from a variety of different sources, servicing a variety of different data environments. You can launch the Data View from the View menu or from the toolbar. Once it's up, you can create a data link by selecting the data providers you wish to use (see Figure 12.1). That's all you need to do to bring the database's schema into your project. When the database is added to your project, you can view the table's data as well as its design. Be careful when viewing data, because your connection to the database is a live one: You can actually change data values and they will be written back to the database.

Data Environment Designer

The Data Environment Designer, shown in Figure 12.2, is a very powerful tool, but only if it is used correctly. Think about this warning as you proceed. The purpose of the Data Environment Designer is to map out the flow of your application. The designer requires you to consider the behavior of your application before you code it.

Figure 12.1 The Data View window.

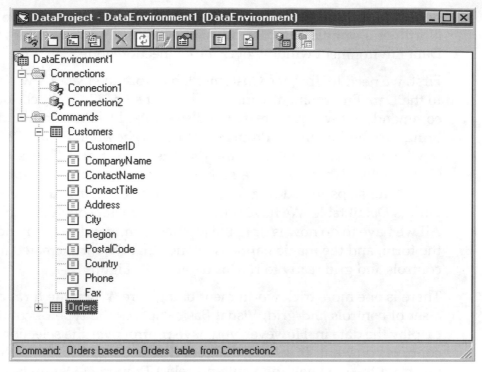

Figure 12.2 The Data Environment Designer.

Let's think for a minute about what the database elements are. We have tables, views, stored procedures, synonyms, and SQL statements. If a database is normalized, we have established relationships between tables: Next we need to determine the hierarchy of the relationships of the tables. This is precisely the function of the Data Environment Designer. If you take the time to design your database layout and your application's behavior in the designer, you have the capability of developing first-class, object-based database systems in record time.

In the following example we walk you through how to create and design a simple project that displays a complex master/detail/detail relationship. You can also use the Data Environment Designer to lay out data reports. We don't cover data reports in this chapter, because you use the same techniques and tools for them as you would to design forms.

If you are ready to start exploring the Data Environment Designer, open the prjCustomer_Detail project on the accompanying CD-ROM and we will walk you through how to create, in less than five minutes, a very complex form that displays customer order detail information.

Because we already have a Data View window with a connection to the Northwind sample database, we will need to drag three tables to the Data Environment window over the connection node.

First, we need to drag the Customer table from the Data View window to the Data Environment window. The next step is to right click on the command that was just created and select Add Child Command. This brings up the Command Property dialog, as shown in Figure 12.3. This is where you select Table as the database object and then select the Orders table. Now select the second command that was just created, repeat the steps for adding a second Child command, and select the Orders Detail table. We have now created a master/detail/detail form. All we have to do now is drag the topmost command—command1—to the form, and the magic happens. Notice that the form created a set of controls and grid ready to run, as depicted in Figure 12.4.

There is one more trick worth mentioning here. When the form creates a set of controls and grid, Visual Basic chooses the type of controls to display the data in. However, you have control over the selection of the controls you want. To select a different type of control, just pick the field out from the data environment and select Properties. Your choices are

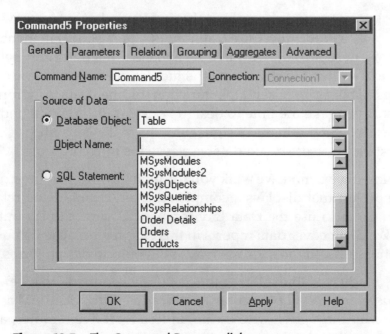

Figure 12.3   The Command Property dialog.

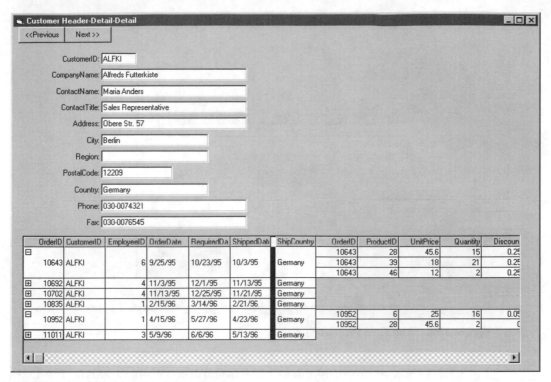

Figure 12.4 A master/detail/detail form.

shown in Figure 12.5. You can pick any type of ActiveX control registered on your machine to associate it with the field.

That's it; you are now ready to run the project.

Data Object Wizard

This is as close as we get to COM when we discuss database access. The Data Object Wizard is a very powerful tool that can assist you in generating code. As the name implies, it generates objects. The wizard is capable of generating two types of objects: A Class object, to which other objects can bind data, and a User Control object that binds to an existing Class object (see Figure 12.6). It can also create middle-tier objects bound to the data environment or UserControls.

Before using the Data Object Wizard, you must design a data environment. The Object Wizard relies on the commands and stored procedures that you create in the data environment.

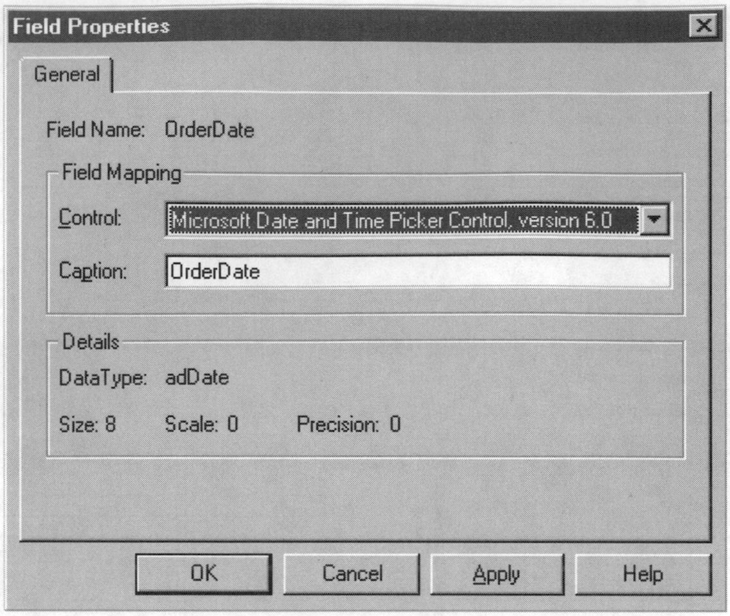

Figure 12.5 The Field Properties dialog.

Let's first look at creating Class objects. Unlike other wizards, the Data Object Wizard requires planning and knowledge of the design of your database. You must understand the layout of your database tables before you can use the wizard, because the wizard asks you to decide which fields are null and which are primary keys so that it can build the class accordingly. You must also understand the design you created in the Data Environment Designer, because you use the Data Environment commands to map the lookup functionality. The Class object created by the wizard will also map the Insert, Update, and Delete functionalities from the data environment into your Class object. This can be a very elegant way to wrap stored procedures into objects you can call methods on.

The generated class contains properties that correspond to the fields in your mapped Data Environment commands; methods for database navigational operations such as MoveNext and MovePrevious; and methods for inserts, updates, and batch operation.

As indicated earlier, the second type of object the Object Wizard can generate is a user control or an ActiveX control. In order to create an ActiveX control you must have a class that already exists and was originally generated by the Object Wizard itself. This is the classic case of

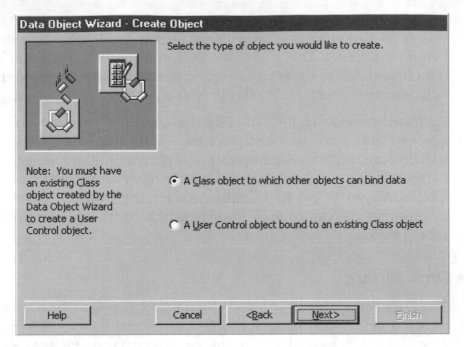

Figure 12.6 The Data Object Wizard.

the chicken-egg conundrum: This wizard gives you the option of creating two types of objects. The first is a Class object to which other objects can bind data, and the second is a User Control object bound to an existing Class object—but you can't create one without the other.

Let's get the steps clear before we continue.

In order to fully use and understand the Object Wizard you need to do the following:

1. Design a data environment. This is where you've laid out your commands and data relationships.

2. Let the Data Object Wizard create a class based on the design depicted by the data environment.

3. Once the class is generated, use the Object Wizard to create an ActiveX control based on that class.

Now that you've selected the appropriate class, you have some choices to make regarding the type of ActiveX control you want the Object Wizard to create. Currently, your choices are limited to a single record control, a data grid, a list box, or a ComboBox. After you select a control type, a new ActiveX control is generated for you ready for use. Because this is an Object Wizard, you don't always know what is going on behind the scenes. That's why we walk you through the creation of a data-bound ActiveX control later in this chapter. This example should help you understand all the steps involved in creating data controls.

As stated previously, the Data Object Wizard is a very powerful tool. You can walk through the steps of the wizard to create a Class object that you can call from within your project or compile and use externally to insert, update, and delete Recordsets. In other words, you can use the Object Wizard to create a framework for the updates, inserts, and deletes that you can compile and reuse as a standalone component in other projects.

Data Form Wizard

The Data Form Wizard, shown in Figure 12.7, is one of the easiest wizards found in Visual Basic. It enables you to create forms very quickly. One of the things we like about this new wizard is that it allows you to select the binding type for the form that it creates. This means that you can choose to use the ADO control, have the Data Form Wizard generate ADO code, or even create a class that you can use to call methods on. By now you've probably guessed that any wizard that allows you to use classes or COM objects is a good wizard.

You can use the Data Form Wizard to generate a variety of forms from simple, single-table forms to complex, master/detail-type forms with one-to-many data relations. You can also create grid-style forms (Figure 12.8). The Data Form Wizard is usually used in conjunction with the ADO control, which we discuss next.

The ADO Data Control

If you've used the DAO control, you should be very familiar with the ADO control. The ADO Data control is the facility to data-bind controls that offer a Data Source property.

Although you can use the ActiveX Data objects directly in your applications, the ADO Data control has the advantage of encapsulating basic database navigational capabilities, such as the Back and Forward buttons, plus an easy-to-use interface that allows you to create database applications with a minimum of code—or no code at all if you prefer (see Figure 12.9).

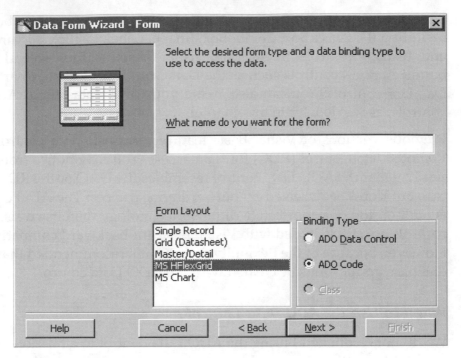

Figure 12.7   The Data Form Wizard.

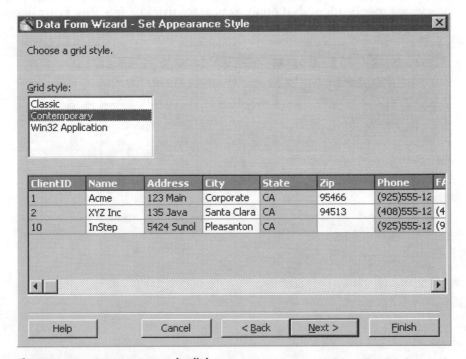

Figure 12.8   Appearance style dialog.

Several of the controls found in Visual Basic's toolbox are data-bound, including the CheckBox, ComboBox, Image, Label, ListBox, PictureBox, and TextBox controls. In addition, Visual Basic includes several data-bound ActiveX controls such as the DataGrid, DataCombo, Chart, and DataList controls. You can also create your own data-bound ActiveX controls, as we do later in this chapter.

Previous versions of Visual Basic featured intrinsic data control and Remote Data Control (RDC) for data access. You may notice from Figure 12.9 that the ADO Data control resembles the DAO or the RDC control, but don't be deceived by outward appearances: The ADO control is built on top of a completely different technology than its rivals. Both controls are still included with Visual Basic for backward compatibility. However, because of the flexibility of ADO, it's recommended that new database applications be created with the ADO Data control.

When to Use the ADO Data Control

We do not recommend using the ADO Data control in a mission-critical application setting, because binding data into controls and forms goes against the tiered design and mechanism discussed throughout this book. We do, however, use the ADO Data control for prototyping. It's a very fast mechanism that enables you to quickly see how your users view

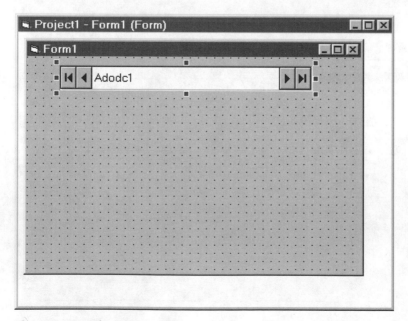

Figure 12.9 The ADO control.

and manipulate data. You can quickly prototype sets of screens that mock the workflow of your application before you start writing the code.

The ADO Data control can also be used to test connection settings for benchmarking performance before you start writing a lot of code. You can test the effects of changing cache sizes, cursor types, and locations before you start coding your classes. It is very important to find out up front what to expect from your application when it comes to performance. These results will help you develop better designs.

How to Create a Sample ADO Data Control Project

To create a client or front-end database application, add the ADO Data control to your forms just as you would any other Visual Basic control. Although your forms can contain as many ADO Data controls as you need, it's important to note that highly graphical controls and controls that carry heavy functionality can be very costly in terms of overhead. For example, each ADO Data control uses at least two connections for the first control and one more for each subsequent control. Be careful how you use these controls.

How to Create a Front-End Database Application with Minimal Code

As you will see, we create an entire database application using minimum code by setting a few properties at design time. We use an OLE DB data source. In order to use this data source, we must first create a Microsoft data link name on your machine. So let's create a data link.

How to Create an OLE DB Data Link

An essential step in accessing data is to create an OLE DB data link for each database you want to access. Use the following steps to create such a data link for the Nwind.mdb (Northwind) supplied with Visual Basic. You need to create this only once, and we use it in several examples. So, let's use the following steps:

1. Open Windows Explorer.

2. Open a directory where you want to create the OLE DB data source. In this example, open Program Files, Microsoft Visual Studio, and VB98. Right click the right pane of Explorer, and then click New on the Context menu. From the list of file types, click Microsoft Data Link.

3. Rename the new file Nwind.UDL. Right click the file and click Properties on the Context menu to display the NWind.UDL Properties dialog box (see Figure 12.10).

4. Click the Connection tab, then click the Provider box and select Microsoft Jet 3.51 OLE DB Provider.

5. Click the Next button to go to the Connection tab. Click the Browse button next to the Database Selection Field box.

6. Use the Select Access Database dialog box to navigate to the nwind.mdb file. This is installed in the Program Files\Microsoft Visual Studio\Vb98 directory.

7. Click Test Connection to check the connection. If the connection passes, click OK.

You have just created an OLE DB data link that you can use in your sample project.

Creating a Simple Front-End Database Application

In order to create a simple front-end database application, draw an ADO Data control on a form. Next, select its properties in the Properties window and click ConnectionString to display the ConnectionString dialog box. Select the Microsoft data link file (Nwind.UDL) we just created.

In the Properties window, set the RecordSource property to a SQL statement. For example,

```
SELECT * FROM Customers
```

Place a Data-Bound Grid control on the form to display the result of the query. In the Properties window, set the DataSource property for DataGrid1 to the name of the ADO Data control (ADODC1). This binds the Grid to the ADO Data control. Press F5 to run the application. You can use the four arrow buttons on the ADO Data control to move to the beginning of the data, to the end of the data, or from record to record through the data.

The running project should look like Figure 12.11, unless you got creative and discovered how easy it is to manipulate data and add some additional clause to the select statement. This is not a bad thing to do, since the demonstrative approach we just took to explain how the ADO Data control works may cause some locking problems in a multiuser environment if we retrieve the entire rows of the table.

We have just created a project with very little code. Except for writing the Select statement, you can also create the connection to the ADO

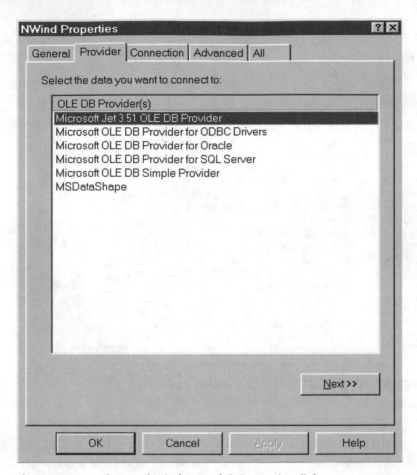

Figure 12.10 The NorthWind Data Link Properties dialog.

Data control programmatically upon loading the form by writing the following code.

```
Private Sub Form_Load()
With Adodc1
.ConnectionString = "FILE NAME=C:\Program Files\Microsoft Visual _
Studio\VB98\Nwind.UDL"
      .RecordSource = "Select * From Customers"
 End With

 Set DataGrid1.DataSource = Adodc1

End Sub
```

You have seen how we can bind the controls that ship with VB to an ADO Data control at design time. Although this process is quite simple, there is frequently a need to group a set of controls together to create

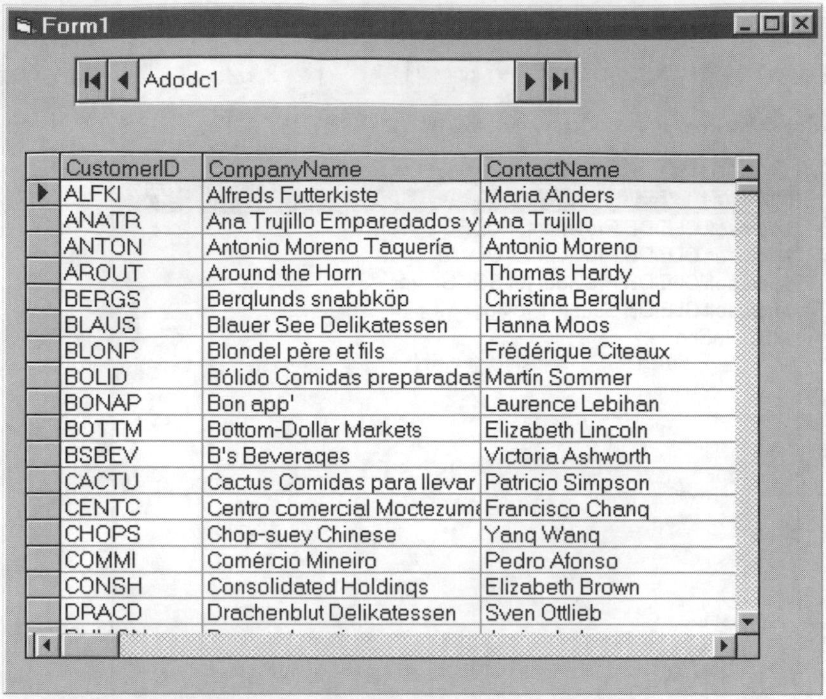

Figure 12.11 The ADO Data control bound to a grid.

your own type of ActiveX control. For example, this could be helpful with an Address control that groups a set of text boxes, or with Combo boxes and so on to create a single control that you can repeat on multiple forms.

Creating a Data-Bound ActiveX Control

Earlier in this chapter we created a User Control object with the Data Object Wizard. We mentioned that we were isolated from the details involved in creating this control because the wizard did all the work. We are now going to design a data-aware ActiveX control without using the Data Object Wizard so that you can see what is involved in creating the control. At the beginning it will seem like we are just creating a standard VB form, which should be very familiar to you. We then move into the implementation of our control interfaces. So now is the time to pay attention if you're not too crazy about wizards and are into how things work.

The following steps explain what you need to do to create the data-bound control. You can repeat these steps to create any number of data-bound controls that represent the set of related functionality we discussed earlier.

1. Create a new ActiveX Control project.
2. In the Properties window, rename Project1 to prjAXCustomers.
3. In the Properties window, rename UserControl1 to ctlCustomersInfo.
4. Add six TextBox controls, seven Label controls, and one ComboBox control to the form, and set their properties as shown in Table 12.1.
5. On the File menu, click Save Project. Save the project in the new folder using the names provided in the dialog boxes.
6. On the File menu, click Make ProductsCtl.ocx. to save the .ocx.

So far we've created an ActiveX UserControl that we can use in other Visual Basic projects. Notice that we didn't write any code. The control should look like Figure 12.12.

Table 12.1 The Control Types and Settings for Your UserControl

OBJECT	PROPERTY	SETTING
Text1	Name	TxtCustID
Text2	Name	TxtCustName
Text3	Name	txtAddress1
Text4	Name	txtAddress2
Text5	Name	TxtCity
Text6	Name	TxtZipCode
Combo1	Name	CboState
Label1	Caption	CustomerID
Label2	Caption	Customer Name
Label3	Caption	Customer Address 1
Label4	Caption	Customer Address 2
Label5	Caption	City
Label6	Caption	Zip Code
Label7	Caption	State

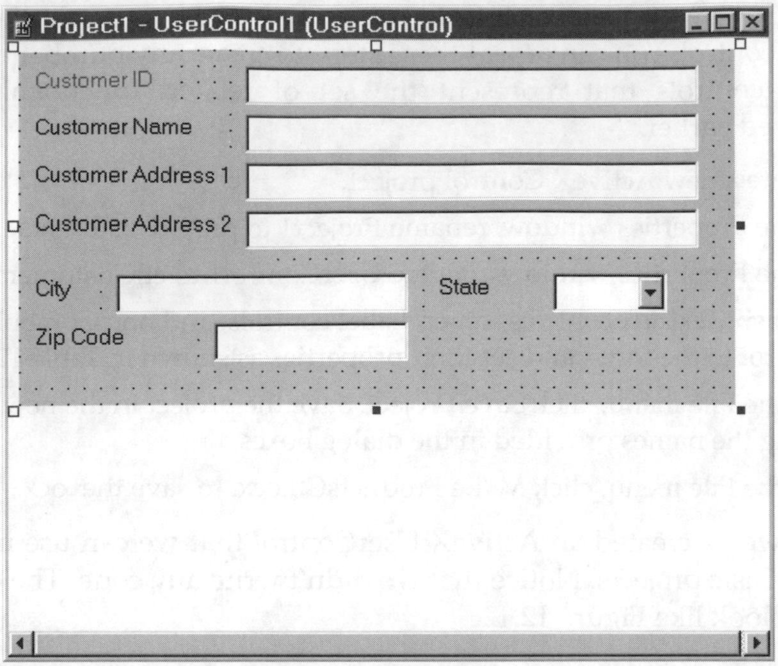

Figure 12.12 The CustomerInfo UserControl.

Binding Our New Control

Now the fun part begins. Let's write some code that will make our control data-aware. All we need to do is to expose the fields we placed on the UserControl as properties with Get and Let, then mark them as data-aware.

The following code shows what we need to place in the UserControl.

```
Public Property Get CustomerAddress1() As String
CustomerAddress1 = txtAddress1.Text
End Property

Public Property Let CustomerAddress1(ByVal newAddress1 As String)
txtAddress1.Text = newAddress1
End Property

Public Property Get CustomerAddress2() As String
CustomerAddress2 = txtAddress2.Text
End Property

Public Property Let CustomerAddress2(ByVal newAddress2 As String)
txtAddress2.Text = newAddress2
End Property
```

```
Public Property Get CustomerCity() As String
CustomerCity = txtCity.Text
End Property

Public Property Let CustomerCity(ByVal newCity As String)
txtCity.Text = newCity
End Property

Public Property Get CustomerState() As String
CustomerState = cboState.Text
End Property

Public Property Let CustomerState(ByVal newState As String)
cboState.Text = newState
End Property

Public Property Get CustomerZipCode() As String
CustomerZip = txtZipCode.Text
End Property

Public Property Let CustomerZipCode(ByVal newZipCode As String)
txtZipCode.Text = newZipCode
End Property
```

Visual Basic allows you to mark properties of your control as bindable. Bindable controls are also known as data-aware controls. You can associate bindable properties with fields in any data source, which makes it easier to use your control in database applications in much the same way we did with the ADO sample project. The controls supplied with Visual Basic can be bound to data source fields using their DataSource and DataField properties. You can select one property of your control to be bound to the DataField property. Typically, this is the most important piece of data your control holds.

Figure 12.13 shows all the options we can choose in making our User-Control bound to data fields. In order to allow the control to be data-aware, we need to select the Advanced button and check the Property is data bound check box as well as two others—This property binds to DataField and Showin DataBindings collection at design time. The This property binds to DataField check box allows us to bind the control to the specific data fields. We show how to do this later in the chapter. The second checkbox allows the control bindable properties to be available when we start using the control in a new project.

Although you can mark only one field as bound to the field specified in the DataField property, you can mark additional properties of your ActiveX control as bindable at runtime. Developers can use the Data-Bindings collection to bind these additional bindable properties to data

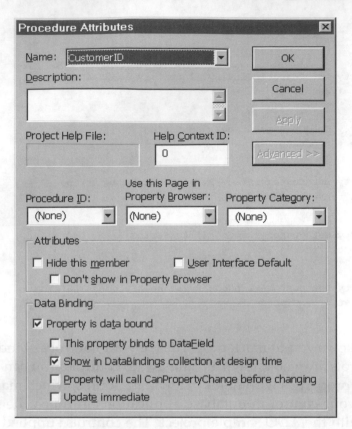

Figure 12.13 The Procedure Attribute dialog.

fields. You can view the Data Binding dialog shown in Figure 12.14 by selecting the Data Bindings Property of our newly created control, and start mapping the fields of the control to data fields.

The DataBindings Collection

The DataBindings collection is a property that is provided by the VB container to users of your control. It allows the developer to access the list of bindable properties on your control. If your control has multiple bindable properties, you must mark one as binding to the Extender object's DataField property. Otherwise, the Extender object will not provide a DataSource property for your control. You can mark a property as binding to a data field by selecting This property binds to DataField in the Procedure Attributes dialog box. The property you mark as binding to a data field can also be bound using the DataBindings collection.

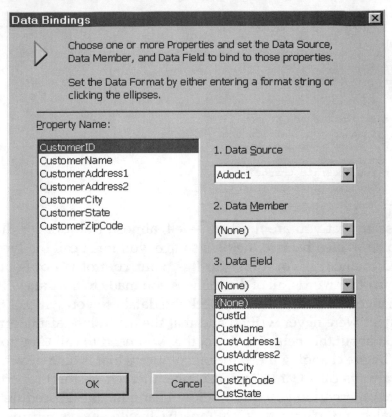

Figure 12.14 The Data Binding dialog.

The mapping between properties of the control and contents of the constituent controls is accomplished by a mechanism called delegation. Delegation is defined as asking someone else to perform certain duties on your behalf. In terms of VB, the Text Box control does all the work of displaying the value and accepting user changes. Because the user can change the value of the property while the text box displays it, you must also mark the property as changed in the text box's Change event, as shown in the following code.

```
Private Sub txtCustID_Change()
PropertyChanged "CustomerID"
End Sub

Private Sub txtCustName_Change()
PropertyChanged "CustomerName"
End Sub

Private Sub txtAddress1_Change()
PropertyChanged "CustomerAddress1"
End Sub
```

```
Private Sub txtAddress2_Change()
PropertyChanged "CustomerAddress2"
End Sub

Private Sub txtCity_Change()
PropertyChanged "CustomerCity"
End Sub

Private Sub txtZipCode_Change()
PropertyChanged "CustomerZipCode"
End Sub

Private Sub cboState_Change()
PropertyChanged "CustomerState"
End Sub
```

It may seem that you are finished—well, almost. In order for the new value to be written back to the data source, you must call the Property-Changed method. If you don't do this, your control is not bound for update. In other words, all of the changes you made to the data will seem to be changed. However, if you check the database you will notice that the changes were never written and that the control is raising errors to warn you about this behavior. To fix this, you need to call CanProperty-Change before changing the value of a property that is data-aware. If the control always calls CanPropertyChange, then check the Property will call CanPropertyChange option before changing the Procedure Attributes dialog box. Currently, CanPropertyChange always returns TRUE in Visual Basic, even if the bound field is read-only in the data source. This does not cause problems with the code shown, because Visual Basic doesn't raise an error when your program attempts to change a read-only field; it just doesn't update the data source. You do need to make sure to let the users know of this behavior or try to avoid it.

Discovering and Setting Bindable Properties at Runtime

If you place an instance of the CustomerInfo control on a form, you can execute the following code to list the bindable properties:

```
Dim dtb As DataBinding
For Each dtb In AddressBox1.DataBindings
    Debug.Print dtb.PropertyName
Next
```

At runtime, the developer can use the following code to bind the AddressLine1 property to the AddrLine1 field, assuming that field was available on the data source specified by the DataSource extender property:

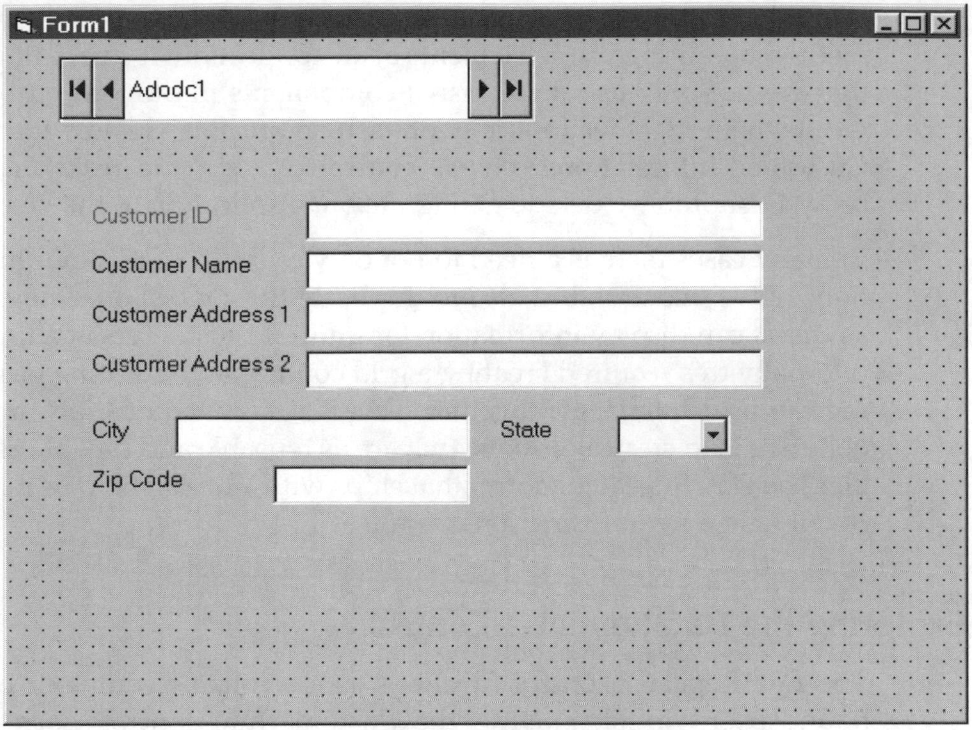

Figure 12.15   The Final CustomerInfo UserControl.

```
AddressBox1.DataBindings("CustomerID").DataField = "CustomerID"
```

You can test the DataChanged property of a DataBinding object to find out if the value of a field has changed. This property functions in the same way as the DataChanged extender property of bound controls.

Finally, we have a control that is ready for use and reuse in different projects. You can simply drop the control on a new form, add an ADO Data control, and bind both of them together, and you are ready to run. If you've followed all of the steps, your form and control should look similar to the one depicted in Figure 12.15.

A Reusable User Interface

What we developed here is a very powerful method for reusing user interface elements. We discussed in detail in Chapter 8, "Understanding COM Internals," how to create reusable COM components that are sharable across different projects. What we aim to achieve here is a method of reusing visual elements of an application. It's very important that we not only use these visual components in our project but also group them together in a generic fashion such as CustomerInfo. The Customer Information ActiveX control can also be used in a Web browser should we decide to migrate our application to the Web.

In many cases there is a need to not only reuse the Customer Information ActiveX control, but also to duplicate the control on a single form so that it can display information for multiple customers at a time. Traditionally this required creating a grid control and rewriting or recreating the user interface altogether. This is a very tedious job, since our objective is to create solutions that are as reusable and flexible as possible. The DataRepeater control that ships with VB6 can help us make use of our Customer Information control.

Exploring the DataRepeater Control

The DataRepeater control functions as a scrollable container of data-bound user controls such as the CustomerInfo control. Each control appears in its own row as a *repeated* control that allows the user to view several data-bound user controls at once. To enable the Data control to repeat ActiveX controls, follow these simple steps:

1. Add the CustomerInfo control that we created and the DataRepeater control to the project.

2. On the Properties window of the DataRepeater, click RepeatedControlName property and select CustomerInfo.

3. Add a data source, such as the ADO Data control, to the form and connect it to a data provider.

4. Set the DataRepeater control's DataSource property to the data source.

5. Right click the DataRepeater control and click DataRepeater Properties, then click the RepeaterBindings tab.

6. Set PropertyName to an appropriate data field and click the Add button.

The DataRepeater control saves computer resources by only displaying a single user control—the active control—at a time. The other controls displayed are simple images that do not maintain individual connections to the data source, as would happen if several user controls were con-

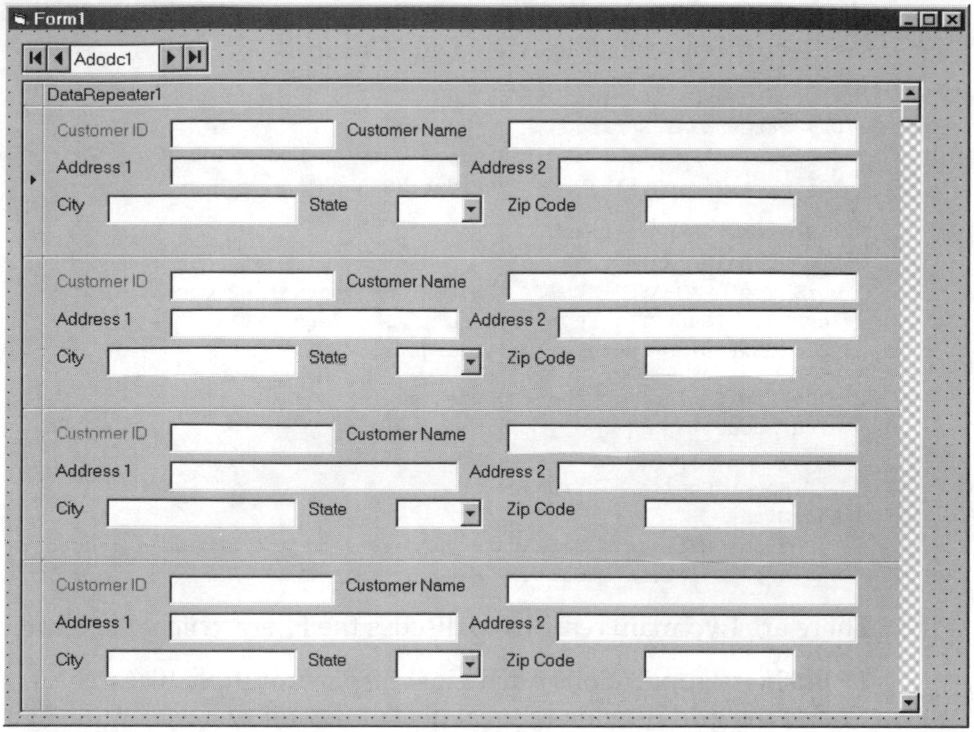

Figure 12.16 The DataRepeater control.

tained on a form. The DataRepeater should now look like Figure 12.16. This is a very cost-effective way to repeat data on a form without consuming too much memory, which is consistent with developing thin clients.

Displaying Hierarchical Data

One of the common business application needs is to display data in a hierarchical view. Performing this task has long required using third-party controls. With VB6 comes a new type of grid called the Hierarchical FlexGrid control. A major feature of the MSHFlexGrid control is its ability to display hierarchical Recordsets—relational tables displayed in a hierarchical fashion. The easiest way to create a hierarchical Recordset is to use the Data Environment Designer and assign the DataSource property of the MSHFlexGrid control to the data environment. You can also create a hierarchical Recordset in code using a Shape command as the RecordSource for an ADO Data Control.

```
' Create a Connection String.
Dim strConn As String
strConn = "Provider=MSDataShape.1;Data Source=Nwind;" & _
"Connect Timeout=15;Data Provider=MSDASQL"

' Use the Shape command.
Dim strShape As String
strShape = "SHAPE {SELECT * FROM 'Customers'} AS Customers " & _
"APPEND ({SELECT * FROM 'Orders'} AS Orders RELATE " & _
"CustomerID TO CustomerID) AS Orders"

' Do the Binding to the ADO control
With Adodc1
   .ConnectionString = strConn
   .RecordSource = strShape
End With
' Set the HflexGrid DataSource property to the ADO Data control.
Set HFlexGrid1.DataSource = Adodc1
```

There are two main reasons to discuss the Hierarchical FlexGrid control.

1. Business applications often must display multiple hierarchies of data, and the grid provides a great deal of flexibility in accomplishing this task.

2. It is necessary to be familiar with the new SQL syntax for shaping and displaying data in a different view; using the Hierarchical FlexGrid control will help get you started.

The ease of use of these new controls combined with the data wizards makes the presentation of the data a snap. If you've followed all of the steps, the hierarchical view of the previous code should look like Figure 12.17.

Winding Up

Although it's easy to get carried away with all the bells and whistles of designers and wizards, it is very important to understand their impact. Here are some guidelines to follow when using them:

1. Don't use wizards or designers that hide code information from you—for example, those wizards that create separate files to store the configuration.

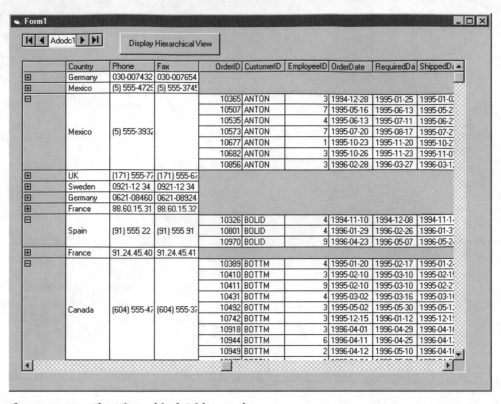

Figure 12.17   The Hierarchical Grid control.

2. Any wizard or designer that generates good, commented code that can be reused or encapsulated is a good wizard.

In the next chapter we will jump back into tier after this quick vacation into the land of wizards. We will discuss Microsoft Message Queue (MSMQ) as a tier in our distributed application. So, pack up your vacation supplies and let's get back to work!

MSMQ as Another Tier

After all the information we've covered so far, you'd think every possible programming need and eventuality has been dealt with. You can talk to components remotely on other computers, handle databases with aplomb regardless of their location, and even manage transactions involving multiple discrete activities. What else is left? Isn't three tiers enough for just about anyone?

Normally, yes: However, there are often special circumstances that require additional tiers. For example, your application might need to send large amounts of e-mail in an automated fashion. To accomplish this, you might introduce Microsoft Exchange into the application framework to handle the mail load.

But don't get too worked up about the term *tier*. Adding tiers does not necessarily mean another server is required for your application. Tiers can be logical as well as physical. Putting another tier in the loop might simply mean creating another service or series of components as part of your application. You create the tiers as necessary for your application. Besides, the term *tier* is fairly loose, and you can classify just about any major component as a tier.

There are lots of possibilities for additional tiers in your applications, such as a Web server or transaction-handling subsystem. We're going to give you the highlights of one more that is particularly useful when building N-tier applications: a technology called Microsoft Message Queue (MSMQ). We'll be covering:

- What is MSMQ, and why should I care?

- What are the components of MSMQ?

- How do I use MSMQ?

This chapter will give you enough information to understand what MSMQ is all about and why it is important to N-tier applications.

What Is MSMQ, and Why Should I Care?

Imagine you are building an N-tier application that involves client programs that talk to each other. Your first client starts a task, which submits an order to a warehouse. When it gets there, the warehouse software is supposed to read it and display the contents of the order for the warehouse personnel, who then approve it, fill it, and mark it as complete. With the technologies we know so far, we might decide to implement the warehouse client as a DCOM component on another server that the original client can connect with. The warehouse would stay connected until the order was marked as complete, after which a success or failure return status would be sent to the client.

What's the problem with this? Well, suppose the warehouse attendants are at lunch and can't fill the order until almost an hour after it has been sent. In this case, the client and the warehouse DCOM component would sit there using a valuable network connection until the warehouse attendants wandered back from lunch (and they're known for taking long lunch breaks). How does this problem, and many others like it in the real business world, get solved?

One outstanding solution is to use messaging. Microsoft Message Queue does this for us, providing a fairly easy-to-use interface for making it happen. In the preceding example, the client, instead of connecting directly to the DCOM warehouse component, sends a message to a message queue. The message, which contains the contents of the order and any other information the warehouse staff needs to get the order out, sits in the queue until someone retrieves it. Once the message is sent, which happens nearly instantaneously, the network connection is released and the client can go on its merry way. Perhaps an hour later, the warehouse attendants return from a lengthy lunch break and check the list of orders to be filled. The warehouse client program retrieves all the messages in the message queue and displays them. In the meantime 42 orders have piled up, requiring the attendant to work an extra hour that evening to get them all filled.

Advantages of MSMQ

The most obvious advantage of this technique is that clients and components on any server or machine can communicate with each other in an asynchronous fashion without worrying about holding on to valuable network resources. While this technique is hardly new to the world of programming, it is new to the Windows platform. Microsoft implements it using Microsoft Message Queue, available as part of the Windows NT Option Pack in a limited version or for purchase on a licensed basis for software with higher demands.

There are other benefits that MSMQ specifically provides:

Guaranteed one-time-only message delivery.   When using MSMQ, you can be assured that every message you send will either be delivered exactly once or return with a delivery failure. This means that two receivers will not accidentally get the same message, and a message won't get lost without your knowledge. This feature provides the level of reliability required for real software systems that your customer or company can depend on.

Delivery of messages without the need for a receiver.   Messages can be sent using MSMQ without the need for an active receiver: They will sit in the queue until the receiver comes along and gets them. This is an ideal feature for clients that frequently work remotely in a disconnected state, or for systems that need to work continuously, even during server outages.

Event-based messaging.   Normally, one part of your software will send messages to a queue and another part will check for messages when it needs them or is ready for them. However, MSMQ also supports event-based messaging. This means that when a message is sent, it raises an event. The receiver can set up an event handler to automatically get the message when it arrives, so you won't have to check for messages periodically because your event handler will do it automatically. While this will not always be the route you want to take, it is a great feature to have at your disposal when you need it. It's even pretty easy to use.

Transactionality. You can send and receive messages as transactions. If your transaction involves sending multiple messages—for example, updating the message queues of several task queues at one time—you can treat all the messages as an all-or-nothing situation. If any message fails, you can cancel the entire transaction.

Sounds pretty good. MSMQ is looking like a distinct possibility if you need this sort of message-based capability in your application.

Disadvantages of MSMQ

To be perfectly honest, there aren't many disadvantages of MSMQ. It's a great piece of software, and it should make message-based programming easy and efficient for your N-tier application. Just make sure you need it before you implement it. If you have no need for message-based communication, don't use it. It would just be an extra layer of implementation that would use up your valuable development time.

What Are the Components of MSMQ?

There are two basic elements of the MSMQ system that you need to understand before you can dive in and start programming. They are almost too obvious to mention, but we will anyway. They are the queue and the message. The queue holds messages. Messages contain the information you are sending.

The queue itself has all sorts of properties. Its primary purpose is to receive and store messages sent by any part of your application until they are needed by another part. There can be as many queues as you like, and each has a unique name, allowing you to target a message to a specific queue. Queues can also be local or remote—that is, located on the same machine as the originator of the message (opening up all kinds of possibilities for local asynchronous storage) or on another server. Each queue also has a GUID to make darn sure it is unique.

Queues can also be public or private. A public queue is created in a centralized MSMQ database called the Message Queue Information Store (MQIS). Many components and programs can access the MQIS given the right security. Private queues are created on the machine where the component or software creating them resides, and can only be created locally. Public queues are good for intercomponent or interapplication communication across servers. Private queues are good for local communication between components on the same computer, and are much faster to create than public queues.

The message contains the actual data you want to send somewhere. Messages also have a set of properties in addition to the actual data. Like e-mail messages, they can have a priority. They can also have a deadline, causing a message to expire if it is not received within a preset time limit.

NOTE
MSMQ messaging is a powerful technology. However, it does have its limitations. One in particular is important. An MSMQ message is limited to 4 megabytes of data. While this is not a problem for most messaging jobs, it is important to note this before you start planning that project that sends the text of an encyclopedia volume to your customers.

The queue and the message are critical to getting anything done with MSMQ. They are the foundation of the object model, through which you do all your MSMQ work.

The MSMQ Object Model

Like most Microsoft technologies, MSMQ exposes an object model that programmers use to access its features and functionality. There are about eleven objects in the MSMQ object model, but you only have to worry about four of them to get most of your work done. They are all listed here, with the four most important objects first.

MSMQQueueInfo. This object allows you to create and get information about a single queue. You will need to create one of these in your program before you can create a queue. It contains such methods as Create, Delete, Update, Refresh, and Open, all of which are used to access queues.

MSMQQueue. This object is the queue itself, and is used to manage the messages that are sent to it. It has methods such as Receive, ReceiveCurrent, Peek, PeekNext, PeekCurrent, Close, and Reset. You can use these methods to get the messages out of a queue or just to look and see what messages are there.

MSMQMessage. The MSMQMessage object represents a single message sent through MSMQ. It has numerous properties that tell you all kinds of information about the message, such as Body, Arrived-Time, Priority, BodyLength, MaxTimeToReceive (like an expiration date), SenderID, and SentTime. It has only two methods. The first, AttachCurrentSecurityContext, obtains the current security context and attaches it to the message before the message is sent. This is useful when impersonating a user, and helps MSMQ authenticate messages. The most important method, however, is Send, which actually forwards a prepared message to a queue.

MSMQEvent. This object represents an MSMQ event, which can be one of only two possibilities: a message arrival or an error notification. By creating an instance of the MSMQEvent object and then attaching it to a queue, you can make sure you are notified when these events occur and react to them. Your code could easily go along its merry way doing its normal job, and then when a message arrives, the event handler is fired and you can deal with the new message.

The preceding objects are the most important ones you will be using in MSMQ. The rest are listed next, each with a short explanation. You will probably be using these at one time or another if you decide to use MSMQ, but the objects just covered are the cornerstones of MSMQ.

MSMQQuery. This object is used to locate a queue or collection of queues. It returns an MSMQQueueInfos object.

MSMQQueueInfos. This is a collection of MSMQQueueInfo objects. It is returned by the MSMQQuery object's LookupQueue method. If you need to locate a queue on a network, use these two objects together.

MSMQCoordinatedTransactionDispenser. Gets an MSMQTransaction object. Once you have this, you can send or receive messages as part of an external transaction.

MSMQTransactionDispenser. Gets an MSMQTransaction object. Once you have this, you can send or receive messages as part of an internal transaction.

MSMQTransaction. Allows you to send and receive messages as part of a transaction. It provides two methods—Abort and Commit—that allow you to cancel or complete the transaction.

MSMQApplication. This object has only one method, which gets the machine identifier of a computer.

Once you understand the MSMQ object model, you can begin to see how the whole thing works together. It's actually pretty simple, and when you get to the code, you'll see that programming MSMQ is straightforward.

How Do I Use MSMQ?

MSMQ is pretty simple to understand. It's a component-oriented messaging system, with some enhancements like event-based message reception and message transactions. Messages go into a queue, then get pulled out of the queue. While there are a few technical details beyond the basic concept—for example, implementation, security, and the MSMQ setup—the general idea is fairly clear. To make use of the MSMQ facilities, you'll need to know some more about the details and see how the code works.

Setting Up MSMQ

Before you can get going with MSMQ, you have to install it. It is available on the Windows NT Option Pack CD-ROM, or you can download it from Microsoft's Web site. There is no big trick to installing it. Just load the CD-ROM and follow the on-screen instructions. There are two small points to take note of, however.

First, when installing from the NT Option Pack, you have to tell it to install MSMQ by selecting the option in the Setup dialog. Second, when installing MSMQ, you will be asked if you want to use a dependent or independent client. Make sure you select independent for the purpose of playing around with MSMQ. This will allow you to create queues on your local computer without the need for a server. Dependent queues require that you be connected to an MSMQ server in order to use MSMQ functionality.

After installation, the MSMQ Explorer will be at your disposal. A program group has been installed called Windows NT Option Pack. You'll find the MSMQ Explorer under this program group. Figure 13.1 illustrates what it looks like. You will use the MSMQ Explorer to manage queues and message traffic.

Now that you are ready to roll with MSMQ, a little more explanation and some code is in order.

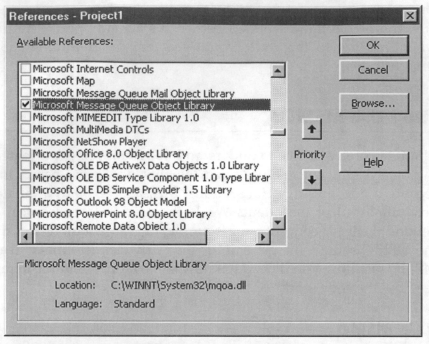

Figure 13.1 The MSMQ Explorer.

The Basic MSMQ Scenario

The whole idea behind MSMQ is that one piece of code sends a message and another piece receives it. You can send anything you like, from grocery lists to secret launch codes. Everything else with MSMQ is just part of the options package. So that you can take the basic model for a test drive, we're going to walk you through the steps required to actually send and receive a message. We'll do the sending part first, then the receiving part.

Actually, first we'll do a "Step 0" that will get us ready to use MSMQ. When you fire up Visual Basic with a new project, you need to give your project access to the MSMQ library. Do this by selecting the References item from the Project menu. When the dialog appears, turn on the Microsoft Message Queue Object Library, as illustrated in Figure 13.2.

Once you have access to the MSMQ library, Visual Basic will know all about the MSMQ object model and will give you automatic access to it and its methods and properties, as well as the named MSMQ constants used in this chapter.

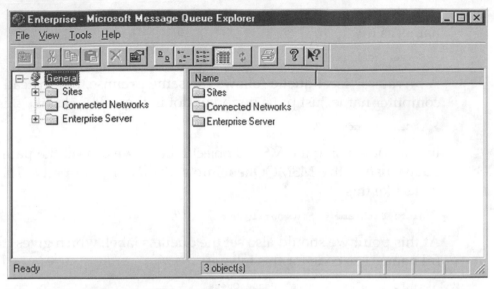

Figure 13.2 The MSMQ Library Reference Setting.

Sending a Message

Sending a message with MSMQ is actually pretty easy. You just have to do things the MSMQ way and follow the little rules. The steps involved are:

1. Create an MSMQQueueInfo object.
2. Set a path to the queue.
3. Create and open the queue.
4. Create an MSMQMessage object.
5. Fill in the contents of your message.
6. Send the message.
7. Close the queue.

First, let's create an MSMQQueueInfo object. The MSMQQueueInfo object is sort of like a base object that gives you access to queues and information about them. You use it primarily to create and open queues. Creating a queue is fairly simple, and it is the first step toward sending a message. Code for it looks like this:

```
Dim qInfo As MSMQQueueInfo
Set qInfo = New MSMQQueueInfo
```

Next, we set a path to the queue. The path to the queue tells MSMQ where to create or access the queue. The basic format for a public queue is the computer name followed by a backslash and then the queue name, as in:

```
Server1\GeneralQueue
```

A private or local queue follows the same premise, but instead of the computer name, just put a period or dot in there. It looks like this:

```
.\GeneralQueue
```

In our code, using the MSMQ object model, we can set the path to the queue using the MSMQQueueInfo's PathName property. The code looks like this:

```
qInfo.PathName = ".\GeneralQueue"
```

At this point we should also set the queue's label, which gives it a useful name. The code for this follows:

```
qInfo.Label = "General Usage Queue"
```

Now that we have set the stage, we can create the queue we will use to send and contain our message. We need to create an MSMQQueue object and then open it using the MSMQQueueInfo object we just built. We'll use the MSMQQueueInfo's Create method to create the queue, and Open to open it (imagine that). The code, which adds on to what we've done so far, follows:

```
qInfo.Create   ' Creates the queue with the info we set earlier.
Dim qQueue as MSMQQueue
Set qQueue = qInfo.Open(MQ_SEND_ACCESS, MQ_DENY_NONE)
```

The parameters on the Open method are the Access and Share modes. The Access mode can be Send, Receive, or Peek, which will let you send and receive messages as well as peek at what's in the queue without actually receiving the messages. The Share mode will allow you to prevent other applications or components from receiving messages from the queue or, as in the preceding code, allow complete access to the queue by anyone.

Now that we have the queue ready to send and receive, we need to create an instance of the MSMQMessage object to contain whatever important information we need to send somewhere. The code looks like this:

```
Dim qMsg As MSMQMessage
Set qMsg = New MSMQMessage
```

Let's fill in the contents of your message. There are a zillion properties attached to the MSMQMessage object (okay, 28). However, only three are important enough for this example to fill in before you can send the message: the label, the body, and the priority. The label is a short description of the message you can peek at without actually receiving the message. The priority is a value between 0 and 7 (0 being the lowest and 7 being the highest) that indicates how important the message is. The default priority is 3. The body of the message is the actual content of the message you are sending. When using the message body in Visual Basic, you treat the Body property as a variant. The receiver will either have to know the type being passed or else use the Visual Basic Type functions, like TypeOf, to determine the type of the data in the message body. The nice part is that, because the message body is a variant, you can send just about any data type you like, including currency, date, an array of bytes, and even a Recordset.

There are many other properties of a message that you can use to your advantage; you can look these up in the MSMQ reference. For example, the MaxTimeToReceive property allows you to set the number of seconds a message will exist before it is received, including time spent getting to the queue. If it is not received within the specified time limit, it is discarded by MSMQ and sent to the dead letter queue. Make sure you cruise through the message properties so you can gain the maximum benefit of the MSMQ message.

Having said all that, we're going to send a simple string. The code for getting a message set up and sending it looks like this:

```
qMsg.Priority = 1    ' We're not that important
qMsg.Label = "Our sample message"
qMsg.Body = "The singularly uninteresting body of a sample message."
```

Sending the message is the easy part, and the code for it is as follows:

```
qMsg.Send qQueue
```

The single parameter used here is the queue to which the message is sent. In this case, we listed the queue we just created in Step 3. Once sent, the message sits in the queue until someone receives it.

One last cleanup detail involves closing down the queue. The code looks like this:

```
qQueue.Close
```

Once the queue is closed, no messages can be sent to it. However, the queue still exists. If you want to send something else through it later, you can simply reopen the queue as we did in Step 3.

Now our message is sent and we can move on to receiving it.

Receiving a Message

The process for receiving a message looks amazingly like sending a message. We still create an MSMQQueueInfo object, set its path, then create a queue and open it. Once that's complete, we can receive the message. Let's run through the setup code quickly, since you've already seen it.

```
Dim qInfo As MSMQQueueInfo
Set qInfo = New MSMQQueueInfo
qInfo.PathName = ".\GeneralQueue"   ' Using a local, private queue.
Dim qQueue as MSMQQueue
Set qQueue = qInfo.Open(MQ_RECEIVE_ACCESS, MQ_DENY_NONE)
```

Now our queue is open. We did not need to create it; the sending code did that for us. Queues hang around until they are explicitly deleted. To receive the message, we simply call the queue's Receive method. The code looks like this:

```
dim qMsg as MSMQMessage
Set qMsg = qQueue.Receive(,,,10000)
```

The last parameter filled in is the receive timeout in milliseconds. We've set ours to 10 seconds. Once this call completes, you can check to see whether any message was actually received by detecting if the message object is set to nothing. If it is, then no message was received.

```
If qMsg Is Nothing Then
    ' Handle the no-message-received situation
Else
    ' Do something to process the message
End If
```

Once the message has been received—or otherwise—remember to close the queue as we did when we sent the message. Note that when you receive a message using the Receive method, the message has been removed from the queue and cannot be received again by the receiving code or any other. If you want to simply look into a queue, use the Peek method to look around without receiving the messages. For example, the following code will examine the first message in a specific queue. Note the change in the access method when we open the queue.

```
Set qQueue = qInfo.Open(MQ_PEEK_ACCESS, MQ_DENY_NONE)
qQueue.Peek(10000)
```

The parameter on Peek is the timeout in milliseconds—essentially, how long the Peek method should wait for a message to show up. You can also use the PeekCurrent and PeekNext methods to move through all the messages in a queue.

The basic scenario for sending and receiving a message is pretty simple as long as you follow the few rules and procedures illustrated here. However, there is one more major aspect of messaging that needs to be covered: events.

Using MSMQ Events

You've seen the basic send and receive mechanism that MSMQ provides. Pretty cool, right? However, there is one aspect of the whole thing that has so far eluded us. We can send a message at any specific point in time, and we can receive one at a specific point in time. However, what if we don't know exactly when a message will arrive? It could show up in a queue at any time. We need a mechanism to tell us when a message is in the queue, so that when it arrives we can go and get it, and until then we can go about other business.

It so happens that Microsoft thought of this when they designed MSMQ. We can have our program notified of the arrival of a message as an event, so that we can write an event handler for the arrival of a message just like we do for a button click. This allows us to receive messages asynchronously.

The event model for MSMQ is very simple. There are only two possible events: the arrival of a message and a message error. To get rolling with events and MSMQ, you will do the following:

1. Create a Message Event object using WithEvents.

2. Open the queue, then set up the event and associate it with the queue.

3. Create the event handler to deal with the arrival of a message.

Let's take a look at the actual process in a little more detail.

Because the queue and the Event object have to stick around beyond the scope of a function in order for the event handler to work, we should create our Event object and queue at the top of a code module, outside of any function. We also need to create the Event object using the Visual Basic WithEvents keyword so that it can actually receive events. The code looks like this:

```
qQueue as MSMQQueue
WithEvents qEvent As MSMQEvent
```

Now the stage is set to deal with messaging events. We need to create and initialize our queue and the event. This can be done any time before the receipt of your first message. In the example we're building, we are putting it in a Sub Main routine, but you could just as easily put it in a Form_Load event.

```
Sub Main
    ' Set up the QueueInfo object so we can access the queue.
    Dim qInfo As New MSMQQueueInfo
    qInfo.PathName = ".\GeneralQueue"   ' Local private queue.
    ' Open the queue we created outside the function
    Set qQueue = qInfo.Open(MQ_RECEIVE_ACCESS, MQ_DENY_NONE)
    ' Create an MSMQEvent and make it active.
    Set qEvent = New MSMQEvent
    qQueue.EnableNotification qEvent
End Sub
```

The EnableNotification method hooks up a queue with an Event object. This actually wires the event into our queue and makes it active. After this point, message arrivals will show up as events.

Now that we can receive Message Arrival events, we need to do something if a message actually shows up. To do this, we create an event handler using the Event object for the Arrived event. A sample event handler is listed next.

```
Sub qEvent_Arrived(ByVal Queue As Object, ByVal Cursor As Long)
    Dim aQueue As MSMQQueue
    Set aQueue = Queue
    Dim qMsg As MSMQMessage
    Set qMsg = aQueue.Receive(,,,0)
    ' Write some code to do something with the message.
    ' ...
    aQueue.EnableNotification qEvent, MQMSG_NEXT
End Sub
```

Once you receive the message, you can do as you like with it. The important part here is the last line. If you would like to continue to receive messages, you need to call EnableNotification at the end of the event handler. Make sure you use the Queue object that gets passed in to the function as your message queue.

That's the basis behind the MSMQ event story. This part of MSMQ is what makes it work, the part that makes it really useful. You can add this little twist to your messaging and not have to worry about when messages arrive. You'll be told when they get there, and you can do other useful things when there are no messages to process.

MSMQ Transactions

How do transactions and MSMQ fit together? There are times when you may be sending or receiving a series of messages that need to be treated as a single, coherent unit; if one of the messages fails, they all need to be canceled or called back. Sending your messages as part of a transaction will do this. MSMQ provides its own transaction mechanism, just like SQL Server does. However, you can also send messages as part of an MTS transaction if you are so inclined.

The basic premise works just like an MTS transaction. You start the transaction, then set up your messages and send them. If everything works, you can call the Commit method on the transaction to close it and send all the messages. If any message or part of your process fails, you can call the Abort method on the transaction to cancel the messages. Note that until you call the Commit function, none of the messages are sent. Once Commit is called, all the messages are sent. This is important to keep in mind, since you won't want to wait too long before committing your MSMQ transaction. If you do, the transaction will stay open too long, hogging resources, and may even be canceled automatically.

Building an MSMQ Transaction

Just like with regular transactions and MSMQ messages, there are a few basic steps you have to follow to build the transaction, start it up, send your messages, and close out. The steps we'll be covering in more detail are as follows:

1. Create a transaction dispenser.
2. Create and start an MSMQ transaction.
3. Send or receive your messages.
4. Commit or abort your transaction.

Let's take a look at each step in more detail.

The transaction dispenser, represented by the MSMQTransactionDispenser object, is used to actually create a new Transaction object as well as start the transaction. Create the transaction dispenser in the standard Visual Basic fashion, as follows:

```
Dim qDispenser As New MSMQTransactionDispenser
```

Now you need to use the dispenser to create and return the actual transaction object. Once you do that, you can use the transaction object to start the transaction. The code looks like this:

```
Dim qTrans as MSMQTransaction  ' Don't create an actual instance!
Set qTrans = qDispenser.BeginTransaction()
```

You've already seen how to set up for and send or receive messages using MSMQ, so we're just going to stick the code in here to do it. Our queue setup code follows:

```
Dim qInfo As MSMQQueueInfo
Set qInfo = New MSMQQueueInfo
qInfo.PathName = ".\GeneralQueue" ' Using a local, private queue.
Dim qQueue as MSMQQueue
Set qQueue = qInfo.Open(MQ_SEND_ACCESS, MQ_DENY_NONE)
```

In this example, we'll just send a couple messages. You can send or receive your messages any time after you call the BeginTransaction method, and any messages will be contained within that transaction. There is only one trick to sending (or receiving) messages in a transaction: you have to send the transaction object to the Send and Receive methods when you call them. The code for sending the messages looks like this:

```
Dim qMsgA As New MSMQMessage
Dim qMsgB As New MSMQMessage
qMsgA.Label = "Sample Message A"
qMsgA.Body = "Sample Message A Body"
qMsgB.Label = "Sample Message B"
qMsgB.Body = "Sample Message B Body"
' Send both messages as part of our transaction.
qMsgA.Send qQueue, qTrans
qMsgB.Send qQueue, qTrans
```

At this point, both messages are sitting in stasis, waiting to be sent. Because they are part of the transaction, they will not be sent until you commit the transaction.

The last step is to decide what to do with the transaction. Assuming everything went well up to now, you can commit the transaction and force all messages to actually be sent. If something went wrong, you can abort the transaction and cancel the sending of the messages. A simple line of code takes care of the process:

```
qTrans.Commit
```

Should you decide that you want to cancel all messages, simply call abort instead, like this:

```
qTrans.Abort
```

Note that if you are receiving messages instead of sending them as part of a transaction, the messages come in immediately. If the transaction is later aborted, the messages that have been received are actually put back in the queue.

So messaging fits in the transactional model just like anything else, which is a boon for those of us who need to write N-tier applications. Transactions allow us to ensure action and data integrity in a distributed environment, and messaging is a big part of a distributed environment.

Winding Up

As another tier, MSMQ fits nicely into any N-tier application that requires message-based communications. Because we define tiers rather loosely to include any major service-oriented subsystem in an application that could possibly reside on a server or client computer, MSMQ fits the model for another tier. Other products, such as Microsoft's Internet Information Server, can also be considered tiers.

While there are all kinds of possibilities for tiers, some of which are part of the Microsoft DNA architecture, don't feel you have to use them all. Tiers and their functionality are there for your use if you need them, but they are not mandatory. Don't get caught in "tier mania," adding them because they look good on your product features list. Every tier you add to your systems also adds complexity and could potentially reduce performance, so choose them carefully.

Putting It All Together

CHAPTER 14

Putting It Together

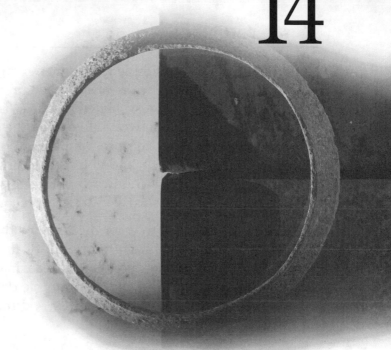

This book has taken you on a whirlwind tour of N-tier application development, focusing on COM and Visual Basic. You've been exposed to many different topics that are commonly encountered when developing N-tier applications, including business rules, databases, fat and thin clients, messaging, communications, servers, remote DLLs, transactions, and more. The last aspect we need to cover about all this wondrous technology and capability is how to make all of it work together to actually create useful software. After all, that's why you get paid the big bucks.

In this chapter, we construct a small but useful program that employs some of what we have learned so far, including:

- The design and construction of components and their interfaces
- Client communication with and use of remote components
- Passing ADO Recordsets from components to clients

Hopefully, you will walk away from the final chapter in this programming story with a reasonable picture of how several technologies and techniques work together to solve problems for you and your customers. If we've done our job, and you woke up on the right side of the bed, you'll have fun doing it as well. There is also an exercise at the end of the chapter that you can try yourself to enhance the program.

What You Need

There are a few simple requirements for the sample program, but they are all optional. The database we are providing is in an Access database, and the ADO drivers that come with Visual Basic will do fine for reading the data. If you would like to do the exercise at the end of the chapter that converts the program's component from a DLL to a remote DCOM component, and you are running a Windows95 client, you will need DCOM for Windows95. This is available as a free download from Microsoft's Web site (www.microsoft.com).

If you prefer not to enter the code for this example program manually, even though you'll get more out of it and feel like you have accomplished something, you can instead load it from the companion CD-ROM. The code, project files, sample database, and compiled versions are located in the \Examples\Ch14 directory.

Program Overview

The program we are building is not especially large or complex: The confines of a book limit what we can do to some extent. However, this program does illustrate some of the principles covered in this book and might actually be specified and used by a real company. The program is described in a general sense, then detailed through requirements that have been provided by our imaginary customer.

Description

We are the sole proprietors of an imaginary software consulting firm called Barking Mad Software. We have just acquired a new customer, Bertha's Exotic Pets, which is a small chain of pet stores in the Northern Virginia area of the United States. Business is doing well, but the company has experienced a business phenomenon whereby most customers enter the store, prowl around, and leave without making a purchase. This worries Bertha, and she wants a software solution to help out with the problem.

Bertha envisions a program that runs on a computer in each store. Customers can walk up to the computer, answer a few simple questions, and receive a recommendation for a pet. Bertha came up with this idea a couple of nights ago, and has since filled in some of the details. She would like our company to construct the solution for her and her stores.

Requirements from the Customer

When building a program of any reasonable size, it pays to plan it out and make sure you're building the right thing. Whether you are dealing with customers internal to your company or external paying ones, you will get a list of requirements from them. These requirements may be as simple as a wish list of features drawn on a lunch napkin, or as elaborate as a 500-page document outlining every feature to the smallest detail. Whatever the case, if you don't get these requirements, make sure you extract them from your customer.

In the case of Bertha's Exotic Pets, we received most of the requirements from Bertha and gathered the rest ourselves in a short interview. Bertha knew all the primary functionality the application should support, or all the business rules; we asked questions about how often the database of pets would be updated and determined where the data and components should reside and what sort of client technology would be appropriate. The following list details everything the program needs to do in the form of requirements:

1. The program will ask customers a series of questions intended to find out what sort of pet would be appropriate for them.

2. The program will not ask more than five questions. Bertha does not want her customers to get bored with the process before they have the chance to purchase something.

3. The program will make suggestions for pets to purchase based on customers' answers to the questions.

4. The program will only suggest pets that are currently in stock in the pet store.

5. The database of pets should be located in a centralized location, because stock is controlled from one location.

6. The algorithm that figures out which pets match the answers to the questions should be easy to change from a central location.

7. A Win32 client will be sufficient for this version of the program.

Our program must meet all the requirements specified. After reading through them, we decide we can do it with no problem. After seeing requirement 4, we became especially impressed with Bertha's willingness to be a ruthless businessperson.

Program Design

An application as simple as Bertha's will not require a large design effort. However, we'll go through the design process to make sure we don't miss anything. We will first run through Bertha's requirements and think about how we can meet them. This will lead us to our high-level design. Once that's done, we can work out the details. Detailed design is a formal stage in larger projects, but for our purposes, we'll do most of it in the code.

The Problem We Are Solving: Basic Requirements Analysis

The first step in any requirements analysis is to state the overall problem we are solving. Bertha's problem statement is fairly simple and reads like this:

> Encourage customers to purchase a pet by helping them decide which pet, currently in stock, best suits them. The process should be quick, painless, and pleasant.

Pretty easy to understand, isn't it? This will keep our efforts focused throughout the course of the project. Next we need to look at the requirements and decide how we will deal with each in our program. Let's get going, working down the list one item at a time.

Requirement 1. The program will ask customers a series of questions intended to find out what sort of pet would be appropriate for them.

This is pretty simple. Our program can display questions for the user in a dialog box. In order to help meet a small part of our problem statement—that the process should be pleasant—we'll display a nice petlike graphic on the dialog for each question. This will keep the process light and amusing.

Requirement 2. The program will not ask more than five questions. Bertha does not want her customers to get bored with the process before they have the chance to purchase something.

The first problem we need to deal with here is how to get an accurate customer profile in five questions or less, so that the pet recommended will be suitable. After speaking with Bertha and a bunch of our friends who own pets, we have decided on the following questions:

1. Why do you want a pet?

2. How much do you want to spend on your pet?

3. How much time will you spend with your pet?

4. How much space will your pet have in which to live?

5. How often will your pet be around children?

This should give us a decent picture of the customer's needs. The second issue we need to deal with is the answers. In order to make the customer's time with the program as short as possible, we will provide multiple choice answers. To further maximize time, and to make life easier for us, we will limit the answers to three possible choices per question.

Requirement 3. The program will make suggestions for pets to purchase based on the customer's answers to the questions.

This is the interesting part. We need an algorithm to match the customer's answers with the pets available in the database. This will also affect our database design, because we will need to store data about the pets that enables us to do the matching. The actual algorithm and database design will be covered a little later in this chapter, but for now, the important point is to note this requirement's impact on our design.

Requirement 4. The program will only suggest pets that are currently in stock in the pet store.

This requirement is a marketing tour de force. Bertha is doing her best to make sure that a customer can act on impulse, purchasing any of the recommended pets immediately. While this is highly unethical with respect to the future welfare of the pet, we are not in a position to argue, especially with Bertha. In order to make this happen, we will have to track pet stock by store in the database. This will also affect our pet matching algorithm, because it will have to take the customer's location into account when it matches pets to answers.

Requirement 5. The database of pets should be located in a centralized location, because stock is controlled from one location.

This means that the database used by our program will not ultimately be located on the same computer as the questions client program. For the purpose of this example, we will be locating the database on the client. The process of moving it to a remote server is the subject of one of the exercises at the end of the chapter.

Requirement 6. The algorithm that figures out what pets match the answers to the questions should be easy to change from a central location.

This can be accomplished by placing the algorithm in a component that can be hosted on a remote server. We can build it, for the purpose of this example, as an ActiveX DLL and run it locally. It would be a simple process to rebuild the component as an ActiveX EXE, so it can run as a DCOM component on a remote computer.

Requirement 7. A Win32 client will be sufficient for this version of the program.

This will be easy enough. It simply makes our choice of client for us. If we were not a consulting firm, or if Bertha had specified it, we could make the user interface replaceable. If we did this, when Bertha was ready, people could access the questions and results from any Internet browser. For now, we'll do it as quickly as we can, using a standard Win32 Visual Basic client.

This gives us a picture of the program we have to build. Our next step is to plan how to go about implementing it. We do this by specifying some detail about it in the form of a design.

Our Design

Because our program is simple and our requirements are small, our design will also be short and sweet. We have decided that we can place our customer answer analysis algorithm and the database lookup code into a single component, because the functionality is logically all related to pet information processing. We will build it as an ActiveX DLL, or COM component, for the purposes of the example. Later we can recompile it as a DCOM component in the form of an ActiveX EXE when we need to move it to a remote server. The database, being very limited in requirements, will be implemented in an Access database.

The details we need to work out include the layout of the database, the organization of the component, and the basic user interface design.

The Database

Our database needs to track two basic types of information: type of pet and specific stock of pets. The pet information will be located in the first of two tables, and will be used to match customer answers to pets. The second table will contain information about specific pets in stock, and will be used to look up pets that can be purchased immediately. The table layouts are illustrated in Figure 14.1.

PetData Table	PetSelectionData Table
PetID (long) PetType (string) Gender (string) PetName (string) Cost (currency) PetLocation (string) QuantityOnHand (long)	PetType (string) CostRange (string) AttentionReqd (string) ResidenceReqd (string) ChildrenRating (string) GoodFor (string)

Figure 14.1 The database layout for our example program.

The database we have provided on the companion CD-ROM contains some sample data that can be used with the program. It is located with the rest of the example files in the \Examples\Ch14 directory. Copy it into the same directory from which you will be running the program. Later, as part of an exercise at the end of the chapter, we will consider its relocation to a server.

The Component

Our component will contain the functionality for matching customer question answers to pet types, as well as the code to use those matches to pull available pets in stock for display to the customer. It will have some basic properties that can be used to set the answers to the questions, which must be filled in before the other functionality of the component can be used. There are two major functions in the component that will be used once the answer properties are set: GetPetSelection, which will perform the question-to-pet matching, and GetPetInfo, which will retrieve stock information about the selected pets.

For the GetPetSelection function we have chosen a simple algorithm. The answers to the questions must make an exact match to the same parameters in the pet database. For example, the question that asks how much money the customer wants to spend on a pet has three possible values that equate to a high, medium, and low amount. To find a match in the database, our component will match the value exactly. If the user chooses the medium amount, the algorithm will only retrieve pets that have the medium setting in the cost column. Because we chose to use a simple algorithm, we will use a SQL statement to perform the matching functionality.

The GetPetInfo function will accept a specific pet type, and for that type will retrieve pets that are currently in stock. It will also use a SQL statement to perform this simple match. This information will be used by the client to display available pets to the user.

Both of these functions will use an ADO Recordset to retrieve the information required, as well as to pass the information back to the calling function.

The User Interface

To keep things simple for the user, our user interface will be designed so that it displays one question at a time. It will also be appealing to look at, with some nice colors and graphics, to attract attention in the store. The basic layout for a question form looks like Figure 14.2.

We will implement the question interface as a single form. For each question, we will simply change the text of the question label and the answer radio buttons. A simple Next Question button will move to the next question.

A second form will be displayed when the results of the search are known and will show users a list of the pets that match their needs. If

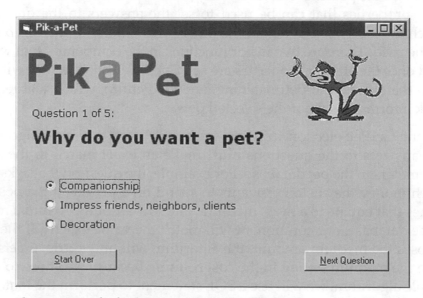

Figure 14.2   The basic questionnaire form layout.

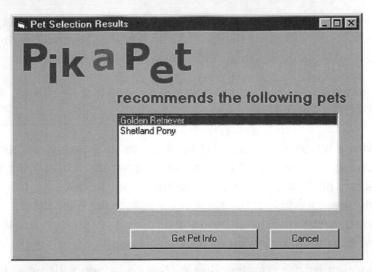

Figure 14.3 The pet search results form design.

there are no pets in stock, the form will display a message box that says so in friendly terms. If the user selects one of the pets in the list, a small third form will appear that simply displays some details about the specific pet chosen. These two forms are illustrated in Figures 14.3 and 14.4.

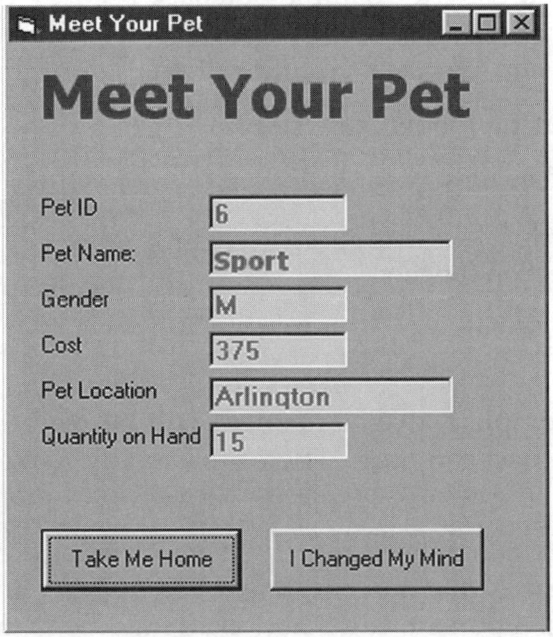

Figure 14.4 The pet information form design.

Now that we have a basic design that will act as our road map, we can begin implementing our program. The code is detailed in the next section.

Program Implementation

Now we move on to the best part of any programming project: the implementation. We will be building our program using two Visual Basic projects. The first is for the component that performs our matching and database lookups, and the second is for our user interface. We build the component first, because the user interface project must reference the component in its project.

In the discussion of the construction of the code, we will be skipping some of the details, specifically the general Visual Basic programming you already know. Instead we will concentrate on the N-tier aspects of the code and the details you need to know to get it running.

The Component Project

We will get things rolling by building our COM component. As a reminder, make sure you copy the sample database used by the program from the companion CD-ROM to the directory in which you will be building the component. The database file will act as our third tier.

To construct the component, follow these steps:

1. Create the project and its files.
2. Create the supporting code.
3. Create the GetPetSelection function.
4. Create the GetPetInfo function.
5. Compile the project.

Once these steps are complete, our component will be ready to use. We'll then move on the user interface, where we actually make use of our new component.

The first step is to create our project. Fire up Visual Basic and create a new ActiveX DLL project. Name the component PetAnalyzer and save it. To begin coding the component, add a new class module to the project and name it CPetAnswers. Finally, add a standard code module to the project and name it whatever you like. We'll only be using it for global variables.

Now open the Project Properties dialog from the Project menu and add a reference to the Microsoft ActiveX Data Objects 2.0 Library. This will give us access to the ADO functions and objects we need to talk to the database.

The supporting code includes all the Get and Set properties for the question answers, as well as the Terminate and Initialize functions for the class. The only two functions of note here are the latter two; these will be covered shortly. For now, enter the following code into the class module CPetAnswers:

```vb
Option Explicit

' Local variable(s) to hold property value(s)
Private mvarWhy As Variant 'local copy
Private mvarMoney As Variant 'local copy
Private mvarTime As Variant 'local copy
Private mvarSpace As Variant 'local copy
Private mvarAroundKids As Variant 'local copy

Public Property Let AroundKids (ByVal vData As Variant)
mvarAroundKids = vData

End Property

Public Property Set AroundKids(ByVal vData As Variant)

    Set mvarAroundKids = vData

End Property

Public Property Get AroundKids() As Variant

    If IsObject(mvarAroundKids) Then
        Set AroundKids = mvarAroundKids
    Else
        AroundKids = mvarAroundKids
    End If

End Property

Public Property Let Space(ByVal vData As Variant)

    mvarSpace = vData

End Property

Public Property Set Space(ByVal vData As Variant)

    Set mvarSpace = vData

End Property
```

```
Public Property Get Space() As Variant

    If IsObject(mvarSpace) Then
        Set Space = mvarSpace
    Else
        Space = mvarSpace
    End If

End Property

Public Property Let Time(ByVal vData As Variant)

    mvarTime = vData

End Property

Public Property Set Time(ByVal vData As Variant)

    Set mvarTime = vData

End Property

Public Property Get Time() As Variant

    If IsObject(mvarTime) Then
        Set Time = mvarTime
    Else
        Time = mvarTime
    End If

End Property

Public Property Let Money(ByVal vData As Variant)

    mvarMoney = vData

End Property

Public Property Set Money(ByVal vData As Variant)

    Set mvarMoney = vData

End Property

Public Property Get Money() As Variant

    If IsObject(mvarMoney) Then
        Set Money = mvarMoney
    Else
        Money = mvarMoney
    End If

End Property

Public Property Let Why(ByVal vData As Variant)

    mvarWhy = vData

End Property

Public Property Set Why(ByVal vData As Variant)

    Set mvarWhy = vData
```

```
    End Property

Public Property Get Why() As Variant

    If IsObject(mvarWhy) Then
        Set Why = mvarWhy
    Else
        Why = mvarWhy
    End If

End Property

Private Sub Class_Initialize()

    ' Setup connect string
    connectstring = "Provider=Microsoft.Jet.OLEDB.3.51;" & _
        "Persist Security Info=False;Data Source=" & _
        App.Path & "\pets.mdb"

    ' Create connection object
    Set cn = New ADODB.Connection

    ' Assign connectstring to connection object
    cn.ConnectionString = connectstring

    ' Specify client side cursor
    cn.CursorLocation = adUseClient

    ' Open connection
    cn.Open

End Sub

Private Sub Class_Terminate()

    ' Free up all the memory we have used.
    Set rsset = Nothing
    Set cn = Nothing
End Sub
```

The Class_Initialize function is of interest. It is called when the component is created. We use this event to set up and open our connection to the database. Once open, the component can freely speak with the database. The Class_Terminate function is called when the class shuts down; we use this event to free up all the memory taken up when we created objects during the execution of code in the component.

Now open the code module we created at the beginning of this project and add the following code. It is a list of the global variables we will be using as part of this component.

```
Global rsset As ADODB.Recordset
Global cn As ADODB.Connection
Global connectstring As String
Global anerror As ADODB.Error
```

All the code in this step forms the infrastructure that any component requires—specifically properties it needs to make public. Next we get into the interesting part of the component, in which we speak with the database and actually retrieve pet data.

The GetPetSelection function will use the customer's answers, which were previously fed into this component by the calling code, in order to retrieve pets that fit the specified criteria. We use a SQL statement to perform the match and retrieve the list of matching pets into an ADO Recordset. Once it is loaded, the list is then passed back to the client.

This technique can be used to pass large lists of data back to calling routines. An ADO Recordset can remain connected, in which case the client can update the values in the database directly using the Recordset. If the Recordset remains connected, at least one connection is maintained to the database. This may or may not be desirable. If you are creating remote components, you don't want to hold on to those connections too long.

You can also send back a disconnected Recordset. In this case, you set the connection object in the Recordset to Nothing, then pass the Recordset back to the client. This works very well for read-only data, does not keep a connection to the database open all the time, and prevents the client from making updates directly to the database without the business tier knowing about it. This is important when you are updating data as part of a transaction.

For now, we just use a regular Recordset, because our connection is open for only a moment. Add the following code to the component class.

```
Public Function GetPetSelection() As ADODB.Recordset

    Dim sSQLString As String

    ' Create the Recordset to retrieve selected pets
    sSQLString = "Select PetType, CostRange, AttentionReqd,
        ResidenceReqd, ChildrenRating, GoodFor
        From PetSelectionData
        Where (GoodFor = '" & mvarWhy & "') AND
            (AttentionReqd = '" & mvarTime & "' ) AND
            (ResidenceReqd = '" & mvarSpace & "' )AND
            (ChildrenRating = '" & mvarAroundKids & "' )"
    ' Run the query and return the record set.
    Set rsset = cn.Execute(sSQLString)
    Set GetPetSelection = rsset

End Function
```

Now we can search the database for matching pets. The Recordset can be iterated through by the client and the contents extracted for display to the user.

The last step in the construction of the components is to create functionality that allows the client to get information about a specific pet in stock from the database. This code takes a parameter that is a specific pet to locate and enables information about it to be retrieved from the database and returned to the client. The code looks like this:

```
Public Function GetPetInfo(ByVal PetType As String) As _
ADODB.Recordset

    Dim sSQLString As String

    ' Create the recordset to retrieve the inventory Count
    sSQLString = "Select PetID, PetType, Gender, PetName, Cost,
        PetLocation, QuantityOnHand
        From PetData
        Where (PetType = '" & PetType & "')"

    ' Run the query and send the information back in the Recordset.
    Set rsset = cn.Execute(sSQLString)
    Set GetPetInfo = rsset

End Function
```

This function does a simple lookup in our database and returns the results from the query in an ADO Recordset. Once the client has it, the data can be extracted and displayed to the user.

Now we can build the project. Select the Build PetAnalyzer.Dll option from the File menu to compile the DLL. Once compiled, the component will be registered on your local computer automatically by Visual Basic. It is now ready for use, so we should go ahead and build the client.

The User Interface Project

Our component is ready to roll, so let's put it to use. We will be building a user interface to present users with questions that they can answer by making a simple radio button selection and pressing a button. Once the users have answered the five questions we provide, our component will kick in and figure out which pets should be displayed for potential purchase.

To build the user interface, we follow these steps:

1. Create the user interface project and its files.

2. Design the three forms we will be using.

3. Write the code behind the forms to do the work.

4. Build the program and run it.

Our program will be ready to go when these steps are complete.

Create a new Standard EXE project in Visual Basic, and name it PikaPet (Bertha thought up the name of the program). Add three forms—frmQuestions, frmPetResults, and frmPetInfo—to the project. Add one code module and name it Module1. Save your project before a power outage occurs.

Next, we design the forms. There are three forms that make up the user interface. The first, frmQuestions, is used to display the questions to users and collect their answers. The second, frmPetResults, displays the results of the pet search, listing all the matching pets found in stock. The last form, frmPetInfo, lists the details about a single, specific pet selected from the search results form.

The forms are fairly simple to design. Add controls to the forms so that they approximate the forms shown in Figures 14.5, 14.6, and 14.7.

When you are finished putting controls on the forms, you can name the controls according to the information listed in Table 14.1. You can, of course, name them anything you like, but you'll have to change the code to match your own names.

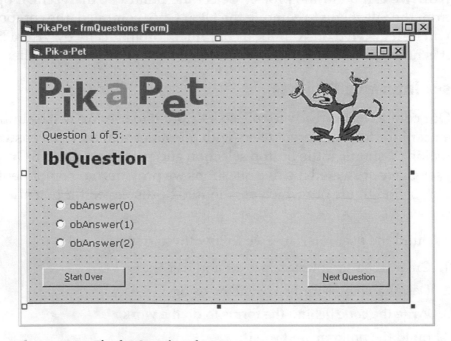

Figure 14.5 The frmQuestions form.

Figure 14.6 The frmPetResults form.

Figure 14.7 The frmPetInfo form.

Table 14.1 The Project Forms and Their Controls

CONTROL	NAME	PURPOSE
frmQuestions		
Label	lblQuestionNum	Displays current question number out of the total number of questions
Label	lblQuestion	Displays the current question
Option button (control array from 0 to 2)	obAnswer	Displays three radio buttons for the answers to the question
Picture	picPet	Displays the cartoon pet image for each question
Command button	cmdStartOver	Restarts the questionnaire from the beginning
Command button	cmdNext	Displays the next question
frmPetResults		
List box	List1	Displays the list of matching pets
Command button	Command1	Displays frmPetInfo with pet information
Command button	Command2	Removes frmPetResults from the screen
frmPetInfo		
Text box	Text1	Displays the pet ID
Text box	Text2	Displays the pet's name
Text box	Text3	Displays the pet's gender
Text box	Text4	Displays the cost of the pet
Text box	Text5	Displays the pet's location
Text box	Text6	Displays the quantity on hand for this type of pet

Set the AutoSize property for the Picture control to True. We have provided some original pet clip art images on the companion CD-ROM for use with this program. They are located in the \Examples\Ch14 directory. Once the form designs are complete, we can start writing code behind them.

Start by adding a small amount of code to the module we added to the project. It contains a PetInfoType that stores the customer's answers to the questions, a global variable or two, and a small utility function that centers a form on the page when it is called. Go ahead and type the following code into the code module:

```
Type PetInfoType
    Why As String
    HowMuch As String
    TimeDevoted As String
    WhereLive As String
    AroundKids As String
End Type

Global rsset As ADOR.Recordset

Public Sub CenterForm(f As Form)

    f.Left = (Screen.Width - f.Width) \ 2
    f.Top = (Screen.Height - f.Height) \ 2

End Sub
```

Now we can move on to the fun stuff. Most of the code for this program is located in frmQuestions. This is the first time we will access the component we created to retrieve data about matching pets. The following code listing shows the simple supporting code required to make the program work. Go ahead and add it to the code section of the frmQuestions form. Afterward we'll add the code that makes use of our component.

```
Option Explicit

Dim PetInfo As PetInfoType
Dim currQuestion As Integer

Private Function WhySelected() As String

    ' Get names we can use to match values in the database.
    If obAnswer(0).Value Then
        WhySelected = "Companionship"
    ElseIf obAnswer(1).Value Then
        WhySelected = "Impress"
    Else
        WhySelected = "Decoration"
    End If

End Function

Private Sub cmdStartOver_Click()

    ' Restart the questionnaire
    cmdNext.Caption = "&Next Question"
    currQuestion = 1
    Start

End Sub
```

```
Private Sub Form_Load()

    ' Start the questionnaire rolling.
    CenterForm Me
    Start

End Sub

' The next set of functions set up and ask the questions
' when they are called.

Private Sub Question1()

    currQuestion = 1
    SetAnswer
    lblQuestionNum.Caption = "Question 1 of 5:"
    picPet.Picture = LoadPicture(App.Path + "\monkeyC.gif")

    lblQuestion = "Why do you want a pet?"
    obAnswer(0).Caption = "Companionship"
    obAnswer(1).Caption = "Impress friends, neighbors, clients"
    obAnswer(2).Caption = "Decoration"

End Sub

Private Sub Question2()

    currQuestion = 2
    SetAnswer
    lblQuestionNum.Caption = "Question 2 of 5:"
    picPet.Picture = LoadPicture(App.Path + "\lizardC.gif")

    lblQuestion = "How much do you want to spend on your pet?"
    obAnswer(0).Caption = "Money is no object"
    obAnswer(1).Caption = "Not too much, but I'm no tightwad"
    obAnswer(2).Caption = "Keep it cheap"

End Sub

Private Sub Question3()

    currQuestion = 3
    SetAnswer
    lblQuestionNum.Caption = "Question 3 of 5:"
    picPet.Picture = LoadPicture(App.Path + "\catC.gif")

    lblQuestion = "How much time will you spend with your pet?"
    obAnswer(0).Caption = "All day"
    obAnswer(1).Caption = "Some time each day"
    obAnswer(2).Caption = "A little time on the weekend"

End Sub

Private Sub Question4()

    currQuestion = 4
    SetAnswer
    lblQuestionNum.Caption = "Question 4 of 5:"
    picPet.Picture = LoadPicture(App.Path + "\snakeC.gif")
```

```
    lblQuestion = "How much space will your pet have in which to
live? _"
        obAnswer(0).Caption = "Inside an apartment or house"
        obAnswer(1).Caption = "A large backyard"
        obAnswer(2).Caption = "A farm with lots of open land"

End Sub

Private Sub Question5()

    currQuestion = 5
    SetAnswer
    lblQuestionNum.Caption = "Question 5 of 5:"
    picPet.Picture = LoadPicture(App.Path + "\allig8rC.gif")

    lblQuestion = "How often will your pet be around children?"
    obAnswer(0).Caption = "All the time"
    obAnswer(1).Caption = "Occasionally"
    obAnswer(2).Caption = "Never"

End Sub

Private Function WhichSelected() As String

    If obAnswer(0).Value Then
        WhichSelected = "High"
    ElseIf obAnswer(1).Value Then
        WhichSelected = "Medium"
    Else
        WhichSelected = "Low"
    End If

End Function

Private Sub SetAnswer()
    Dim Value As Integer
    Select Case currQuestion
    Case 1
        obAnswer(PetInfo.Why - 1).Value = True
    Case 2
        obAnswer(PetInfo.HowMuch - 1).Value = True
    Case 3
        obAnswer(PetInfo.TimeDevoted - 1).Value = True
    Case 4
        obAnswer(PetInfo.WhereLive - 1).Value = True
    Case 5
        obAnswer(PetInfo.AroundKids - 1).Value = True
    End Select

End Sub

Private Sub Start()

    ' Initialize the question answers and fire the
    ' first question.
    PetInfo.AroundKids = 1
    PetInfo.HowMuch = 1
```

```
        PetInfo.TimeDevoted = 1
        PetInfo.WhereLive = 1
        PetInfo.Why = 1

        Question1

End Sub
```

This code takes care of routine tasks, such as displaying the questions as they are needed. Our next chunk of code actually runs the show and is the event handler for the click event on the Next button. Each time it is clicked, the next question is displayed and its answer is collected. Go ahead and enter it into the frmQuestions code section.

```
Private Sub cmdNext_Click()

    ' This function asks the questions.
    Dim bAnalysisComplete As Boolean
    Dim oPetAnalyzer As CPetAnswers

    Select Case currQuestion
    Case 1
        'Find out why they want the pet
        PetInfo.Why = WhySelected()
        Question2
    Case 2
        'Find out how much the level of pay
        PetInfo.HowMuch = WhichSelected()
        Question3
    Case 3
        'Find out the level of time devoted
        PetInfo.TimeDevoted = WhichSelected()
        Question4
    Case 4
        'Find out how much space
        PetInfo.WhereLive = WhichSelected()
        Question5
        cmdNext.Caption = "See Results"
    Case 5
        'Level around children
        PetInfo.AroundKids = WhichSelected()
        bAnalysisComplete = True
    End Select

    ' If the user is finished answering questions, then we
    ' can run the analysis.
    If bAnalysisComplete = True Then
        ' Create a new instance of our COM component.
        Set oPetAnalyzer = New CPetAnswers
        ' Set the component properties (the answers to the
        ' questions).
        With oPetAnalyzer
```

```
            .Why = PetInfo.Why
            .Money = PetInfo.HowMuch
            .Time = PetInfo.TimeDevoted
            .Space = PetInfo.WhereLive
            .AroundKids = PetInfo.AroundKids
        End With

        ' Figure out what pets match the user's answers.
        Set rsset = oPetAnalyzer.GetPetSelection

        ' If there were matches, then display them in our
        ' PetResults form. If not, tell the user with a
        ' polite message that none were found.
        If rsset.RecordCount <> 0 Then
            frmPetResults.Show
            frmPetResults.List1.Clear
            While Not rsset.EOF
                frmPetResults.List1.AddItem rsset.Fields("PetType")
                rsset.MoveNext
            Wend
            frmPetResults.List1.Selected(0) = True
        Else
            MsgBox "Sorry, we could not find any pets " & _
                "to match your needs"
        End If
    End If

    ' Free up the memory we have used.
    Set oPetAnalyzer = Nothing

End Sub
```

Once the last question is answered, this function begins the analysis. It first creates an instance of our component, using the code line

```
Set oPetAnalyzer = New CPetAnswers
```

This allocates and initializes our component, which is now ready for use. The code then populates all the properties of the component with the answers the user has entered. It next calls the component method Get-PetSelection. The component then checks the database, matching up suitable pets with the answers provided. When the list is built, it is returned in an ADO Recordset, which is the return value of the function. Our rsset variable is a pointer to that Recordset.

If there are any records returned from the GetPetSelection function, the code iterates through the Recordset, adding each pet to the list box on the frmPetResults form we are about to show. If there are no pets that match, a polite message box is displayed instead. The frmPetResults form is then displayed.

The other forms are much simpler. In fact, there is no code for the frm-PetInfo form. The data fields are populated by frmPetResults before it is displayed. So we can skip that one—it's done. The frmPetResults form has a little code and is listed next. Go ahead and type it into the code window for that form:

```
Private Sub Command1_Click()

    Dim sSelectedPet As String
    Dim oPetAnalyzer As CPetAnswers

    ' We need to get information about the selected pet.
    sSelectedPet = List1.Text
    ' Create an instance of our CPetAnswers COM component.
    Set oPetAnalyzer = New CPetAnswers
    ' Get info about the pet the user selected.
    Set rsset = oPetAnalyzer.GetPetInfo(sSelectedPet)

    ' Show and populate the form with the pet information.
    frmPetInfo.Show
    frmPetInfo.Text1.Text = rsset.Fields("PetID")
    frmPetInfo.Text2.Text = rsset.Fields("PetName")
    frmPetInfo.Text3.Text = rsset.Fields("Gender")
    frmPetInfo.Text4.Text = rsset.Fields("Cost")
    frmPetInfo.Text5.Text = rsset.Fields("PetLocation")
    frmPetInfo.Text6.Text = rsset.Fields("QuantityOnHand")

End Sub

Private Sub Command2_Click()

    frmPetResults.Hide

End Sub
```

When the Command1 button, which reads Get Pet Info, is clicked, the form gets and displays information about a pet selected in the list. It uses our component again to make this happen. After creating an instance of the component, just like the last form did, it calls the component method GetPetInfo. The component hits the database and retrieves the information about the pet specified. When the data is returned, the form populates the fields of frmPetInfo and displays it. Its job is done. And so is ours!

This part you know well: Compile and run the program. The sample database does not contain data for every possible combination of answers, but feel free to add more data to accommodate the missing cases. Bertha's stock is a little low. If you just want to try it out, one case that works for sure is to select the first answer for each question. You'll get a few database hits with that combination of answers.

Our example N-tier program is now complete. More functionality, such as a messaging or transaction system, could be added later, either as additional components or completely new tiers. We can save our ideas for additional functionality until Bertha comes up with some more capital.

Exercise: Enhancing the Program

Because of the nature of creating examples for books, we have implemented our program in three tiers that are all intended to be run on one machine. However, Bertha would clearly prefer that the component and database reside on a server at her headquarters. This was stated in requirements 5 and 6. Converting our current program to a remote component and database is the subject of this exercise. You can do this in the great quantities of spare time you have at work. We will provide you with guidelines, and you can use the knowledge you have gained by reading this book to make it happen.

Our first step is to rebuild the component as DCOM ActiveX EXE and move it to a remote server. You can do this by changing the project type on the Project Properties dialog on the General tab. Change the project type from ActiveX DLL to ActiveX EXE. Then, on the Component tab of the same dialog, make sure to turn on the Remote Project Files option. This will create a .VBR file that will be used to allow the component to be run remotely by adjusting the registry. You can now move the component and the database to a directory on the server. It must be registered there using the .VBR file.

The last step is to rebuild the client. You must change the reference in the project properties from the local version of your component to the remote one. Once you do, you can recompile it and run the program.

This little exercise should keep you busy for an afternoon. Save it for a rainy day.

Winding Up

The example program in this chapter touches on many aspects of the distributed N-tier applications you will be implementing using COM and Visual Basic. While the previous chapters covered a large number of topics individually, this example illustrates how to put some of them together to solve a problem using an N-tier software solution. Now that you have seen some of the possibilities, no doubt you'll begin coming up with your own combinations of these technologies to solve your own problems.

This pretty much winds up our coverage of N-tier development with COM and Visual Basic. Make sure you check the appendices of this book for additional supporting information. Appendix B, "Project Considerations," is a chapter unto itself and details some of the setup and execution of a larger distributed software project. It will help you get your project organized and off to a good start. Appendix A, "What's New in Visual Basic 6.0," covers the new features of Visual Basic 6.0 that are specifically relevant to N-tier development. Appendix C, "What's on the CD-ROM," details the contents of the companion CD-ROM and will help guide you through all the examples and software.

Now you can head out into the N-tier jungle equipped with the knowledge and tools necessary to tame it and bend it to your will. Best of luck to you!

What's New in Visual Basic 6.0

Y ou've probably already read through the Visual Basic 6.0 brochures that Microsoft sent you in the mail, hyping all the shiny new features. Perhaps you've toyed with some of those new features yourself, creating little test programs to try them out. You might even have read through the Microsoft Developer Network (MSDN) to find out what Microsoft built into Visual Basic 6.0—it's over 12 pages long. There are lots of new goodies in Visual Basic 6.0, and it can take a long time to weed through them to figure out which ones are useful and how they can help you out.

Well, we've done some of that for you. Listed in this appendix are some of the more useful features of Visual Basic 6.0, particularly the ones related to building N-tier applications. Take a few minutes to read through them and commit the interesting ones to memory.

New Project Types

Visual Basic 6.0 adds a few new project types you can use to get you going. It had several to start with, and the number has increased. You can create your own project types by developing a template and placing it in the VB98\Template\Projects directory. You can even change the existing templates if they don't suit your needs.

All that aside, the following new project types are of interest to those programmers developing N-tier enterprise applications with Visual Basic 6.0.

DHTML Project. This project type helps you to construct applications that are based on Dynamic HTML. It creates a Web page, which can be used as a user interface, and an ActiveX DLL to contain the code behind the DHTML Web page. The project includes a limited DHTML page designer you can use to assemble a Web page interface without heavy knowledge of HTML (Chapter 7, "Web and Internet Clients"). It is a good project template because it takes care of tying your code in an ActiveX DLL to your Web page interface. This hides code normally visible in HTML script in a compiled ActiveX DLL, which is not visible to your customers and will run faster because it is compiled.

To use this project type effectively, you will need some knowledge of DHTML and the Document Object Model. One good thing about the DHTML Designer is that it has a nice object-oriented view of your DHTML document. You will probably also want to use a third-party HTML editor, because the DHTML Designer that comes along as part of this project is very limited and generates HTML code that is difficult to read or modify.

IIS Applications and WebClasses. With Visual Basic 6.0, you can now create Internet Information Server (IIS) Applications and Web-Classes that allow you to take action on your servers in response to user actions on Web pages. For example, a user can make a request for new data on a Web page, and your WebClasses, in conjunction with Internet Information Server, can fetch the data and send it to the user's browser. WebClasses and IIS Applications can create Web content dynamically, even Dynamic HTML, as required at a specific moment in time. In combination with Dynamic HTML, WebClasses and IIS Applications should be able to handle almost all your Web development needs. Visual Basic 6.0 even provides a new designer to help you create Web-Classes.

Data Project. An enhanced version of the Standard EXE project, this project type adds a Data environment and a Data Report. Data-oriented applications can use the Data Environment to connect to, create, and modify databases, and the Data Report can easily create data-bound reports (Chapter 12, "Data Access with Visual Basic 6"). This project might be useful to anyone creating a new database project. It is a good place to start because it provides you with a report template ready for data binding, as well as a new Data Environment that you can use to get your database going.

Database Tools

Visual Basic 6.0 adds a large number of new database features to make N-tier development easier and more pleasant. From ADO to the Data Environment, access to any data source is now possible. You can even write your own data sources. Remote data access from one machine to another is improved as well. Visual Basic is now a formidable force as a database development environment.

ActiveX Data Objects (ADO).　The latest Microsoft data access technology, ADO provides a universal mechanism for talking to just about any data source that acts as an OLE DB data provider. ADO is especially good at creating database applications for the Internet. And now you have access to it through Visual Basic (Chapter 12). Most new controls and databases, including all those that Microsoft produces, support ADO and can be used with Visual Basic 6.0. If you are planning a new application that uses a database (and who isn't?), then ADO is probably in your future.

ADO Data Control.　An updated version of the original Data Control, the ADO Data Control provides enhanced access to OLE DB data sources as well as to the new data-bound controls (Chapter 12). Like its earlier cousin, the ADO Data Control allows you to bind a Recordset to any number of controls while keeping your actual coding to a minimum.

Data Environment.　This is an environment for creating new ADO data objects (Chapter 12). You can add a data environment to just about any type of project, and you will have access to the Visual Database Tools (see following). This can be very convenient while developing an application that deals with a database. For example, we were busy creating some MTS COM components that retrieved and saved data to and from a database for client software. During development, we were constantly adding data, modifying the schema, and creating new queries. With a Data Environment in our project, we could connect to the SQL

Server 7.0 database and have complete access to every aspect of it. This is immeasurably convenient, especially when you need to quickly add some test data to a few tables. Get to know this feature—you'll become very fond of it.

Visual Database Tools.   A collection of tools that are part of the Data Environment, these allow you to easily create and change database designs, schemas, and queries, as well as to modify the data itself. You can do all this without leaving Visual Basic, making it extremely convenient to design databases and database applications from the ground up (Chapter 12). You can create new connections, maintaining as many as you like. You can add, remove, and update tables, their design, and the data they contain. You can even create database diagrams of your tables, establishing relationships between tables by dragging and dropping them in the diagram. Create queries on the fly and save them in the database. All this can be done remotely from your development computer, and all the changes are updated on your SQL Server database, even if it is on a server somewhere else. Of course, these tools work with databases other than SQL Server as well.

Data Sources.   You can now create your own data sources with Visual Basic. They act like any other data source, and can be bound to data-aware controls. For example, you could create a data source to access a proprietary data file format from a legacy application (Chapter 12). While not everyone will need this feature, and it takes a little while to learn how to use it, you'll be very glad it's there when you do need it.

ADO Recordsets.   You can create ADO Recordsets that contain any number of records from a database based on a query. These Recordsets not only allow you to access the data they contain, but can be passed to and from functions and components, even across the network (Chapter 12). A function can actually have a return type of ADO Recordset. This makes returning data from the network and updating it from the client much easier than before. You can even create a Recordset from the database, disconnect it from the database, and pass the Recordset back to the client. These disconnected Recordsets will allow clients to receive data from your server components without the danger of their being able to update the data without your knowledge. Once they update the data in the Recordset, they can pass it back to your component on the server, and your component can reconnect the Recordset to the database and update the data in a more controlled fashion. This technique has the added benefit of releasing the connection to the database for the Recordset as soon as possible, and then reconnecting only when necessary, freeing valuable database connections for others to use.

The DataRepeater Control. This allows you to create a data-bound user control of your own and repeat it as many times as you like on a form. Each control acts as a row on the form (Chapter 12). This can make it easier to create complex data forms much quicker than was previously possible.

Data Consumers. Essentially, this allows you to create your own data-bound controls or classes. If you need a custom control that talks to data, such as a graphical gauge, you can now create it with Visual Basic (Chapter 12).

Components

Microsoft is preaching a new story that involves COM and components. If you're not currently building components, you will be in the near future. In order to support the component-based architecture of the Windows distributed environment, Microsoft has updated Visual Basic with some new features to help you build components.

Lightweight controls. Lightweight controls are more efficient with resources than normal controls, and are particularly useful for creating controls intended for the Internet. Visual Basic provides support for windowless and transparent controls (Chapter 9, "DCOM Details").

Component compatibility. Visual Basic now helps you to manage and keep track of component versions and their compatibility with other projects. The Project Compatibility option is especially useful for components during the initial development phase (Chapter 8, "Understanding COM Internals").

CreateObject enhancements. You can now call the CreateObject function and specify a location from which the object is to be created. This allows you to tell your program to create objects on remote servers from inside your code (Chapter 9, "DCOM Details").

Support for Microsoft Transaction Server. You can now specify the behavior of your components in a transaction through code and properties. This makes Microsoft Transaction Server components easier to set up and provides the programmer with more control over transactions (Chapter 10, "Microsoft Transaction Server").

Threading.   Visual Basic now supports Apartment-model threading. This is useful for creating efficient server-side ActiveX COM components (Chapter 9, "DCOM Details").

Language Additions

Every release of Visual Basic has had a few new features added to the Basic language, and version 6.0 is no exception. While not all are listed here, the language additions that are relevant to N-tier development in particular are included. Check out the Visual Basic 6.0 readme file for the complete scoop if you're interested.

Data Validation.   This provides language support for the validation of data in controls before the control loses focus, making field-level data validation much easier than before, without the need for checking Lost-Focus events.

Arrays.   Functions and components can now return arrays as a return type, making it easier to pass around larger amounts of data. You can also use a dynamic array on the left side of an assignment, making it possible to copy an entire array in one statement.

User-Defined Types.   Now you can create user-defined types that can be returned by public methods. This makes passing data between components more type-safe, which is something Visual Basic can certainly use more of.

Dictionary Object.   The Dictionary Object is an associative array that allows you to store name-value pairs, as in a dictionary. It could store a word as the first part of an entry and its definition as the second part. This can be useful in many applications that need to provide a lookup capability.

One Last Note

While Visual Basic 6.0 adds many new features to make our programming lives easier and more productive, it is not all wine and roses. It is important to note that not only does Visual Basic 6.0 have a fair number of bugs, but it is actually slower in a few areas (the PSET function, for example). Service packs in the near future may address some of these problems, but until they are available, keep your eyes open. Overall, however, it is a great improvement over previous versions, adding enough new projects and features for everyone to find something useful.

Project Considerations

N-tier enterprise development projects tend to be large ones. They can involve the development of many components, can encompass a great deal of functionality, and can require very large databases. They can also involve a lot of people. In this appendix, we discuss how to organize and run a large software development project.

If you are developing in Visual Basic, it is especially important to run your project correctly and formally. In the past, most developers and sometimes complete development groups treated Visual Basic development more as playing around than as actual software development. If you were creating a complex program using C++, would you just dive in and start coding? We doubt it. C++ is too complicated and dangerous to use in a large project without serious planning. It is usually much easier to leap into Visual Basic, just start coding, and come up with something useful the same afternoon.

A typical project cycle involves several phases, including planning, design, implementation, and testing. A solid project management team with a plan can make a project go much more smoothly than one that is run in an ad hoc fashion. Other tools, such as standards and schedules, are also important to the successful completion of a multitier development effort. Each of these aspects of an N-tier project deserves a discussion of its own.

While a complete development plan and process is beyond the scope of this book, we'll give you a framework to use as a starting point. The information presented here describes techniques and processes that we have used before and that have worked well.

The Project Cycle

Every project is made up of a series of activities, some of which are sequential, while others can be run in parallel. The activities themselves and the orchestration of these activities make up the project cycle: planning, design, implementation, testing, and deployment.

Before the first line of code is written or the first object identified, the project must be planned. In the planning phase, the developers choose a development methodology and define the activities of the project. During design, the entire project is architected and the major software components are laid out. The implementation phase sees the actual construction and coding of your project. Testing usually goes on at the same time as implementation and ensures that your code is in good working order. Deployment involves getting your software to your users, and this can be an involved process for large distributed systems. While your choice of development methodology may rearrange the order of some of these phases, or cause them to repeat, the basic concepts are the same. Some of the early activities you can look forward to in this phase include defining the user interface, prototyping and usability testing, creating or reviewing program requirements, establishing a methodology and documenting its procedures, and defining project standards.

They're all worthwhile tasks, but you may not need all of them for your project. There is a point at which a project is small enough that the overhead of all these tasks may hinder your efforts. It will ultimately be your call as to which tasks are appropriate for your project, but we will give you as much help as we can.

You've just been assigned to lead the company's new development project. What do you tell your teams to do? Get them involved in the project planning. Start by defining your tasks. We've been through many development efforts, and over the years we've gotten a pretty good feel for some things that work and some things that don't. Here's our approved list of useful tasks from which you can choose.

Establish Requirements

One of the most important tasks in a project is establishing requirements. The requirements define what the software is supposed to do. In most cases, this is a project management task done by the project manager and a design group that understands the application and the users, with input from the development group. It is important to have development involvement, because the requirements dictate what development is agreeing to build. Read the requirements as you would a legal contract before you agree to them, because once you sign on the dotted line, you're obliged to implement everything in that document.

Establishing requirements is a task recommended for all but the tiniest projects. The time to perform this task is at the very beginning of the project, as soon as the big guns approve it.

Rapid Prototyping

Rapid prototyping is the process of very quickly creating a version of the program that has minimal functionality. There are typically two sorts of prototypes. The first is basically a user interface prototype that is built for the purpose of *usability testing*, wherein real potential users interact with a prototype to help you determine if your user interface is a good one (more on this topic follows). The second prototype is called a *proof-of-concept prototype*, used to test out architectural concepts. For example, if you decide to create a Dynamic HTML user interface that talks to Microsoft Internet Information Server (IIS) and Microsoft Transaction Server (MTS) you would create a simple end-to-end test program to see if it works.

If you have a potentially complex architecture (as N-tier projects are wont to be), or you deem that usability testing is important to your project, then we'd recommend some degree of rapid prototyping. If your project is a large one, some degree of rapid prototyping is still in order.

This task is usually started near the beginning of the project. Architectural prototypes can begin as soon as the requirements are finalized. This will prevent you from going too far down one technical alley before realizing it won't work. User interface prototyping can occur any time. However, do not start too early, before you have a clear idea of what your program is supposed to do (the requirements), or too late, when it is much harder to factor in usability study results.

CAUTION

It is very important for everyone on the project to understand that prototypes are *throwaway code.* This means that when the purpose of the prototype has been fulfilled—that is, the concept has been proven or the user interface has been evaluated—the code is *not* used again for any part of the actual project. The reason for this is that prototypes are built with speed in mind, not quality, maintainability, or usability. They are not appropriate to put into any real code base. Make sure that everyone in the project understands this from the first second of the project. If they do not, they'll see some prototype intended for testing and say, "Hey, that looks great! Why don't we just keep it—we'll save time!" If this happens, you'll have to find a way to throw away the code surreptitiously!

Define the User Interface

You can't create an N-tier application without designing a user interface. The design of your user interface will go much better if you plan it first. The most important part of planning your user interface is getting the right team on the job. While defining a user interface is an important task, we would not leave it solely to software engineers. We have seen many good user interfaces designed by engineers, but we have seen even more bad ones. If you have engineers that you feel are good interface designers, then by all means, put them on the job. If your engineers are not visual-design-oriented, leave this task to a team of user interface designers and analysts who understand the users and the application. However, make sure that you have an engineer or two in all of their design meetings. You need to keep a rein on the designers so they don't design an interface that's impossible to implement.

User interface definition occurs as soon as you start to receive requirements from the management team. As the user interface designs are completed, you can begin prototyping and design.

Establish a Methodology

A development methodology is the process used during development. Most people are familiar with the traditional waterfall method, in which one task is completed before the next can begin. For example, requirements are completed before design begins, and design is completed before coding begins. There are many other methodologies from which to choose (see Table B.1 for a synopsis of the popular ones).

The important thing is to choose one that's right for your project. An iterative development cycle would probably be too much for a small project, while a project that needs to be done quickly cannot afford to use a waterfall methodology. Choose your methodology as soon as you know the scope of the project. Begin using it and educating your team as soon as possible.

While you should choose a methodology that is right for your project, don't switch around too often. If you use four methodologies in two years, your team doesn't have time to get good at any of them.

Table B.1 Some Development Methods

METHODOLOGY	DESCRIPTION	WHEN TO USE
Code-and-fix	Very little planning. Get the requirement, maybe some basic design, then code it. Most time spent in coding and bug fixing.	Use for small and short-term projects when little formalism is required.
Waterfall	Very structured and organized. Takes longer than most because it is very sequential. Hard to go back and rework earlier stages.	Use in low-trust situations like contract development. Lots of sign-off potential.
Spiral	Similar to iterative and waterfall combined. Run through requirements, design, code, test, then do it again.	Easy to understand (waterfall) with the ability to rework any part of the project (iterative).
Iterative	Characterized by short development cycles (a month or so) that run through the entire process of design, implement, and test.	Good for projects where the requirements are less clearly defined. Allows constant redefinition of requirements and the project.

Devise Standards

Standards ensure consistency and quality throughout your project. There are many types, including process standards, programming standards, and visual standards. They can be more formal or less so, brief and simple or extensive and complex. When creating your standards, remember their purpose and that they are there to help, not to hinder, your project. Specific standards and the details of coming up with them are discussed in the section titled *Programming Standards* later in this appendix.

Standards should be created early in the project—as soon as you know your project's scope. Experience shows that you will not have time to create and document them later, so you'd better do it at the beginning.

Usability Testing

You can either assume that the user interface you've designed is perfectly usable and that your users will love it and find it productive, or you can test and confirm it. Many times we've come up with a brilliant user interface, full of capability and usable by an exceptionally dim chimp, only to find out that *we* were the undereducated simians in the equation. Usability testing has proven us wrong many times, and exceptionally wrong on occasion. Once in a while, we get something right. The point is that users rarely do what you expect them to, and you need a sizable sampling to figure out if your user interface is usable. We highly recommend this process, even though it involves some time and expense. You'll have much happier users who will tell other users, who in turn become happy users and tell more users, and so on.

A professional does usability testing best. There are people who specialize in this, and they can be hired either as consultants or employees. They can run the tests, come up with the results and conclusions, and render a report with the results. All you have to do is build time for it into the schedule. Oh, and pay for it, of course.

Usability testing is an ongoing process. It usually starts fairly early in the project, after user interfaces have been designed. You can run a test as many times as you like during your development cycle, but you usually do at least two: one early, during user interface design, and one later on, when interface design is considered complete.

Set Logistics

Now that all these wonderful processes and tasks have been defined, how do we go about doing them? It's important to set up guidelines defining how everyone goes about their daily jobs. Status reports every Wednesday morning, new product builds every Friday morning, team leader meetings every Thursday afternoon, running your unit tests after each module is complete. Logistics is the glue that holds the project together, that allows your team to run like clockwork. (Table B.2 offers some guidelines.)

This part of the process may seem trivial, but it can make the difference between a smooth and a troubled project. Lay out the team members' routine tasks and how to perform them. For example, if you expect status reports from all team members, have them submitted on a specific day—Thursday mornings by 10 A.M.—and use a specific template in Microsoft Word to elicit the information you need. You'll always get a consistent report.

Table B.2   Summary of Tasks and When They Should Be Completed

TASK	WHEN TO DO IT	WHO SHOULD DO IT
Establish a methodology	As soon as you know the scope of your project.	Medium to large projects.
Establishing requirements	As soon as you know the project has been approved.	All but the tiniest projects.
Rapid prototyping	As soon as user interface designs start rolling in.	Projects with a complex architecture or user interface.
User interface definition	After requirements start filing in.	All projects with a user interface.
Devise standards	As early as you can—you won't have time later.	Any project that can afford the time.
Usability testing	As soon as you have some user interface to test.	All can benefit, but usually only the largest projects can afford it.
Setting up logistics	Start early—you're going to run out of time to do it.	All but the smallest projects—especially for large teams.

Formalism

Formalism is the amount of procedure you build into your project. Generally, the smaller your project, the less formalism you'll need. For example, in a large project it would be important for the programmers to perform formal unit testing and record the results in a document that would be available to the rest of the team and the team leadership (not to mention the quality assurance department). However, a smaller project might simply require the programmers to unit-test their code to their own satisfaction, without documenting the results. Formalism can apply to any of your project tasks. Table B.3 lists some examples of tasks with varying degrees of formalism.

Table B.3　Project Tasks with Varying Degrees of Formalism

TASK	MORE FORMALISM	LESS FORMALISM
Establishing requirements	Project has a requirements-definition phase. Results in requirements document.	Project description written down in a document.
Rapid prototyping	UI and architectural prototypes created to test concepts. Prototypes are thrown away when complete. Results are formally documented.	Some prototypes may be built for testing purposes. These may simply be illustrations of the dialog boxes printed on paper.
User interface definition	All dialogs are designed and documented. All UI functionality is defined. Program UI concept is created.	UI concept is defined. Most important dialogs designed and documented.
Establish a methodology	Appropriate methodology selected. Process for using it is defined and documented.	Perhaps only a partial methodology is defined and used.
Devise standards	All or most standards are used and defined. Standards compliance checks are made periodically.	Only the most important standards are defined and used. Maybe only coding standards are used.
Usability testing	Complete usability tests performed and results documented. Tests performed using external potential customers.	Informal usability tests performed, perhaps using paper models, on internally available subjects.
Setting up logistics	Document all daily processes, including status reporting, daily tasks, and regular meetings.	Require status reporting. Occasional meetings.

While you're thinking about which tasks your project needs, think also about how much formalism each task should have.

Project Management

Project management is the glue that holds your project together. It involves organizing and building teams, scheduling and tracking the project, and establishing effective communication mechanisms. If you are part of the management team of your project, from team lead to development director, this section is for you. It will give you some great ideas and guidelines for managing your project and making sure everything runs more smoothly.

If you are a team member, a quality assurance engineer, or perhaps a software engineer, this section will also be useful. You'll know what the management team is planning for you.

Team Organization

Consider this hypothetical telephone conversation you may have overheard:

"Who needs team organization? I have a great bunch of people. Put too much management in their way and they freak out. I don't want anything slowing them down. Let them do what they do best and you'll get a great product at the end."

"I really don't know if we're on schedule."

"Quality's great, take my word for it."

"Fred? Oh, he stalked out. He hates it when Cheryl reformats his code. Don't worry, he'll be back."

"The next build? We'll build when the team is ready for it, that's when! Hey, get off my back, will ya! You'll get it, you'll get it!"

"What do you mean, fired?"

Who needs team organization? Well, our speaker here, for one. He couldn't answer any questions about the project; he couldn't guarantee any degree of quality; he had no control over his people; and he couldn't say whether or not the project was on schedule. As a team leader or a project manager, you will need to be able to answer these questions, because they will most certainly be asked of you. Having an effective team organization will help us answer these questions. An effective team organization works well together, communicates regularly, knows where the project is and what's coming next, gets work done on time, and goes home in time for dinner. Creating an effective team is largely a matter of organization and management.

There are several ways to organize your teams, each with pros and cons. They include the team hierarchy, the team of teams, and resource pooling.

Team Hierarchy

A team hierarchy is a traditional and easily understood team layout that involves successive layers of a reporting structure. It's made of layers of organization (the fewer the better). Typically, a project manager sits on top. Underneath the project manager might sit a quality assurance (QA) manager and a development manager. The development manager has a host of software engineers who build the product, and the QA manager has a team of QA analysts who test it out (among other quality assurance tasks). Figure B.1 illustrates the team hierarchy.

Team of Teams

A team of teams is a very flat organizational structure with only two real layers of management. At the top is the project leadership. This includes at least a project manager, but may also include a product

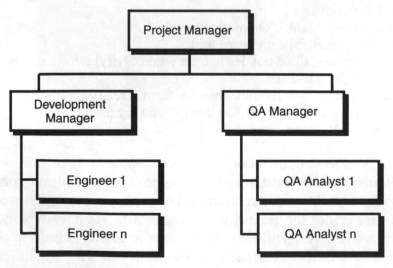

Figure B.1   The team hierarchy.

manager. Underneath the project leadership is the group of teams, arranged according to your specific needs. The number of teams is usually a function of the size of the project. The larger the project, the more teams it will have.

Here's a hypothetical example of how a larger team might be organized. Our project is an N-tier application with a standard Win32 client written in Visual Basic, business components written for Microsoft Transaction Server, and Microsoft SQL Server for a database. We decide that we need seven teams underneath the project leadership team:

1. **Client Development Team.** This group designs and constructs the client portion using Visual Basic. The team consists of a technical team leader and four engineers.

2. **Business Logic Development Team.** This team designs and constructs all the business logic as MTS components.

3. **Database Development Team.** This group designs and develops the interface code to the database, writes all the stored procedures, and creates any supplementary functionality relating to the database.

4. **Web Services Team.** This team is responsible for implementing the Internet Information Server layer as well as all of the dynamic functionality behind it.

5. **Quality Assurance Team.** This team performs testing on the product, enforces standards adherence for all teams and processes, participates in design reviews, and uses automated tools to ensure code quality.

6. **Services Development Team.** These developers design and implement system level and common services used by the entire development project staff, such as the internationalization code, including tools for internal use.

7. **Architecture Team.** This group is responsible for the high-level design of the software, including the organization of the components, which tools to use, and ensuring consistency during development.

While these are fairly discrete teams, communication between them is critical. Occasionally, the teams will overlap or share team members. Beware of creating too many small teams. Although it's tempting to establish a small team for every component in your project, this situation can become unmanageable in short order. (Figure B.2 illustrates the team of teams organization.)

Resource Pooling

Another technique for organizing teams is called *resource pooling*. In this structure, engineers are not organized into long-term teams, but rather pulled from the pool. An engineer who finishes a task moves on to the next one, wherever he or she is needed.

Resource pooling has advantages, especially at the beginning of the project when the activities may be less defined and organized. For example, a pool of engineers might work on a usability prototype for a couple of weeks. When the architectural team needs more people because the prototype needs suddenly increase, a couple people from the UI task move over to work on the architectural prototypes for a while. When they're done, they can move on to the next task.

This team topology can work well on smaller projects or at the beginning of larger ones because it's easy to organize and understand and you don't need complete knowledge of your project's detailed architecture. However, it can be difficult to manage with large groups of people, and it can get out of control quickly, particularly as the size of the pool grows. This can happen because it gets difficult to track what each team member is working on, when they switched tasks, and where they should go next. You may end up spending a large amount of time planning the tasks for your team members. If poorly managed, it will be difficult for any of the engineers on the project to focus for any length of time on a specific part of the program.

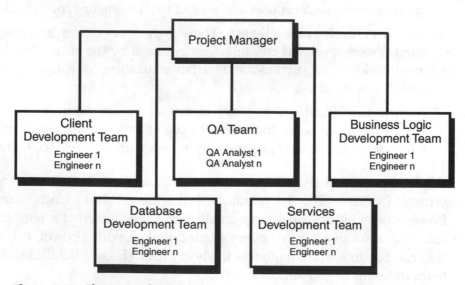

Figure B.2 The team of teams.

Project Scheduling

Schedules are the pulse and the disease of every software development project. They are a necessary evil. Without schedules, software projects would languish and die before they were ever close to deployment. However, they are also usually abused, because people—especially management—assume that the schedule represents a firm commitment for the project's completion date. There are ways to manage schedules, however, to make them work for you.

The Nature of the Schedule

Contrary to most people's expectations, a schedule is a yardstick against which the software project should be measured. A schedule is a planning tool that allows us to estimate when a project will be complete and to help us measure progress. It is not a time box into which a software project is wedged.

The problem with schedules is that most people don't understand what they are or how they should be used. The key is to set expectations correctly. Make sure everyone related to the project understands that a schedule is an *estimate*, not a fact, and that it is a *living document*, subject to revision as new information becomes available. Schedules are usually made toward the beginning of a project, when the least is known, and new information constantly becomes available as the project progresses. Therefore, regular schedule revisions are a fact of life for the software development project.

It's important to manage everyone's expectations for the schedule. Team members need to understand the following:

- A schedule is an estimate based on incomplete information. You cannot possibly know in advance everything that will come up or be required for a software project.

- A schedule will undergo regular revisions as new information becomes available or as the development team changes direction. It is normal for a schedule to change.

- A projected ship date may need to change. Get everyone in project management involved and make sure they understand the whole situation. This is always the touchiest part of a project schedule, so make sure the facts are laid out and emotions held in check.

- Adding functionality to a project will extend the schedule. You'd be surprised how many people do not understand this, so make sure you actually say it.

- Development teams really do want to finish on schedule. They just don't want to promise something they can't deliver, and this is hard to forecast at the beginning of a project.

If you communicate all these concepts to everyone involved in the project, there will be far fewer misunderstandings during the course of the project. Because schedule strife is typically the most common source of conflict during a project, this can go a long way toward a more productive and enjoyable effort for everyone.

Time Estimates

Whether you are an engineer on a development project or the project leader, you will be involved in scheduling and creating time estimates. If someone asks how long it will take to implement that recipe-ingredients calculation module, you can't respond, "I dunno. Three weeks?"

A newspaper article about the time estimates for implementing software said that programmers will come up with one of only three possible estimates: 15 minutes, 2 weeks, or 6 months. While this is an exaggeration, the article was right about one thing: Developers usually don't put much work into their estimates. They quickly scan the functionality required of them, look thoughtful for a minute, and spit out their gut feeling about how long it will take. Sure, the painful and annoying estimation process is now over, but you'll be feeling a lot more pain later when you're three weeks late on it because you didn't look at it more carefully. Everyone who is depending on that ingredients calculation module will also be delayed.

There is a better way. It will take a little longer to estimate, but this is trivial compared to how much happier you'll be when your development efforts are closer to the mark. When you are asked to estimate a particular piece of functionality, make sure you consider all the following details:

- How long will it take to *design* this piece of functionality, including a design review and changes to the design?

- How long will it take to *fully document* the design of this functionality?

- How long will it take to *implement* this piece of functionality, including code review and changes to the code?

- How long will it take to *fully comment* this code?

- How long will it take to *fully unit-test* this functionality, including documenting the results and making corrections based on the results of the tests?

- How much time will using the *source code control system* add to the estimate?

The idea is to think more carefully about everything involved in the task that you're being asked to estimate. Make sure you cover as many details as you can. Consider everything you have to do during the development of that functionality, because everything you do takes time.

Looking at schedules from a more general viewpoint, keep in mind that as a project progresses, estimates will become more accurate. As you gain more experience with the project, knowing more about it will enable you to make more accurate estimates. You'll also have a better feel for the quality of the early estimates and will be able to make more accurate revisions.

Scheduling Hints

In addition to creating more accurate estimates, there are a few other things you can do to make your schedules more realistic.

- Schedule only 80 percent of your people's time instead of 100 percent. You can do this by setting the length of a workday in your scheduling program to only 6.4 hours instead of 8 hours. It's difficult to account for distractions, meetings, and other assorted delays. The unallocated 20 percent will build in some time for those activities.

- Make sure you schedule in vacations. Overlooking this factor can really throw off your schedule. To help out with this, ask your team to plan vacations as far ahead of time as possible.

- As mentioned before, base your estimates on the experience of past projects. Try to equate current tasks with those of another project, and use an estimate based on the actual time it took to perform a similar task. If you do not have any historical data, you should start to collect it now.

- Rather than having one or two people perform the estimates for the entire team, involve the team as a whole in the estimation procedure. Engineers are more likely to buy into estimates they've created themselves.

The most important thing to remember about schedules is that they are estimates based on current knowledge, and they will change over the course of time as you learn more about the project. Make sure that everyone on the project understands this from day one. This will set their expectations early in the project, and everyone will experience fewer schedule-related disappointments.

Communication

We once worked with a project manager who used to say, "Unless you're tired of hearing from me, I'm not communicating enough." We completely agree with this statement. Communication is key to a successful development effort, and to get it you have to plan for it.

There are all kinds of information to communicate during a project, and many ways to communicate it. The trick is to communicate the most important information in the most effective way. These things will probably vary from project to project, but there are a few things we've found to be universally important.

- Project schedule and progress information is critical. Everyone wants to know where the project is and how it's doing, and regular updates of this information can be beneficial. You can keep people informed by distributing a simple printout of the schedule on a regular basis or by posting it on a project intranet.

- Document your project. This includes programming standards, the project requirements, domain glossaries, user interface standards, and anything else people on the team need to know about. We don't know how many times we've seen people trying to find a document they needed, and the search held up the work they were doing.

- Publish a code repository. Make sure everyone on the development team knows what code is out there, what it does, and where to get it. We have seen the same function implemented more than 10 times in the same project because the developers either didn't know it existed or knew it was there but couldn't find it.

Communication is one of those touchy-feely skills that are difficult to grasp sometimes, and because of this, people tend to shy away from it. However, it's really not that difficult to establish some effective communication mechanisms that will help your project run more smoothly.

TIP

Have a goal. One project management and communication technique we've found invaluable is to make sure your project has a clear, specific, well-communicated goal. This goal can help keep your teams focused on the job at hand and establish project scope. John F. Kennedy did a fabulous job at this when he stated his goal for the space program. It was simple and clear: Land a man on the moon and return him safely to Earth by the end of the decade. Because of this, everyone on the project knew exactly what the ultimate goal was and the time frame in which it was to occur. It also helped establish scope. This works just as well with software projects. A sample goal might read: "We will build the next generation of Cajun cooking software that contains all known recipes, ingredients, and historical information. It will have endorsements from at least two famous chefs, will be flexible enough to accommodate the needs of our varied target customers, and will be affordable to any computer-equipped family." It establishes scope (no Mexican or French recipes) and defines exactly what the product is supposed to be. The team knows what they're building, and "feature creep" will be kept to a minimum.

Techniques for Good Communication

The many techniques for communication could become a complete discussion topic by themselves. Without sounding too much like a self-help book, here are some useful tips on communication within a project.

It's okay to repeat information. Some of your team may hear the same thing a few times, but this can be beneficial. It confirms things they thought they heard earlier, plus it reaffirms your commitment to what you're saying.

Assume everyone knows nothing. This way, you'll be sure to tell everyone anything that's important, and no one will be missed. If you communicated something at the team meeting, make sure you repeat it at the management meeting.

Establish regular status meetings. While it is a good idea to keep meetings out of the way of the development teams, one regular update can be very useful. Updates ensure that your team members are all on the same page about the project, its issues, and the current status. The frequency can be adjusted based on need.

Encourage frank and open questions.   Communication is a two-way connection. You must establish an environment in which people feel free to communicate issues, problems, and suggestions without fear of retribution of any kind. This is the only way you'll be able to get an accurate pulse reading on your project and its people. And one more thing. I've seen people reprimanded many times for bringing up a problem without suggesting a solution. The trouble with this is that if the person cannot think of a solution, you'll never hear about the problem in the first place. It's better to encourage people to bring problems to the table than to be surprised by them later.

Create an information and status repository.   It's a great idea to have a place on the network where people can go to get information about the project, including status, project documents, information about the teams, and the latest project news. This not only prevents unnecessary meetings, but it's asynchronous—people can get information anytime they like. You can use a project intranet, workgroup software, or a custom solution for this. The only drawback to this communication method is that it requires constant maintenance. You'll have to make it someone's responsibility to keep it up-to-date. If you don't update it regularly, people will stop visiting and it will fall into disuse.

These techniques have worked well for us in the past. As projects become larger and more people join the team, communication becomes more important. Formal communication mechanisms that everyone knows about will go a long way toward making good communication automatic.

Standards

Standards are lists of rules and guidelines that tell us how to run a development project and how to create the software we intend to build. Successful standards are designed to help (not to hinder) us during the development process. They should answer our questions and streamline our work. They should not create a mountain of paperwork for us to do, distract us from the real job at hand, or become an entire job in themselves. A useful standard would tell you what comes next in the development process, how to design a dialog box, or help to make your code consistent.

The primary focus of standards is to ensure that the project maintains a high level of quality, consistency, and maintainability. Quality levels often vary wildly and can especially suffer during crunch times. If you adhere to the standards, quality levels should stay on an even keel. Consistency is also important. If you need to work on a completely different section of the code, consistency will make it easier to grasp what is going on when you get there. Consistency is also very important when designing your user interface. Similarly, standards can make your programs more maintainable. If your coding standards require in-line comments in all code, it will be much easier to make changes to that code when the sales department comes running into your office six months from now screaming about some new UNIVAC import feature they've just gotta have by next week.

We focus on two types of standards in this appendix: *programming standards* and *visual design standards.* Programming standards help developers create consistent, maintainable, and often reusable code; provide a standardized development process so everyone knows what to do and what's coming; ensure an appropriate standard of quality; and guide the design decisions programmers face every day. Visual design standards define a consistent look and organization to the user interface; establish specific design rules for user interface designers; and ensure that your software will be easy to use, helping your users get their work done quickly and accurately.

The standards we've found to be useful, and some techniques for creating them, are discussed in the following sections. Make sure you give these standards fair consideration. They can do wonders for your project across the board.

TIP

Keep the faith! During stressful times in a project, especially when the development effort is behind schedule, it is very tempting to abandon your process and standards in favor of good old-fashioned, 14-hour coding days. During these difficult periods, most projects ignore their process and standards, assuming that they take more time than they are worth. In fact, this is the time when standards are the most important—they can actually get you out of trouble. When standards are abandoned, quality drops significantly, bug counts shoot through the roof, and development actually takes longer. Keep the faith, baby; it'll pay off.

Programming Standards

Programming standards help establish consistency among the work of many different people. They establish many useful guidelines for programmers: how their code should be organized, what algorithms to use, and how components should communicate. This makes your project more maintainable and easier to understand by others. However, when it comes to programming standards, most developers are prepared to look the other way. In fact, they prefer to. Why should they change the way they do design work and write code? After all, they've thought long and hard about how they work, and it's clearly the best way to do things. Any other way is flawed, and they won't change.

We know some people like that. We're usually part of that group. However, we have learned to be tolerant of standards because they work for a higher purpose.

Implementing Programming Standards

There are, in fact, big and important reasons to use programming standards such as consistency, maintainability, and quality. Without standards, there would be chaos. We would not be able to guarantee any degree of consistency; the program would be far less maintainable; quality would suffer. The program could even suffer severe functional problems if architectural and construction standards are not followed.

How do you get programmers to agree to a set of standards? The best way is to have them participate in the process of creating the standards. Programmers are more likely to succumb if they feel the standards are their own. Even if they don't get their own way on everything, at least they had a chance to voice their opinions and fight for them. One guideline to follow during the negotiations: Everyone may have a chance to present their preferences and arguments for each standard, but once the standards are finalized, everyone is expected to back them and use them.

Once your standards have been defined and agreed upon, you have to make sure they are used. Normally, everyone is gung ho about them at first and uses them religiously. Shortly thereafter, you begin to see usage decline. When the project gets really busy, people worry about content, not form, and the standards are often completely ignored. To help out with this, enlist your QA team! They can regularly spot-check the code, design documents, and the day-to-day activities to make sure the standards are being used. But remember, don't call them the "Standards Police," or you're asking for trouble. They need to be viewed as part of the team, as professionals just doing a job.

Standardizing the Development Process

A standard is simply a process that everyone follows. This applies to the development process itself. It is important to create and document your development process so everyone knows what tasks are involved and the sequence in which they are to be performed.

Any team member should be able to reference a development standard and know how to go about his or her tasks. For example, Pete the Programmer has just been assigned to implement the joystick interface for the new corporate accounting software package you are building. He's not sure where to start, so he consults your project's development process standard. He discovers that the sequence of events looks like this:

1. Review the requirements carefully and make a list of all the functionality you will have to implement.

2. Begin your design by identifying objects in the area of functionality you are implementing. Once complete, identify the services you will have to provide.

3. Document the design completely using the Microsoft Word and Visual Modeler software packages.

4. Schedule and hold a design review that follows the design review standard. Incorporate any results from the design review.

5. Code the functionality using the language defined by the architectural team.

6. Schedule and hold a code review that follows the code review standard. Incorporate any results from the code review.

7. Fully unit-test the code using the unit-testing procedures defined for the project.

8. Once the code has passed all unit tests, schedule testing time with the QA department. Incorporate any changes required to fix bugs uncovered during testing.

9. File the code into the source code control system and label it as Code Complete for the piece of functionality you are implementing.

Pete will understand exactly what he has to do and in what order. This will ensure that all parts of the project undergo the same rigorous implementation and quality processes. It will also aid communication, prevent confusion, and deter Pete from asking a million questions and annoying everyone around him.

The Standards Themselves

Because a development process is made of several different tasks, you will need several different types of standards. You can, of course, pick and choose which ones are right for your project. As with any process, you want to make sure it helps your development project and does not hinder it. Smaller projects will need fewer standards because they have fewer formal tasks. Here's a list of some possible standards:

Coding standards. These standards dictate the specifics of programming in a given language. They can operate at the lowest level of detail, containing such information as bracing style, number of spaces per indent level, and variable naming rules.

Programming standards. The programming standards are the next level up, governing such things as standard algorithms to use, approved data structures, and design patterns. Some people include these standards as part of the coding standards, just to eliminate the need for a second document (good idea, in our opinion).

Architectural standards. As the architects on your project come up with their high-level design, they can be creating an architectural standard. This standard includes rules to help programmers adhere to the architecture for the project. For example, if your project needs to be international, you might create an architectural standard that says the user interface code will not have any string literals in it, but will instead get them from a resource DLL.

Visual standards. Visual standards define the rules for creating your user interface. They help ensure that the user interface build is consistent and implements all your usability research. Typically, they are very detailed, including such information as font standards, standard button placement, color usage, dialog layout guidelines, usability guidelines, and rules for wording all messages displayed to the user. Visual standards are especially important if your engineers are designing the user interface as part of the development process, because they may not have the time or training to do a thorough and correct job of it.

Designing the User Interface

User interface design is an incredibly important task. Even though your client application may be as intelligent as dirt, it still encompasses all the usability of your software. Your users will make a first-impression judgment of your software based on its user interface. They will also remember your software, good or bad, based on their experience with the user interface. The process of designing a good user interface usually involves getting a complete understanding of your users and the job they are trying do, acquiring a clear impression of the problem you are trying to solve with the interface, and actually designing the user interface, incorporating feedback from real, potential users. To do this, you need to get the right people involved in this process.

As we've said before, it is usually not a good idea to have software engineers designing your user interface. They are usually not trained in good user interface design; they are much better at *implementing* them. However, there are exceptions to this rule, and sometimes it's appropriate for the engineering department to get involved with user interface design:

- If your engineers are, in fact, trained in usability and user interface design, by all means, have them tackle the job.

- If your project is a small one, it may not be worth involving designers and increasing the size of your team and the cost of your project.

- If your project has only a small amount of user interface (perhaps you are designing a simple utility), then it may be overkill to get designers involved, or even to bother with user interface standards.

- If your project is a program for use by other programmers, engineers might be good designers for the effort. Because they are themselves target customers, they will know what other programmers like.

At a minimum, you must have an engineer or two present during the user interface design sessions. They will keep the user interface designers from creating a UI that cannot be implemented.

Defining Your Look

Your user interface, to users, is your entire program. It's how they interact with it; it's what they see every minute they are using it. You want it to look clean and professional, and you want it to help them get their work done. With that in mind, there are a couple of decisions you have to make before you sit down and start whipping out dialog boxes.

Windows or the Web?   Whether you have chosen to host your client in a Web browser or write it as a standard Win32 application, you'll have to decide how you want it to look. These days, a Web-like look is very popular, but users are more used to the standard Win32 application look. It's not an absolute choice, either, but more of a sliding scale. At one end is the straitlaced, short-haircut Win32 Windows standard. Most everyone understands it. At the other end is the easygoing, completely Web-hosted, Web-like user interface, with lots of flash and graphic appeal. It is possible, however, to fall somewhere in the middle. You might have a Win32 application with graphic appeal and Web-like features, or a Web-hosted application that looks as much like a standard application as possible.

The bottom line is, you will find that your user interface design goes much more smoothly if you decide ahead of time what style you will use. It will help to guide your decisions.

What is the overall standard we will use?   It started with Windows. Microsoft invented it and soon thereafter produced a user interface standard that matched it. You can still, of course, follow the Windows user interface standard. You might even decide to use a slight derivative of the Microsoft standard. However, more and more companies today are establishing a company look and feel. It has to do with a marketing concept called *branding,* the idea that all the applications developed by a company look the same and use the company's signature style.

If your company has user interface guidelines already, you can stick to those. If not, maybe you can suggest developing them, explaining the benefits of doing so (buy a marketing book for details). If you would rather not stir up trouble, go for the Windows standard.

A unified look for your user interface will help establish consistency across the interface. Making these decisions before you start design will save you a boatload of trouble. You'd hate it if you had just put the finishing touches on your last dialog box and then found out your company already had a standard.

Interface Usability

The basic idea behind interface usability is that the user can be productive with it; it acts and responds as they expect it to. A novel concept, yes? Usability and its study is an entire science by itself. It can be expensive and time-consuming, but in general, it will yield a program that users will find more satisfying and productive. We have done this before, and it reveals how even basic assumptions about ease of use can be completely wrong. It's a complex equation to match user interface standards, users in your target market, and how they do their jobs.

If you want to do formal usability testing on your project, hire or lease a usability expert. They know what usability is all about, how to conduct usability tests and what equipment is required to do it, and how to interpret results and draw accurate conclusions. They also know how to make recommendations for changes to your user interface based on those conclusions.

However, if you can't afford to do usability testing, or your project is too small to warrant it, you can still make a more usable program by understanding and utilizing some basic usability concepts—general techniques for designing your user interface to make it less intimidating, more streamlined, and easier to use. You could purchase an entire book on the subject (or several). However, we are going to save you the $50 to $100 you would spend and give you a list of a few real-world usability techniques. (You're welcome!)

Don't interrogate the user. Users hate to be asked questions. They are trying to get work done. They do not have time to answer a bunch of questions. There should always be a way to fill in the answers to these questions, but there should also be a way to launch the functionality and have the program simply execute it. For instance, a program might have an option to create a calendar in a document. There are all kinds of options available, and you could access these options by selecting Create Calendar from the menu. However, if the user clicks on the Create Calendar option on the toolbar, it would create a calendar right away without asking the user a single question. It would figure out what all the options are, either based on the user's previous choices or by making a guess. (Which date should it use? How about today?)

Less user interface is better. Any time users spend operating the user interface is time they are not getting their work done—time the program is robbing from them. The less UI you build, the less the user will have to operate.

Keep the user in command.   Always strive to keep the user in command of the software instead of the software commanding the user. For instance, instead of the program telling users that they have to close the current window before opening a new one (which forces them to respond to the program's command to get what they want), simply close the window for them and open the new as requested.

Provide useful feedback.   Ever get an error message like "Fatal error saving file"? Lots of people have. The problems with this message are many. The word *fatal* scares the heck out of users, leading them to believe they have done some sort of irreparable damage to the file or the computer. The error occurred during a save operation, while the user was committing the work already completed. Did the user lose it all? Probably. It doesn't say. And worst of all, the user doesn't know why the error occurred or how to fix it.

When designing feedback for the user, make sure it is not intimidating, tells the user what happened and why, explains the ramifications of the error, and suggests at least one possible solution to the problem.

Provide modeless feedback.   When users get going with the software, they can be very productive if they can establish operating patterns and stick to them. For example, if they have a lot of data entry to do, they learn the proper keystrokes and can really fly through the software—and their work. This is an ideal situation. However, if a message box pops up for every error or warning that occurs, this work flow is interrupted. The user is forced to stop, interpret the error message, clear it, and move on. Or worse, if it happens too often, the user will start to ignore the messages and clear them automatically without reading them. Users will lose the benefit of having error information reported to them *and* they will be annoyed.

A better way is to provide *modeless* feedback. This is an indicator or area on the interface that communicates information to users without interrupting their work flow. For example, you might have a feedback area at the bottom of the window that displays short messages to the user. Or you could have a small graphic indicator next to each field on a form that would indicate a warning or error condition with the field. In the latter case, the user can completely enter the data for a form without looking at the screen and, when finished, give the screen a once-over before saving the data and correct any problems before the save. The user is far more productive in this situation than if he or she is required to stop on each error and deal with it then.

Don't make the user feel stupid. There's not much worse in a user interface than making the user feel stupid. If users feel stupid, they will avoid using the program altogether, and you've got shelfware. This can occur if users cannot figure out how to use the software, if the software reports inexplicable errors that users do not know how to deal with, or if the software behaves in an unexpected fashion. Avoid these situations at all costs.

We're all software users. Think about putting yourself in the place of *your* users when you design a user interface. You'll be surprised how many times you go back and change something, thinking, "I'd never put up with that!"

Poor Man's Usability

You can conduct some basic usability studies on your own without incurring the cost of a formal effort. The process involves using people from your own company instead of outside users and using paper models of your user interface instead of a functional prototype.

Your coworkers can fill in as usability test subjects. Try to select subjects that are as close as possible to your actual users in terms of the job they do, and make sure they are not part of your current project. Make paper prototypes by drawing pictures of your dialog boxes and windows on paper. Then present them to the users one at a time, giving them specific tasks to accomplish. For example, "Here's a dialog. You task is to run a monthly report." Then ask them what they would do with the user interface, such as clicking a button or making a menu selection. When they answer, show them the next sheet of paper, representing the new window or dialog box they just opened. Watch their reactions. Can they can figure out how to accomplish the task? Ask them questions: "Did you understand how to use the interface to accomplish the task you were asked to perform?" "What do you think of the overall organization of the interface?"

The results from this sort of study are not of the same quality as a real usability study, because the test subjects are not real customers and they're not using real software, but it will give you some valuable information you can use to guide your user interface designs.

User Interface Standards

User interface standards serve two purposes. They are guidelines that the user interface designers use to come up with designs that match the agreed-upon standards. Second, they are detailed enough to aid the engineers when they are coding the interface. It is important to create user interface standards and make them as complete as possible so that your resulting interface is consistent throughout.

What does a user interface standard look like? It contains high-level design guidelines such as usability techniques listed earlier. It also contains very specific details, including, for example, the following interface information.

- *Standard button placement guidelines.* "All buttons are located in the bottom right corner of the dialog. The rightmost button is always the Cancel button. If the dialog contains a tab strip, the buttons specific to a tab are located on the property page itself. These buttons are also located in the bottom right corner of the property page."

- *Font specifications.* Example: "All dialogs will use the Verdana typeface at an 8-pt. size. All graphic dialog titles will use Arial at the 14-pt. size in a bold weight."

- *Dialog-positioning information.* Example: "The initial placement of all dialogs will be centered in the client area of the program. If the user moves the dialog, the new position will be saved, and when the dialog appears the next time, it will use the last saved position. These dialog positions will be saved on a per-user basis."

- *Color information.* Example: "For all standard dialog elements, the program will use the standard user-defined system-provided colors. All warning indicators will be yellow. All error indicators will be red."

- *Tab order.* Example: "Tab order will generally be left-to-right, top-to-bottom. If a grid control is in the tab order, tab will revert to navigating the grid while it has focus. If the user hits tab and the focus in the grid is in the last cell, the focus will move out of the grid and to the next control."

If you spend the time to create user interface standards, you won't be sorry. There will rarely be a question as to how a dialog should be designed or when to use a specific font. The quality assurance group can even use it to help test your interface and catch inadvertent inconsistencies. It will entail some work up front, but will save more time in the long run.

Winding Up

This appendix has addressed some of the issues you'll be facing when planning a sizable N-tier project. You can establish methodologies and standards, set up logistics, understand user interface planning, and have a grip on the timing of these early project tasks.

About the CD-ROM

The companion CD-ROM for this book contains all the example source code from the book and additional software that will be helpful to you when developing N-tier applications.

All the source code for the examples are organized by chapter and are located in separate directories under the \Examples directory on the CD-ROM. Each example includes all the source code and project files needed to rebuild the program, as well as a compiled, ready-to-run version. Of course, a few of the programs will require some configuration, such as installing a component in MTS, before they will run correctly.

There are also full working versions and trial additions of professional software packages on the CD-ROM:

- *The CSS Style Sheet Editor.* This program is an HTML style sheet editor that helps you to easily create and edit CSS1 style sheets for use with Web clients. We wrote it just for you. See Chapter 7 for more details about it.

- *Allaire Homesite.* This program is one of the best HTML editors we have ever seen. The version included on the CD-ROM is a 30-day evaluation copy that will convince you to buy it.

- *Rational Software's Visual Quantify.* Visual Quantify is an advanced performance profiling tool that automatically pinpoints application performance bottlenecks. Visual Quantify also delivers repeatable timing data for all parts of an application, including components, not just the parts for which you have the source code. It provides graphical views of performance data, and integrates directly with Visual Basic.

- *Rational Software's Visual PureCoverage.* Visual PureCoverage for Windows NT is an easy-to-use coverage analysis tool that automatically pinpoints untested code in your C, C++, Java or Visual Basic components and applications.

- *Riverton Software's HOW.* HOW is a component modeling tool and deployment framework for building business applications. HOW makes it straightforward for mainstream developers to build distributed and Internet applications using Visual Basic, Microsoft Transaction Server, DCOM, and other enterprise technologies from Microsoft.

- *Platinum Technologies' Platinum ERwin.* PLATINUM ER*win*, the industry leader, is a powerful, award-winning, easy-to-use database design tool. Its rich set of design techniques and unique iterative approach provide exceptional productivity for implementing transactional systems and data warehouse across the enterprise. This fully functional evaluation version of ER*win* 3.5.2 will help jump-start you into data modeling and database design. To activate this product evaluation you will need to use an evaluation key code. You can obtain an evaluation by contacting PLATINUM technology at 800-442-6861 or 630-620-5000.

- *Methods Bay's Infraset.* Infraset is a repository-driven and model-based COM business object framework and RDBMS persistence layer for component-based archectures. The InfraSet business object framework enables any middle-tier business class to Create, Retrieve, Update, and Delete its objects within standard relational database through the developer's configuration of an Active Repository of design information.

Feel free to cruise around the CD-ROM and run the examples or play with the software. It will give you feel for what's to come in the book, and hopefully get you wound up about N-tier development.

Hardware Requirements

To use the CD-ROM, your computer will need to run Visual Basic 6.0 with adequate memory (32 MB RAM for Windows NT, 16 MB RAM for Windows95 and Windows98). Each software package has its own requirements, so check the individual packages' READMEs for more information.

User Assistance and Information

The software accompanying this book is being provided as is without warranty or support of any kind. Should you require basic installation assistance, or if your media is defective, please call our product support number at (212) 850-6194 weekdays between 9 am and 4 pm Eastern Standard Time. Or, we can be reached via e-mail at **wprtusw@wiley.com**.

To place additional orders or to request information about other Wiley products, please call (800) 879-4539.

To use this CD-ROM, your system must meet the following requirements:

Platform/Processor/Operating System. Windows95, Windows98, or Windows NT.

RAM. 16MB for Windows95 and Windows98, or 32MB for Windows NT.

Hard Drive Space. See individual software packages for more information.

Peripherals. CD-ROM drive, Internet browser installed to navigate CD-ROM.